The Complete
WORLD
ATLAS

The Complete

WORLD
ATLAS

Silverdale Books

Published by
Silverdale Books
an imprint of Bookmart Ltd

Registered Number 2372865
Trading as Bookmart Ltd
Desford Road
Enderby
Leicester LE9 5AD

ISBN 1-85605-502-0

Printed in Singapore

Contents

Saint Mary Lake, Glacier National Park, Montana

NORTH
AMERICA
AND THE
CARIBBEAN

NORTH AMERICA

North America is the third-largest continent after Asia and Africa. North America stretches 3,300 miles west to east from the Pacific coast of Washington State to St. John's in Newfoundland (Canada). The continent extends 3,500 miles north to south from the icy shores of the Arctic Ocean to the warm blue waters of the Gulf of Mexico. North America's total land area is more than 9.3 million square miles.

The continent is a land of contrasts, with every imaginable kind of scenery and habitat. Frozen **tundra** (permanently frozen ground) and dark pine forests in the far north give way to the colorful **deciduous** woodlands of New England and the Appalachian Mountains and then to the vast Great Plains of the American heartland. The Coast Ranges, the Rocky Mountains, and the Mexican Highlands dominate the western one-third of the continent. The southwestern states and Mexico contain some of the world's most spectacular desert scenery. The subtropical forests and swamps of the deep south and Florida and the long chain of Caribbean islands complete this kaleidoscope of landforms.

More than 400 million people live in North America. There are 270 million in the United States, 97 million in Mexico, and 30 million in Canada. More than 30 million additional people make their homes on the thousand or more islands and cays (keys) of the Caribbean.

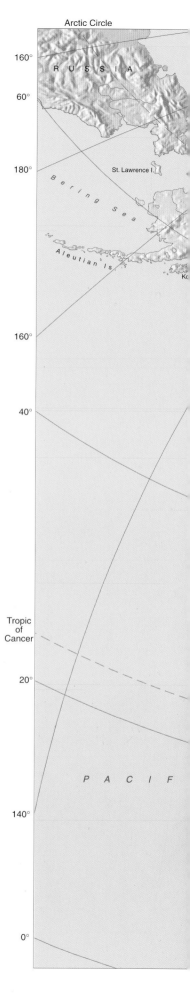

North America is a land of stunning contrasts. People come from all over the world to see the glorious fall colors in New England (*left*) and the spectacular scenery of the Grand Canyon (*below*).

The Arctic Regions

The Arctic regions consist of the Arctic Ocean and the land that nearly encircles it. The northernmost edges of Alaska, Canada, Norway, Sweden, Finland, and Russia form this land ring. Hundreds of islands and island groups called **archipelagoes** dot the Arctic Ocean. The largest island group, known as the Canadian Archipelago, lies off Canada's northern coast. The biggest single island is Greenland. Fewer islands—most notably Spitzbergen (part of Norway) and the three Russian island groups, Franz Josef Land, Novaya Zemlya, and the New Siberian Islands—exist on the European and Asian side of the Arctic Ocean.

Abyssal plains (very deep regions) separated by underwater mountain ranges cover much of the Arctic Ocean's floor. The deepest area is the Pole Abyssal Plain, which plunges near the North Pole to more than 15,000 feet below sea level. The Lomonosov Ridge rises to 10,000 feet and bounds the plain on one side. On the other side of the plain is the Arctic Mid-Ocean Ridge, a volcanic mountain range of molten rock rising through cracks in the seafloor. Shallow **continental shelves**, up to 1,000 miles wide, skirt the ocean's edge. Thick ice covers the Arctic Ocean in winter, but in summer much of the ice melts over the continental shelves, allowing boaters to reach some of the world's richest fishing grounds.

Most of the Arctic landscape is tundra—low plains covered in deep snow in winter and frozen solid for many hundreds of feet down. In summer the snow and the top layer of soil melt, turning the ground into a patchwork of **muskeg** and drier ground clothed in mosses, lichens, grasses, wildflowers, and small shrubs. Native peoples in the Arctic include the Inuit of North America—historically hunters of seals, whales, and walruses—and the Sami (Lapps) of Scandinavia and the Chukchi and Samoyed of northern Russia, who traditionally herd reindeer.

Selected Arctic Facts

• Nearly 1,700 different plant species grow in the Arctic. Almost 1,000 are flowering plants.

• There are about 830,000 native peoples spread across the icy lands of the Arctic regions.

• The highest spot in the Canadian Arctic is Barbeau Peak (8,544 feet) on Ellesmere Island.

• Robert Peary, Matthew Henson, and four Inuit companions are credited with being the first people to reach the North Pole, on April 6, 1909.

• In Siberia, the average temperature in January is -40°F.

• In Russia, the permafrost can extend down to 5,000 feet.

• At 5.4 million square miles, the Arctic is the smallest of the oceans. Its average depth is 4,360 feet.

• Canada's mainland Arctic coastline is more than 12,400 miles long.

About 120,000 Inuit (Eskimo) live in the Arctic regions of Canada, Alaska, Greenland, and northern Russia. Most of them live in towns and small settlements and work in the fishing, mining, oil, and construction industries. Many incorporate the old way of life—fishing, hunting seal and caribou, and traveling by dogsled.

Since 1973 polar bears have been protected by their own international treaty. It has been so successful that the number of bears has increased from about 5,000 to 25,000 in the last 25 years.

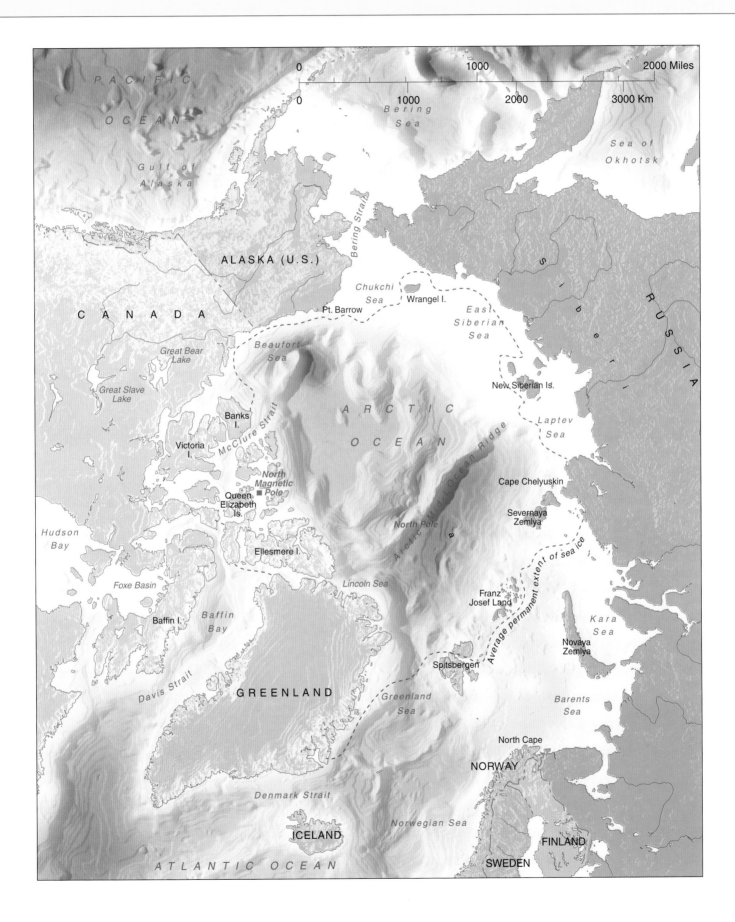

PACIFIC OCEAN

Gulf of Alaska

Bering Sea

Sea of Okhotsk

0   1000   2000 Miles

0   1000   2000   3000 Km

Bering Strait

ALASKA (U.S.)

Chukchi Sea

Pt. Barrow

Wrangel I.

East Siberian Sea

S i b e r i a

R U S S I A

CANADA

Great Bear Lake

Beaufort Sea

New Siberian Is.

Great Slave Lake

A R C T I C

O C E A N

Laptev Sea

Banks I.

McClure Strait

Victoria I.

Cape Chelyuskin

North Magnetic Pole

Severnaya Zemlya

Queen Elizabeth Is.

North Pole

Hudson Bay

Ellesmere I.

Lincoln Sea

Arctic Mid-Ocean Ridge

Foxe Basin

Franz Josef Land

Kara Sea

Baffin I.

Baffin Bay

Average permanent extent of sea ice

Novaya Zemlya

Davis Strait

GREENLAND

Spitsbergen

Greenland Sea

Barents Sea

North Cape

NORWAY

Denmark Strait

Norwegian Sea

ICELAND

FINLAND

SWEDEN

A T L A N T I C   O C E A N

Greenland, the Faeroe Islands, Iceland

Greenland (Kalaallit Nunaat)

Status:	Province of Denmark
Area:	840,000 square miles
Population:	58,000
Capital:	Nuuk (Godthåb)
Languages:	Greenlandic, Danish
Currency:	Danish krone (100 øre)

Iceland

Status:	Republic
Area:	38,707 square miles
Population:	300,000
Capital:	Reykjavík
Language:	Icelandic
Currency:	Icelandic króna (100 aurar)

Greenland—in the local Greenlandic language, Kalaallit Nunaat—is the world's largest island. It is 1,650 miles long and 750 miles wide and lies to Canada's northeast. Only 16 miles from the coast of Ellesmere Island, Greenland is a self-governing province of Denmark, which is located 1,300 miles away. Many Greenlanders have both European (mainly Danish) and Inuit ancestors and most speak Greenlandic. Greenlandic place names are replacing most of the island's Danish titles.

A huge ice cap, 5,000 feet thick, covers nearly 85 percent of the island. The only permanently ice-free areas are in **fjords** and bays—mainly along the southwestern coast, where the natural vegetation consists of grasses and clumps of birch, alder, and willow trees. The island has very little farming, but Greenlanders plant a few vegetables and grow hay to feed their cows and sheep.

Greenland's primary industries are fishing and canning of halibut, cod, shrimp, and salmon; hunting for fox, polar bear, and seals; and mining cryolite—a mineral used to make aluminum. The island also has deposits of lead, zinc, uranium, and gold.

The Faeroes are a cluster of 18 small islands between Iceland and Scotland. They, too, are a self-governing province of Denmark. The islanders make a living by fishing, raising sheep, and selling seabird eggs and feathers.

Iceland lies 160 miles southeast of Greenland and 500 miles northwest of Scotland. Volcanic eruptions on the Mid-Atlantic Ridge created the island. At least 200 eruptions have occurred since the island was first inhabited 1,000 years ago. In 1963 an eruption on the seafloor near Iceland created a new island named Surtsey. Ten years later, volcanic activity destroyed part of the town of Vestmannaeyjar on nearby Heimaey Island.

Ice covers much of Iceland, but about one-fifth is rough grassland where the islanders graze cattle and sheep. Islanders produce all the meat and dairy goods needed and export wool and sheepskins. Iceland's primary industry is fishing, mainly for Atlantic cod, and 70 percent of Iceland's exports consist of fish and fish products such as fish oil and fish meal.

The island's volcanic activity creates an endless supply of **geothermal energy**. Steam is piped from deep underground directly to heating and electrical systems in homes and offices in the capital city of Reykjavík. This cheap energy source powers the island's main manufacturing industries—cement making and aluminum smelting (using imported bauxite, the main aluminum ore). Icelanders use geothermal energy to heat greenhouses for year-round food production.

Right: Svartsengi power station in Iceland uses the heat of volcanic rocks to produce the steam to drive its turbines and produce electricity. Water from the Blue Lagoon—a volcanically heated lake—is believed to cure skin problems and other aches and pains.

Opposite: The Icelandic Parliament building in Reykjavík is home to the world's oldest parliament. Called the Althing, it dates back to A.D. 930.

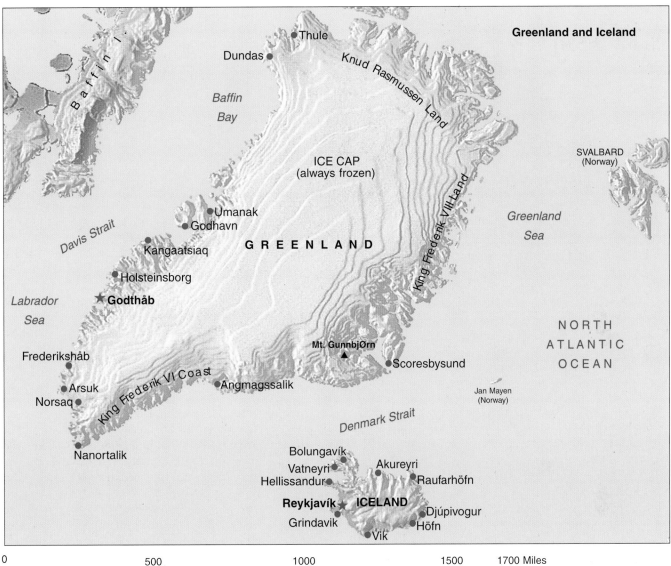

Baffin I.

Thule

Dundas

Baffin
Bay

Knud Rasmussen Land

ICE CAP
(always frozen)

SVALBARD
(Norway)

Umanak

Godhavn

Davis Strait

Kangaatsiaq

G R E E N L A N D

Greenland
Sea

Holsteinsborg

King Frederik VIII Land

Labrador
Sea

★ **Godthåb**

NORTH
ATLANTIC
OCEAN

Frederikshåb

Mt. Gunnbjørn
▲

Scoresbysund

Arsuk

King Frederik VI Coast

Angmagssalik

Jan Mayen
(Norway)

Norsaq

Denmark Strait

Nanortalik

Bolungavík

Vatneyri

Akureyri

Hellissandur

Raufarhöfn

Reykjavík ★ **ICELAND**

Djúpivogur

Grindavik

Höfn

Vík

0		500		1000		1500	1700 Miles

0	500	1000	1500	2000	2500 Km

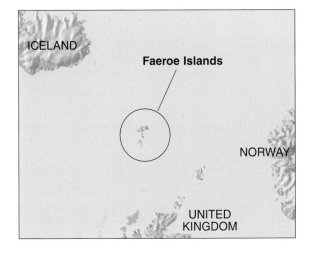

ICELAND

Faeroe Islands

NORWAY

UNITED
KINGDOM

Canada

Canada

Status:	Constitutional Monarchy and Parliamentary Democracy
Area:	3.55 million square miles
Population:	30.6 million
Capital:	Ottawa
Languages:	English and French
Currency:	Canadian dollar (100 cents)

Canada is the world's second-largest country after Russia. This vast expanse covers more than half of North America, from Canada's shared border with the United States to the Arctic Ocean and from the Pacific Ocean (excluding Alaska) to the Atlantic shore.

Canada's far north consists of the Arctic islands and tundra of the Northwest Territories. South of the tundra lies a broad belt of dense **coniferous** forest dotted with lakes and crossed by the country's major rivers, such as the Fraser, the Mackenzie, the Saskatchewan, and the St. Lawrence. Continuing south the forests open to the flat open grasslands of the central prairies.

Canada's west contains some of North America's most dramatic mountain scenery. The Rocky Mountains rise to more than 13,000 feet. Beyond them are the Pacific Coast Mountains and the spectacular fjord coast of British Columbia. Low mountain ranges snake along the eastern half of the country, and gently rolling hills drop to the Great Lakes lowlands, the St. Lawrence River, Québec, and the Maritime Provinces of Newfoundland and Labrador, Nova Scotia, New Brunswick, and Prince Edward Island. The eastern region, claiming some of the most fertile farmland in Canada, is home to most of Canada's people.

An arctic climate embraces Canada's far north. Winters are long and bitterly cold. In the brief cool summer, the average temperature doesn't rise much above 50°F. On Canada's western coast, the Pacific Ocean creates a gentler, wetter climate. Winter temperatures are around 35°F, rising to 65°F in summer. The western region also receives the most rain. Moisture-filled winds blow in from the Pacific and drop their rain over the mountains. As a result, the prairie regions farther inland are relatively dry, with very cold winters. Winters in the eastern lowlands are long and cold with temperatures around 14°F, but the summers are much warmer, with average temperatures of 68°F.

The city of Québec, on the St. Lawrence River, is the oldest city in Canada. Founded in 1608 by the French explorer Samuel de Champlain, Québec City is the capital of the province of Québec. The city has a huge tourist industry, and its busy port handles 15 million tons of goods every year.

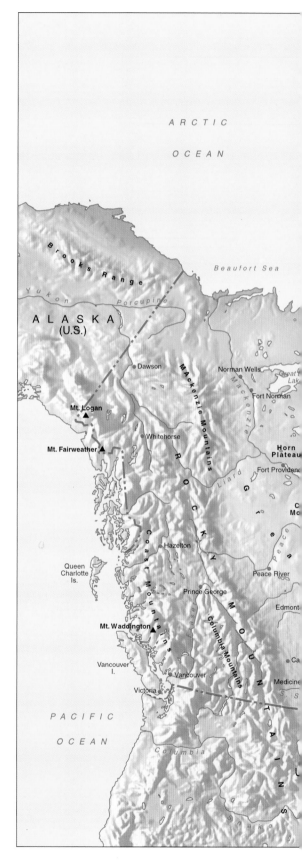

Lincoln Sea

Barbeau Peak ▲

Ellesmere I.

GREENLAND

ICELAND

Melville I.

Devon I.

Baffin Bay

Denmark Strait

Victoria I.

Baffin Island

Davis Strait

Foxe Basin

Cumberland Sound

Amadjuak Lake

Southampton I.

Frobisher Bay

Baker Lake

Hudson Strait

Labrador Sea

Dubawnt Lake

Coats I.

Mansel I.

Nain

Feuilles

Hudson Bay

Churchill

Smallwood Reservoir

Happy Valley-Goose Bay

Reindeer Lake

Churchill

Nelson

Belcher Is.

La Grande

Gander

St. John's

James's Bay

Fort George

Monts Otish

Pelbancantien Platea

Severn

Akimiski I.

Laurentien Plateau

Anticosti I.

Prince Albert

Lake Winnipegosis

Fort Albany

Gulf of St. Lawrence

atoon

Albany

Charlottetown

Lake Winnipeg

St. Lawrence

Quebec

Regina

Lake Manitoba

Lake Nipigon

Fredericton

St John

Halifax

Winnipeg

Thunder Bay

Montreal

Lake Superior

Ottawa

STATES OF AMERICA

Georgian Bay

Lake Michigan

Lake Huron

Toronto

Lake Ontario

Niagara Falls

Missouri

Mississippi

Lake Erie

ATLANTIC OCEAN

500

1000

1500 Miles

0

0

500

1000

1500

2000 Km

15

Canada

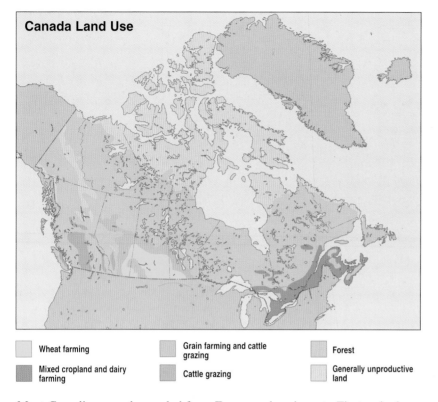

Canada Land Use

Wheat farming	Grain farming and cattle grazing	Forest
Mixed cropland and dairy farming	Cattle grazing	Generally unproductive land

Most Canadians are descended from European immigrants. First arrivals to the region were French settlers, who came in the 1760s, followed quickly by the Scots and later by the English and Irish in the 1800s. Europeans immigrated to Canada in great numbers following World War II, resulting in a population tracing its roots to Germany, Italy, Greece, Hungary, Ukraine, Poland, Norway, Sweden, and the Netherlands. Since then the bulk of immigrants has been from Southeast Asia. The largest non-English-speaking group is the French Canadians, who account for about 28 percent of the population. Nearly five million French Canadians live in French-speaking Québec. Another four million reside in the eastern half of the country. Some members of the **separatist** movement want an independent French-speaking Québec republic. Others simply want to preserve their French culture while remaining part of Canada. Native peoples of Canada account for about 2 percent of the population. Inuit claims to be properly recognized resulted in the new territory of Nunavut being formed in 1997.

Canada's mines produce a wide range of mineral ores, including iron, nickel, copper, zinc, molybdenum, uranium, gold, and platinum. The country also claims rich deposits of sulfur, asbestos, potash, and gypsum. These resources make Canada one of the world's largest mineral exporters. Hydroelectric power from the country's many large rivers, along with coal, oil, and natural gas, provide energy for homes and industry.

Much of Canada is forested, and the country is a major exporter of lumber (sawn wood), plywood, wood pulp, paper, and cardboard. The rich prairie soils of Alberta, Saskatchewan, and Manitoba produce most of Canada's wheat, oats, barley, and rye and feed crops for large herds of beef cattle. The eastern lowlands, with their milder climate, produce corn, vegetables, fruit, tobacco, and poultry and dairy products.

Lincoln Sea

Ellesmere I..

GREENLAND

Greenland Sea

Denmark Strait

ICELAND

Devon I.

Baffin Bay

Davis Strait

Victoria I.

N   U   N   A   V   U   T

Baffin Island

Auyuittuq
N.P.

Foxe Basin

ition

smith

Southampton
I.

Baker Lake

Hudson Strait

Dubawnt
Lake

Coats I.

Mansel I.

Nain

NEWFOUNDLAND
AND
LABRADOR

Lake
abasca

Churchill

Hudson Bay

Happy Valley-Goose Bay

Feuilles

Smallwood
Reservoir

Reindeer Lake

D A

Nelson

Churchill

Belcher Is.

La Grande

Gander

MANITOBA

Severn

James
Bay

Fort George

QUÉBEC

Peribonca

NEWFOUNDLAND
AND LABRADOR

St John's

Anticosti I.

ONTARIO

Akimiski
I.

Fort Albany

Albany

St. Lawrence

Gulf of St. Lawrence

Prince Albert

Lake
Winnipeg

PRINCE
EDWARD I.

Charlottetown

Saskatoon

Lake
Winnipegosis

NEW
BRUNSWICK

NOVA
SCOTIA

Riding
Mountain
N.P.

Lake
Manitoba

Lake
Nipigon

Québec

Fredericton

★ Regina

KATCHEWAN

Winnipeg ★

Thunder Bay

Pukaskwa
N.P.

St John

★ Halifax

Lake
Superior

Montréal

ATLANTIC

D STATES OF AMERICA

Lake Michigan

Georgian
Bay

Lake Huron

Ottawa

OCEAN

Toronto

Lake Ontario

Lake Erie

United States of America

United States of America

Status:	Federal Republic
Area:	3.53 million square miles
Population:	270 million
Capital:	Washington D.C.
Language:	English
Currency:	U.S. dollar (100 cents)

The United States forms the world's third-largest country by population and the fourth-largest by size. Only China and India have more people, and only Canada, China, and Russia have greater land areas. The United States occupies the entire central section of the North American continent, as well as Alaska in the far northwest and the Hawaiian Islands in the middle of the Pacific Ocean. A 5,500-mile border separates the United States from Canada, which is America's most important trading partner. In the south, Mexico and the United States share a 1,930-mile boundary. The U.S. Pacific coastline is 1,300 miles long. The East Coast runs for nearly 3,700 miles along the Atlantic Ocean and around the Gulf of Mexico.

The country's varied climate, fertile farmlands, and vast resources of timber minerals, **fossil fuels**, and water power make it one of the world's richest nations. In fact, some of its 50 states are like small countries in terms of their size, their population, and the amount of food and industrial goods they produce.

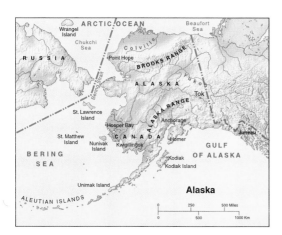

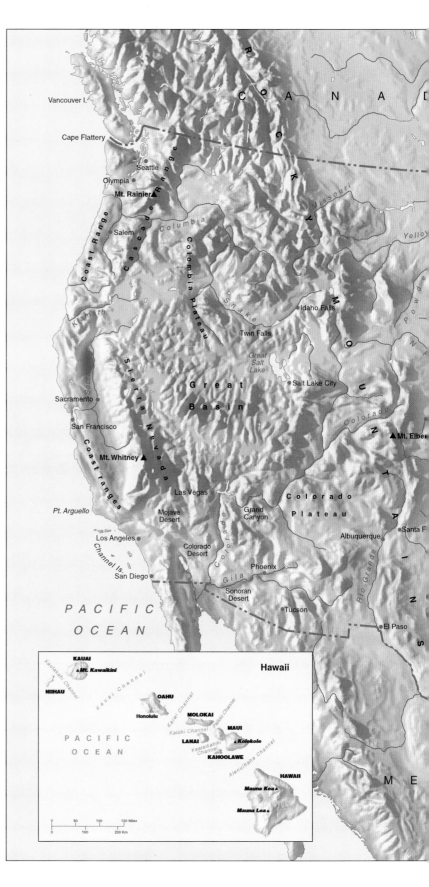

Gulf of
St. Lawrence

C A N A D A

Cape Sable

Lake Superior

Georgian
Bay

Lake Huron

Lake Ontario

Connecticut

Boston
Cape Cod

Minneapolis

Hudson

Niagara Falls

Sioux Falls

Madison

Grand Rapids

Lake Michigan

Detroit

Lake Erie

New York

Chicago
Gary

Pittsburgh

Philadelphia

Susquehanna

Delaware Bay

U N I T E D   S T A T E S
O F   A M E R I C A

Washington, D.C. ★

Indianapolis
Cincinnati

Ohio

James

Chesapeake Bay

Kansas City

Roanoke

Cape Hatteras

Missouri

Missouri

Red

James

Mississippi

G r e a t   P l a i n s

Nashville

White

Cape Fear

Oklahoma City

Memphis

Tennessee

Atlanta

Augusta

Savannah

Arkansas

Savannah

Chattahoochee

Cimarron

sas

Red

Mississippi

Tombigbee

Altamaha

Dallas

Sabine

Red

Brazos

Trinity

Alabama

A T L A N T I C

Colorado

New Orleans

O C E A N

Austin
Houston

Cape Canaveral

San Antonio

Mississippi Delta

Orlando

B A H A M A S

Nueces

Lake
Okeechobee

Grand
Bahama I.

G U L F   O F   M E X I C O

The Everglades

Miami

Rio Grande

Key West

Florida Keys

Andros I.

Turks & Caicos
Is.

O

Straits of Florida

Great
Inagua I.

| 0 | | 500 Miles | |
| 0 | 500 | | 1000 Km |

C U B A

United States of America

The United States is a federal republic, comprised of 50 states and the District of Columbia (D.C.)—where the country's government meets. In the federal system, the federal government makes decisions regarding foreign policy, defense, the justice system, health services, agricultural and industrial policy, and many aspects of taxation. These laws apply to the entire country. State and local governments discuss and regulate other issues such as education, public health, crime control, and local taxation.

Throughout its history, the United States has attracted immigrants from all over the world. The U.S. population mix is roughly 73 percent white—mainly of European origin—12 percent African American, 11 percent Hispanic, 3 percent Asian, and about 1 percent Native American. Nearly three-quarters of the population live in cities and towns.

Geology and climate have created a variety of natural resources. The West Coast—a region of forested mountains and fertile valleys—has a mild climate that is wet in the north and much drier in the south. Inland from the coast lie broad valleys and basins, rising to the rugged peaks of the Rocky Mountains. This basin and range area has few people but contains valuable minerals and is a vital mining and manufacturing area. Cattle graze in the north. To the south lie the deserts of Utah, Nevada, and California.

The Great Plains east of the Rockies have relatively little rainfall, but the rain they do receive falls mainly in summer, allowing these fertile plains to produce huge quantities of grain, meat, and dairy products. New England and the Atlantic states along the East Coast are famous for their historic sites and scenery but also have rich farmland and industrial centers such as Philadelphia, Buffalo, and Pittsburgh. The southern lowlands traditionally produce cotton, tobacco, and other warm-climate crops. The oil industry, manufacturing, and tourism are also essential to the economy of the south.

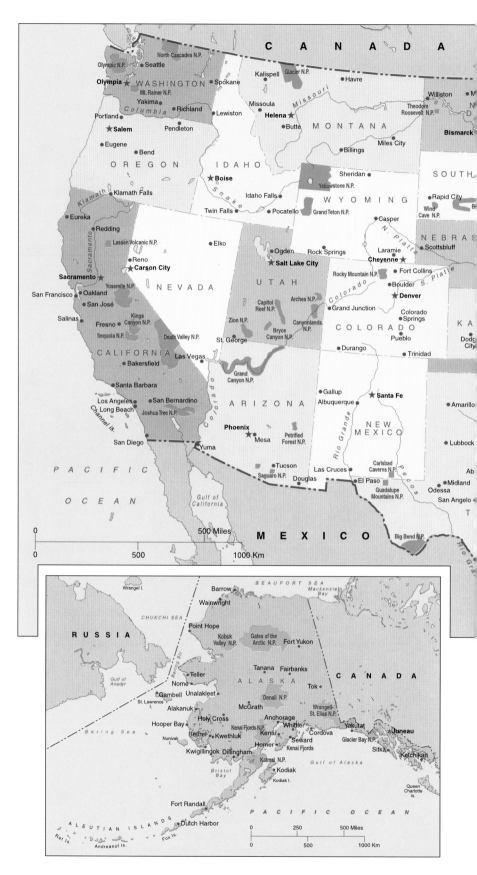

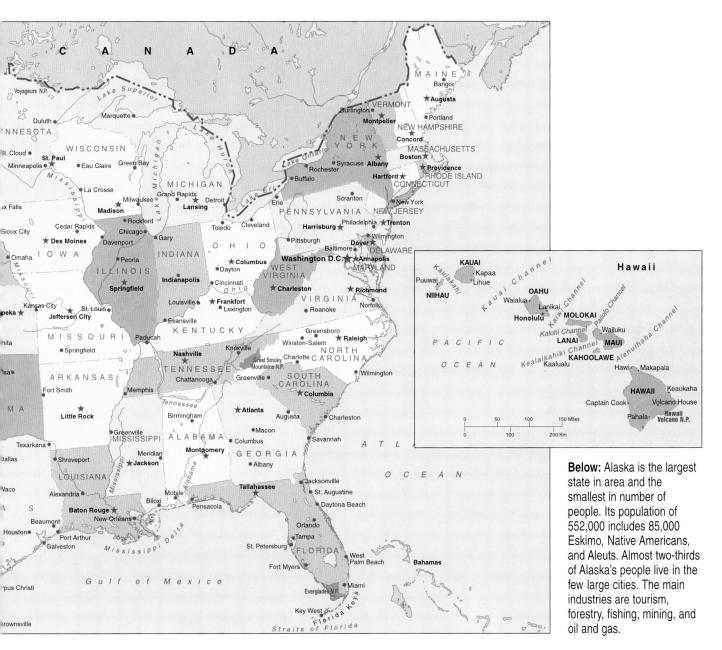

C A N A D A

Voyageurs N.P.

Lake Superior

Duluth

Marquette

M I N N E S O T A

St. Cloud

St. Paul ★

Minneapolis ●

Sioux Falls

Eau Claire

La Crosse

W I S C O N S I N

Green Bay

Milwaukee

M I C H I G A N

Lake Michigan

Lake Huron

Grand Rapids

Lansing ●

Detroit ●

Lake Erie

M A I N E

Bangor

Augusta ★

VERMONT

Burlington

Montpelier ●

NEW HAMPSHIRE

Concord ★

Portland

MASSACHUSETTS

Boston ★

N E W
Y O R K

Rochester ●

Syracuse ●

Albany ★

Providence ★

RHODE ISLAND

Hartford ★

CONNECTICUT

Buffalo ●

Scranton

New York

Erie

Madison ★

Rockford

Chicago ●

Gary ●

P E N N S Y L V A N I A

NEW JERSEY

Philadelphia ●

Trenton ★

Cedar Rapids

I O W A

Davenport

I N D I A N A

Columbus ★

Harrisburg ★

Dayton ●

Pittsburgh ●

Baltimore ●

Wilmington

Dover ★

DELAWARE

Des Moines ★

Peoria

I L L I N O I S

Indianapolis ★

O H I O

Cincinnati ●

WEST
VIRGINIA

Ohio

Washington D.C. ★

Annapolis ★

MARYLAND

Omaha

Kansas City

St. Louis ●

Springfield ★

Louisville ●

Frankfort ★

Lexington

Charleston ★

Richmond ★

V I R G I N I A

Topeka ★

Jefferson City ★

M I S S O U R I

Springfield

Paducah

K E N T U C K Y

Evansville

Roanoke

Norfolk

Wichita

Greensboro

Winston-Salem

Raleigh ★

N O R T H
C A R O L I N A

Tulsa

Nashville ★

Knoxville

Charlotte ●

A R K A N S A S

Fort Smith

Memphis ●

T E N N E S S E E

Great Smoky
Mountains N.P.

Chattanooga

Greenville

S O U T H
C A R O L I N A

Wilmington

Tennessee

Columbia ★

OKLAHOMA

Little Rock ★

Birmingham

Atlanta ★

Augusta

Charleston

Greenville

M I S S I S S I P P I

A L A B A M A

Macon

Savannah

Texarkana

Meridian

Montgomery ★

Columbus

G E O R G I A

Dallas

Shreveport

Jackson ★

Albany

L O U I S I A N A

Mississippi

Alabama

A T L A N T I C

Waco

Alexandria

Mobile

Biloxi

Pensacola

Jacksonville

Tallahassee ★

St. Augustine

Baton Rouge ★

New Orleans ●

Daytona Beach

O C E A N

Beaumont

Houston ●

Port Arthur

Galveston

Mississippi Delta

Orlando ●

Tampa ●

St. Petersburg

F L O R I D A

West
Palm Beach

Bahamas

Corpus Christi

G u l f   o f   M e x i c o

Fort Myers

Everglades N.P.

Miami ●

Brownsville

Key West

Florida Keys

Straits of Florida

H a w a i i

KAUAI

Kauaikahi Channel

Kapaa

Lihue

Puuwai

NIIHAU

Kauai Channel

OAHU

Waialua

Honolulu ●

Lanikai

Kaiwi Channel

MOLOKAI

Kalohi Channel

P A C I F I C

O C E A N

LANAI

Paliolo Channel

Wailuku

MAUI

Alenuihaha Channel

Kealaikahiki Channel

KAHOOLAWE

Kaalualu

Hawi

Makapala

HAWAII

Captain Cook

Keaukaha

Volcano House

Pahala

Hawaii
Volcano N.P.

0   50   100   150 Miles

0   100   200 Km

Below: Alaska is the largest state in area and the smallest in number of people. Its population of 552,000 includes 85,000 Eskimo, Native Americans, and Aleuts. Almost two-thirds of Alaska's people live in the few large cities. The main industries are tourism, forestry, fishing, mining, and oil and gas.

Right: Los Angeles, California, (*right*) is a thriving city with 3.5 million people in the city itself and another 3.5 million in the rest of Los Angeles County. Its richly varied population includes Hispanics, Asians, Pacific Islanders, and African Americans. The city is a major seaport, the home of the movie industry, and a center for the aviation and petroleum industries.

United States of America

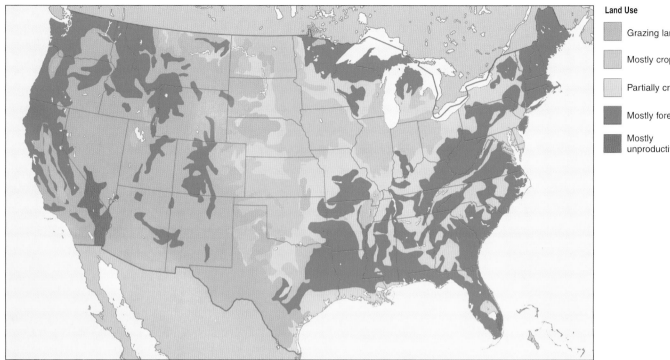

Land Use

- Grazing land
- Mostly cropland
- Partially cropland
- Mostly forest land
- Mostly unproductive land

Above: The United States is rich in natural resources. The fertile soils of the Midwest, the eastern states, and California produce cereal grains, vegetables, and fruit. Farmers in these areas also raise pigs, poultry, and dairy cattle. The drier western and southern grasslands produce prime beef. Forest lands yield both hardwood and softwood lumber, and the country has large deposits of coal, oil, gas, iron ore, copper, and other minerals. Compare the land use map (*above*) with the rainfall map (*below*). You can see at a glance what an important influence rainfall has on the way people use the land.

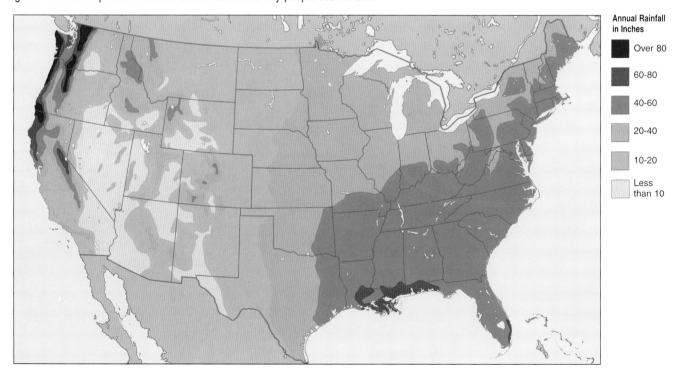

Annual Rainfall in Inches

- Over 80
- 60-80
- 40-60
- 20-40
- 10-20
- Less than 10

When the first European settlers arrived in North America during the early 1600s, the French settled mainly in the northeast in what would become Canada. The British traveled along the East Coast, and the Spanish stayed near the Gulf coast and settled the lands west of the Mississippi. By the 1750s, the population of these colonies had grown to almost 1.5 million. Life was difficult, but people eager to build a new future continued to arrive from Europe. Many were fleeing religious persecution. Some were adventurers. Others had no choice. Peoples from Africa were enslaved and shipped to North America, where they were sold to wealthy landowners as plantation workers and domestic servants.

By 1763, after winning the bitter Seven Years' War with France in Europe, Britain controlled most of eastern North America. By this time, however, the British colonies along the East Coast had become thriving, successful communities. The colonists resented British rule. The arguments grew bitter, eventually erupting in the American Revolution, which lasted from 1775 to 1783. At the war's end, the world had a new nation—the United States of America.

The United States continued to grow and prosper, gaining more territory from Britain, France, Spain, and Mexico. Farmers, ranchers, prospectors, and traders moved farther west, reaching the Pacific Coast by the mid-1800s. But America's troubles were not over. Between 1861 and 1865, the nation was torn, north to south, by the bitter struggle of the Civil War. In 1867 the United States bought the territory of Alaska from Russia, and it officially became the forty-ninth state in 1959. The Hawaiian Islands became the fiftieth state in the same year.

Top: By the mid-1700s, the 13 original British colonies lined the East Coast from Massachusetts to Georgia, with French territory to the north and west and Spanish territory to the south.

Center: The Treaty of Paris in 1783 ended the American Revolution. The United States gained territory stretching west to the Mississippi River. British territory was to the north, and Spanish colonial lands lay to the west and south.

Below Left: In 1803 President Thomas Jefferson almost doubled the size of the United States when he bought Louisiana from France, which had taken over the territory from Spain some years earlier.

Below Right: By the mid–1800s, the United States stretched all the way to the West Coast. Britain gave up its claim to Oregon in 1846, and huge areas were won from Mexico after the war of 1846–1848.

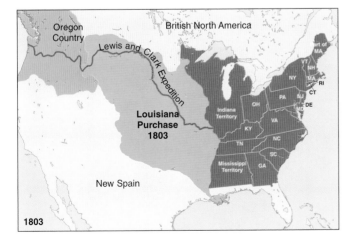

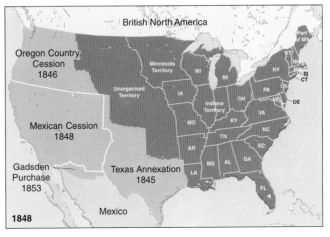

Mexico

Mexico

Status:	Federal Republic
Area:	736,946 square miles
Population:	97.5 million
Capital:	Mexico City
Language:	Spanish
Currency:	Mexican Peso (100 centavos)

Roughly one quarter of the Mexican people are farmers, and most of them work small farms in the highlands. Most of the country's wealth comes from its vast oil reserves and from minerals, textiles, forestry, and tourism.

Mexico has a variety of topographical features. North of the capital, Mexico City, the land is dominated by two north-south mountain ranges. The western Sierra Madre has peaks rising to 11,000 feet, and the eastern Sierra Madre reaches heights of more than 13,000 feet. Between the two ranges lies the Mexican Plateau. The northern part of the plateau is dry. It merges into the desert regions that stretch north and west to the U.S. border and the 760-mile-long desert peninsula of Baja (Lower) California. The plateau's southern section hosts a milder climate with more rain, and its rich volcanic soils support much of Mexico's fertile farmland.

A narrow coastal plain runs along the Pacific Coast. A wider plain, which snakes along the Gulf Coast and goes north of the seaport of Tampico, is covered with thorn bush and scrub. South of the city, the climate is more moist, and the vegetation becomes richer as it becomes part of the tropical rain forests of southeastern Mexico. The Yucatán Peninsula, a low limestone region, juts into the Gulf of Mexico. Dry scrubland covers the northern peninsula, but the southern end merges with the tropical forest claiming most of the narrow Isthmus of Tehuantepec.

More highlands dominate southern Mexico. To the south of Mexico City, a range of volcanic mountains cuts across the country. This range contains Mexico's highest peak—the 18,410 foot Pico de Orizaba—and many active volcanoes, including Iztaccíhuatl and Popocatepétl, both more than 17,000 feet above sea level. The Chiapas Highlands line the Pacific Coast in the far south, stretching into the Central American nations of Guatemala and El Salvador.

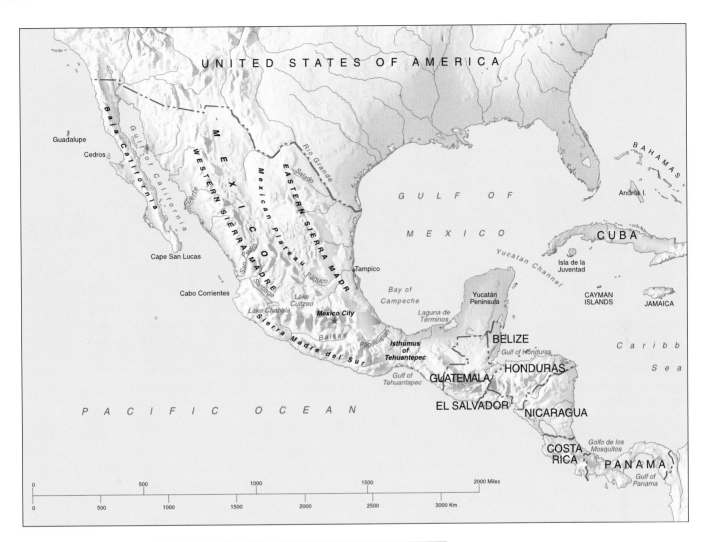

United States of America

Guadalupe
Cedros
Baja California
Gulf of California
M E X I C O
WESTERN SIERRA MADRE
EASTERN SIERRA MADRE
Mexican Plateau
Rio Grande
Salado
Cape San Lucas
Cabo Corrientes
Tiete
San Pedro
Santiago
Lake Chapala
Lake Cuitzeo
Pánuco
Tampico
Mexico City
Balsas
Papaloapan
La Sierra Madre del Sur
Isthmus of Tehuantepec
Gulf of Tehuantepec
Bay of Campeche
Laguna de Términos
Yucatán Peninsula
Yucatan Channel
Gulf of Honduras
BELIZE
GUATEMALA
EL SALVADOR
HONDURAS
NICARAGUA
COSTA RICA
PANAMA
Golfo de los Mosquitos
Gulf of Panama
GULF OF MEXICO
PACIFIC OCEAN
BAHAMAS
Andrós I.
CUBA
Isla de la Juventad
CAYMAN ISLANDS
JAMAICA
Caribbean Sea

| 0 | 500 | 1000 | 1500 | 2000 Miles |
| 0 | 500 | 1000 | 1500 | 2000 | 2500 | 3000 Km |

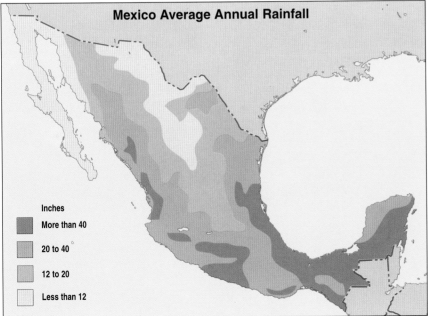

Mexico Average Annual Rainfall

Inches

- More than 40
- 20 to 40
- 12 to 20
- Less than 12

Mexico

Mexico has a long history. By 2000 B.C., large farming villages were dotting the southern highlands. Around 1000 B.C., Mexico had sizable towns, with elaborate temples and stone carvings. And by 400 B.C., the Olmec Indians had invented the calendar and systems for writing and counting. The great empires of the Mayan, Olmec, Mixtec, Toltec, and Aztec peoples flourished for centuries. In A.D.1521, Spanish soldiers conquered the Aztecs. For the next 300 years, Spain ruled the country as one of its colonies. In fact, most modern Mexicans are **mestizos**—people who have both Indian and European ancestors.

Mexico gained its independence from Spain in 1821, but a century of wars and unrest followed. Successive governments have introduced land reforms and have encouraged industry, but the country still struggles with a weak economy, high unemployment, and a growing population. The birthrate is very high, and more than half the people are less than 20 years old. Poverty troubles both rural and urban areas. Mexico City has a population of more than 15 million, and five other cities have more than a million people.

Roughly one-fourth of Mexico's people make their living from farming, mainly in the southern part of the plateau and in the valleys of the south. The northern regions are so dry that farmers must irrigate their crops. The primary agricultural products are corn, wheat, coffee, cotton, and a wide variety of fruits and vegetables. Beef cattle, sheep, and goats graze in the north. Dairy cows thrive mostly in the south where the pasture is better. The eastern Sierra Madre contains rich deposits of coal and iron ore, and Monterrey is home to the iron and steel industry. Other manufacturing centers include Mexico City, Guadalajara, Chihuahua, Mexicali, Puebla, Tijuana, and Veracruz. Workers produce cars, foods, beverages, chemicals, petroleum products, cement, and fertilizers. New factories built near the U.S. border manufacture car components and electrical goods for the United States. The oil industry operates from platforms in the Gulf.

Above: Mexico has hundreds of ancient monuments, such as this Mayan pyramid, and many colorful local traditions.

Below: Veracruz, on the Gulf of Mexico, is the country's main port. It was founded in 1519 by Hernán Cortés.

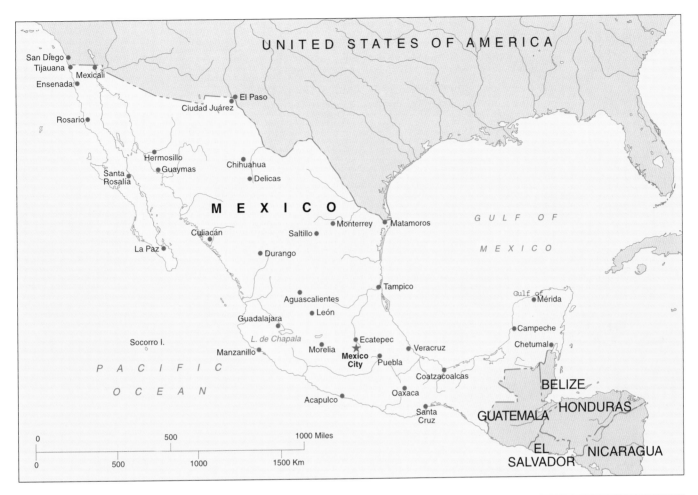

UNITED STATES OF AMERICA

San Diego
Tijuana
Mexicali
Ensenada

Rosario

El Paso
Ciudad Juárez

Hermosillo
Guaymas

Chihuahua
Delicas

Santa
Rosalía

MEXICO

GULF OF

MEXICO

Monterrey
Matamoros

Culiacán
Saltillo

La Paz
Durango

Tampico

Aguascalientes
León

Gulf of
Mérida

Guadalajara
L. de Chapala

Campeche

Socorro I.
Manzanillo
Morelia
Ecatepec
Mexico City
Puebla
Veracruz
Chetumal

PACIFIC
OCEAN
Coatzacoalcas
BELIZE

Acapulco
Oaxaca
GUATEMALA
HONDURAS

Santa
Cruz
EL
SALVADOR
NICARAGUA

| 0 | 500 | 1000 Miles |
| 0 | 500 | 1000 | 1500 Km |

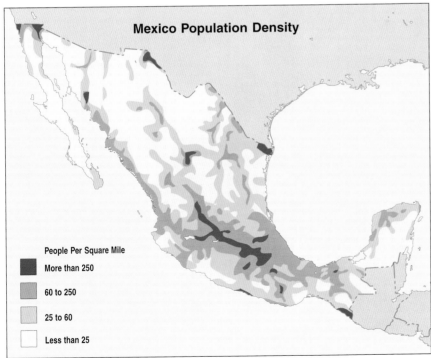

Mexico Population Density

People Per Square Mile

More than 250

60 to 250

25 to 60

Less than 25

Above: Despite improvements in fuel quality and vehicle emission standards, Mexico City's three million automobiles and thousands of trucks and buses make it still one of the world's most polluted cities.

27

Bermuda, Bahamas, Turks and Caicos Islands

Bermuda

Status:	Self-governing British Crown Colony
Area:	21 square miles
Population:	65,000
Capital:	Hamilton
Language:	English
Currency:	Bermudan dollar (100 cents)

Turks and Caicos Islands

Status:	British Dependency
Area:	166 square miles
Population:	13,000
Capital:	Cockburn Town
Language:	English
Currency:	U.S. dollar (100 cents)

The Turks and Caicos group contains about 30 small islands located at the southeastern edge of the Grand Bahama Bank. Eight of the islands are inhabited, and the people earn their living from tourism and banking. Grand Turk, the largest island, houses an important U.S. missile tracking station. Both France and Spain once claimed the islands, which Britain has governed since 1766.

Bermuda is a cluster of more than 300 small islands, 580 miles off Cape Hatteras, North Carolina. Most of the islands are tiny. Only 20 of them are inhabited, and the largest, Great Bermuda, is linked by bridges and causeways to the five other main islands. The islands are made of limestone—the remains of ancient **coral reefs**—and they are still surrounded by living reefs. The warm, mild climate, sandy beaches, pastel-colored buildings, and pro-fusion of wildflowers attract more than 500,000 visitors each year. Tourism is the main industry, along with banking and insurance. The islands have no rivers or lakes, so rainwater is collected from roofs and stored in underground tanks. There are a few small farms, but most of the islands' food supplies are imported.

Left: Hamilton is the capital and chief port of Bermuda. It is a popular tourist resort, and cruise ships can tie up right alongside the city's main street, Front Street. Pastel-painted buildings and sunshades for the traffic police all add to the city's charm.

Below: Golden beaches and subtropical vegetation make the Bahamas a vacationers' paradise.

Bahamas

Status:	Independent Nation
Area:	5,365 square miles
Population:	300,000
Capital:	Nassau
Languages:	English, Creole
Currency:	Bahamian dollar (100 cents)

The Bahamas consist of 27 inhabited islands and nearly 3,000 uninhabited small islands and cays. These small landforms are scattered across 90,000 square miles of limestone and coral reefs known as the Grand Bahama Bank in the western Atlantic. The islands nearest the U.S. mainland lie 60 miles off the Florida coast, while the southernmost islands in the archipelago are just 50 miles from the Caribbean island of Cuba. The Bahamas enjoy a subtropical climate, and the economy is based on tourism, sport fishing, gambling, and banking. Many historians believe that Columbus's first landfall in 1492 was on the Bahamian island of San Salvador.

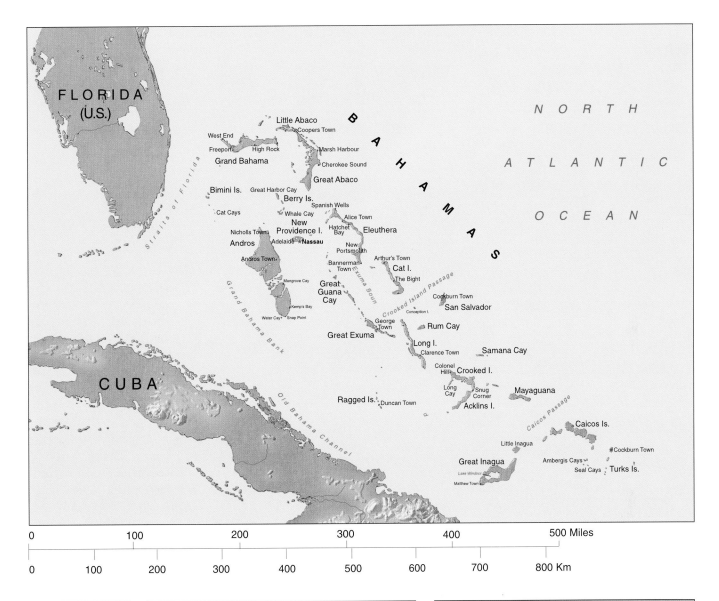

FLORIDA
(U.S.)

N O R T H

A T L A N T I C

O C E A N

B
A
H
A
M
A
S

Little Abaco
West End
Coopers Town
Freeport
High Rock
Marsh Harbour
Grand Bahama
Cherokee Sound
Great Abaco
Bimini Is.
Great Harbor Cay
Berry Is.
Spanish Wells
Cat Cays
Whale Cay
Alice Town
New
Providence I.
Hatchet
Bay
Eleuthera
Nicholls Town
New
Portsmouth
Andros
Adelaide
Nassau
Arthur's Town
Andros Town
Bannerman
Town
Cat I.
The Bight
Mangrove Cay
Great
Guana
Cay
Cockburn Town
Conception I.
San Salvador
Kemp's Bay
George
Town
Rum Cay
Water Cay
Snap Point
Great Exuma
Long I.
Samana Cay
Clarence Town
Colonel
Hill
Crooked I.
Ragged Is.
Duncan Town
Long
Cay
Snug
Corner
Mayaguana
Acklins I.

Straits of Florida
Grand Bahama Bank
Old Bahama Channel
Exuma Soun
Crooked Island Passage
Caicos Passage

CUBA

Little Inagua
Caicos Is.
Ambergis Cays
Cockburn Town
Great Inagua
Seal Cays
Turks Is.
Lake Windsor
Matthew Town

0	100	200	300	400	500 Miles

0	100	200	300	400	500	600	700	800 Km

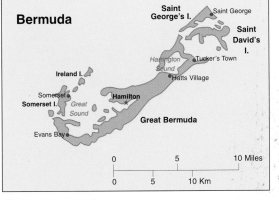

Bermuda

Saint
George's I.
Saint George
Saint
David's
I.
Harrington Sound
Tucker's Town
Ireland I.
Hatts Village
Somerset
Somerset I.
Hamilton
*Great
Sound*
Great Bermuda
Evans Bay

0	5	10 Miles

0	5	10 Km

Right: Bermuda's financial services and generous tax laws make the islands a popular base for international businesses and wealthy individuals as well as a major tourist destination.

Cuba

Cuba

Status:	Socialist Republic
Area:	42,402 square miles
Population:	11.1 million
Capital:	Havana
Language:	Spanish
Currency:	Cuban peso (100 centavos)

Cuba lies 90 miles south of the tip of Florida. The largest of the Caribbean islands, Cuba is 120 miles wide and more than 750 miles long. The landscape is varied with high mountains to the west, middle, and east. Nearly three-quarters of the land consist of low rolling hills, fertile valleys, and broad plains. Cuba's climate is subtropical, with a warm dry season lasting from November to April and a mild rainy season occurring from May to October. Hurricanes frequently hit the island in the second half of the rainy season, often causing great damage to crops and buildings.

Spain ruled Cuba for nearly 400 years, but the island gained its independence in 1898. Decades of political

Above right: Royal palms dot the sugarcane fields of the "Valley of the Sugarmills" near the old town of Trinidad on the island of Cuba.

Right: Small farms on Cuba grow tobacco, sugarcane, and fruit and sell all their produce to the government.

troubles followed. For 12 years, the country had a democratic government that Fulgencio Batista overthrew in 1952. He, in turn, was ousted by Fidel Castro in 1959. President Castro's Communist govern-ment took control of the island's industries and most of the farmland. Under the Communist regime, education and health improved. Roughly 94 percent of the population can read and write, and life expectancy is 75 years.

Tobacco and coffee are grown on the higher ground, along with Cuba's main crop, sugarcane, which dominates more than half of all the cultivated land and accounts for nearly 80 per-

cent of the island's exports. Bananas, citrus fruits, rice, tomatoes, and a wide variety of vegetables thrive on the fertile lower ground, and beef and dairy cattle graze on the rich grasslands. Fishing is another state-run industry. In addition to chromium, iron, manganese, copper, and silver, Cuba has one of the world's largest deposits of nickel. The country exports these minerals in great quantities and manufactures cement and fertilizers for export. Cuba's factories produce farm tools, paper, rum, textiles, and cigars.

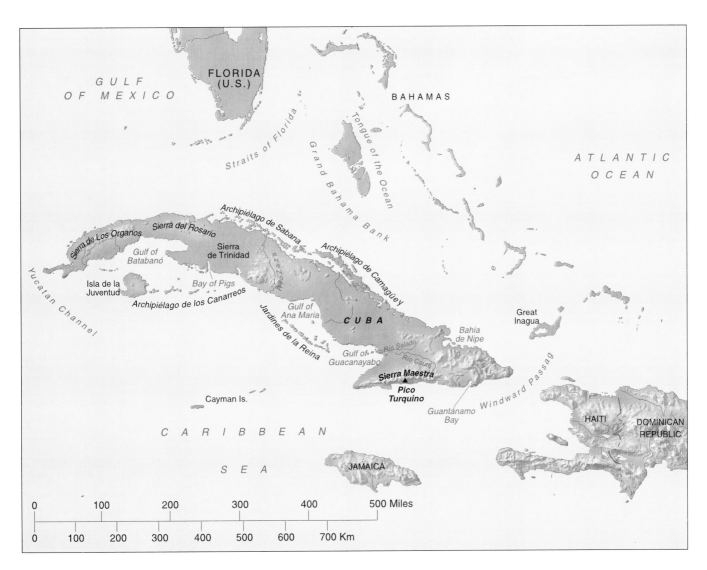

GULF
OF MEXICO

FLORIDA
(U.S.)

BAHAMAS

ATLANTIC
OCEAN

Straits of Florida

Tongue of the Ocean

Grand Bahama Bank

Sierra de Los Organos

Sierra del Rosario

Archipiélago de Sabana

Sierra
de Trinidad

Archipiélago de Camagüey

Gulf of
Batabanó

Río Zaza

Isla de la
Juventud

Bay of Pigs

Archipiélago de los Canarreos

Gulf of
Ana María

CUBA

Great
Inagua

Jardines de la Reina

Río Salado

Bahía
de Nipe

Gulf of
Guacanayabo

Río Cauto

Yucatan Channel

Sierra Maestra

▲
Pico
Turquino

Guantánamo
Bay

Windward Passag

Cayman Is.

HAITI

DOMINICAN
REPUBLIC

CARIBBEAN

SEA

JAMAICA

0	100	200	300	400	500 Miles

0	100	200	300	400	500	600	700 Km

Havana   Matanzas

Marianao   Cárdenas   Sagua la Grande

Artemisa

Colón

Pinar del Río

Santa
Clara

Guane

Aguada
de Pasajeros

Caibarién

Nueva
Gerona

Cienfuegos

Sancti-Spíritus

Trinidad

Santa Fé

Isla de la
Juventud

Florida

Camagüey

CUBA   Banes

Jardines de la Reine

Holguín

Yucatan Channel

Manzanillo

Baracoa
Guantánamo

Santiago
de Cuba

Cayman Islands

h

0	100	200	300 miles

0	100	200	300	400 Km

Jamaica and the Cayman Islands

Jamaica

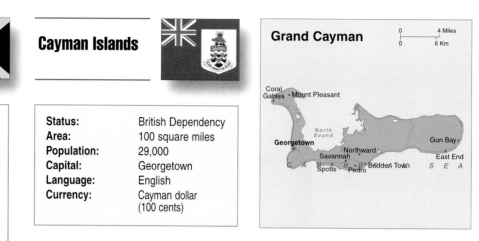

Status:	Constitutional Monarchy
Area:	4,181 square miles
Population:	2.6 million
Capital:	Kingston
Languages:	English, Creole, Hindi, Spanish, Chinese
Currency:	Jamaican dollar (100 cents)

Cayman Islands

Status:	British Dependency
Area:	100 square miles
Population:	29,000
Capital:	Georgetown
Language:	English
Currency:	Cayman dollar (100 cents)

Grand Cayman

0 — 4 Miles
0 — 6 Km

Coral Gables • Mount Pleasant

North Sound

Georgetown

Northward
Savannah
Spotts • Pedro • Bodden Town

Gun Bay •
East End

SEA

The third-largest of the Caribbean islands (after Cuba and Hispaniola), Jamaica is located about 100 miles south of the eastern end of Cuba. The 145-mile-long, 50-mile-wide island is mountainous, with Blue Mountain Peak rising to 7,400 feet above sea level near its eastern end. Moisture-bearing winds blowing from the west carry up to 200 inches of rain a year to the high-lands, most of it falling between May and October. Jamaica's lowlands are drier, with an average of 80 inches a year.

Jamaicans are an interesting mix of people. Most are of African descent, but others are descended from British, Portuguese, Spanish, German, Indian, and Chinese im-migrants. Claimed by Christopher Columbus in 1494, Jamaica was ruled by Spain until 1655, when Britain took control.

Thin soils on top of limestone make farming difficult, but sugar-cane, fruits, coffee, cacao beans, and spices do well in the fertile valleys and coastal plains. Jamaica exports much of its produce, mainly from the cities of Kingston and Montego Bay. Most of the island's income derives from tourism and from mining and exporting bauxite—the principal ore of aluminum and of alumina.

Columbus claimed the three tiny Cayman Islands for Spain in 1503, but they have been governed by Britain since 1670. About 75 percent of the people are of African descent. The rest are mainly British and American. The islands are made of limestone and are fringed by coral reefs. Temperatures range from 55°F to 95°F, and rainfall is low at around 56 inches annually. The islands support a small fishing industry, and farmers raise tomatoes, bananas, pigs, cows, and poultry. The Cayman Islands' principal businesses are finance and tourism. Very liberal tax laws have attracted the headquarters of nearly 18,000 companies and more than 400 banks. Luxury tourism and the world's most expensive beachfront real estate provide 70 percent of the islands' total income.

Below: Jamaica is one of the world's leading producers of bauxite, shown here, the mineral ore from which aluminum is made. The country's mines also produce gypsum, which is used to make plasterboard and other construction materials.

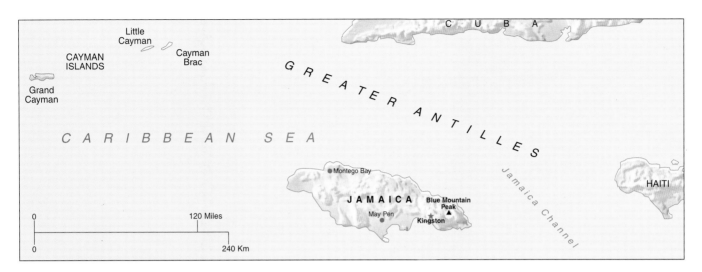

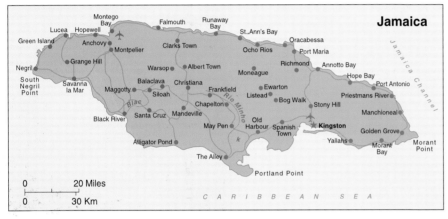

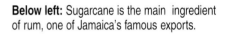

Below left: Sugarcane is the main ingredient of rum, one of Jamaica's famous exports.

Below: Some stretches of the coast are a tourist's paradise, while others provide loading points for the bauxite carriers.

Haiti and the Dominican Republic

Haiti

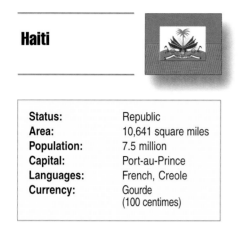

Status:	Republic
Area:	10,641 square miles
Population:	7.5 million
Capital:	Port-au-Prince
Languages:	French, Creole
Currency:	Gourde (100 centimes)

Haiti makes up the westernmost one-third of the island of Hispaniola, the second-largest island in the Caribbean. Haiti is a mountainous nation, with very little farmland and few natural resources. It is also heavily populated and, as a result, is one of the poorest countries in the world. Almost two-thirds of the people just manage to make a living on small farms in the valleys and on steep hillsides or by fishing along the coast.

From 1697 until 1804, France ruled Haiti. The country gained its in-dependence after a slave revolt, giving Haiti the distinction of being the world's oldest black republic. Nearly 200 years of turmoil followed. Among the worst periods was the brutal father-son regime of François and Jean-Claude Duvalier. It lasted from 1957 to 1986. In 1990 the first democratically elected president, Jean-Bertrand Aristide, took office but seven months later was forced into exile by supporters of the old regime. In 1994 the United States sent troops to restore democracy and to return Aristide to power. Haiti's later governments have continued to struggle for stability.

Dominican Republic

Status:	Republic
Area:	18,680 square miles
Population:	8.3 million
Capital:	Santo Domingo
Language:	Spanish
Currency:	Dominican Peso (100 centavos)

The Dominican Republic has fared much better than its neighbor on Hispaniola. The land is dominated by mountains, including the highest peak in the Caribbean, the 10,414 foot Duarte Peak. But the country also has fertile valleys, lowlands, and coastal plains. The climate is tropical, with average temperatures around 77°F, and ample rainfall, especially in the summer.

The Dominican Republic produces sugarcane, coffee, rice, and tobacco, as well as cacao beans, fruits, and vegetables. In rural areas, most people farm small holdings, producing enough for their families and a small surplus to sell in the local markets. In the lowland areas, privately owned estates employ large numbers of workers in the sugarcane fields and coffee and cacao plantations. Mineral exports include bauxite, nickel, silver, and gold. The Dominican Republic is also developing its tourist industry by building resorts along the northern coast. Visitors increased from 5,000 to 65,000 between 1987 and 1990, and numbers continue to rise. Most of the tourists are from Canada, the United States, and Europe.

Big hydroelectric projects can sometimes be environmental disasters. When this dam was built at Pelgré in Haiti, the surrounding forests were cut down. With no trees to protect them, the hillside soils were soon washed away by the heavy rains, and the reservoir was clogged with silt.

Opposite: Troops patrol the streets in Haiti after a disturbance. Political unrest is common in countries where a few people hold most of the wealth, while the rest struggle to survive in poor housing, with not enough food or adequate medical services.

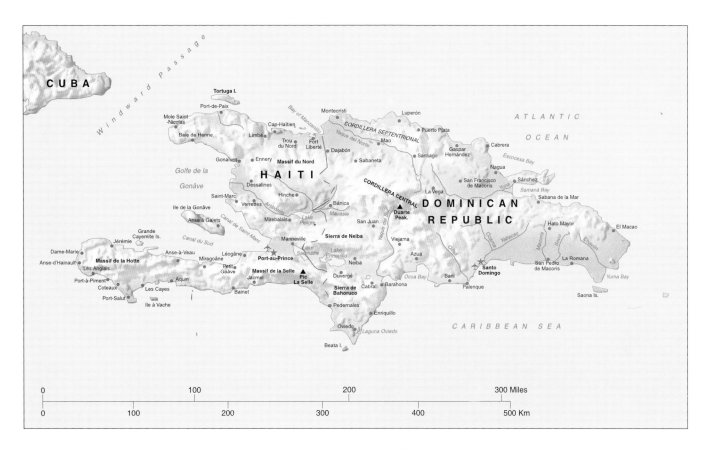

35

Puerto Rico

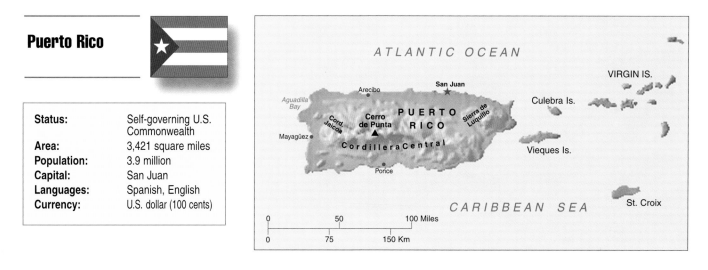

Puerto Rico

Status:	Self-governing U.S. Commonwealth
Area:	3,421 square miles
Population:	3.9 million
Capital:	San Juan
Languages:	Spanish, English
Currency:	U.S. dollar (100 cents)

Puerto Rico is about 100 miles long and 35 miles wide. It is mountainous, with a narrow coastal plain, so agricultural land is scarce. The best land is used for growing sugarcane, coffee, bananas, tobacco, tropical fruits, and spices. The climate is tropical, creating good growing conditions on the moist northeastern side of the island, but the island lies in the track of Atlantic hurricanes and often suffers devastating storms.

Since a referendum (a public vote) in 1952, Puerto Rico has been a self-governing commonwealth of the United States. The island creates its own laws, as long as they don't conflict with those of the United States, and its people can travel freely to the mainland. Puerto Ricans can vote in U.S. presidential primaries but not in the actual elections. The government of Puerto Rico is based on that of the United States, with a Senate, a House of Representatives, and a president who is elected every four years. Health and education have improved faster than anywhere else in the Caribbean. Free medical and dental care is available to everyone, life expectancy has increased from 46 years to 74, and 90 percent of the population can read and write.

Compared to most other Caribbean islands, Puerto Rico is heavily industrialized, and a large proportion of the people make their homes in urban areas. Nearly half the population lives in or around the capital, San Juan, working in factories that produce textiles, clothing, electrical goods, leather goods, and processed foods. More than 85 percent of the country's exports and 65 percent of its imports are with the United States. Other major employers are the huge petroleum refinery and chemical works on the southwestern coast; the mining and smelting of copper; and the growing tourist industry.

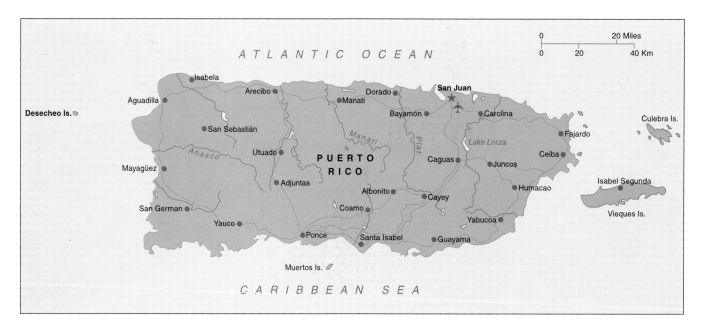

Above: An aerial view shows one of the large rum distilleries in San Juan, Puerto Rico. Rum—made from sugarcane—is one of the traditional exports of the Caribbean.

Right: Puerto Rico's lowlands are mainly farmed, but the inland areas still contain large tracts of untouched tropical rain forest.

Below: Puerto Rico has one of the fastest-growing economies in the Caribbean. The country's success is shown by the modern buildings in Hato Rey—San Juan's financial district.

Leeward Islands

The Leeward Islands form the northern section of the long island arc known as the Lesser Antilles, which stretches from just east of Puerto Rico to the coast of South America. The Leeward Islands extend from the Virgin Islands to Guadeloupe, while the Windward Islands continue the island chain almost to the coast of Venezuela. The Leeward and Windward Islands are the tops of a chain of submarine volcanoes that mark the line on the seabed where two sections of the earth's rocky crust meet. They form a natural breakwater of islands and coral reefs separating the Caribbean Sea from the Atlantic Ocean.

The Leeward group contains about 15 main islands and hundreds of small islets. It totals roughly 1,500 square miles and is home to about 700,000 people. Arawak and Carib Indians were the original inhabitants, but immigration and exploration resulted in a mixed population—descendants of Europeans, Africans brought in as slaves, Indian workers, and settlers from Asia and North and South America. The Leeward Islands contain two independent countries, as well as several dependencies of the United States, Britain, France, and the Netherlands.

The islands have warm, dry, tropical climates, with temperatures around 80°F for most of the year and total annual rainfall of 30 to 40 inches. Local farmers grow tobacco, cotton, sugarcane, and a wide variety of fruits and vegetables. Tourism is essential to most of the islands' economies. The beautiful scenery, colonial architecture, sandy beaches, clear water, and opportunities for leisure activities attract thousands of international visitors.

Tourism is the basis of Antigua's economy, with beautiful white sand beaches and a warm sunny climate drawing tourists from all over the world.

UNITED STATES OF AMERI

GULF OF MEXICO

Yucatan Channe

Campeche Bay

MEXICO

BELIZE

Gulf of Honduras

Gulf of Tehuantepec

GUATEMALA

HONDURAS

EL SALVADOR

NICARA

PACIFIC OCEAN

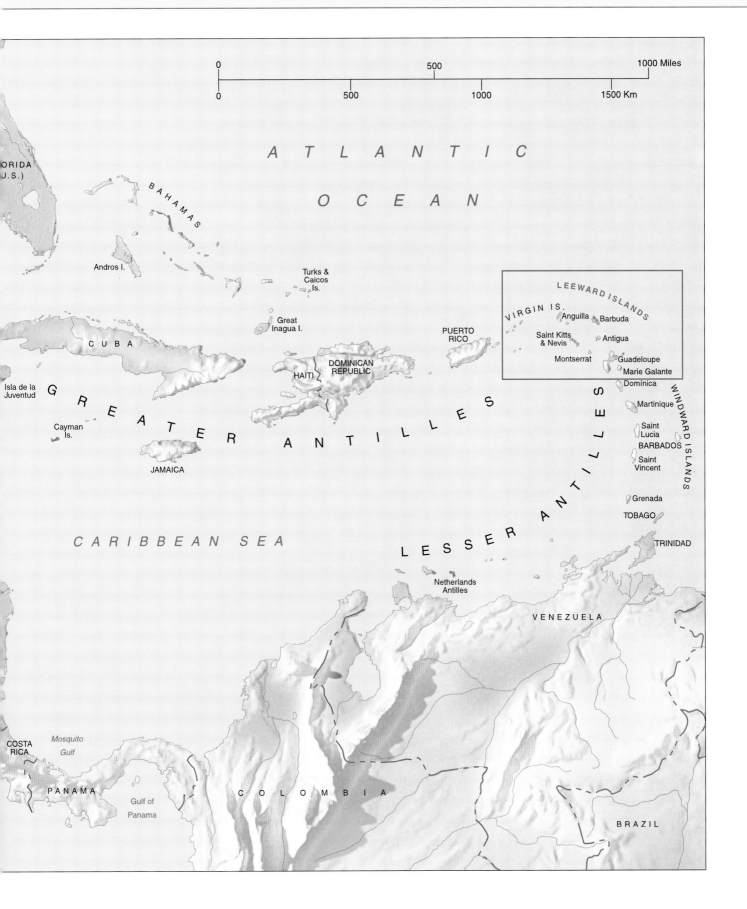

ATLANTIC

OCEAN

0   500   1000 Miles

0   500   1000   1500 Km

FLORIDA (U.S.)

BAHAMAS

Andros I.

Turks & Caicos Is.

Great Inagua I.

PUERTO RICO

LEEWARD ISLANDS

VIRGIN IS.

Anguilla   Barbuda

Saint Kitts & Nevis   Antigua

Montserrat   Guadeloupe

Marie Galante

Domínica

CUBA

Isla de la Juventud

Cayman Is.

JAMAICA

G R E A T E R   A N T I L L E S

HAITI

DOMINICAN REPUBLIC

Martinique

Saint Lucia

BARBADOS

Saint Vincent

WINDWARD ISLANDS

L E S S E R   A N T I L L E S

Grenada

TOBAGO

TRINIDAD

CARIBBEAN SEA

Netherlands Antilles

VENEZUELA

COSTA RICA

Mosquito Gulf

PANAMA

Gulf of Panama

C O L O M B I A

BRAZIL

Leeward Islands

U.S. Virgin Islands

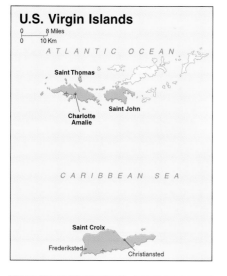

U.S. Virgin Islands

Status:	Self-governing U.S. Territory
Area:	130 square miles
Population:	102,000
Capital:	Charlotte Amalie (on Saint Thomas)
Language:	English
Currency:	U.S. dollar (100 cents)

U.S. Virgin Islands

Most of the population of this island group lives on the largest islands—Saint Thomas, Saint Croix, and Saint John—but the territory also covers 65 smaller islands. Residents are U.S. citizens. Tourism is the primary industry, but Saint Croix also has oil refineries and bauxite processing plants.

British Virgin Islands

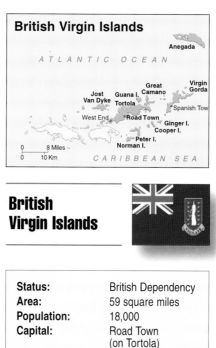

British Virgin Islands

Status:	British Dependency
Area:	59 square miles
Population:	18,000
Capital:	Road Town (on Tortola)
Language:	English
Currency:	U.S. dollar (100 cents)

British Virgin Islands

This British island group contains 4 main islands and 36 smaller ones. About 75 percent of the people live on the largest island, Tortola. The islands receive more than 325,000 visitors each year and are a popular tax haven. Rum is the main export.

Barbuda / Antigua

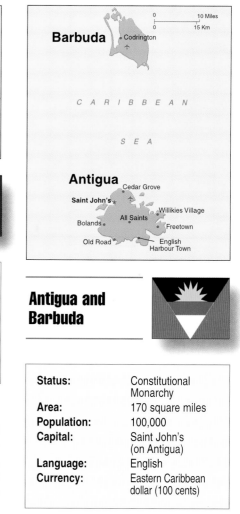

Antigua and Barbuda

Status:	Constitutional Monarchy
Area:	170 square miles
Population:	100,000
Capital:	Saint John's (on Antigua)
Language:	English
Currency:	Eastern Caribbean dollar (100 cents)

Antigua and Barbuda

Antigua is hilly and rugged, made of volcanic rocks that create good soils in the valleys and lowlands. Barbuda is a low, mainly wooded coral island. Tourism is important, in addition to fishing (especially for lobster), market gardening, and Sea Island cotton production.

Left: The cable car at Charlotte Amalie on the island of Saint Thomas in the U.S. Virgin Islands provides a spectacular view of the bay, dotted with yachts and visiting cruise ships.

Far Left: The town of Charlotte Amalie on the island of Saint Thomas

Saint Kitts and Nevis

Status:	Constitutional Monarchy
Area:	139 square miles
Population:	40,000
Capital:	Basseterre
Language:	English
Currency:	Eastern Caribbean dollar (100 cents)

Saint Kitts and Nevis

These twin volcanic islands feature peaks of more than 3,000 feet above sea level that are covered with lush tropical rain forests. The lowlands are fertile and are used mainly for growing sugarcane, cotton, and tropical fruits. Tourism is the biggest industry, but the islands also produce textiles, leather, and electronic goods.

Montserrat

Status:	British Dependency
Area:	40 square miles
Population:	12,500
Capital:	Plymouth
Language:	English
Currency:	Eastern Caribbean dollar (100 cents)

Montserrat

Rugged and hilly with dense forests, Montserrat is famous for its volcanic eruptions. Volcanic rocks provide fertile soils and dark-colored sandy beaches. Tourism supplies one-quarter of the island's income, but Montserrat also exports Sea Island cotton, tropical fruits and vegetables, and manu-factured electrical goods.

Anguilla

Status:	British Dependency
Area:	37 square miles
Population:	8,900
Capital:	The Valley
Languages:	English, Creole
Currency:	Eastern Caribbean dollar (100 cents)

Anguilla

This long, thin coral island is very flat—rising only to 200 feet above sea level. Low rainfall and poor soil hamper farming. The main crops are peas, beans, corn, and sweet potatoes. Anguilla's economy relies mostly on tourism and on exporting lobsters. Many of the island's most beautiful reefs have been damaged by removing coral to sell as tourist souvenirs.

Guadeloupe

Status:	Overseas Department of France
Area:	653 square miles
Population:	400,000
Capital:	Basse-Terre
Language:	French
Currency:	French franc (100 centimes)

Guadeloupe

Guadeloupe is a group of eight islands, the two largest being mountainous and volcanic Basse-Terre and lower Grand-Terre. The islands export sugar, bananas, and rum but depend heavily on aid from France.

Windward Islands and Barbados

From north to south, Dominica, Martinique, Saint Lucia, Saint Vincent and the Grenadines, and Grenada make up the Windward Island group. Barbados, lying about 40 miles to the east, is considered a separate island because it is not geologically connected to the Windward Island chain. Total land area of the Windward Islands is approximately 1,000 square miles, and the population numbers roughly 720,000.

Like the Leeward Islands to the north, Arawak Indians originally inhabited the Windward group, which Europeans (mainly British and French) settled on in the early 1600s. Martinique has remained a French possession, while the other territories became British colonies and later gained their independence. Years of migration has resulted in a population of mainly African descent, with small numbers of immigrants from Europe and North and South America.

Some of the smaller islands are composed of limestone and coral and therefore have very thin and infertile soils. These islands rely mainly on tourism. The larger islands are volcanic, and their mountainous interiors are covered in dense forests. The volcanic rocks produce rich soils that collect in the valleys and coastal plains, providing good farmland. Primary agricultural products are bananas, cacao beans, sugarcane, arrowroot, nutmeg, and mace. A few of the islands have small industries, but tourism is generally the most important source of income.

Small-scale fishing in the shallow coastal waters is a traditional way of life in Grenada. These fishing crews will sell most of their catch in the local market.

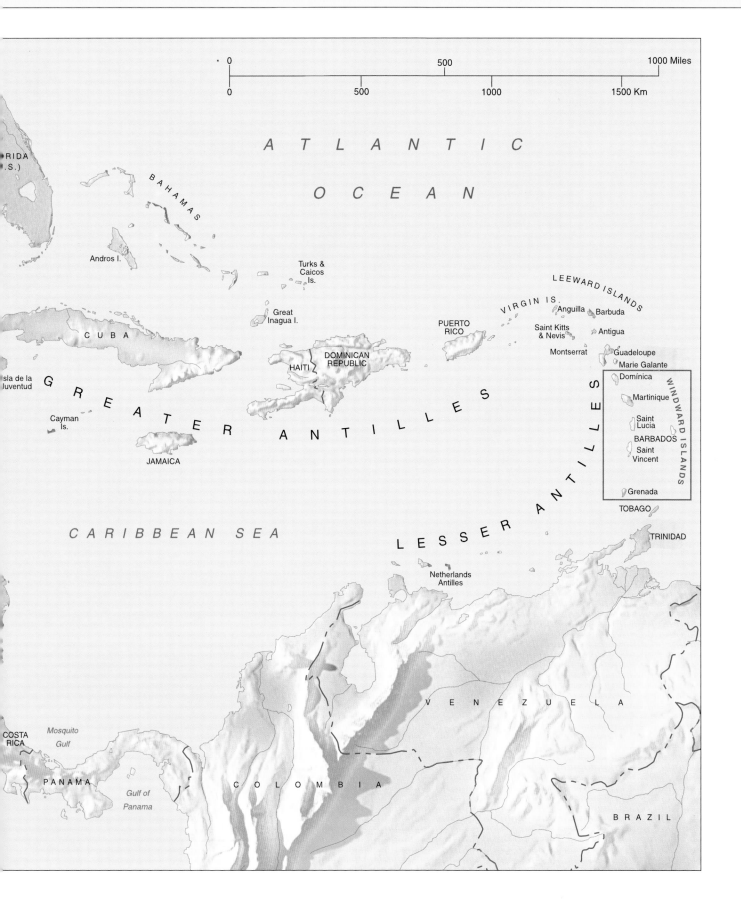

0   500   1000 Miles

0   500   1000   1500 Km

A T L A N T I C

O C E A N

RIDA
.S.)

BAHAMAS

Andros I.

Turks &
Caicos
Is.

Great
Inagua I.

PUERTO
RICO

LEEWARD ISLANDS

VIRGIN IS.

Anguilla   Barbuda

Saint Kitts
& Nevis   Antigua

Montserrat   Guadeloupe

Marie Galante

Dominica

Martinique

Saint
Lucia

BARBADOS

Saint
Vincent

Grenada

TOBAGO

TRINIDAD

WINDWARD ISLANDS

C U B A

Isla de la
Juventud

G
R
E
A
T
E
R
   A N T I L L E S

Cayman
Is.

HAITI

DOMINICAN
REPUBLIC

JAMAICA

L E S S E R

A N T I L L E S

C A R I B B E A N   S E A

Netherlands
Antilles

V E N E Z U E L A

COSTA
RICA

*Mosquito
Gulf*

PANAMA

*Gulf of
Panama*

C O L O M B I A

B R A Z I L

43

Windward Islands and Barbados

Dominica

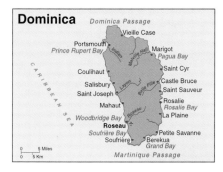

Status:	Republic
Area:	290 square miles
Population:	100,000
Capital:	Roseau
Languages:	English, French patois
Currency:	Eastern Caribbean dollar (100 cents)

Dominica

The island is mountainous, volcanic, and densely forested. Its climate is hot, averaging 80°F, and wet, with 70 inches of rain falling annually on the coast and well over 200 inches blanketing the hills. A small tourist industry exists, but the islanders primarily support themselves by exporting bananas, coconuts, oranges, and grapefruits—mainly to the United States and Britain.

Martinique

Status:	Overseas Department of France
Area:	409 square miles
Population:	400,000
Capital:	Fort-de-France
Languages:	French, Creole
Currency:	French franc (100 centimes)

Martinique

Martinique's highest peak is the volcano Mont Pelée (4,583 feet above sea level), which erupted in 1902, engulfing the town of Saint-Pierre and killing 30,000 people. Farmers grow tropical fruits for export and vegetables for local use. Other islanders work in tourism and in the oil refineries, rum distilleries, and sugar-processing factories.

Saint Lucia

Status:	Constitutional Monarchy
Area:	236 square miles
Population:	150,000
Capital:	Castries
Languages:	English, French patois
Currency:	Eastern Caribbean dollar (100 cents)

Saint Lucia

Saint Lucia is mountainous, with dense forests and deep, fertile valleys. About one-third of its people work in agriculture—producing bananas, cacao beans, and copra for export. Light industries operate in the **free-trade zone** at Vieux Fort, a deepwater port for transferring oil between tankers. Cruise ships dock at the modern harbor of the city of Castries.

Left: Pineapples thrive on a big plantation in Martinique.

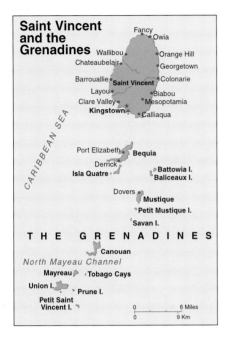

Saint Vincent
and the
Grenadines

Status:	Constitutional Monarchy
Area:	151 square miles
Population:	100,000
Capital:	Kingstown
Languages:	English, French patois
Currency:	Eastern Caribbean dollar (100 cents)

Saint Vincent and the Grenadines

This small country consists of the island of Saint Vincent and the northern-most islands of the Grenadines group, including Union and Bequia. Bananas and arrowroot are the primary export crops. Tourism is essential to the economy, and some of the smaller islands are the lavish hideaways of the world's wealthy.

Grenada

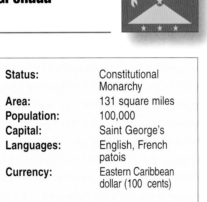

Status:	Constitutional Monarchy
Area:	131 square miles
Population:	100,000
Capital:	Saint George's
Languages:	English, French patois
Currency:	Eastern Caribbean dollar (100 cents)

Grenada

An independent nation since 1974, this island country includes the island of Grenada and the southern islands of the Grenadines, the largest of which is Carriacou. Grenada is the world's foremost producer of nutmeg and mace. Other exports include bananas, citrus fruits, and cacao beans.

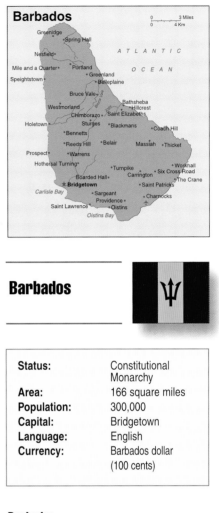

Barbados

Status:	Constitutional Monarchy
Area:	166 square miles
Population:	300,000
Capital:	Bridgetown
Language:	English
Currency:	Barbados dollar (100 cents)

Barbados

Barbados has a warm, pleasant climate that supports a growing tourist industry. Nearly 500,000 visitors a year come mainly from the United States and Britain. Sugar and sugar products such as molasses and rum are important agricultural exports, but the island is also developing new industries such as banking and data processing. Barbados is one of the most densely populated countries in the world but has good health and educational systems.

The Netherlands Antilles, Aruba, Trinidad and Tobago

The Netherlands Antilles consists of two groups of islands 500 miles apart. The two largest islands, Curaçao and Bonaire, lie about 50 miles off the coast of the South American nation of Venezuela. The other territory lies at the northern end of the Leeward Islands, about 160 miles east of Puerto Rico. Comprised of the southern part of Saint Martin Island and the islands of Saba and Saint Eustatius, the Netherlands Antilles is a self-governing entity of the Kingdom of the Netherlands.

Trinidad and its tiny companion Tobago lie a few miles off the coast of Venezuela. The islands have high mountains in the north and lower ranges of hills across the central and southern regions. Between these highlands sit broad plains and swamps. Nearly half the island nation is forest. Islanders grow sugarcane, coffee, cacao beans, rubber, and tropical fruits for export, but the islands' main wealth comes from oil and natural gas and from the petrochemical industries based on those resources. Trinidad is also the world's largest source of asphalt—a thick, tarry substance used internationally for paving roads. Food processing, cement making, and textiles are other major employers.

Aruba sits 48 miles west of Curaçao and until 1986 was also part of the Netherlands Antilles. The island was scheduled to achieve full independence in 1996, but the people chose instead to remain a self-governing part of the Kingdom of the Netherlands. Many Arubans and citizens of the Netherlands Antilles work in tourism, banking, and other financial services, all of which are essential island industries. The islands have no mineral resources and no industries apart from local crafts. Local businessowners operate refineries that process Venezuelan oil for export, mainly to the Netherlands. Other mineral exports include phosphates from Curaçao and salt from Bonaire. The islands are not very fertile, growing only sorghum, groundnuts, aloes, and tropical fruits.

Netherlands Antilles

Status:	Self-governing Region of the Kingdom of the Netherlands
Area:	309 square miles
Population:	200,000
Capital:	Willemstad
Languages:	Dutch, English, Spanish, and Papiamento
Currency:	Guilder (100 cents)

Netherlands Antilles

Nearly 80 percent of the population lives on the largest island, Curaçao. The standard of living is high, with efficient health services and schools and almost 100-percent literacy. The soils are too poor for large-scale farming, but tourism, banking, and industries ensure a high rate of employment.

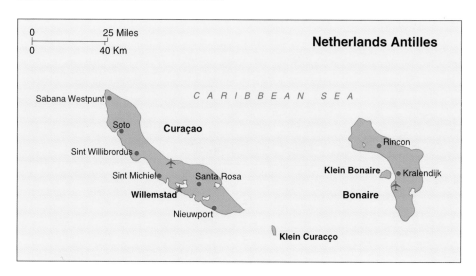

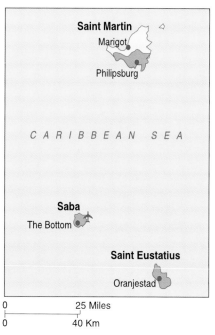

46

Aruba

Status:	Self-governing Island of the Kingdom of the Netherlands
Area:	75 sq mi
Population:	69,000
Capital:	Oranjestad
Languages:	Dutch, English, Spanish, and Papiamento
Currency:	Aruban florin (100 cents)

Aruba

Almost half the people of Aruba are descended from the Arawak Indians, the island's original inhabitants. On most Caribbean islands, the Indians were wiped out by European settlers or by the diseases they brought to the islands. The modern Aruban economy depends on oil refining, fertilizer production, food exports, and tourism.

Trinidad and Tobago

Status:	Republic
Area:	1,981 square miles
Population:	1.3 million
Capital:	Port-of-Spain
Languages:	English, French, Spanish, Hindi
Currency:	Trinidad and Tobago dollar (100 cents)

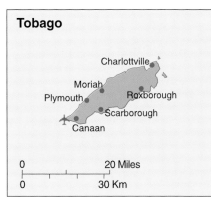

Trinidad and Tobago

Trinidad's population is 43 percent Afro-Caribbean, 40 percent East Indian, and 16 percent mixed background. Settlers from Europe, China, the Middle East, and elsewhere comprise the other 1 percent. This blend reflects the island's colonial past, when huge plantations produced sugarcane for Spanish, French, and British owners. The economy combines agriculture, tourism, financial services, and petrochemical industries.

Below: Trinidad is one of the world's main producers of asphalt—a sticky black tarlike material used for surfacing roads. The asphalt occurs naturally—oozing up through the ground. Eighty percent of the island's international trade comes from asphalt.

Rio de Janeiro, Brazil

CENTRAL AND SOUTH AMERICA

CENTRAL AND SOUTH AMERICA

Seven countries—Belize, Guatemala, Honduras, El Salvador, Nicaragua, Costa Rica, and Panama—occupy the **isthmus** of Central America, a narrow strip of land joining North and South America. A total land area of 201,000 square miles supports about 35 million people. A volcanic mountain chain stretches 800 miles along the west side of the isthmus from Mexico to Panama, with peaks rising to 12,000 feet. Lowland plains of dense rain forest cover the eastern coast, which is frequently struck by hurricanes that sweep in from the Caribbean Sea.

The Mayan civilization, which had developed great cultural and economic advances, occupied part of Mexico and Central America for 1,500 years. Spanish invaders conquered this remarkable people in the 1520s and ruled Central America for 300 years. In 1823 five of the countries merged into a **federation** but disbanded in 1838. In the intervening years, Central America has suffered bitter conflicts between rich and poor and a succession of military dictatorships, revolutions, and wars.

The continent of South America stretches 4,600 miles from north to south and 3,200 miles from west to east. It covers an area of 6,898,579 square miles and has a population of more than 339 million. The Andes—the world's longest mountain chain—and the world's mightiest river, the Amazon, dominate the landscape. South America's climate and vegetation zones range from the rain forests of Brazil, through **savanna** and scrub in Paraguay and northern Argentina, to Chile's Atacama Desert—the driest place on earth.

The continent is rich in mineral resources. Exports include iron ore, manganese, copper, silver, mercury, gold, and emeralds, as well as the nitrates and phosphates used to make fertilizers. South America has very little coal, which has limited heavy industrialization in most countries. Oil and hydroelectric power are the primary sources of energy. South America exports hardwoods, beef, coffee, maize, cacao beans, cotton, and fresh fruits and vegetables, mostly to the United States.

Sugarloaf Mountain (Pão de Açúcar) is a towering rock landmark rising 1,300 feet above the blue waters of Guanabara Bay, Rio de Janeiro. Visitors who take the six minute cable-car ride to the top enjoy spectacular views of the city.

80°

Caribbean Sea

LESSER ANTILLES

COSTA RICA

Barranquilla

Maracaibo

Caracas

Port-of-Spain TRINIDAD & TOBAGO

10°

PANAMA

Gulf of Panama

VENEZUELA

Orinoco

N O R T H

Medellín

Guiana Highlands

GUYANA

Georgetown

Paramaribo

A T L A N T I C

C. Corrientes

Bogotá

FRENCH GUIANA

Cayenne

Cali

COLOMBIA

Huila

Orinoco

SURINAME

O C E A N

Quito

Chimborazo

Macapá

0°

Guayaquil ECUADOR

Marañón

Putumayo

Japurá

Negro

Amazon

Marajó I.

Belém

São Luis

Fortaleza

Pta. Negra

A N D E S

Huascarán

Juruá

Purus

Madeira

Tapajós

Xingu

Tocantins

Araguaia

Caatingas

Cape São Roque

S e l v a

Recife

PERU

MOUNTAINS

Mamoré

Guaporé

Atinos

B R A Z I L

Sobradinho Reservoir

10°

Lima

Lake Titicaca

Illampu Peak

Plateau De

Brazilian Highlands

São Francisco

Salvador

La Paz

BOLIVIA

Mato Grosso

Brasília

Campos

Parnaíba

Arica

Altiplano

Lake Poopó

Atacama Desert

ANDES

MOUNTAINS

Gran Chaco

PARAGUAY

Paraná

20°

Antofagasta

CHILE

Llullaillaco Volcano

Pilcomayo

Asunción

Itaipu Res.

São Paulo

C. Frio

Rio de Janeiro

Tropic of Capricorn

Cerro Ojos del Salado

Salado

Serra do Mar

S O U T H

Mar Chiquita

Uruguay

A T L A N T I C

Mount Aconcagua

ARGENTINA

Porto Alegre

Lagoa dos Patos

O C E A N

30°

Santiago

Rosario

Buenos Aires

URUGUAY

Montevideo

Lagoa Mirim

Pampas

Rio de La Plata

P. Sur del Cabo San Antonio

Colorado

Bahia Blanca

P A C I F I C

Negro

Blanca Bay

O C E A N

San Matias Gulf

P. Valdés

Central America

Chiloé I.

Chubut

MEXICO

40°

L. Buenos Aires

San Jorge Gulf

BELIZE

Caribbean

Archipelego de Los Chonos

C. Tres Puntas

GUATEMALA

HONDURAS

Sea

EL SALVADOR

NICARAGUA

Gulf of Mexico

FALKLAND Is. (ISLAS MALVINAS)

Grande Bay

West Falkland

East Falkland

P A C I F I C

COSTA RICA

Archipelago Reina Adelaide

Strait of Magellan

O C E A N

PANAMA

Punta Arenas

Tierra del Fuego

C. San Diego

S C O T I A   S E A

South Georgia

50°

Cape Horn

90°   80°   70°   60°   50°   40°   30°   20°

0   500   1000   1500   2000 Miles

0   500   1000   1500   2000   2500   3000 Km

Belize and Guatemala

Belize

Status:	Constitutional Monarchy and Parliamentary Democracy
Area:	8,865 square miles
Population:	200,000
Capital:	Belmopan
Languages:	English, Spanish, Mayan
Currency:	Belize dollar (100 cents)

This former British colony changed its name from British Honduras to Belize in 1973 and became a fully independent nation in 1981. British troops remained in Belize until 1994 as protection from a possible invasion by neighboring Guatemala. The troops were withdrawn when Guatemala recognized Belize as a **sovereign state.**

Belize is a small country with forest-covered mountains in the south and patchy savanna and forest in the north, dotted with lakes and marshes. The country has a swampy coastal plain, and the **coral reef** that lies offshore is the world's second longest after Australia's Great Barrier Reef. More than half the population lives along the coast, 50,000 of them in Belize City, the former capital. In 1970 Belizeans built a new capital city, Belmopan, 50 miles inland—safe from the hurricanes that frequently hit the coast.

Belize City is the country's principal port, exporting tropical hardwoods, coconuts, bananas, sugarcane, and fresh fish and lobsters from the local fisheries—products account-ing for 65 percent of Belize's foreign trade. Tourism continues its rapid expansion, contributing to the country's **foreign exchange.** To lessen tourism's impact, the government has set aside some coastal land as conservation areas to protect the fragile mangrove forests and reefs from hotel and road construction and other developments.

A bunch of bananas ripen on a young banana "tree"—which is not actually a tree at all. The plant is a giant herb, and the trunk consists entirely of tightly wrapped leaves.

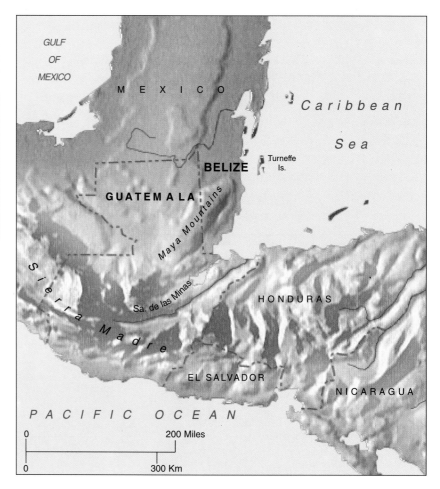

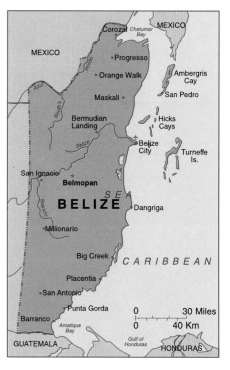

Guatemala

Status:	Republic
Area:	42,042 square miles
Population:	12.3 million
Capital:	Guatemala City
Languages:	Spanish, Amerindian languages
Currency:	Quetzal (100 centavos)

Guatemala's landscape is distinguished by three major land regions. The Petén region in the northeast is a flat, low, limestone **plateau** covered in tropical forests, which hide impressive Mayan ruins. Not many people inhabit this remote area, but the government is encouraging logging and new farming settlements—a plan Guatemalan conservation groups oppose.

Most of Guatemala's population live in the highlands in the southern half of the country. The climate there is cooler, and rainfall is moderate. Farmers grow coffee on the lower hillsides (up to about 5,000 feet) and plant maize and beans at the higher elevations. Cardamom, a valuable spice, is an important crop along the southern edge of the highlands. This region also contains the country's main urban centers, including the national capital, Guatemala City.

Guatemala's third region, the Pacific coastal plain, boasts fertile volcanic soil and an abundance of water tumbling from the Sierra Madre range. Coastal farmers produce fruits, vegetables, cotton, sugarcane, rice, and beef for both local use and export.

Cash-poor and heavily populated, Guatemala supplements its agriculturally based economy with the mining of oil, nickel, lead, and zinc. Industrial workers produce processed foods, clothing, textiles, and traditional crafts for export.

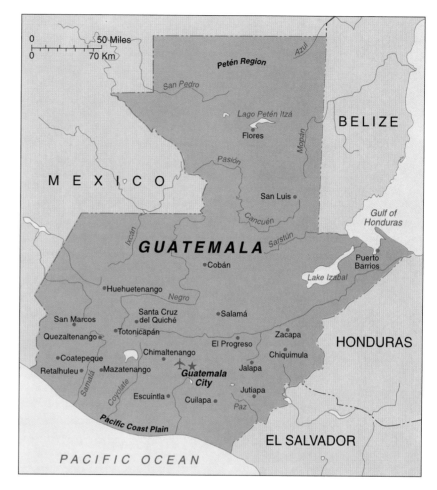

Huge stepped pyramids with wide, steep, stone stairways are typical of the Mayan ruins hidden in the forests of northern Guatemala's Petén region and Mexico's Yucatán Peninsula.

Honduras and El Salvador

Honduras

Status:	Republic
Area:	43,278 square miles
Population:	5.9 million
Capital:	Tegucigalpa
Languages:	Spanish, Indian languages
Currency:	Lempira (100 centavos)

Most of Honduras is mountainous, with several western peaks that rise to more than 8,000 feet. Oak and pine forests cover the foothills. Evergreen **cloud forests** grace the higher elevations. Nearly 60 percent of Hondurans live in small, scattered highland communities. Most are peasant farmers who own or rent small plots of land and produce just enough food for themselves, with a little extra to sell in local markets.

Narrow lowland plains run along the country's short Pacific coast and its longer Caribbean coast. Rich volcanic soil on the Pacific coastal plain supports large farms and cattle ranches. Farmers on the northern coast grow an abundance of bananas, which account for more than 30 percent of the country's exports. Honduras's only railroads snake through the northwestern coastal region, carrying bananas from the plantations to the port of Puerto Cortés. Coffee, sugarcane, beef, timber, and shrimp comprise the country's other major exports. Farmers grow maize and beans for local use.

Honduras has built few roads, and the interior of the country is largely undeveloped. Schools are few, especially in rural areas, and more than 40 percent of the population cannot read or write. About 15 percent of the people work in food processing, textile, furniture, and paper factories—industries situated in Tegucigalpa and San Pedro Sula, the country's two largest cities. Honduras abounds in minerals. Workers have mined only a small portion of the country's resources, such as silver, gold, lead, zinc, and cadmium.

Military dictators ruled Honduras for much of this century until 1981 when the Honduran people elected their first civilian government. It and the succeeding goverments have pledged to improve the country's living standards.

El Salvador

Status:	Republic
Area:	8,125 square miles
Population:	5.9 million
Capital:	San Salvador
Languages:	Spanish
Currency:	Colón (100 centavos)

El Salvador, the smallest of the Central American countries, has the third-largest population after Guatemala and Honduras. Nearly three-quarters of its people live in the country's central region—a wide rolling plateau with average temperatures of 73°F and about 45 inches of annual rain. Farms and ranches scattered across the plateau employ nearly half of El Salvador's workers. Small family farms grow beans, rice, maize, and other crops for home consumption and to sell at local markets. Many farmers also keep cows, pigs, and poultry. Most of the land belongs to large ranches raising beef and dairy cattle and to plantations of coffee—El Salvador's primary export crop. Plantations on the coastal plain grow sugarcane and cotton, which thrive in the hotter, wetter lowland climate. The Sierra Madre, a low mountain range created by ancient volcanic eruptions, forms El Salvador's northernmost boundary.

Most Salvadorans are mestizos (people of mixed Spanish and Indian ancestry), and the vast majority are poor. The wealthiest 2 percent of the population own most of the land in contrast to the nearly 20 percent who own none. This gulf between rich and poor led to a civil war that raged from 1980 to 1990. More than 75,000 people died, hundreds of thousands were left homeless, and the monetary drain on the country was enormous. Salvadorans are slowly rebuilding their country.

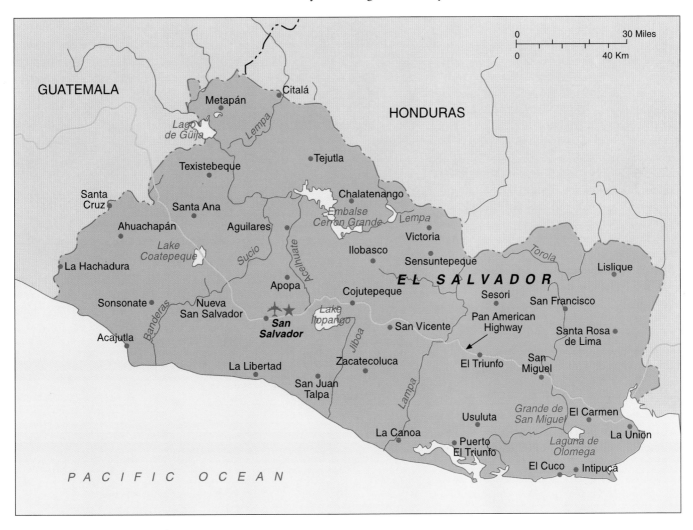

Nicaragua and Costa Rica

Nicaragua

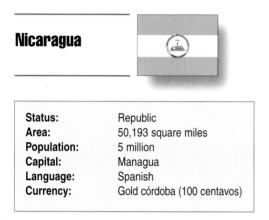

Status:	Republic
Area:	50,193 square miles
Population:	5 million
Capital:	Managua
Language:	Spanish
Currency:	Gold córdoba (100 centavos)

Three distinct land regions divide Central America's largest country. The Pacific region consists of a fertile coastal plain, a range of hills and volcanoes, and a long depression containing Lake Nicaragua and Lake Managua—Central America's two largest lakes. The region enjoys a warm climate with ample rain from May to November. Local farmers cultivate cotton, sugarcane, and bananas for export and rice and vegetables for local consumption. The bulk of Nicaragua's people and industries inhabit this region, an area often hit by earthquakes. Seismic activity nearly destroyed the capital city of Managua in 1972.

The Central Highlands, although cooler than the Pacific region, also receive most of their rain between May and November. Highlanders primarily grow coffee—one of the country's major exports—and maize and beans for local consumption.

Nicaragua's third region is the flat, low-lying Caribbean coast where the climate is hot (average temperature of 80° F) and wet. More than 165 inches of rain fall each year in the dense tropical rain forest and coastal swamps and lagoons. Very few people live in this part of the country.

Nicaraguans recently endured one of Central America's most bitter civil wars. In 1979, the left-wing Sandinista movement forced from office their corrupt president, Anastasio Somoza. Right-wing Contras, supported by the United States, opposed the Sandinistas. After a decade of conflict, the two factions agreed to a cease-fire in 1989, but outbreaks of fighting continued until 1994 when the Sandinistas signed a peace agreement with the last of the Contras.

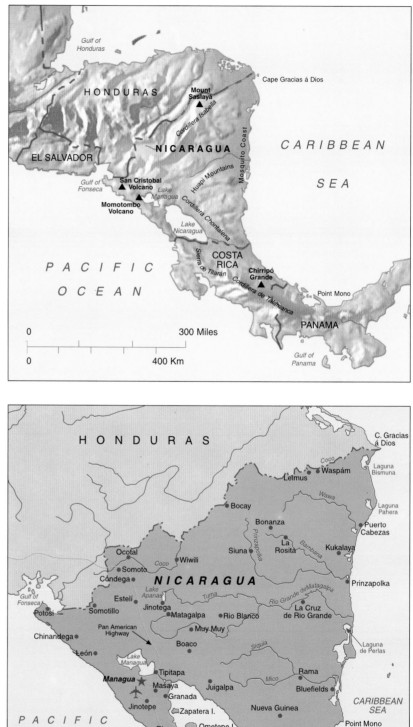

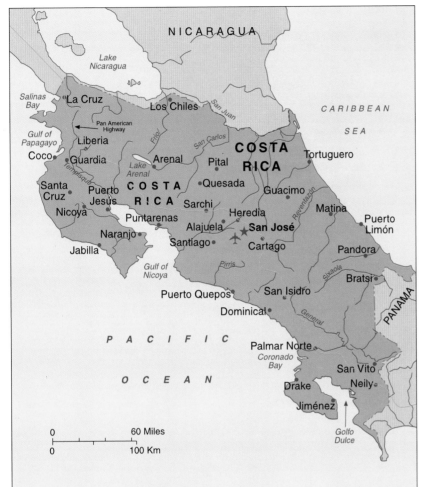

Costa Rica

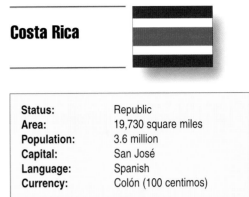

Status:	Republic
Area:	19,730 square miles
Population:	3.6 million
Capital:	San José
Language:	Spanish
Currency:	Colón (100 centimos)

Costa Rica is a **republic** and one of the most stable countries in **Latin America.** The president and the 57 deputies of the Legislative Assembly are elected every four years, and all citizens 18 years of age or older are required to vote. Local government oversees such basic services as fire fighting and access to water supplies.

Most of Costa Rica's terrain is mountainous, and high plateaus run northwest to southeast across the country. These highlands contain two large areas of very fertile land, surrounded by rugged peaks. Roughly three-quarters of Costa Ricans live in the highlands, many of them employed by the coffee plantations that produce the country's second most significant **cash crop.** Highlanders also grow maize, cacao beans, rice, potatoes, and beans. To the west, a narrow coastal plain runs along the Pacific shore. The coastal climate is ideal for growing bananas, Costa Rica's major export. Coastal farmers supplement their banana crops with sugarcane and tropical fruits. The Caribbean Lowlands to the east are hot and humid, with some of the world's richest rain forest vegetation and wildlife. The coast alternates between swamps and forests and long sandy beaches.

Although Costa Rica depends largely on agriculture, the country also produces fertilizers, cement, machinery, furniture, cosmetics, and pharmaceuticals and enjoys a healthy tourism industry.

Coffee trees produce small white flowers and then bright red cherries that contain the coffee beans. Workers remove the soft flesh of the fruit and dry the beans in the sun before packing them for export.

Panama and the Canal

Panama

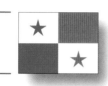

Status:	Republic
Area:	29,158 square miles
Population:	2.8 million
Capital:	Panama City
Languages:	Spanish, English
Currency:	Balboa (100 cents)

Narrow and S-shaped, Panama is the southernmost country on the isthmus linking North and South America. Bisected by the world's most famous canal, Panama is 450 miles long and 30 to 130 miles wide. Mountains run west to east across the country. The chain begins with Barú Volcano—an 11,400 feet peak near the border with Costa Rica—drops to the low rounded hills of the Canal Zone, and then rises again to 6,000 feet in the east. Very few people inhabit this forest-covered territory. More than 90 percent of the population lives in Panama's central region (near the canal) or on the Pacific coastal plain, where rich volcanic soil provides the country's most fertile farmland.

Panama City, at the canal's southern end, and Colón, at its northern end, are the country's largest cities and its centers of commerce and industry. Colón's Free Trade Zone allows companies to import and export goods without having to pay duties. Although not highly industrialized, Panama produces cement, beer, cigarettes, and processed foods. An oil refinery near Colón processes crude oil from other countries. Small farms grow **subsistence crops** of rice, maize, and beans. Larger farms and estates mass-produce bananas and other cash crops—sugarcane, coffee, and tobacco—for export to the United States and Europe.

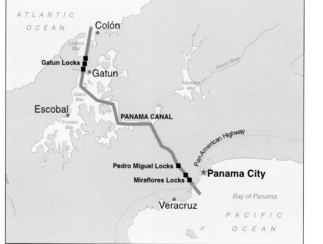

The Canal

The Panama Canal, which links the Atlantic Ocean with the Pacific Ocean, is one of the world's most significant waterways. Built by the United States between 1904 and 1914, the canal allows an average of 36 ships to pass through it each day, cutting thousands of miles from the long trip around South America. On the first stage of the 40-mile transit, a series of **locks** transports a ship 85 feet up to Gatun Lake. After crossing the lake, the ship enters the Gaillard Cut, a one-way channel just 160 yards wide that slices through the hills for more than eight miles. A second series of locks then lowers the ship to sea level again. After passing the city of Balboa, the ship sails under the Thatcher Ferry Bridge and heads into the Gulf of Panama.

A 1903 treaty between the United States and Panama allowed the United States to build the canal (at a cost of $380 million) and govern the Panama Canal Zone—a 10-mile-wide strip of land enveloping the canal. For years Panama tried to gain control of the canal and the Canal Zone. A treaty signed in 1977 returned territorial sovereignty of the Canal Zone to Panama in 1979 and gave Panama full operational control of the canal in 1999.

Left: Powerful electric locomotives running on tracks haul a cargo ship into one of the locks on the Panama Canal. Tugboats are used in addition to the locomotives when very large ships have to be maneuvered into place.

Right: This map shows just how important the canal is to ship operators. The 7 to 8 hour transit from the Pacific to the Atlantic saves 7,800 miles on a trip between New York and California—well worth the canal fee of about $30,000.

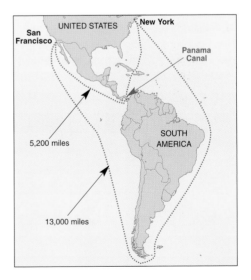

59

Colombia and Venezuela

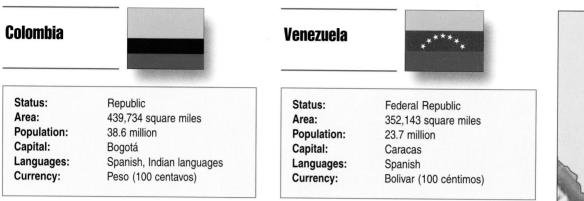

Colombia

Status:	Republic
Area:	439,734 square miles
Population:	38.6 million
Capital:	Bogotá
Languages:	Spanish, Indian languages
Currency:	Peso (100 centavos)

Venezuela

Status:	Federal Republic
Area:	352,143 square miles
Population:	23.7 million
Capital:	Caracas
Languages:	Spanish
Currency:	Bolivar (100 céntimos)

Long coastlines on the Pacific Ocean and the Caribbean Sea cradle Colombia, South America's fourth-largest country. The rugged Andes Mountains dominate the western landscape, fanning across the country in three separate ranges. The Cauca and the Magdalena—Colombia's two largest rivers—flow through the valleys on either side of the central range. This vast highland region supports the country's richest farmland and many of its larger towns—Bogotá, Cali, Medellín, Armenia, and Manizales. Colombia's narrow Pacific coastal plain is swampy and wet with very few inhabitants. The Caribbean coast is quite busy by comparison because most of the country's exports pass through the ports of Santa Marta, Barranquilla, and Cartagena. East of the highlands, treeless grassy plains called **llanos** stretch nearly 500 miles to the Venezuelan border. Cattle ranching provides the most employment in this hot, dry region. Farther south the plains give way to the dense tropical rain forest of Amazonia.

Colombia produces more coffee than any other country except Brazil. Farmers also grow rice, potatoes, rubber, sugarcane, and bananas. Abundant coal reserves and massive oil production bolster the economy. Colombia is also rich in platinum and gold and produces 95 percent of the world's emeralds.

Most of Venezuela's people live in the highland regions of the north and northwest and on the narrow coastal plain. A vast llano lies between the northern mountains and the Orinoco River. South of the Orinoco, a mixture of savanna and forest covers the rest of the country, rising to the Guiana Highlands in the southeast. The climate varies from a dry north to a very wet south.

Venezuela is the largest oil producer in South America. Petroleum and refined petroleum products account for 94 percent of its exports. The country also has rich reserves of iron, bauxite (the source of aluminum), copper, nickel, manganese, gold, diamonds, and coal. Rivers provide hydroelectric power for the steel and aluminum industries. Venezuelans also process sugar and manufacture textiles, furniture, leather goods, paper, chemicals, and light machinery.

Venezuelan soil is not very fertile, so much of the land, especially the llanos, is used for cattle ranching. Rice, corn, sorghum, coffee, sugarcane, cotton, and tropical fruits are the major crops in more fertile areas. The country has untapped resources in its forests and coastal fisheries, and Venezuela's tourist trade is minimal, considering the country harbors the world's longest waterfall—the 3,212-foot Angel Falls in the Guiana Highlands.

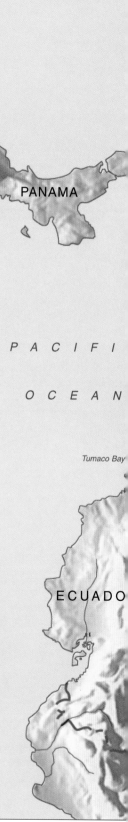

Music and dance play an important part in Colombian life, from the traditional songs and dances of rural villagers, like these members of a Bora Indian community, to the lavish carnivals of the big cities.

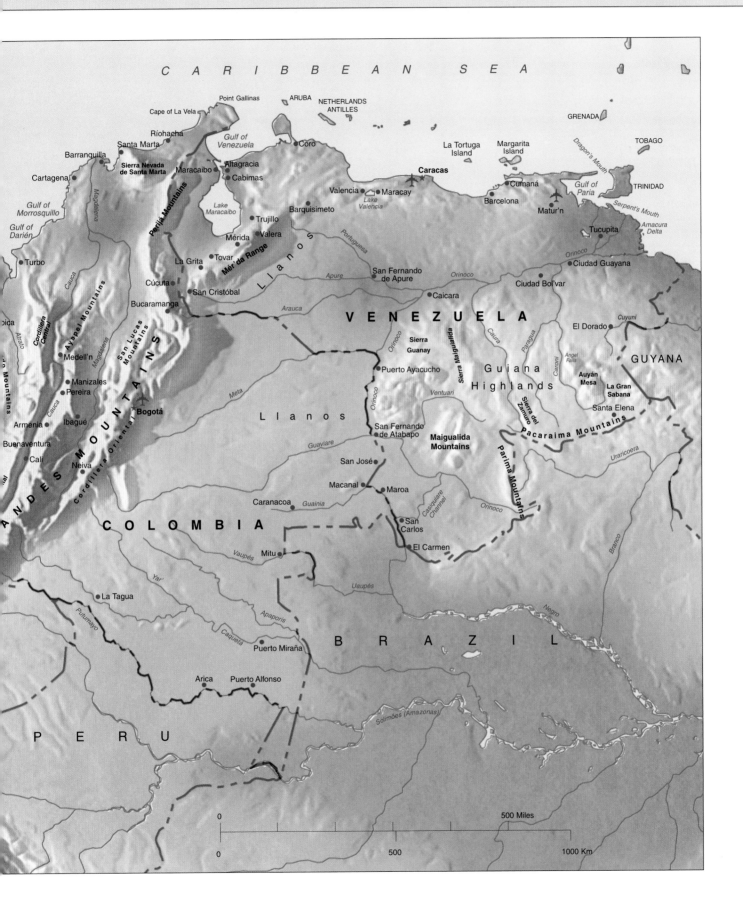

CARIBBEAN SEA

Point Gallinas
Cape of La Vela
ARUBA
NETHERLANDS ANTILLES
GRENADA
TOBAGO
Ríohacha
Santa Marta
Gulf of Venezuela
Coro
La Tortuga Island
Margarita Island
Barranquilla
Sierra Nevada de Santa Marta
Maracaibo
Altagracia
Cabimas
Caracas
Cumaná
Dragon's Mouth
Cartagena
Valencia
Maracay
Barcelona
Gulf of Paria
TRINIDAD
Lake Valencia
Gulf of Morrosquillo
Lake Maracaibo
Barquisimeto
Matur'n
Serpent's Mouth
Gulf of Darién
Perijá Mountains
Trujillo
Mérida
Valera
Portuguesa
Tucupita
Amacura Delta
Turbo
La Grita
Tovar
Mér'da Range
Llanos
Apure
San Fernando de Apure
Orinoco
Orinoco
Ciudad Guayana
Cúcuta
San Cristóbal
Caicara
Ciudad Bol'var
Cuyuni
Bucaramanga
Arauca
VENEZUELA
El Dorado
GUYANA
Cordillera Central
Ayapel Mountains
San Lucas Mountains
Magdalena
Orinoco
Sierra Guanay
Sierra Maigualida
Caura
Paragua
Angel Falls
Auyán Mesa
La Gran Sabana
Medell'n
Manizales
Pereira
Meta
Puerto Ayacucho
Guiana Highlands
Caroni
Santa Elena
Cauca
Bogotá
Orinoco
Ventuari
Sierra del Zamuro
Armenia
Ibagué
Cordillera Oriental
Llanos
Pacaraima Mountains
Buenaventura
Guaviare
San Fernando de Atabapo
Maigualida Mountains
Uraricoera
Cali
Neiva
San José
Parima Mountains
ANDES MOUNTAINS
Macanal
Maroa
Caranacoa
Guainia
Casiquiare Channel
Orinoco
COLOMBIA
San Carlos
Vaupés
Mitu
El Carmen
Negro
La Tagua
Yar'
Uaupés
Putumayo
Apaporis
BRAZIL
Branco
Caquetá
Puerto Miraña
Arica
Puerto Alfonso
Solimões (Amazonas)
PERU
0
500 Miles
0
500
1000 Km

Guyana, Suriname, French Guiana

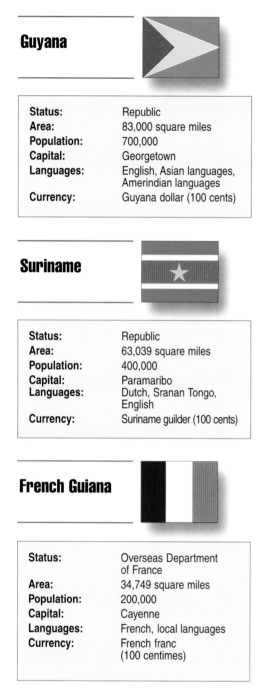

Guyana

Status:	Republic
Area:	83,000 square miles
Population:	700,000
Capital:	Georgetown
Languages:	English, Asian languages, Amerindian languages
Currency:	Guyana dollar (100 cents)

Suriname

Status:	Republic
Area:	63,039 square miles
Population:	400,000
Capital:	Paramaribo
Languages:	Dutch, Sranan Tongo, English
Currency:	Suriname guilder (100 cents)

French Guiana

Status:	Overseas Department of France
Area:	34,749 square miles
Population:	200,000
Capital:	Cayenne
Languages:	French, local languages
Currency:	French franc (100 centimes)

These three locations on South America's northern coast have many similarities—hot, wet, tropical climates; average temperatures of 80°F; and average annual rainfall of 80 to 126 inches. Each has a narrow coastal plain, wherein lives the majority of the population. Savanna and woodlands merge into densely forested highlands farther inland.

Guyana began as a Dutch colony in 1581, coming under British control 250 years later (as British Guiana). The country gained independence in 1966 and became a republic in 1970. Most Guyanans are descended from African slaves and Asian laborers brought in to work the sugar plantations. The population also includes Europeans (mainly Portuguese) and Chinese. Guyana's economy depends entirely on exports. Sugarcane and bauxite each account for about 32 percent of the country's income, with rice, rum, gold, and diamonds comprising the balance.

Suriname, formerly Dutch Guiana, gained independence in 1975. Dutch is still the primary language, but people also speak English and a local **patois** called Taki-Taki. Children are required to attend school, and most of the population can read and write. Since the 1920s, Suriname has been the world's chief supplier of bauxite, but during the 1980s antigovernment guerrillas attacked the mines and processing plants, causing extensive damage. Farmers grow oil palms, rice, sugarcane, coffee, and tropical fruits on Suriname's fertile coastal plain. The government is helping to develop a fishing industry—primarily for shrimp.

French Guiana, an Overseas Department of France since 1946, has been under French rule since 1817. Most of the people are descendants of slaves brought to the territory in the 1600s and 1700s to work the sugarcane plantations. Later, the French built penal colonies, including the infamous Devil's Island offshore, to hold convicts sent from France. The country's economy is underdeveloped and depends on France for financial support. Guiana has iron, copper, silver, gold, lead, bauxite, and diamonds—but so far only gold is produced in any quantity. French Guiana is working with France to develop a shrimp fishing industry, and the country is also the site of the European Space Agency's launch facility.

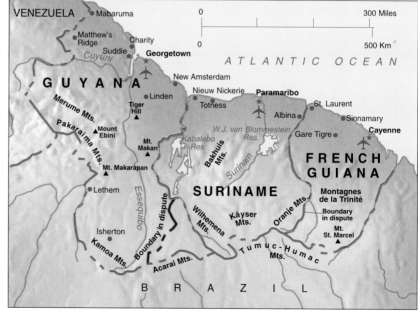

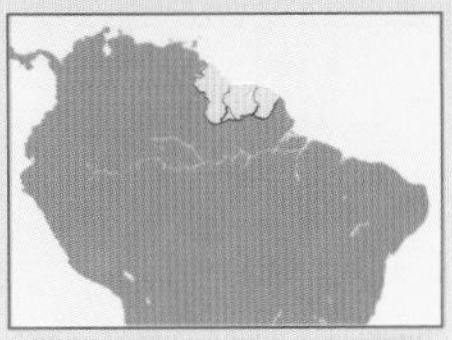

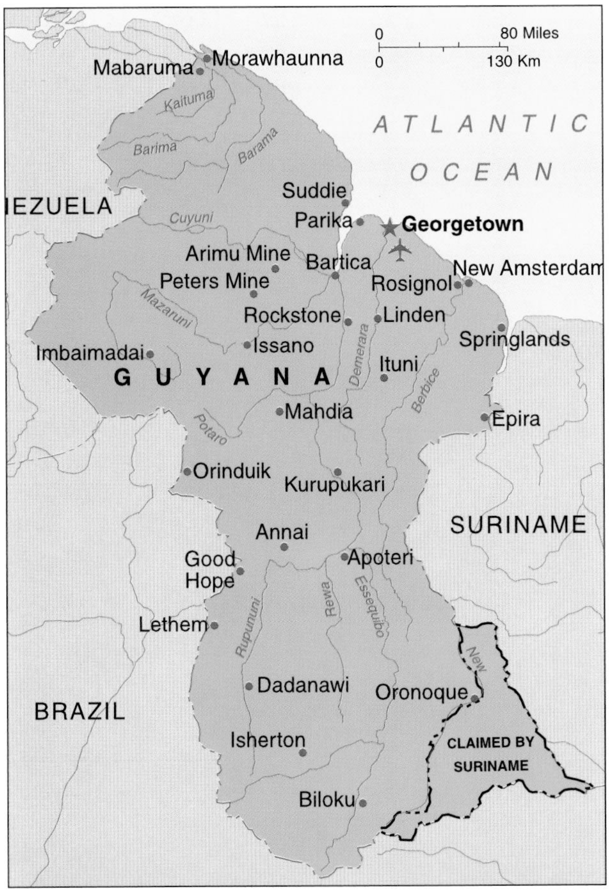

0 80 Miles
0 130 Km
Mabaruma
Morawhaunna
Kaituma
Barima
Barama
ATLANTIC
OCEAN
IEZUELA
Cuyuni
Suddie
Parika
Georgetown
Arimu Mine
Bartica
Peters Mine
Rosignol
New Amsterdam
Mazaruni
Rockstone
Linden
Springlands
Issano
Imbaimadai
GUYANA
Demerara
Ituni
Berbice
Mahdia
Epira
Potaro
Orinduik
Kurupukari
Annai
SURINAME
Good Hope
Apoteri
Rewa
Essequibo
Rupununi
Lethem
New
Dadanawi
Oronoque
BRAZIL
Isherton
CLAIMED BY SURINAME
Biloku

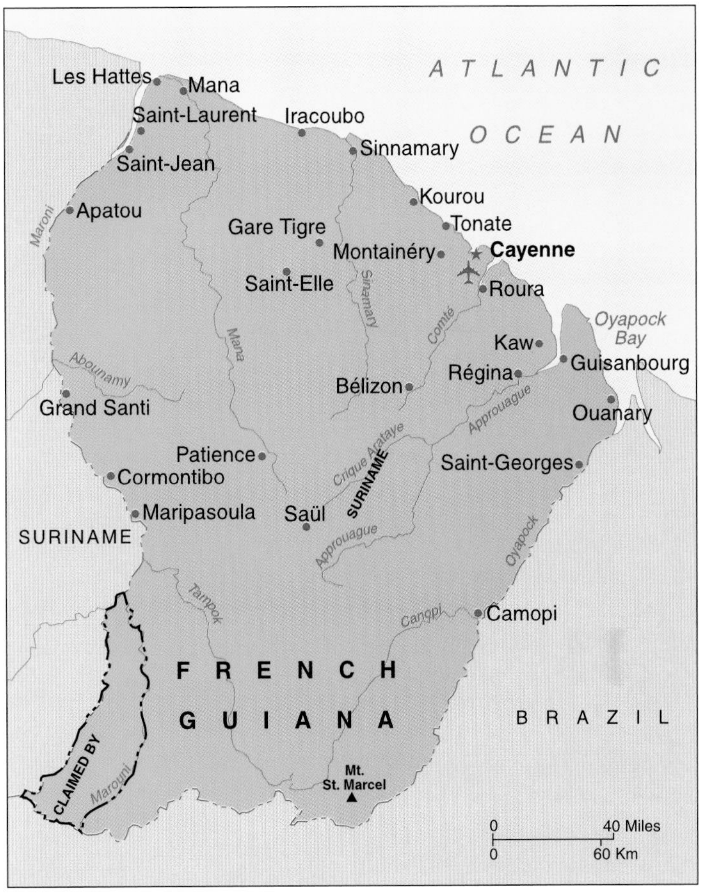

Les Hattes
Mana
ATLANTIC
Saint-Laurent
Iracoubo
Sinnamary
OCEAN
Saint-Jean
Kourou
Apatou
Tonate
Maroni
Gare Tigre
Montainéry
Cayenne
Saint-Elle
Roura
Sinnamary
Comté
Oyapock Bay
Mana
Kaw
Abounamy
Guisanbourg
Bélizon
Régina
Grand Santi
Approuague
Ouanary
Patience
Crique Arataye
Saint-Georges
Cormontibo
SURINAME
Maripasoula
Saül
SURINAME
Approuague
Oyapock
Tampok
Camopi
Camopi
FRENCH
GUIANA
BRAZIL
CLAIMED BY
Marouini
Mt. St. Marcel
0 40 Miles
0 60 Km

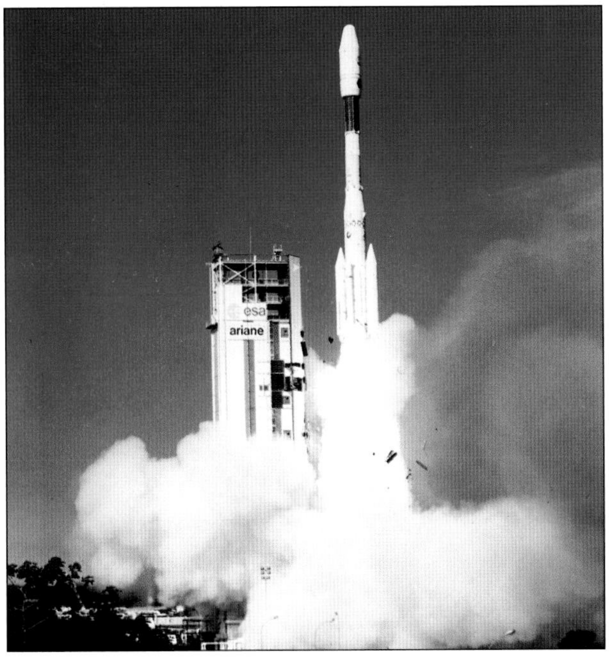

esa
ariane

Rockets launched toward the east from the European Space Agency's facility at Kourou, French Guiana, gain a 1,500 feet-per-second boost from the earth's spin.

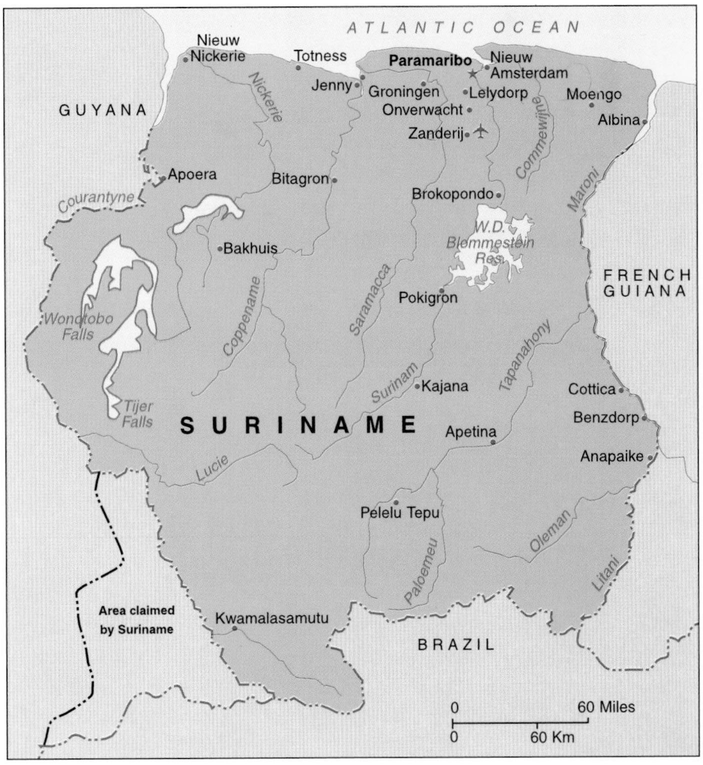

ATLANTIC OCEAN
Nieuw Nickerie
Totness
Paramaribo
Nieuw Amsterdam
GUYANA
Jenny
Groningen
Lelydorp
Moengo
Nickerie
Onverwacht
Albina
Zanderij
Commewijne
Apoera
Bitagron
Maroni
Courantyne
Brokopondo
W.D. Blommestein Res.
Bakhuis
FRENCH GUIANA
Saramacca
Pokigron
Wonotobo Falls
Coppename
Tapanahony
Surinam
Kajana
Cottica
Tijer Falls
SURINAME
Benzdorp
Apetina
Anapaike
Lucie
Pelelu Tepu
Oleman
Paloemeu
Litani
Area claimed by Suriname
Kwamalasamutu
BRAZIL
0 60 Miles
0 60 Km

Ecuador and the Galápagos Islands

Ecuador

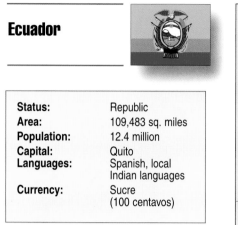

Status:	Republic
Area:	109,483 sq. miles
Population:	12.4 million
Capital:	Quito
Languages:	Spanish, local Indian languages
Currency:	Sucre (100 centavos)

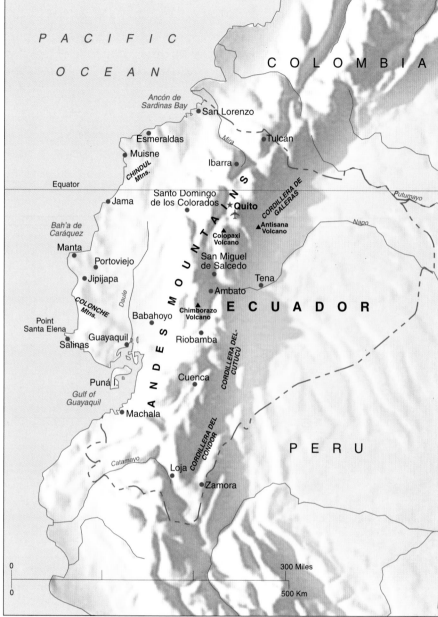

Spain ruled Ecuador from 1534 until 1822 and was responsible for many influences, including the country's name. Ecuador is Spanish for "equator"—the line of 0° latitude that runs across the country just north of the capital city of Quito.

Ecuador has three contrasting regions—a wide coastal plain, the mountains and high plateaus of the Andes, and an eastern lowland region sloping down into the Amazon Basin. The country also lays claim to the Galápagos Islands, which are located more than 600 miles to the west in the Pacific Ocean. Ecuador's coastal plain, 100 miles wide in places, supports a rich soil of mud and silt washed down from the Andes. The climate is hot and wet year-round. Plains farmers harvest bananas, coffee, and cacao beans for export from the port of Guayaquil and rice and sugarcane for local consumption. Coastal shrimp are another significant export.

Ecuador's Andean plateaus and valleys have a cooler, temperate climate ideal for cattle ranching and growing grains. The **haciendas** provide a much-needed paycheck for local citizens. Workers in the industrial cities of Quito, Ambato, Riobamba, and Cuenca produce textiles, shoes, and other leather goods. These cities lie on the **Pan-American Highway,** which runs from Santiago, Chile, to the border between Mexico and the United States.

The eastern half of the country is covered in rain forest. This region is largely uninhabited, apart from small groups of Indians and the oil crews who are opening up the rich oil fields in the north. Oil has been Ecuador's most valuable export since the early 1970s. The country has become South America's second largest oil producer after Venezuela.

Thirteen volcanic islands and scores of rocks and reefs form the Galápagos Islands. Barren rock covers the shores, but dense forests blanket the inland mountains. The Galápagos Islands are famous for their unique animal life, including 500-pound giant tortoises and 5-foot-long marine iguanas. Naturalist Charles Darwin developed his theory of evolution after visiting the islands in 1835.

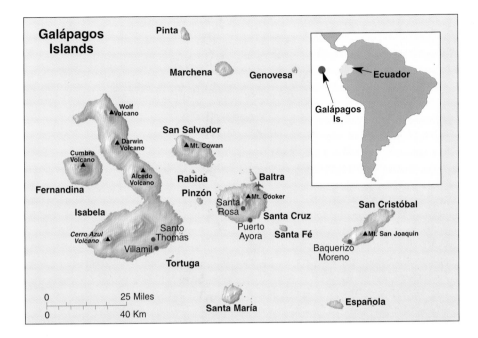

Galápagos Islands

Pinta

Marchena   Genovesa

Ecuador

Galápagos Is.

Wolf Volcano

Darwin Volcano

Cumbre Volcano

San Salvador

▲Mt. Cowan

Alcedo Volcano

Fernandina

Rabida

Pinzón

Baltra

Isabela

Mt. Cooker

Santa Rosa

Santa Cruz

Cerro Azul Volcano

Santo Thomas

Puerto Ayora

Santa Fé

San Cristóbal

Villamil

▲Mt. San Joaquin

Baquerizo Moreno

Tortuga

0   25 Miles
0   40 Km

Santa María

Española

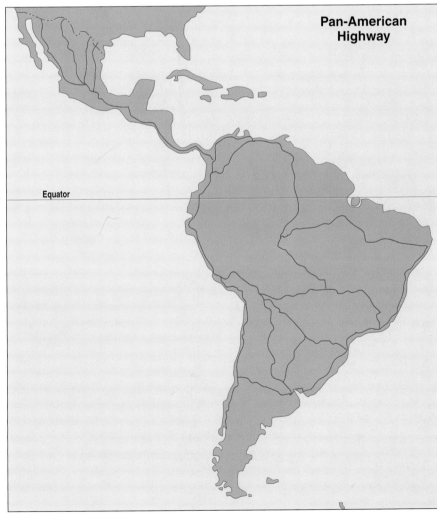

Pan-American Highway

Equator

Above: The marine iguana is just one of many unusual animals found on the Galápagos Islands. These prehistoric-looking creatures live on the rocky shores but feed on algae growing on rocks below sea level. The iguanas, giant tortoises, and unique birdlife of the islands inspired Charles Darwin's ideas on the evolution of life on earth.

Left: The Pan-American Highway runs from Santiago, in Chile, to the U.S. border with Mexico. Work started on the highway in 1936, and much of the work in Central America was financed by the United States. This amazing highway crosses deserts, plains, tropical rain forests, and 15,000-foot mountain passes.

Peru

Peru

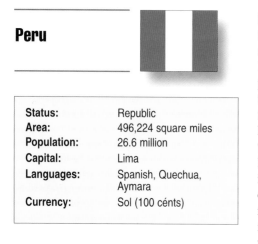

Status:	Republic
Area:	496,224 square miles
Population:	26.6 million
Capital:	Lima
Languages:	Spanish, Quechua, Aymara
Currency:	Sol (100 cénts)

Andean villagers often sell handcrafted goods at the roadside. These women are selling decorative gourds, used to carry and drink water, and colorful handwoven clothes, rugs, and blankets.

South America's third-largest country enjoys a variety of climates and scenery. Peru's coastal plain is a 100-mile-wide strip of desert with patches of scrubby vegetation moistened only by winter fog that rolls in from the sea. Yet this barren plain is home to 45 percent of the population, to the country's capital, to its largest farms, and to its primary industries. Desert farmers produce cotton and sugarcane for export and rice, fruits, and vegetables for city markets. They irrigate farmland with water from mountain streams, a resource shared with people in nearby cities.

Peru's nearness to the ocean influences several areas of the local economy. Fishing crews catch vast quantities of sardines and anchovies each year. Most of the catch is processed into fish meal and exported as animal feed. The southern coast supports iron ore mining, and oil fields dot the northern coast. Peruvians even mine offshore islands for **guano** (manure used as fertilizer), which is exported from the chief port of Callao, near Lima.

Approximately 40 percent of the population lives in the Andes Mountains, where plateaus at 10,000 to 15,000 feet above sea level break around towering peaks of 21,000 feet. Fertile soil and a temperate climate enable farmers to grow coffee on the lower slopes and grains and potatoes on higher ground. Large flocks of sheep, alpacas, and llamas graze in the grassy valleys. Peruvian mountains are also rich in minerals. The country exports great quantities of copper, lead, silver, gold, and zinc.

Peru's eastern landscape consists of the lower slopes of the Andes and the Amazon Basin's rolling plain, all covered in dense rain forest. The area is inhabited primarily by small groups of native Indians.

Above: The Indians of the Peruvian highlands wear colorful traditional costumes of handwoven cloth made from the wool of llamas, alpacas, and guanacos. Warm clothing, a thick shawl, and an embroidered cap keep this young girl warm despite the cold of the high mountains.

Left: Visitors travel from around the world to marvel at the ruins of Machu Picchu, an ancient Incan settlement perched above the Urubamba Valley, 7,875 feet up in the Peruvian Andes. The site is famous for its fine architecture and the terraced fields on the steep surrounding hillsides. Machu Picchu was discovered in 1911 by the American archaeologist Hiram Bingham.

Brazil

Brazil

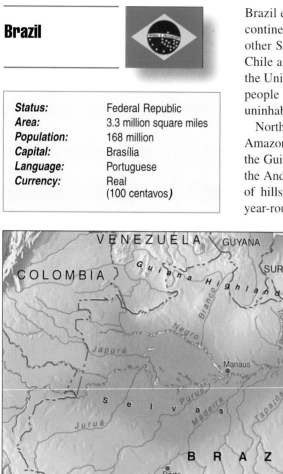

Status:	Federal Republic
Area:	3.3 million square miles
Population:	168 million
Capital:	Brasília
Language:	Portuguese
Currency:	Real
	(100 centavos)

Brazil encompasses nearly half of the continent, sharing borders with every other South American country except Chile and Ecuador. Nearly as large as the United States, Brazil has far fewer people and much of its interior is uninhabited.

Northern Brazil consists of the vast Amazon Basin, which is bordered by the Guiana Highlands in the north and the Andes in the west. This huge area of hills and plains is warm and wet year-round. Covered by the world's largest tropical rain forest, northern Brazil embraces the world's greatest river system—the Amazon and its main tributaries, which flow for nearly 4,000 miles from the Andes to the Atlantic Ocean. The river is so big and so deep that oceangoing ships can easily navigate it for more than 1,000 miles inland.

The southern half of the country consists of the Brazilian Highlands— on of high plateaus and deep valleys. The climate is seasonal.

Above: Carnival time in Rio de Janeiro is one of the noisiest and most colorful spectacles in the world.

Left: Iguazú Falls, on the border between Brazil and Argentina, consist of 275 separate waterfalls plunging 280 feet from a 2.5-mile-wide escarpment.

Below: Enormous open-pit iron ore mines scar the landscape at Belo Horizonte in the Minas Gerais province of southeastern Brazil.

Brazil

The south has cool winters and rain-drenched summers, perfect for the treeless savanna. Farmers graze cattle and sheep at the higher elevations and farm the fertile valleys and coastal plains. Roughly 80 percent of Brazil's population lives within 200 miles of the Atlantic coast. São Paulo, Rio de Janeiro, Salvador, and Recife—Brazil's major cities—lie on the country's southeastern coast.

Brazil produces more crops, timber, minerals, and manufactured goods than any other country in South America. Major commercial crops are coffee, cacao beans, soybeans, bananas, tobacco, sugarcane, maize, and oranges. Brazil raises beef cattle, horses, pigs, and sheep. The country is one of the world's chief exporters of iron ore, bauxite, beryllium, chrome, tin, manganese, magnesium, gold, and diamonds. Oil and gas wells along the coast produce fuel, as well as the raw materials for the country's petro-chemical industries. Brazil is the most heavily industrialized country in South America, and its exports include cars, aircraft, textiles, cement, chemicals, electrical goods, machinery, and paper.

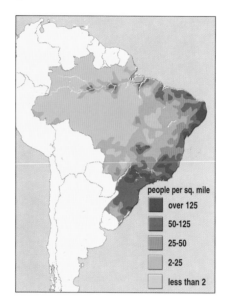

inches
- over 80
- 60-80
- 40-60
- less than 40

people per sq. mile
- over 125
- 50-125
- 25-50
- 2-25
- less than 2

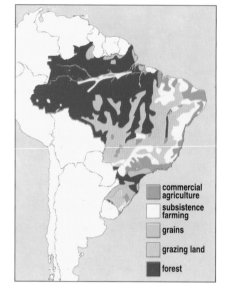

- commercial agriculture
- subsistence farming
- grains
- grazing land
- forest

Right: The National Congress is one of many stunning modern buildings in the capital, Brasília, 3,500 feet above sea level on the central plateau. Work started on the city in 1957, and the government moved there from Rio de Janeiro in 1960.

70

Bolivia

Status:	Republic
Area:	424,162 sq. miles
Population:	8.1 million
Capital:	La Paz
Languages:	Spanish, Aymara, Quechua
Currency:	Boliviano (100 centavos)

Above: The Cathedral of San Francisco overlooks this busy square in the Bolivian capital of La Paz. La Paz was founded by the Spanish in 1548, on the route between the Potosi silver mines and the port at Lima on the coast of Peru. At 12,000 feet above sea level, La Paz is the highest capital city in the world.

Bolivia, like many of its South American neighbors, has three contrasting regions. The high plateaus of the **altiplano** dominate the west, surrounded by the snow-covered peaks of the Andes. The highland climate is cold and dry, with nighttime temperatures often falling below freezing. Despite the harsh conditions, most Bolivians live in this area. Herders raise llamas and alpacas for their wool on the sparse grasslands of the highlands. In the more fertile areas—around Lake Titicaca and the cities of Cochabamba and Sucre—farmers grow potatoes, maize, quinoa, wheat, and oca, an edible tuber. Coffee, cacao beans, beans, rice, cotton, and fruits comprise the major crops in the eastern lowlands.

The climate is humid in northern Bolivia where dense forests merge with the Amazon rain forest. Southern and central Bolivia enjoy gentle hills and wide valleys, and in the southeast, semi-arid grasslands merge with the **Gran Chaco** of Paraguay. Ranchers raise cattle on the drier plains. Nearly half of Bolivia's workers are employed as farm laborers, but the country is very poor, barely producing enough food for its own needs. Peasant farmers in many areas illegally grow coca, the source of cocaine.

Mines in the altiplano produce tin, copper, lead, tungsten, silver, and zinc. Large oil fields and natural gas fields lie beneath the eastern plains.

Hydroelectric power stations on major rivers produce energy for the country's industries. Bolivia's principal exports are minerals (chiefly tin), natural gas, and textiles. The goods are shipped overland by road through Chile and Peru or south by river through Paraguay.

Paraguay and Uruguay

Paraguay

Status:	Republic
Area:	157,046 sq. miles
Population:	5.2 million
Capital:	Asunción
Languages:	Spanish, Guarani
Currency:	Guarani (100 céntimos)

The Paraguay River divides this land-locked country in two. A vast plain lies to the west of the river, rising gently from marshy bottomland near the river to the semi-arid Gran Chaco in Paraguay's northwest. Chaco vegetation is a mixture of coarse grasses, cacti, and thorny scrub—land best used for grazing cattle. A region of higher land lies east of the river, with alternating areas of grassland and hardwood forest. About 90 percent of Paraguayans live in this fertile eastern area. In addition to raising livestock, farmers grow maize, cassava, rice, and sugarcane for local use and tobacco, soybeans, and cotton for export.

Because Paraguay lacks a coast, the country's exports are shipped down the Paraguay River and on to the Atlantic Ocean, 1,000 miles away. The river, however, is so deep that 1,700-ton ships are able to sail upriver as far as the capital of Asunción.

Paraguay's chief energy source is hydroelectricity. And the country produces enough to export some to its neighbors. The gigantic Itaipu Dam on the Paraná River, built in partnership with Brazil, is the world's largest hydroelectric installation. With Argentina's help, Paraguay is nearing completion on a second huge hydro-electric plant at Yacyreta.

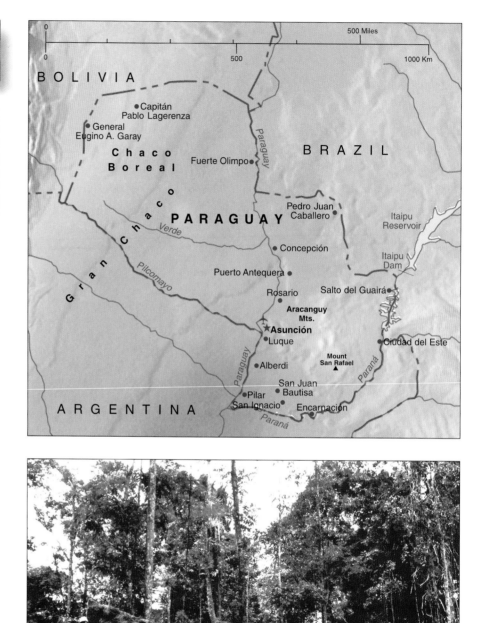

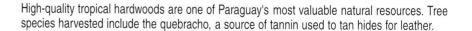
High-quality tropical hardwoods are one of Paraguay's most valuable natural resources. Tree species harvested include the quebracho, a source of tannin used to tan hides for leather.

Uruguay

Status:	Republic
Area:	68,498 sq. miles
Population:	3.4 million
Capital:	Montevideo
Language:	Spanish
Currency:	Uruguayan peso (100 centésimos)

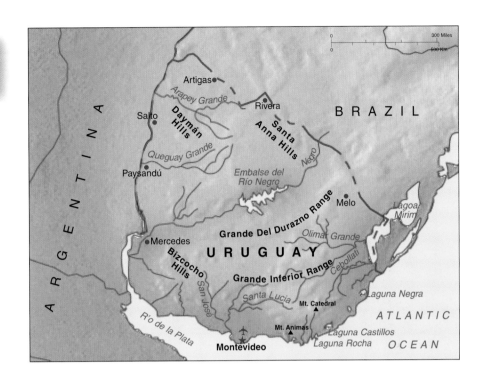

Uruguay, one of South America's smallest countries, is dwarfed by its neighbors, Brazil and Argentina. Its landscape consists of gently rolling long-grass prairies with ribbons of woodland growing alongside its rivers. Uruguay's highest point is just 1,640 feet above sea level. The climate is temperate, with warm summers and cool winters. Rain falls throughout the year. The country's many large rivers provide plenty of hydroelectric power, and the Paso de los Toros on the Río Negro has created the largest artificial lake in South America—the Embalse del Río Negro reservoir.

Uruguay's grasslands are ideal for grazing livestock. Local ranchers raise about 10 million cattle and 20 million sheep. Beef, wool, and leather goods are some of the country's main exports. The fertile soil of Uruguay's coastal plains supports a diversity of agriculture—wheat, rice, sorghum, maize, potatoes, and sugar beets—as well as milk and dairy products for the home market.

Most Uruguayans live in the coastal region—about half of them in the capital of Montevideo and the surrounding area. Beautiful beaches have helped boost tourism, a vital source of jobs and income. Uruguay has no mineral wealth, so machinery, cars and trucks, chemicals, and many other goods must be imported.

Well-developed educational, health, and welfare systems help Uruguay remain one of the most stable Latin American countries, despite some political unrest.

Chile

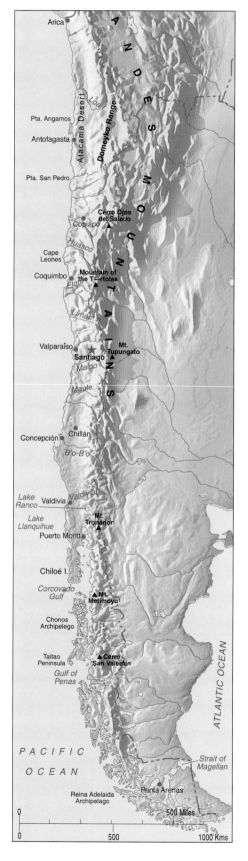

Chile

Status:	Republic
Area:	292,135 square miles
Population:	15 million
Capital:	Santiago
Language:	Spanish
Currency:	Peso (100 centavos)

Chile is one of the world's most unusual countries in shape and climate. A narrow strip of land extending 2,600 miles from north to south, Chile's green bean shape averages only 110 miles wide. The country's northernmost point is well inside the **tropics** and yet contains one of the driest deserts on earth. Far to the south, Chile's Cape Horn lies at the tip of Tierra del Fuego and is a land of forests, glaciers, and rocky mountain peaks jutting into the wild Southern Ocean. The country's narrow width slivers into three contrasting landscapes. Steep, rocky cliffs dominate the western coastline. Just inland lies a fertile central valley—home to most of the country's population, agriculture, and industry. The Andes Mountains rise steeply in the east, separating Chile from neighboring Argentina and Bolivia.

Chile enjoys one of South America's strongest economies, relying primarily on its significant mineral resources. The country is one of the world's chief producers of copper, and it also has large reserves of iron ore, lead, zinc, gold, silver, iodine, sulfur, and borax. Chile is one of the few South American countries with large coal deposits, although hydroelectric power and oil account for most of the country's energy supplies. Timber, manufactured goods, fruits and vegetables, fish, and by-products such as fish oil and fish meal also contribute to the local economy.

From 1973 to 1990, Chile was ruled by a military **junta** led by General Augusto Pinochet. In 1990 the country returned to democratically elected government, with a 120-member Chamber of Deputies and a 38-member Senate. Since the mid-1960s, all Chilean schoolchildren have had access to free primary education, and the country has one of the highest literacy rates in Latin America.

Above: An oil production platform sits off Punta Arenas in southern Chile. The oil fields in this region produce about half the country's fuel needs.

Left: Torres del Paine National Park in the Chilean Andes contains some of the finest scenery—and most demanding mountain climbing—in the entire Andes range.

Right: Significant resources of both metallic and nonmetallic ores, plus coal, oil, and hydroelectric power, make Chile one of the world's leading exporters of minerals.

Map labels:
500 Miles
0   500   1000 Kms
BOLIVIA
Iquique
Tocopilla
Mejillones
Calama
Pedro de Atacama
Point Tetas
Antofagasta
Atacama Salt Flat
Taltal
Catalina
Point San Pedro
Chañaral
Caldera
Point Medio
Copiapó
Huasco
Vallenar
La Serena
Coquimbo
Ovalle
Illapel
Viña del Mar
Valparaíso
Santiago
Rancagua
PACIFIC
OCEAN
ARGENTINA
Talca
Chillán
Concepción
CHILE
Valdivia
Lake Ranco
Lake Llanquihue
Puerto Montt
Gulf of Ancud
Chonos Archipelego
Taitao Peninsula
Gulf of Penas
ATLANTIC OCEAN
Reina Adelaida Archipelego
Punta Arenas
Londonderry I.
Cape Horn

Argentina

Argentina

Status:	Republic
Area:	1.07 million sq. miles
Population:	36.6 million
Capital:	Buenos Aires
Language:	Spanish
Currency:	Peso
	(100 australes)

South America's second-largest country is more than 2,170 miles long from north to south and 870 miles across at its widest point. Nestling into Chile's curved eastern border, Argentina covers most of the southern part of the continent. A varied landscape begins in the west with the Andes Mountains, whose highest peak, Aconcagua, towers over the region at 22,831 feet. The chaco in the northeast is damp and subtropical, with forested plains and swampy areas. The bulk of the country east of the Andes consists of rolling lowland plains. Flat and fertile, the **pampas** blanket most of eastern and central Argentina, from the dry west to the humid east where moist winds blow in from the Atlantic. South of the pampas lies the dry, windswept region of Patagonia and beyond that are the low mountains of the southern Andes and Tierra del Fuego, with their snowcapped peaks, ice fields, and glaciers.

Argentina's pampas boast large areas of fertile soil, a necessity for the country's agriculturally based economy. Farmers in the moist temperate regions produce wheat, maize, rye, soybeans, and linseed for export and fruit and vegetables for home consumption. In the drier regions, gauchos (cowboys) manage vast herds of beef cattle. Meat packing and food processing are primary industries, but Argentina also produces cars and trucks, iron and steel, cement, chemicals, textiles, and petroleum products. The country has few mineral resources apart from coal, iron ore, and uranium. Hydroelectricity provides about half of the country's energy. Coal and petroleum supply the rest. Locally mined uranium could be used for fuel rods should the country decide to use nuclear energy. Pine, larch, and oak forests in the flatland of Patagonia provide valuable timber for both local use and export, and Argentina's fishing crews catch hake, mackerel, anchovies, tuna, and squid.

Good schools and excellent medical services allow Argentinians to enjoy one of the highest standards of living in South America. Argentina

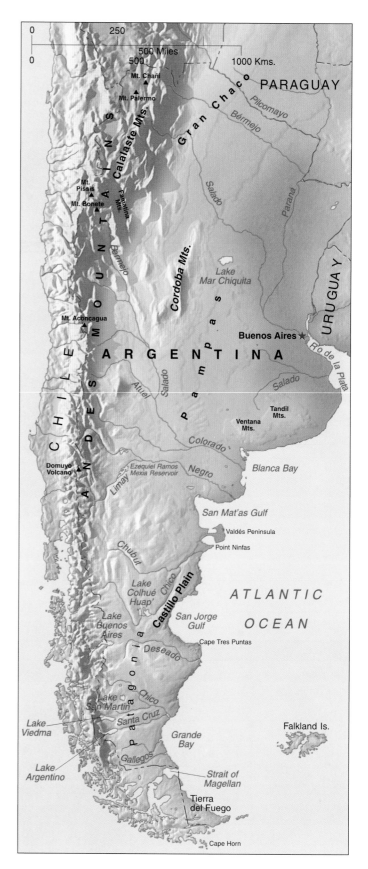

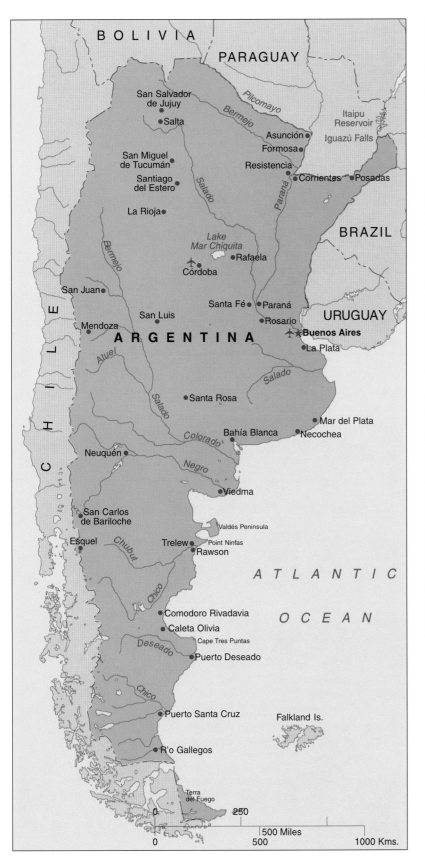

BOLIVIA

PARAGUAY

San Salvador
de Jujuy
● Salta

Pilcomayo

Bermejo

Itaipu
Reservoir

Asunción ●

Iguazú Falls

Formosa ●

San Miguel
de Tucumán ●

Resistencia ●

Santiago
del Estero ●

Salado

Corrientes   ● Posadas

Paraná

La Rioja ●

BRAZIL

Lake
Mar Chiquita

Bermejo

Rafaela

✈ Córdoba

San Juan ●

Santa Fé ● ● Paraná

San Luis

Mendoza ●

● Rosario

URUGUAY

A R G E N T I N A

✈✦ **Buenos Aires**

Atuel

● La Plata

Salado

● Santa Rosa

Salado

● Mar del Plata

Colorado

Bahía Blanca ●

● Necochea

Neuquén ●

Negro

● Viedma

Valdés Peninsula

San Carlos
de Bariloche

Point Ninfas

Esquel ●

Chubut

Trelew ●

● Rawson

A T L A N T I C

Chico

O C E A N

Deseado

Comodoro Rivadavia

● Caleta Olivia

Cape Tres Puntas

● Puerto Deseado

Chico

● Puerto Santa Cruz

Falkland Is.

● R'o Gallegos

Terra
del Fuego

C H I L E

0   250

500 Miles

0   500   1000 Kms.

Top: Like cowboys everywhere, the gauchos of the Argentinian pampas enjoy showing off their skill with horses.

Above: Buenos Aires—the capital and main cultural, business, and industrial center—has a population of about 3 million. More than 10 million people inhabit the metropolitan district. The residents proudly call themselves *portenos*, which means "people of the port."

Atlantic Islands

The vast Atlantic Ocean is home to less than 100 islands, relatively few compared to the Pacific Ocean. Large islands lie close to the mainland. Smaller islands, most of them the tops of submarine volcanoes (some extinct, some still active), rise from the **Mid-Atlantic Ridge**. The islands are rugged and mountainous, with steep slopes ending in sheer sea cliffs. People who inhabit these remote islands make their living primarily from subsistence farming, fishing, and tourism—the Azores, Madeira, Canary, and Cape Verde Islands entertain many foreign visitors each year. Cape Verde in the North Atlantic is an important refueling stop for transatlantic ships and aircraft, and Ascension Island in the South Atlantic has a U.S. military base and a satellite tracking station. Most of these islands are overseas territories of Britain, Spain, and Portugal, and they rely financially on their parent countries for the essentials such as food and fuel. Cape Verde is an independent nation, which receives financial help from international aid organizations and from Cape Verdians who work abroad.

The Falkland Islands, 320 miles east of South America, rise from the South American continental shelf, rather than from the deep ocean floor. Low and windswept, the Falklands are covered in tussock grass and peat bogs. Islanders raise sheep for their livelihood. Mineral resources in the surrounding seas could also supplement the island's economy, but the industry has not yet been developed. Both Argentina and Great Britain claim ownership of this island group.

Madeira

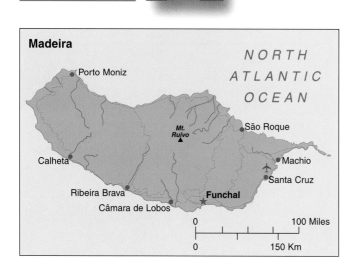

The Azores

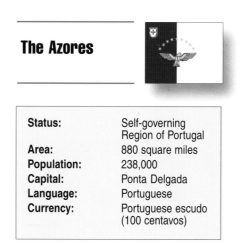

Status:	Self-governing Region of Portugal
Area:	880 square miles
Population:	238,000
Capital:	Ponta Delgada
Language:	Portuguese
Currency:	Portuguese escudo (100 centavos)

The group consists of nine main islands spread over 400 miles of the eastern Atlantic. The Azores are rugged, with a temperate climate. Farmers grow bananas and subtropical fruits at the lower elevations and grains and temperate fruits higher up. Islanders fish for tuna and sardines to export. The islands also have a growing tourist industry.

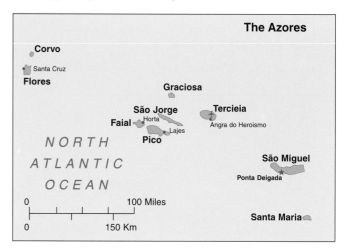

Status:	Self-governing Region of Portugal
Area:	315 square miles
Population:	270,000
Capital:	Funchal
Language:	Portuguese
Currency:	Portuguese escudo (100 centavos)

A warm, temperate climate and rich soil allow the islanders to grow sugarcane, vines, and both temperate and tropical fruits and vegetables. Grapes from the island's vineyards are processed into Madeira wine, a very popular export. Tourism is an important and growing industry.

Newfoundland

NORTH
ATLANTIC
OCEAN

North Eastern
Atlantic Basin

Danube

*Bay
of Biscay*

C. Race
Grand
Banks

Sable I.

Cape Cod

Newfoundland Basin

Mid-Atlantic Ridge

Azores

Cape de São Vicente

Mediterranean Sea

Cape Fear

Bermuda

*Sargasso
Sea*

Madeira

Canary Is.

Canary Basin

Puerto Rico Trench

Cape Blanc

*Caribbean
Sea*

Orinoco

Cape
Verde Is.

Cape Verde

Senegal

Niger

Cape
Verde
Basin

Guiana Basin

Cape Orange

Sierra Leone
Rise

Sierra
Leone
Basin

Cape Palmas

Guinea
Basin

*Guinea
Rise*

Congo

Amazon

Romanche Fracture Zone

Cape de São Roque

Ascension I.

Mid-Atlantic Ridge

St. Helena

Angola Basin

Brazil

Basin

Cape Frio

SOUTH
ATLANTIC
OCEAN

Paraná

Rio Grande
Rise

Walvis Ridge

Orange

Cape San Antonio

Tristan da Cunha

Cape of
Good Hope

Cape Corrientes

Gough I.

Cape
Basin

Cape Rise

Perú-Chile Trench

Argentine

Cape Tres Puntas

Basin

Falkland Is.

Atlantic-Indian Ridge

Scotia Ridge

S. Georgia

Bouvet I.

Cape Horn

Scotia Sea

S. Sandwich Is.

Drake Passage

0	1000	2000	3000	4000 Miles

0	1000	2000	3000	4000	5000	6000 Km

Atlantic Islands

Canary Islands

Status:	Self-governing Region of Spain
Area:	2,800 square miles
Population:	1.5 million
Capital:	Las Palmas
Language:	Spanish
Currency:	Peseta (100 centimos)

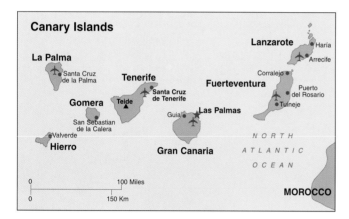

Above: The lowland and coastal areas of Tenerife are lush and fertile, but the island's mountainous interior is wild and rugged. Wind and rain have carved this rock pillar, standing like a sentry on the approach to Pico de Teide volcano.

Most of the islands in this group are rugged and mountainous. Only Lanzarote and Fuerteventura, nearest the African coast, are flat. Pico de Teide volcano on Tenerife erupted in 1909 and towers over the area at 12,156 feet. Fertile soil and irrigation procedures allow farmers to grow sugarcane, coffee, and tropical fruits on low ground and grains and temperate vegetables at the higher elevations. Tourism flourishes on the main islands.

Cape Verde Islands

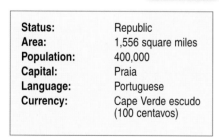

Status:	Republic
Area:	1,556 square miles
Population:	400,000
Capital:	Praia
Language:	Portuguese
Currency:	Cape Verde escudo (100 centavos)

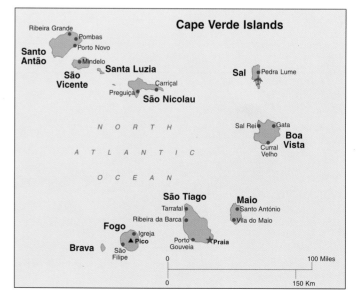

The islands are volcanic, mountainous, and very rugged. Cano Peak on Fogo Island is the highest point at 9,281 feet. The climate is arid, and much of the land is badly eroded. Local farmers grow maize, vegetables, and some fruits on land that has been improved by irrigation and by soil conservation programs. The islands' main exports are rum and fish (mainly tuna and lobster).

Falkland Islands

Status:	Overseas Territory of Great Britain
Area:	4,700 square miles
Population:	2,120
Capital:	Stanley
Language:	English
Currency:	Pound (100 pence)

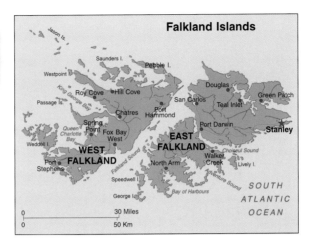

The Falklands consist of two main islands and nearly 200 smaller islands and islets. About half the population lives in the capital, Stanley. The remainder inhabits the outlying sheep stations. Since the war with Argentina in 1982, Britain has maintained a military garrison and air base on the islands.

Saint Helena Island

Status:	Overseas Territory of Great Britain
Area:	47 square miles
Population:	6,700
Capital:	Jamestown
Language:	English
Currency:	Pound (100 pence)

This mountainous island, 1,200 miles from the coast of Africa, is famous as the place where Napoléon Bonaparte died in exile in 1821. The island's small population lives by farming and by creating lace and flax for export. Saint Helena is the administrative center for several smaller British Overseas Territories, including Ascension Island and Tristan da Cunha.

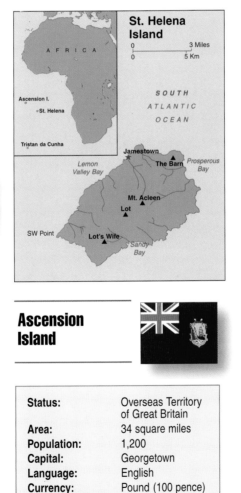

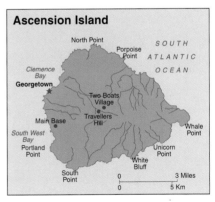

Tristan da Cunha Islands

Status:	Overseas Territory of Great Britain
Area:	40 square miles
Population:	330
Capital:	Edinburgh
Language:	English
Currency:	Pound (100 pence)

The largest of these remote volcanic islands, Tristan da Cunha sits at the southern end of the Mid-Atlantic Ridge. The climate is mild and wet. Islanders grow vegetables and raise sheep and cattle. The entire population was evacuated in 1961 when a volcano erupted. Most returned in 1963.

Ascension Island

Status:	Overseas Territory of Great Britain
Area:	34 square miles
Population:	1,200
Capital:	Georgetown
Language:	English
Currency:	Pound (100 pence)

More than 700 miles northwest of Saint Helena, Ascension Island is most famous for the sea turtles that lay their eggs on its beaches each year. The inhabitants are mainly British and American. Many of them work at the satellite tracking station and the military airfield.

A vineyard and lavender fields in southern France

EUROPE

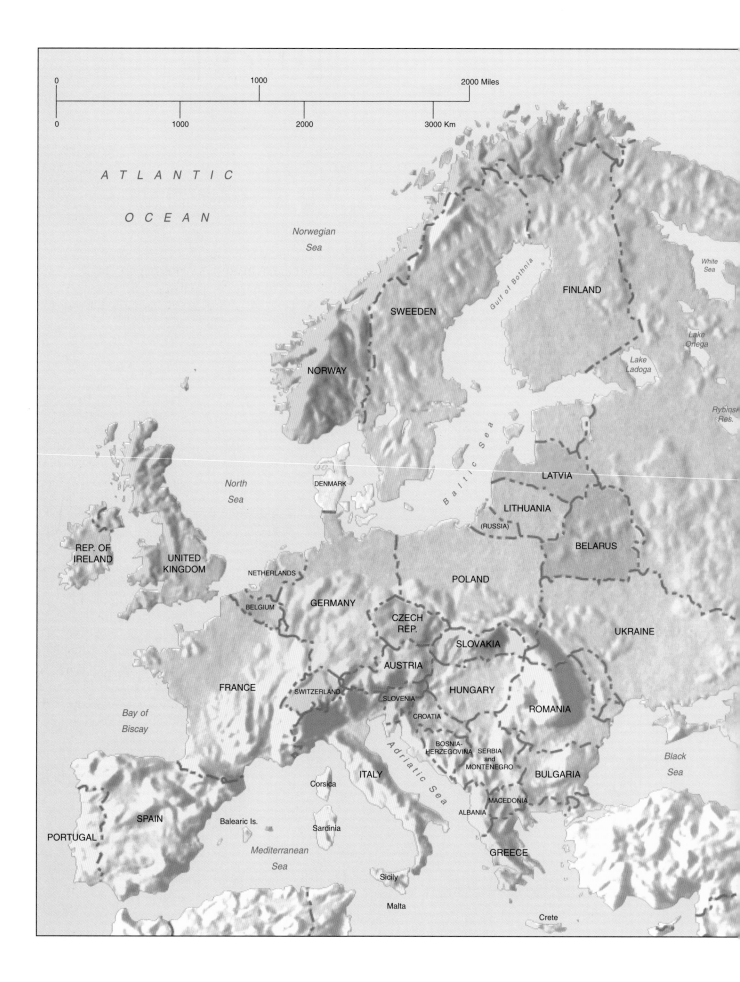

A T L A N T I C

O C E A N

*Norwegian
Sea*

*White
Sea*

Gulf of Bothnia

FINLAND

SWEEDEN

*Lake
Onega*

*Lake
Ladoga*

NORWAY

*Rybinsr
Res.*

*North
Sea*

Baltic Sea

LATVIA

DENMARK

LITHUANIA

(RUSSIA)

BELARUS

REP. OF
IRELAND

UNITED
KINGDOM

NETHERLANDS

POLAND

BELGIUM

GERMANY

CZECH
REP.

UKRAINE

SLOVAKIA

AUSTRIA

FRANCE

SWITZERLAND

HUNGARY

ROMANIA

SLOVENIA

*Bay of
Biscay*

CROATIA

Adriatic Sea

BOSNIA-
HERZEGOVINA

SERBIA
and
MONTENEGRO

*Black
Sea*

ITALY

BULGARIA

Corsica

SPAIN

MACEDONIA

Balearic Is.

Sardinia

ALBANIA

PORTUGAL

GREECE

*Mediterranean
Sea*

Sicily

Malta

Crete

0   1000   2000 Miles

0   1000   2000   3000 Km

EUROPE

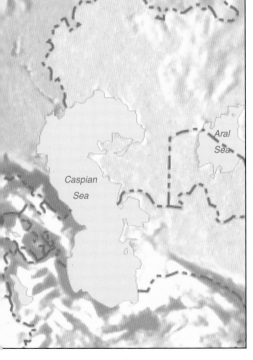

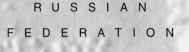

Europe is the second-smallest continent, yet it contains 40 independent countries. If you traveled the 925 miles from London, England, to northern Bosnia-Herzegovina, you would cross 10 countries each with its own history, traditions, and culture—that's 10 countries in the distance between Chicago, Illinois, and New Orleans, Louisiana.

With so many diverse **nationalities** packed into such a small land area, Europe has had a turbulent history. Over the past 2,000 years, great empires have come and gone. New countries have emerged, and old ones have disappeared. National borders have been redrawn time after time as a result of wars, alliances, and treaties.

Europe's landmass stretches 4,000 miles east to west and slightly more than 3,000 miles north to south. An abundance of bays, **fjords**, peninsulas, and inland seas have created a coastline that is nearly 38,000 miles long. The continent has a wide range of climates, soil types, resources, and scenery. It is one of the most densely populated and most productive regions in the world.

Europe has had an immense influence on the world despite its small size. Beginning in the fourteenth century, Europeans expanded their culture through art, music, science, medicine, navigation, industry, and technology. Intellectuals conceived many new ideas about economics, politics, and social justice. The world changed dramatically after World War II (1939–1945). Many European countries were devastated—their cities, industries, farms, and transport systems in ruins. It took many years to repair the damage. The United Kingdom, France, the Netherlands, and Belgium were also weakened by the loss of overseas territories as, one after another, their former colonies became independent nations. The United States and the Soviet Union emerged from the war as the world's superpowers.

Modern Europe continues to change. The former Soviet Union has fragmented into a dozen separate countries. But as one group separates, another develops. Major European countries have joined together as the European Union (EU, formerly the European Community). Its aim is to bring the people of Europe closer together culturally, technologically, and financially.

The European Union (EU)

The European Union has 15 independent states—Austria, Belgium, Denmark, Finland, France, Germany, Greece, Ireland, Italy, Luxembourg, the Netherlands, Portugal, Spain, Sweden and the United Kingdom.

The organization's aims are to bring the people of Europe closer together, to promote economic and social progress, and to make the voice of Europeans heard on the international scene. In March 1998, the EU began a process that will lead to the admittance of 13 more states—Bulgaria, Cyprus, the Czech Republic, Estonia, Hungary, Latvia, Lithuania, Malta, Poland, Romania, Slovakia, Slovenia, and Turkey.

85

Portugal and Spain

Portugal

Status:	Parliamentary Democracy
Area:	35,514 square miles
Population:	10 million
Capital:	Lisbon
Language:	Portuguese
Currency:	Portuguese escudo
	(100 centavos)

Overseas Territories
Azores—Eastern Atlantic Ocean
Madeira—Eastern Atlantic Ocean

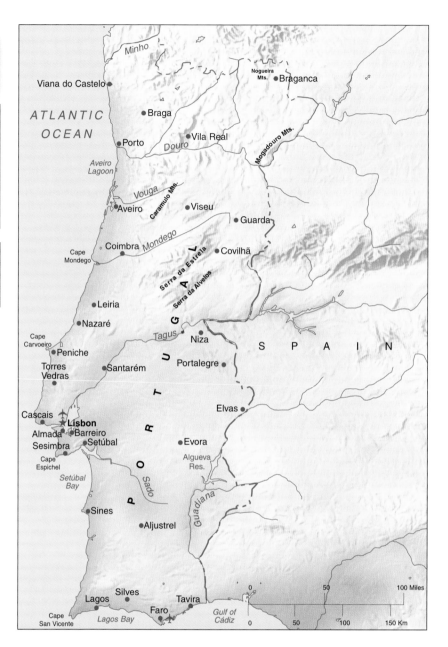

Situated on the westernmost edge of the European continent, Portugal is 350 miles north to south and about 125 miles wide. It covers roughly one-sixth of the Iberian Peninsula, which it shares with its neighbor, Spain. The self-governing islands of the Azores and Madeira in the eastern Atlantic are all that remain of Portugal's once-vast overseas empire.

Northern Portugal is mountainous, with a mild damp climate and a short dry season. Farmers use the poor upland soil mainly for grazing sheep and goats and the forests for producing lumber and wood pulp. The hotter, drier, southern coastal plains are an area of flatland rising inland to the **meseta**—a region of dry highlands cut by broad river valleys. Portugal's most fertile land is found in the valleys and on the coastal plains.

Farmers grow mostly grains—corn in the north and wheat in the south. Other crops include beans for local use and olives, grapes, limes, oranges, and almonds for export. Portugal exports nearly half the world's supply of cork, as well as wine, turpentine, resin, and Atlantic sardines.

Portugal's main mineral resources are tungsten ore, copper ore, and coal. Lisbon and Setúbal have shipbuilding and repair yards, and the manufacturing centers around Lisbon and Porto produce processed food, leather goods, ceramics, glass, and textiles.

Southern Portugal's Algarve coast extends for 60 miles from Cape San Vicente eastward to Faro. Tourists flock to its sandy beaches, coves, and spectacular rock formations. Quiet villages, farmland, and medieval towns provide plenty to explore farther inland.

Spain

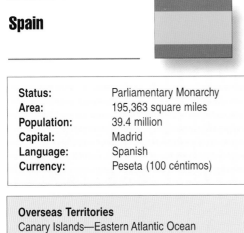

Status:	Parliamentary Monarchy
Area:	195,363 square miles
Population:	39.4 million
Capital:	Madrid
Language:	Spanish
Currency:	Peseta (100 céntimos)

Overseas Territories
Canary Islands—Eastern Atlantic Ocean
Ceuta—North coast of Morocco
Melilla—North coast of Morocco

One of the oldest occupied territories in Europe, Spain has been inhabited for more than 100,000 years. Dry, scrub-covered meseta, lying at 2,000 to 2,500 feet above sea level, covers most of the central region. Numerous mountain ranges run across the middle of the country and along the north and south coasts.

Prime farmland is found on the coastal lowlands of Valencia and Alicante, in the Ebro River Valley, and in the Guadalquivir Basin.

The inland climate is hot and dry in summer and cold in winter. Meseta farmers graze sheep and goats and grow barley and oats. Forestry workers produce lumber, cork, and resin. Farmers in the cool damp northern regions and in the warm mild Mediterranean coastal areas produce wheat, barley, fruits, sugar beets, vegetables, cotton, and tobacco. Olive groves and vineyards cover vast expanses. Spain is the world's primary olive producer and one of the world's leading wine makers.

Tourism contributes a great deal to the economy. Visitors flock to the country's Mediterranean coast, to the historic inland towns, and to the Balearic and Canary Islands. The northern cities of Bilbao, Santander, and Oviedo house the country's iron and steel, shipbuilding, automobile, chemicals, and cement industries. Spaniards mine copper, lead, zinc, silver, mercury, and other metals. Barcelona is the main center for manufactured goods such as textiles, electronics, leather goods, and food processing.

Left: Spain has a daily routine all its own. Most people work until midday, take a three-hour break, then work again until seven. The evening meal is seldom eaten before 10 P.M., and there's still time to sit and talk or to enjoy the country's wealth of traditional dances.

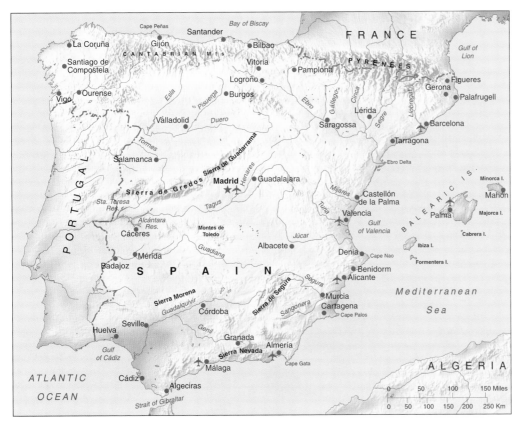

Above: Antonio Gaudi's spectacular Church of the Holy Family is one of many architectural attractions in Barcelona, Spain's second-biggest city. Barcelona is also the country's principal seaport, a center of trade and industry, and a world-famous cultural center.

France

France

Status:	Parliamentary Democracy
Area:	212,934 square miles
Population:	59.1 million
Capital:	Paris
Language:	French
Currency:	Franc (100 centimes)

Overseas Territories
French Polynesia—Mid-Pacific Ocean
St. Pierre and Miquelon—Off
  Newfoundland, Canada
Mayotte—Indian Ocean, off Madagascar
Wallis and Futuna Is.—Western Pacific
  Ocean
New Caledonia—Western Pacific Ocean
Kerguelen—Southern Ocean

Overseas Departments
Guadeloupe—Caribbean
Martinique—Caribbean
French Guiana—South America
Réunion—Indian Ocean

Above: Among the great attractions of Paris are the city's hundreds of sidewalk cafés, where tourists and local residents alike can relax and talk and watch the world go by.

Right: The village of Dieulefit lies in the Rhône Valley in south central France. Local farmers plant crops in the valley's fertile soils, and vines thrive on the hillsides.

France is one of the largest countries in Europe, extending about 600 miles north to south and 600 miles east to west. Fertile plains and rolling hills dominate northern France. The hard granite moors of Brittany jut into the Atlantic Ocean. The capital city of Paris stands in the middle of a huge saucer-shaped hollow called the Paris Basin. The city is home to the Cathedral of Notre Dame, the Eiffel Tower, and the Louvre. Western France is covered in flat plains, rimmed with sandy beaches that attract tourists to the Atlantic coast. Most of France's inland borders are mountainous. The Pyrénées separate France from Spain in the southwest. To the southeast, the Alps form a barrier between France and its neighbors Switzerland and Italy. The lower wooded Vosges and Ardennes Mountains mark France's borders with Germany and Belgium in the east and northeast.

France's **Massif Central** boasts beautiful scenery, opulent chateaus, and three of the country's great rivers—the Loire, the Seine, and the Rhône. Several large industrial centers (Clermont-Ferrand, Limoges, St. Étienne, and Lyon) have developed where these rivers flow into the northern lowlands. France's other important industrial centers lie near Paris, in the Nord-Pas-de-Calais and Lorraine coalfields, and close to the ports of Le Havre and Dunkerque on the English Channel. France has to import most of its coal and oil, but 70 percent of the country's power derives from its nuclear power plants. Mountain rivers and the world's largest tidal power station, at the mouth of Brittany's Rance River, supply energy for France's surging hydroelectric power.

France is the world's fourth-ranked industrial nation—following the United States, Japan, and Germany. The country produces vast quantities of steel and aluminum and is a leading manufacturer of cars, locomotives, aircraft, turbines, and other machinery. Electrical goods, chemicals, pharmaceuticals, and textiles comprise the remainder of its industrial exports. France is also Europe's leading agricultural nation. Sixty percent of the land supports crops and livestock. Northern farmers produce grains, beets, beef, veal, poultry, and dairy products. Mediterranean farmers grow fruits and vegetables. Many French tend grapes to make wine.

ATLANTIC
OCEAN

UNITED KINGDOM

ENGLISH CHANNEL

Strait of Dover

Dunkerque
Calais
Gravelines
Boulogne
St.Omer
Roubaix
Hazebrouck
Lille
Montreuil
Douai
Arras
Valenciennes

BELGIUM

GERMANY

Abbeville
Dieppe
Fécamp
Le Havre
Bolbec
Rouen
Beauvais
Amiens
Montdidier
Bapaume
Cambrai
St. Quentin
Hirson
Charleville-Mézières
Montreuil
Compiègne
Reims

Ardennes
Argonne Plateau
LUXEMBOURG

Meuse
Moselle

Verdun
Metz
Pont à Mousson
Nancy
Strasbourg

Cap de la
Hague
Cherbourg
Channel Is.
(U.K.)
Valognes
Carentan
Caen
St. Lô

Seine
Bay

Roscoff
Morlaix
Granville
St.-Malo
St-Brieuc
Dinan
Fougères

Gulf of
Saint-Malo
Normandy Hills

Elbeuf
Louviers
Lisieux
Evreux
Mantes-la-Jolie
Argentan
St. Germain-en-Laye
Argenteuil
St. Denis
Paris
Versailles
Île-de-Paris
Meaux
Châlons-sur-Marne

Marne

St.Dizier
Wassy
Toul
Spinal

Vosges
Colmar
Mulhouse
Belfort
Basel

Brittany Hills
Rance
Vilaine

Pontivy
Rennes
Vitré
Mayenne
Laval

Alençon
Chartres
Rambouillet
Fontainebleau
Nemours
Sens

Seine

Troyes
Langres

Langres Plateau
Saône

Vesoul
Besançon

La Chaux de Fonds
Pontarlier

SWITZERLAND

Quimper
Lorient
Auray
Vannes
Redon

Groix I.
Quiberon Peninsula
Belle-Île-en-Mer

St. Nazaire
Angers
Nantes
Saumur
Cholet

Le Mans
Orléans
Blois
Tours
Vierzon

FRANCE

Loir
Loire
Cher

Montargis
Gien
Auxerre
Avallon
Dijon
Dôle

Autun
Chalon-sur-Saône
Lons le Saunier
St.Claude

Jura Mountains
Lake
Geneva
Chamonix

Île de Noirmoutier
Île d'Yeu

Bressuire
La Roche-sur-Yon
Les Sables-d'Olonne
Niort

Poitiers
Châtellerault
Châteauroux
La Châtre

Bourges
Nevers
Le Creusot
Montceau les Mines
Moulins

Montluçon

Mâcon
Bourg-en-bresse
Villefranches
Lyon
Villeurbanne

Île de Ré
La Rochelle
Rochefort
Île d'Oléron

Civray
Limoges

Lapalisse

Clermont-Ferrand
Ambert
St.-Étienne

Chambéry
Vienne

Voiron
FRENCH
ALPS
Grenoble
Val d'Isère

Grave Point
Royan
Cognac
Angoulême
Nontron
Barbezieux

Le Mont-Dore
MASSIF CENTRAL

Annonay
Tournon
Romans-sur-Isère

ITALY

Lesparre-Médoc
Pauillac
Blaye
Bourg
Libourne
Bordeaux
Arcachon

Étang de Carcans

Périgueux
Brive-la-Gaillarde
Bergerac
Souillac

Tulle
Mauriac
Murat
St. Flour
Aurillac

Yssingeaux
Le Puy

Prives
Valence

Isère

Montélimar

Durance
Gap

Étang de Cazaux
Étang de Biscarrosse

Mimizan

Bay
of
Biscay

Marmande
Figeac
Lot
Villeneuve
-sur-lot
Agen

Cahors
Villefranche
Espalion
Rodez

Marvejols
Mende
Florac

Tarn

Alès
Orange
Avignon
Carpentras

Rhône

Maritime Alps

Monte-de-Marsan
Castelsarrasin
Condom
Verdun
Moissac
Montauban
Gaillac
Carmaux
Albi

Millau
Le Vigan
Lodève

Nîmes
Montpellier

Apt

Monte Carlo
Nice
Antibes
Draguignan
Cannes

Dax
Biarritz
Bayonne
St. Jean-de-Luz
Pau
Tarbes

Auch
Mirande
Toulouse
Muret

Graulhet
Castres
Mazamet

Carcassonne
Béziers

Tarascon
Arles

Aix-en-Provence

Brignoles
St.Raphael
St.Tropez

Étang
de Berre

Rhône Delta

Marseille
Bandol
Hyères
Toulon
La Seyne-sur-Mer

SPAIN

Lourdes
St. Gaudens
Foix

PYRÉNÉES

Limoux
Narbonne

Gulf
of Lion

Mediterranean
Sea

ANDORRA
Prades
Perpignan

Garonne
Garonne
Adour
Dordogne
Sète

SCALE
0   50   100   150   200 Miles
0   100   200   300 Km

United Kingdom and Ireland

United Kingdom

Status:	Constitutional Monarchy
Area:	94,548 square miles
Population:	59.4 million
Capital:	London
Languages:	English, Welsh, Gaelic
Currency:	British pound (100 pence)

The United Kingdom of Great Britain and Northern Ireland comprises a group of islands separated from mainland Europe by the English Channel, the Strait of Dover, and the North Sea. England, Scotland, the principality of Wales, and Northern Ireland comprise the country's four political divisions.

The United Kingdom's landscape is quite varied. Mountains and **moors** dominate the north. Rolling hills and fertile plains cover the southern and eastern lowlands. The rugged peaks and calm mountain lakes of the Scottish Highlands, England's Lake District, and Snowdon in northern Wales attract many tourists. Upland farmers graze sheep on the high ground and grow grain, hay, and **fodder crops** at the lower elevations. Depending on soil and climate, farmers grow wheat, barley, oats, vegetables, peas, beans, sugar beets, fodder crops, and fruit. Large dairy and beef herds graze on the rich lowland pastures. Agriculture employs only 1 percent of the country's workforce, but farming is highly mechanized and very productive.

The United Kingdom's early economy depended on heavy industries such as coal mining, steel, machinery, automobiles, chemicals, textiles, and pottery. Industrial centers developed in northern England and Scotland, in the western Midlands, and near the ports of London, Liverpool, Glasgow, and Belfast. Modern manufacturing such as light engineering, electrical goods, computers, biotechnology, and food processing have developed in parts of the United Kingdom where the older industries have declined. Although the country's imports exceed its exports, the economy is bolstered by banking, by insurance, by other financial services, and by tourism.

United Kingdom Overseas Territories

Anguilla—Caribbean

Bermuda—Western Atlantic Ocean

British Antarctic Territory—Antarctica

British Indian Ocean Territory—Indian Ocean

British Virgin Islands, Cayman Islands, Montserrat, Turks and Caicos Islands—Caribbean

Falkland Islands—South Atlantic Ocean

Gibraltar—Mediterranean

Pitcairn, Henderson, Ducie, and Oeno Is—South western Pacific Ocean

St. Helena, Ascension, Tristan da Cunha—Southeastern Atlantic Ocean

South Georgia and South Sandwich Is—South Atlantic Ocean

Above: Like New York, London has an instantly recognizable skyline—especially dramatic in the evening sun.

Republic of Ireland

Status:	Republic
Area:	27,135 square miles
Population:	3.7 million
Capital:	Dublin
Languages:	English, Gaelic
Currency:	Irish pound (100 pence)

Southern Ireland's lush green countryside and rich pastures have earned the country its famous nickname—the Emerald Isle. Separated politically from Northern Ireland in 1921, southern Ireland first became the Irish Free State. In 1949 it was renamed the Republic of Ireland (Eire in Gaelic).

The central part of the country is low-lying, with peat bogs and clusters of low rounded hills called **drumlins**. Low rugged mountains rise to about 2,500 feet in the north and west. Southwestern Ireland's long ridges of hard sandstone jut out to sea like fingers, creating long sea inlets and natural harbors. Ireland's hills, lakes, and coastal scenery attract many visitors each year.

Nearly 70 percent of the country is farmland. Atlantic winds carry plenty of rain, and the climate is cool and mild. Farmers raise large dairy herds in the country's southern and midland regions. Smaller herds of beef cattle graze in the east and west. Primary crops are wheat, oats, potatoes, and sugar beets. Farmers also grow barley for cattle feed and to make beer. The Irish enjoy excellent fishing opportunities and export fish, lobster, prawns, and shellfish. Ireland's manufactured goods include machinery, textiles, fine glassware, and electronic equipment. The island's main manufacturing center is a vast government-supported industrial estate near Shannon airport.

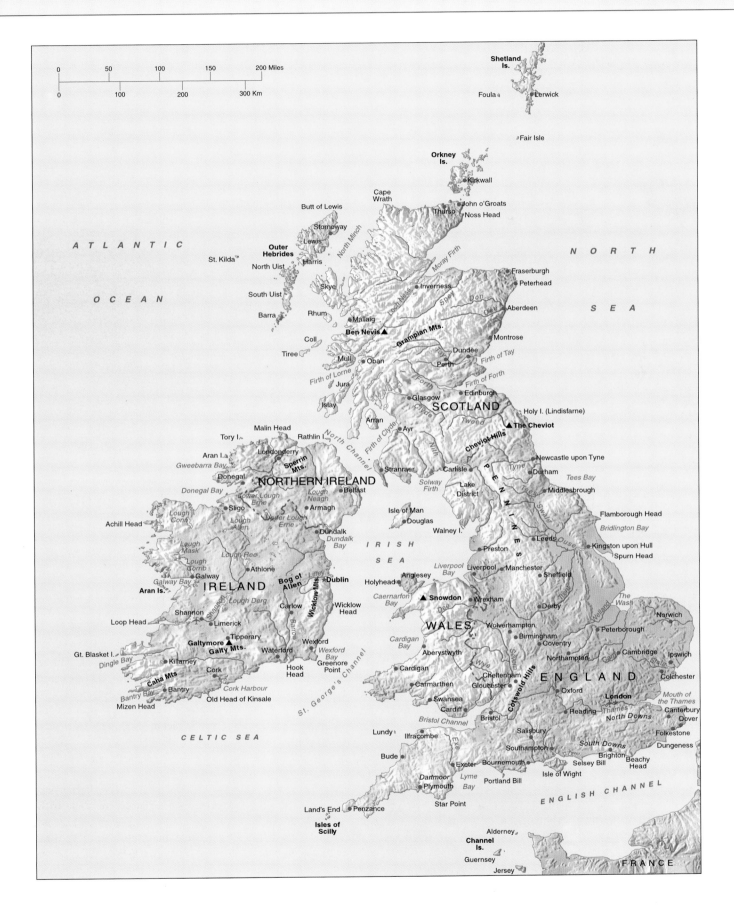

Shetland
Is.

Foula   Lerwick

Fair Isle

Orkney
Is.   Kirkwall

Cape   John o'Groats
Wrath   Thurso   Noss Head

Butt of Lewis

Stornoway
Lewis

Outer
Hebrides   Harris   Fraserburgh
St. Kilda   North Uist   Peterhead

OCEAN   South Uist   Inverness   Aberdeen

ATLANTIC   Skye   Loch Ness   Montrose

Barra   Spey   Don   Dee

Mallaig   Dundee
Coll   Ben Nevis ▲   Grampian Mts.
Tiree   Perth   Firth of Tay

Mull   Oban   Firth of Forth

Firth of Lorne   Forth
Jura   Glasgow   Edinburgh

Islay   SCOTLAND   Holy I. (Lindisfarne)
Arran   Clyde   Tweed

NORTH

SEA

Malin Head   Ayr   ▲ The Cheviot
Tory I.   Rathlin I.   Cheviot Hills
Aran I.   North Channel   Stranraer   Newcastle upon Tyne
Londonderry   Carlisle   P   Durham
Gweebarra Bay   Sperrin   Solway   E   Tyne
Mts.   Firth   N   Tees Bay
Donegal   NORTHERN IRELAND   Lake   N   Middlesbrough
Donegal Bay   Belfast   District I
Lower Lough   Isle of Man   N
Sligo   Erne   Lough   E
Achill Head   Lough   Neagh   Douglas   S   Flamborough Head
Conn   Armagh   Bridlington Bay
Lough   Upper Lough   Walney I.   Kingston upon Hull
Mask   Erne   Preston   Leeds   Ouse   Spurn Head
Lough   Lough Ree   Dundalk
Gorrib   Dundalk   Liverpool   The
Galway   Lough   Bay   IRISH   Bay   Liverpool Manchester   Wash
Galway Bay   Allen   SEA   Anglesey   Sheffield
Aran Is.   IRELAND   Bog of   Holyhead   Snowdon ▲ Wrexham   Derby
Athlone   Allen   Liffey
Shannon   Dublin   Caernarfon   Dee
Loop Head   Shannon   Lough   Carlow   Wicklow Mts.   Bay   WALES   Wolverhampton   Peterborough
Limerick   Derg   Wicklow   Cardigan   Birmingham   Norwich
Tipperary   Head   Bay   Aberystwyth   Coventry   Cambridge
Gt. Blasket I.   Galtymore ▲   Barrow   Wexford   Northampton   Ipswich
Galty Mts.   Waterford   Wexford   Cardigan   Cheltenham   ENGLAND   Colchester
Killarney   Cork   Bay   Greenore   Carmarthen   Gloucester   Cotswold Hills   Oxford
Caha Mts   Hook   Point   Swansea   Severn   London
Bantry   Head   Cardiff   Bristol   Reading   Thames   Canterbury
Bantry Bay   Cork Harbour   St. George's Channel   North Downs   Dover
Mizen Head   Old Head of Kinsale   Bristol Channel   Salisbury   South Downs   Folkestone
Lundy   Brighton   Dungeness
CELTIC SEA   Ilfracombe   Exe   Southampton   Selsey Bill   Beachy
Bude   Isle of Wight   Head
Exeter   Bournemouth
Dartmoor   Lyme   Portland Bill
Land's End   Penzance   Plymouth   Bay   ENGLISH CHANNEL
Isles of   Star Point
Scilly   Alderney
Channel   FRANCE
Is.   Guernsey
Jersey

Norway and Denmark

Norway

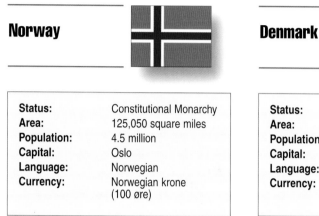

Status:	Constitutional Monarchy
Area:	125,050 square miles
Population:	4.5 million
Capital:	Oslo
Language:	Norwegian
Currency:	Norwegian krone (100 øre)

Denmark

Status:	Constitutional Monarchy
Area:	16,637 square miles
Population:	5.3 million
Capital:	Copenhagen
Language:	Danish
Currency:	Danish krone (100 øre)

Danish Overseas Territories
Greenland—North Atlantic Ocean
Faeroe Islands—North Atlantic Ocean

Below: Norway's fjords—very deep sea inlets—were gouged out by glaciers flowing from the mountains into the sea. They provide the country with one of the most spectacular coastlines in the world.

Norway stretches 1,100 miles north to south, but its coastline has so many bays, headlands, and **fjords** that the country's shoreline is more than 2,100 miles long. The northernmost third of the country lies inside the Arctic Circle, and Hammerfest is Europe's most northerly city. In midsummer, northern Norway sees nearly 24 hours of daylight, giving the country the nickname of Land of the Midnight Sun. More than 150,000 small islands, rocks, and reefs are scattered along Norway's Atlantic coast.

Norway is a mountainous country, and 80 percent of it is more than 500 feet above sea level. The only area of lowland occurs around Oslo in the south. Because Norway has few large **alluvial plains,** Norwegian farms average only about 40 acres. Farmers grow barley and potatoes and raise pigs, beef, and dairy cattle. The climate is cool in summer and cold in winter, but some farmers are able to grow fruit trees on sunny hillsides.

Forestry and fishing are Norway's traditional industries, but the country's abundant hydroelectric power has enabled Norwegians to build many manufacturing plants. Modern industries include lumber and wood pulp, metal goods, paper, processed food, engineering parts, and ship and boat building. Norway also has one of the world's largest merchant shipping fleets. Norway's already high standard of living grew after the country discovered oil and gas fields beneath the North Sea in the 1960s. The country's most significant industry is now the production and export of oil and natural gas.

Nearly surrounded by water, Denmark consists of the low-lying Jutland Peninsula and 482 islands. The country's only link to the mainland is its 43-mile-long border with Germany that runs across the neck of the peninsula. Most Danes live on Sjaelland, Fyn, Lolland, Falster, and Bornholm, but about 100 of the smaller islands are also inhabited.

Nearly 70 percent of Denmark's land area is given over to agriculture. Danish farmers best utilize their fertile soils and mild climate by concentrating on high-value food products such as butter, cheese, bacon, and ham. Most farmers grow barley, green fodder crops, and root crops—used chiefly for animal feed. About 60 percent of the country's food production is exported as meat and dairy products, mainly to the United Kingdom and Germany. Fishing fleets based in West Jutland and on Greenland and the Faeroe Islands catch sand lances, cod, herring, and Norway pout. Factories in Jutland process much of the catch for export.

Denmark's only natural resources are oil and gas from beneath the North Sea and granite and kaolin (a fine white clay) from the quarries on Bornholm. Industrial centers around Copenhagen and other big cities import raw materials, turning them into lucrative products such as machinery, food-processing equipment, silverware, furniture, textiles, chemicals, and pharmaceuticals.

Right: Merchants' houses line the quay (docks) in the port area of Copenhagen, whose Danish name—København—translates as "merchants' harbor."

0 100 200 300 Miles

0 100 200 300 400 500 Km

North Cape
Kjelvik
Berlevåg · Båtsfjord
Hammerfest · Lebesby · Hanningberg
Sørøya · Kistrand · Vadsø · Varanger
Vanna I. · Polmak · Fjord
Ringvassøy I. · Alta · Kirkenes

Kvaløy I. · Tromsø · Karasjok
· Skibotn

RUSSIA

Finnsnes

Vesterålen · Harstad
Hadsel · Narvik
Vagan · Svolvær

Sørfold

NORWEGIAN

Bodø
Beiarn · Rognan

SEA

· Mo

Vega · Mosjøen
Brønnøysund · Grane

Vikna

FINLAND

Folda Fjord · Kjølen Mts.
Namsos · Grong
Fro Fjord · Snåsa
Frøya I. · Steinkjer
· Levanger

SWEDEN

Kristiansund · Hålsa · Trondheim
· Surnadalsøra

Ålesund · Sunndalsøra
Stranda · Røros
Norddal · Dombås
Dovre Mts.
Sande · **Galdhøpiggen**

Gulf of Bothnia

Fåberg
Lillehammer
Voss · Myrdal · Fagernes · Hamar
Bergen · Gjøvik
Åland

Uskedal · Kongsvinger

Skjold · Dalen · Drammen · **Oslo**
Haugesund · Horten · Sarpsborg
Stavanger · Fredrikstad
Bygland · Gulf of Finland
Egersund · Evje · Larvik
· Arendal **ESTONIA**
Mandal · Kristiansand
Hiiumaa

Skagerrak
Saaremaa

Hjørring · Gulf of
Jammer Bay · Riga

Nissum Bay · Ålborg
Lim Fjord · Ålborg · **LATVIA**
Holstebro · Viborg · Bay
Ringkøbing · Silkeborg · Randers · Gotland
· Århus · Öland
DENMARK · Horsens · **LITHUANIA**
Esbjerg · **Copenhagen** · BALTIC SE
Fan I. · Odense
Main I. · SJAELLAND · **(RUSSIA)**
Rømø I. · FYN · Svendborg · BORNHOLM
LOLLAND · FALSTER · Rønne
NORTH
SEA
POLAND

GERMANY

93

Sweden and Finland

Sweden

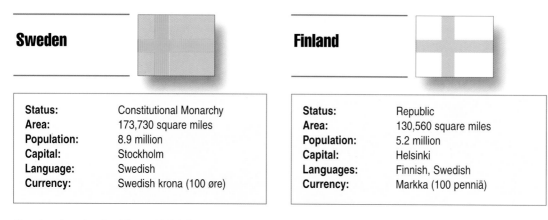

Status:	Constitutional Monarchy
Area:	173,730 square miles
Population:	8.9 million
Capital:	Stockholm
Language:	Swedish
Currency:	Swedish krona (100 øre)

Finland

Status:	Republic
Area:	130,560 square miles
Population:	5.2 million
Capital:	Helsinki
Languages:	Finnish, Swedish
Currency:	Markka (100 penniä)

Sweden is a land of beautiful lakes, snow-covered mountains, and rushing water. The country's population is small compared to its land area, and Swedes enjoy a very high standard of living. Northwestern Sweden's mountainous terrain is dotted with hundreds of small **glaciers**. A broad, forested plateau sloping down from the mountains to the Gulf of Bothnia dominates northeastern Sweden. Hydroelectric power stations perched on the plateau's many rivers provide more than 60 percent of Sweden's energy. High-voltage power lines carry the electricity to the industrial areas of central and southern Sweden. The remainder of Sweden's energy is from nuclear power stations, but Sweden has decided to phase out nuclear energy by 2010.

A broad low-lying region of woodlands and lakes stretches across southern Sweden from Göteborg to the capital city of Stockholm. Natives and tourists flock to this area to camp, hike, and fish. Much of Sweden's manufacturing industry is located around Göteborg in the west and Stockholm and Eskilstuna in the east. Vast reserves of iron ore, copper, gold, lead, and other metals cover much of the Inner Northland. The country is a leading exporter of iron and steel, cars, aircraft, ball bearings, electrical equipment, and household appliances. Sweden also boasts the world's second-largest shipbuilding industry. Other important exports include chemicals, lumber, wood pulp and paper, textiles, and food products.

Swedish agriculture is concentrated in the fertile lowlands at the country's southern tip. Modern, highly mechanized farms specialize in meat and dairy produce. Farmers grow barley, oats, and hay for animal feed and grains, fruits, and vegetables for human consumption.

Finland's capital, Helsinki, lies farther north than any other capital city except Reykjavík, the capital of Iceland. Most of Finland is low and flat. Two-thirds of the country is below 650 feet. Finland's highest point—in the far northwest—is only 4,357 feet above sea level.

Finland has three principal landscapes—the Upland District, the Lake District, and the flat Coastal Lowlands. Peat bogs and forests of pine, spruce, and birch cover the northern uplands, giving way to treeless Arctic **tundra** in the far north. Very few people other than the nomadic Sami (also called the Lapps), along with their reindeer herds, live this far north. South central Finland is a lowland region of bogs, dense forests, and more than 60,000 lakes. Almost one-tenth of the country is covered by water. The lakes are shallow and fill the hollows in the thick layer of clay left behind by ice age glaciers. Coastal plains, 40 to 80 miles wide, extend along the Gulf of Bothnia and the Gulf of Finland.

Finland's forestry workers provide lumber, plywood, wood pulp, and paper for export. The country also mines copper, nickel, iron, zinc, chromium, and other useful metals. Engineering and shipbuilding are Finland's second-largest industries, followed by glass, chemicals, and textiles. Farmers on the coastal lowlands raise dairy and beef cattle, poultry, and pigs. They also grow wheat, barley, and vegetables.

Below: The land around Finland's Saimaa Lake

0   100   200   300 Miles

0   200   400 Km

NORWEGIAN

SEA

BARENTS

SEA

Utsjoki

Inarijärvi

RUSSIA

Lotta

Enontekió

Kiruna   *Torne*   Kittilä   Sodankylä

Vittangi   *Ounasjoki*   Pelkosenniemi

Gällivare   *Torne*   Rovaniemi

Jokkmokk   Övertorneå   *Kemijoki*

Klule   Tornio   Kemi

Boden   Luleå

Sorsele   Arvidsjaur   Piteå   FINLAND

Dikanäs   *Skellefte*   Hailuoto   *Oulujoki*   *Oulujärvi*

Storuman   Åsträsk   Oulu   Raahe

Lycksele   Skellefteå   Kajaani   Vuokatti

Vilhelmina   Hällnäs   Lövånger   Pyhäjärvi   Sukeva

Dorotea   *Ume*   Bygdeå   Kokkola   Iisalmi

Alanäs   Hoting   Umeå   Jakobstad   Kuopio   Outokumpu

Hotagen   SWEDEN   Nykarleby   Joensuu

Offerdal   Gäxsjö   Ådalsliden   *Gulf*   Vaasa   Lapua

Östersund   *Indals*   Örnsköldsvik   *of*   Sejnäjoki   Varkaus

Håsjö   Kramfors   *Bothnia*   Kaskinen   Jyväskylä

Åsarna   Härnösand   Sysma

Klövsjö   Sundsvall   Tampere   Heinola

Linsell   *Ljusnan*   Gnarp   Pori   Kouvola

Lillhärdal   Ljusdal   Rauma   Hämeenlinna   Lahti   Anjalankoski

Särna   Los   Hudiksvall   Forssa   Kotka

Bollnäs   Söderhamn   Hyvinkää   Porvoo

Mora   *Klar*   Rättvik   Gävle   *Gävle Bay*   Naantali   **Helsinki**

Höljes   Leksand   Falun   Åland   Turku   *Gulf of Finland*

Appelbo   Borlänge   Ekenäs

Västerdalal   Mariehamn   Hangö

Årvika   Kopparberg   Uppsala

Karlstad   Västerås

Karlskoga   Örebro   **Stockholm**   Hiiumaa   ESTONIA

Eskilstuna   Södertälje

Katrineholm   Saaremaa

Strömstad   *Vänern*   Motala

Uddevalla   Lidköping   Norrköping   *Gulf of*

Trollhättan   Linköping   *Riga*

Göteborg   Gränna   Gotland

Boras   Huskvarna   Västervik   LATVIA

Mölndal   Jönköping   Visby

Vetlanda   Målila

Varberg   Växjö

Halmstad   Kalmar   Borgholm

Tingsryd   Öland I.

Helsingborg   Karlskrona   *Kalmar Sound*   LITHUANIA

Kristianstad

Malmö   *Hanö Bay*

Ystad   *BALTIC SE*

Trelleborg   Bornholm

(RUSSIA)

BELARUS

GERMANY   POLAND

Kattegat

Top: Stockholm, Sweden's beautiful capital city, extends over 14 islands, linked by almost 50 bridges.

Above: The midnight sun

Estonia, Latvia, Lithuania

Estonia

Status:	Parliamentary Democracy
Area:	17,413 square miles
Population:	1.4 million
Capital:	Tallinn
Languages:	Estonian, Russian
Currency:	Estonian kroon (100 cents)

Latvia

Status:	Parliamentary Democracy
Area:	24,942 square miles
Population:	2.4 million
Capital:	Riga
Languages:	Latvian, Russian
Currency:	Lat (100 santimes)

Lithuania

Status:	Parliamentary Democracy
Area:	25,174 square miles
Population:	3.7 million
Capital:	Vilnius
Languages:	Lithuanian, Russian
Currency:	Litas (100 cents)

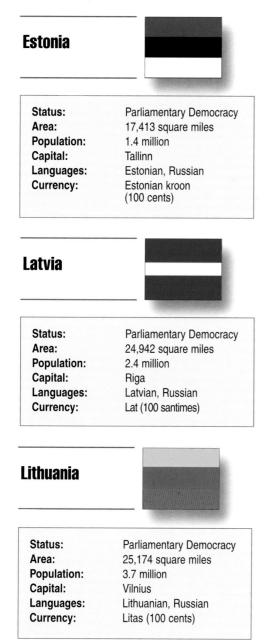

The three small countries known as the Baltic States—Estonia, Latvia, and Lithuania—cluster along the eastern shore of the Baltic Sea. Russia, Belarus, Poland, and the small territory of Kaliningrad—part of the Russian Federation—border the countries on the inland side. Before World War I (1914–1918), the Baltic States belonged to the Russian Empire. When the war ended in 1918, the three states gained independence. In 1940 during World War II, the Soviet Union (a successor to the Russian Empire) seized the three countries. After 50 years under Soviet control, Lithuania declared independence in 1990. Estonia and Latvia broke free the following year.

The three states have very similar geography. The land is flat and low-lying, with large areas of coniferous forest dotted with marshlands, peat bogs, and lakes. The climate is cool and mild at the coast, but farther inland—and in the north—the summers are short and winters are long and very cold.

Estonia's main resources are oil shale, which provides fuel for power plants, and phosphates, which are used to make fertilizer and other chemical products. Shipbuilding, engineering, chemicals, and textiles are the country's primary industries.

Latvia produces telephones and other electronic equipment, railroad cars, machinery, and household appliances. The country has no coal, oil, or gas reserves and imports most of its energy supplies from Estonia.

Lithuania has some oil and gas and a large nuclear power plant near the town of Ignalina. The country imports crude oil, processing it into fuels and other chemical products. Lithuania's factories produce industrial machinery, ceramics, glass, and textiles.

All three countries have fishing fleets and forest-based industries that create lumber, wood pulp, paper, and wood products such as furniture. Farmers in the Baltic States raise beef and dairy cattle, pigs, sheep, and poultry. Essential field crops are rye, oats, sugar beets, potatoes, and other vegetables. Most farmers grow fodder crops, and many specialize in growing flax, which is used to make linen and linseed oil.

The Netherlands

The Netherlands—historically known as Holland—is one of Europe's smallest countries and is also one of the most crowded. Each square mile of land supports almost 1,200 people, compared to 277 per square mile in France and 76 per square mile in the United States. Despite this high **population density**, the Dutch people have one of the highest standards of living in Europe. International trade, many diverse industries, and a very efficient farming system all help support excellent state-funded education, health, and social services. And the population gets a lot of exercise—there are as many bicycles as there are people in the Netherlands.

Nearly one-third of the country's land area is below sea level. The highest point, Vaalser Berg in the Southern Uplands, rises to just 1,053 feet above sea level. This lack of elevation has led people to name the Netherlands and neighboring Belgium the Low Countries. The country's southern delta region is formed by the Maas, Rhine, and Schelde Rivers, which empty into the North Sea. Huge earth-filled dams, called dykes, prevent the North Sea from flooding vast areas of reclaimed land called **polders**. Dutch engineers are world leaders in land reclamation and in designing flood and sea defenses.

Farms occupy nearly 70 percent of the Netherlands, and farmers concentrate on high-value produce such as butter and cheese, flower bulbs, and tomatoes and other vegetables grown in greenhouses. Potatoes, sugar beets, and wheat grow in some areas.

The Netherlands has both oil and natural gas but imports large quantities of crude oil to feed the large refineries at Rotterdam. Imported raw materials support the manufacturing industries clustered around the busy ports of Amsterdam and Rotterdam—the gateways to Europe's inland waterways. Factory workers produce chemicals, vehicles, electrical and electronic equipment, fine china, pottery, and a wide range of food products.

The Netherlands

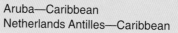

Status:	Constitutional Monarchy
Area:	15,768 square miles
Population:	15.8 million
Capital:	Amsterdam
Language:	Dutch
Currency:	Guilder (100 cents)

Overseas Territories
Aruba—Caribbean
Netherlands Antilles—Caribbean

Top: Tulip fields and windmills—the most typical of all Dutch scenes

Above: More than 100 canals wind through Amsterdam, adding to the charm of this historic capital city.

Belgium

Belgium

Status:	Constitutional Monarchy
Area:	11,787 square miles
Population:	10.2 million
Capital:	Brussels
Languages:	Dutch, French
Currency:	Belgian franc (100 centimes)

Above: A carpet of flowers decorates the Grand' Place (main square) in Brussels, the Belgian capital. The square is lined with ornate houses built in the 1600s for the city's merchant and craft guilds (associations).

Right: In military cemeteries across the Belgian lowlands, thousands of immaculately tended graves witness the tragic losses of two world wars.

Belgium, like the Netherlands, is densely populated and enjoys a high standard of living. Most of the country is flat and low-lying, rising gently to the forested hills of the Ardennes region on Belgium's borders with France and Luxembourg. Reclaimed polders along the coast provide the best cropland, while farmers in the higher inland regions concentrate on livestock and dairy farming. Belgium's main crops are wheat, barley, oats, sugar beets, flowers, vegetables, and hops (used to make the country's famous beers).

Excellent roads, railroads, and waterways link Belgium's manufacturing areas with Europe's main trading ports in the Netherlands. Belgian industries import raw materials for production of exports, such as textiles, glassware, metal goods, and electrical products. Luxury goods include lace and chocolate. Eighty percent of Belgium's energy is nuclear power, one of the highest percentages in the world.

Belgium was a founding member of the EU. Many of the EU's governing bodies are headquartered in the capital city of Brussels alongside the command center of the North Atlantic Treaty Organization (NATO) and other international organizations.

Germany

Germany

Status:	Federal Republic
Area:	137,830 square miles
Population:	82 million
Capital:	Berlin
Language:	German
Currency:	Deutsche mark (100 pfennigs)

Germany is among the world's leading trade nations, is a major international finance center, and is one of the most powerful partners in the EU. Before World War II, Germany was a single country, but at the end of the war the Allied Powers—Britain, France, the United States, and the Soviet Union—divided it in two. The Federal Republic of Germany (West Germany) remained allied with western Europe, while the German Democratic Republic (East Germany) became part of the Communist bloc, controlled by the Soviet Union. The two German states were reunited after the East German people rejected Communism in 1990. But reunification has not been easy.

Western Germany's industry is modern and efficient, and the people have long enjoyed a very high standard of living. By contrast, eastern Germany's industries were badly run-down and inefficient. Roads, utilities, hospitals, and other services were seriously diminished, and the standard of living was low. Since reunification, Germany is investing a great deal of money in eastern Germany's modernization, but the process will take many years.

Germany lacks abundant natural resources. Large coal deposits lie beneath the western Ruhr Valley—the country's main industrial region—and small oil and gas fields dot the northern lowlands, but Germany imports most of its necessary raw materials and energy. The country's economic strength rests on modern industries turning out high-quality manufactured goods such as automobiles, trucks, trams and buses, machine tools, printing presses, precision instruments, and electronic equipment. Germany also exports many chemical and pharmaceutical products.

Northern Germany is a flat lowland plain with patches of fertile farmland and sandy **heathland.** Farmers grow barley, oats, rye, potatoes, and sugar beets. Central Germany consists of rolling uplands and small, fertile river valleys, where farmers concentrate on producing grapes (for wine) and hops (for beer). Cattle, pigs, horses, poultry, and sheep graze throughout the country, but Germany's best pastureland is in the southeast. In southern Germany the land rises toward the spectacular Alps. Forested mountains, beautiful lakes, picturesque castles, and medieval towns full of decorative half-timbered buildings draw thousands of tourists to southern Germany each year.

Above: Koblenz, on the Rhine River, is one of Germany's oldest and most beautiful cities. Most of the old town center was destroyed in World War II but has been painstakingly restored into a major tourist attraction.

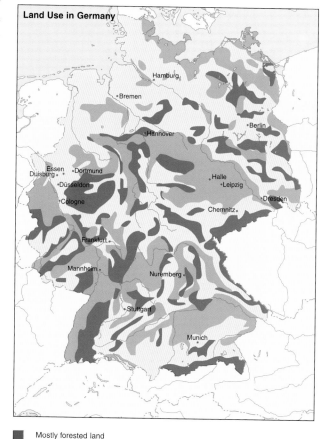

Land Use in Germany

■ Mostly forested land

Mostly cropland

☐ Grazing land mixed with cropland

● Major urban-industrial center

99

Germany

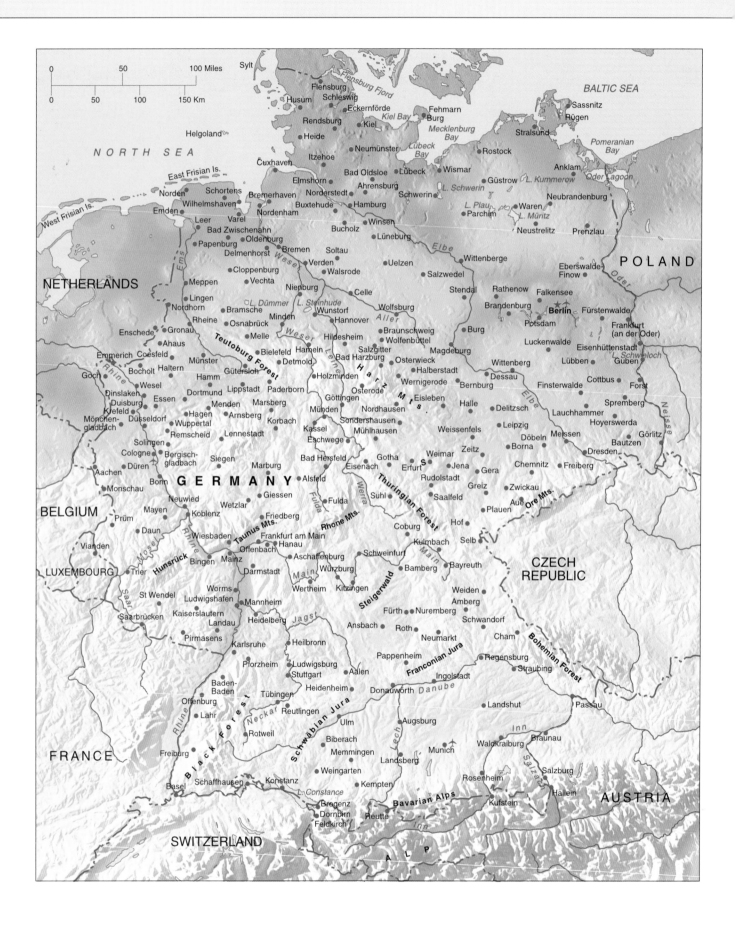

Right: The magnificent Brandenburg Gate stands in the center of Berlin. Before the Berlin Wall was built close by in 1961, the gate was the city's principal east-west crossing point. When the wall came down, thousands flocked to the Brandenburg Gate to celebrate.

Right: The Rhine is one of Europe's most important rivers. It rises in the Swiss Alps and winds for 820 miles across northern Europe, finally emptying into the North Sea. Its valley contains some of Germany's most beautiful scenery and most spectacular castles.

Below: Heidelberg, on the Neckar River in southern Germany, is a beautiful old university city overlooked by a sixteenth-century castle.

Switzerland and Austria

Switzerland

Status:	Federal Republic
Area:	15,942 sq. miles
Population:	7.1 million
Capital:	Bern
Languages:	German, French, Italian
Currency:	Swiss franc (100 centimes)

Switzerland is a small, landlocked country in the center of western Europe. Mountains cover nearly three-fifths of the land. The snowcapped Alps in the south include 15,203–foot Monte Rosa and the dramatic 14,691–foot Matterhorn. The forested Jura Mountains rise in the north to 5,518 feet. Most Swiss people live on the Mittelland—a central plateau of rolling hills, broad river valleys, and beautiful lakes such as Lake Geneva, Lake Lucerne, and Lake Constance.

Switzerland is poor in natural resources. Mountain rivers provide hydroelectric power, but all other fuels and industrial raw materials must be imported. The Swiss have made up for this lack of resources by specializing in the production of high-quality, high-value precision-engineering goods such as clocks and watches, machine tools, scientific instruments, microscopes, and laboratory equipment. Swiss factories also produce glassware, textiles, chemicals, pharmaceuticals, and luxury foods such as chocolate and cheese. Switzerland spends more on imports than it earns from its exports but makes up the difference with a thriving tourist industry—nearly 12 million visitors a year—and the country's world-famous international banking and insurance businesses.

Farmers in the more fertile valleys grow grains, potatoes, sugar beets, vegetables, and fruit. Many farmers also raise beef and dairy cattle. Those in the south take advantage of their nearness to the mountains, grazing their animals on the high alpine pastures in the summer and herding them back to the sheltered valleys for the winter.

Top: Bern, the Swiss capital, lies on the Aare River.

Center: Schönried is a typical Swiss alpine village, surrounded by mountain pastures at 4,000 feet above sea level.

Bottom: The twin towers of Zurich's Grossmünster Church overlook the old city, the Limmat River, and Lake Zurich.

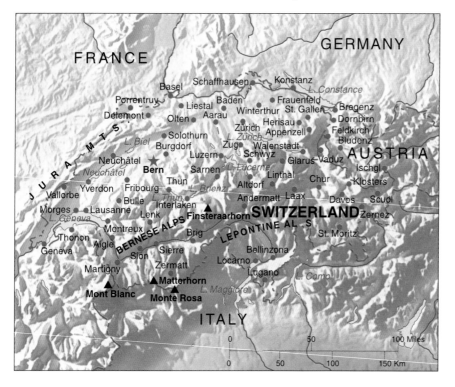

Austria

Status:	Federal Republic
Area:	32,378 sq. miles
Population:	8.1 million
Capital:	Vienna
Language:	German
Currency:	Austrian schilling (100 groschen)

The jagged Austrian Alps and their foothills cover most of western, southern, and central Austria. At 12,470 feet, the Grossglockner towers over this mountainous area. Central Europe's longest river—the Danube—flows through northern Austria's fertile valleys and past the forested hills that border the Czech Republic. Eastern Austria is a broad fertile plain that slopes gently eastward and merges with the great plain of Hungary.

Austria's farmers utilize only about 20 percent of the land, but modern methods and machinery allow them to meet three-quarters of the country's food needs. Meat and dairy production, grains, sugar beets, potatoes, fruits, and vegetables contribute to both the local and export markets. Forests cover about 40 percent of the country. Strict conservation laws control lumber companies, allowing them to produce a steady but replaceable supply of sawed lumber, pulp, and paper.

Graphite, magnesite, and iron ore are Austria's most valuable mineral resources. Hydroelectricity generated by mountain rivers accounts for two-thirds of Austria's energy needs. The balance derives from imported fuels and small local oil and gas fields. Most of the manufacturing industries are located in the Danube Valley and around Vienna, where factories produce iron and steel, automobiles, tractors, machinery, electrical goods, plastics, chemicals, textiles, ceramics, and processed foods. Like most alpine countries, a thriving tourist industry—based on winter sports and cultural attractions such as historic Vienna and the famous Salzburg Festival—bolsters Austria's economy.

Austria's Alps, like those of France and Switzerland, attract thousands of winter sports enthusiasts every year.

Europe's Smallest Nations: Andorra, Monaco, Vatican City, San Marino, Malta

Seven tiny states, two of them smaller than New York's Central Park, nestle among the larger countries of western Europe. They are a reminder of the turbulent history and countless boundary changes that have characterized Europe over the centuries.

Andorra

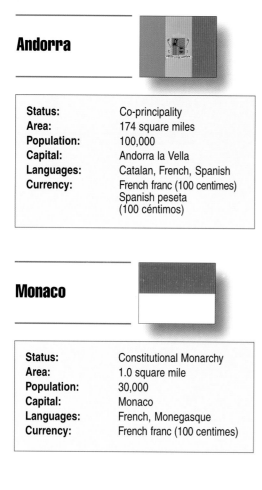

Status:	Co-principality
Area:	174 square miles
Population:	100,000
Capital:	Andorra la Vella
Languages:	Catalan, French, Spanish
Currency:	French franc (100 centimes) Spanish peseta (100 céntimos)

Monaco

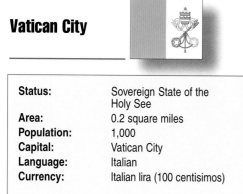

Status:	Constitutional Monarchy
Area:	1.0 square mile
Population:	30,000
Capital:	Monaco
Languages:	French, Monegasque
Currency:	French franc (100 centimes)

Vatican City

Status:	Sovereign State of the Holy See
Area:	0.2 square miles
Population:	1,000
Capital:	Vatican City
Language:	Italian
Currency:	Italian lira (100 centisimos)

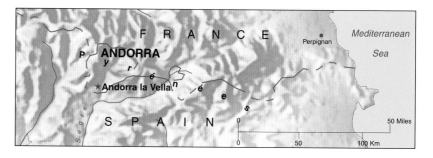

Andorra

Andorra sits on the French-Spanish border, high in the Pyrénées Mountains. Beginning in 1278, the Spanish Bishop of Urgel and the French Comte de Foix (later the French president) became the country's joint heads of state. When Andorra adopted its first constitution in 1993, these co-princes lost most of their power. An elected council with a modern constitution governs the country.

Tourism drives Andorra's economy. Visitors can buy Swiss watches, French wines, and many other luxury items without paying high **duties**. Andorra's few farmers graze sheep and goats on the mountain pastures and grow tobacco, potatoes, rye, and olives in the valleys.

Monaco

Tucked into the Mediterranean coast, Monaco lies nine miles east of the French city of Nice. The capital, also named Monaco, perches on a rocky headland, overlooking the Port of Monaco. Monte Carlo's casinos, luxury hotels, opera house, and famous beaches are just minutes away. Monegasques—natives of Monaco—comprise only 14 precent of the population. French citizens account for nearly half the population, and Italians number about 16 percent. The Grimaldi family has ruled Monaco since 1308, but in the past it accepted protection from and partial control by Italy, France, and Sardinia. Modern Monaco is an independent country with close ties to France.

Some Monegasques work in light industry, but Monaco's economy depends on tourism and banking. Extremely low taxes have encouraged foreign corporations to relocate to Monaco, and many of the world's wealthy and famous people have built lavish homes along the sun-drenched coast.

Vatican City

The walled enclosure of Vatican City lies on the west bank of the Tiber River in the middle of the city of Rome, Italy. The Vatican is the home of the Holy See—the Roman Catholic Church's governing body. Vatican City is also one of the world's great cultural treasure houses, containing museums, galleries, libraries, St. Peter's Basilica, and the Vatican Palace where Michelangelo's famous paintings grace the ceiling of the Sistine Chapel. The pope is head of state, but Vatican City also has a civil administration run by a governor and a Pontifical Commission. Popes have lived in the Vatican since the fifth century, except for a short period in the fourteenth century when they were based in Avignon, France.

Vatican City is all that remains of the **Papal States**, which once occupied most of central Italy and were ruled by the pope. In 1870 the Papal States became part of the Kingdom of Italy, and in 1929 Italy finally recognized the Vatican as an independent sovereign state.

San Marino

Status:	Republic
Area:	23 square miles
Population:	30,000
Capital:	San Marino
Language:	Italian
Currency:	Italian lira (100 centisimos)

San Marino

San Marino, the world's oldest republic, nestles on top of Mount Titano, a limestone peak on the eastern edge of the Apennine Mountains about 12 miles southwest of the Italian port of Rimini. Documents written in the eighth century mention a castle on Mount Titano, but some historians believe San Marino dates as far back as the fourth century A.D.

Many San Marinese work in tourism, hosting two million visitors each year. Other locals labor on small farms, in limestone quarries, or in factories producing leather goods, ceramics, and textiles.

Malta

Status:	Republic
Area:	124 square miles
Population:	400,000
Capital:	Valletta
Languages:	Maltese, English
Currency:	Maltese lira (100 cents)

Malta

The tiny island country of Malta, 60 miles south of Sicily, comprises three inhabited islands—Malta, Gozo, and Comino—and three small uninhabited islands. Formerly a British colony, Malta became independent in 1964.

Low limestone hills cover most of Malta. The soil is thin and dry, and farmers can raise only small crops of barley, wheat, potatoes, grapes, and citrus fruits. The Maltese have to import most of their food and also the fuel and raw materials for the islands' manufacturing industries—ship repairs, textiles, and electrical goods. Most Maltese work in the shipyards, in construction, or in tourism—Malta's fastest-growing industry. With its sunny climate, rocky cliffs, sandy beaches, and a wealth of historic and archaeological sites, Malta attracts visitors from all over the world.

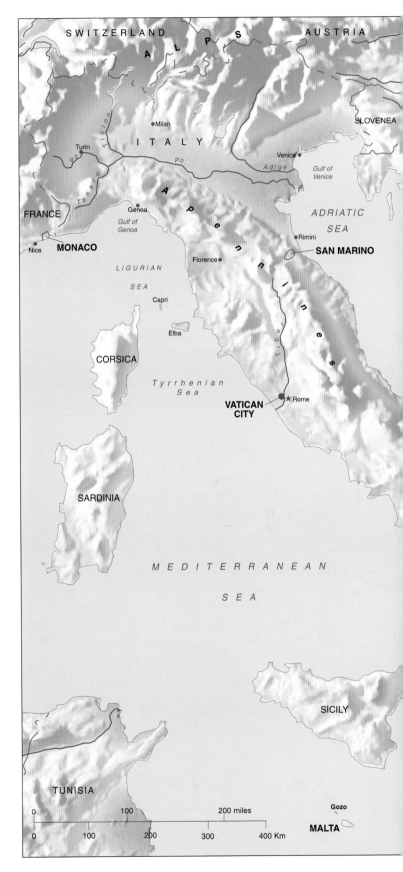

Liechtenstein

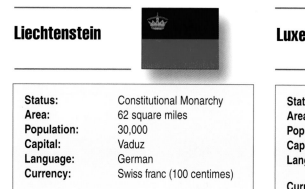

Status:	Constitutional Monarchy
Area:	62 square miles
Population:	30,000
Capital:	Vaduz
Language:	German
Currency:	Swiss franc (100 centimes)

Luxembourg

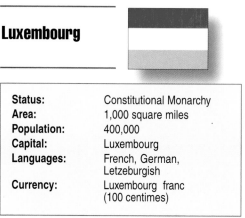

Status:	Constitutional Monarchy
Area:	1,000 square miles
Population:	400,000
Capital:	Luxembourg
Languages:	French, German, Letzeburgish
Currency:	Luxembourg franc (100 centimes)

Liechtenstein

Roughly the size of Washington, D.C., Liechtenstein lies between Austria and Switzerland. A narrow strip of fertile land in the country's northwest runs along the Rhine River. Farmers use this lowland area to raise beef and dairy cattle and to grow grains, vegetables, and fruits—including grapes for wine production. Southeastern Liechtenstein is mountainous and nearly covered with pine forests. Before World War II, Liechtenstein was a farming country. The modern economy is highly industrialized, specializing in machinery, scientific and medical instruments, pharmaceuticals, ceramics, and textiles.

In the Middle Ages (A.D. 500 to A.D. 1500), Liechtenstein consisted of two states, Vaduz and Schellenberg. An Austrian prince named Johann-Adam Liechtenstein bought them in 1719. From 1815 to 1866 the country was part of the German Confederation but kept its independence. Liechtenstein remains a monarchy, ruled by the House of Liechtenstein, but also has a constitution and an elected government.

Luxembourg

The Grand Duchy of Luxembourg shares borders with Belgium, France, and Germany. Wooded hills in the north merge with the Belgian Ardennes. Fertile lowlands in the southern two-thirds of the country provide rich agricultural land where farmers grow barley, wheat, oats, and potatoes and raise pigs and cattle. Luxembourg's main industries are located in the south. Iron ore supplies the primary raw material for a huge iron and steel industry. Luxembourg's workforce also produces chemicals, plastics, synthetic fibers, and computer equipment.

Luxembourg was a founding member of the EU. The country also headquarters both the European Court of Justice and the European Coal and Steel Community. Luxembourg's history traces back to the Holy Roman Empire of the Middle Ages and includes periods of rule by Spain, Austria, France, and the Netherlands. The country gained its independence in 1867.

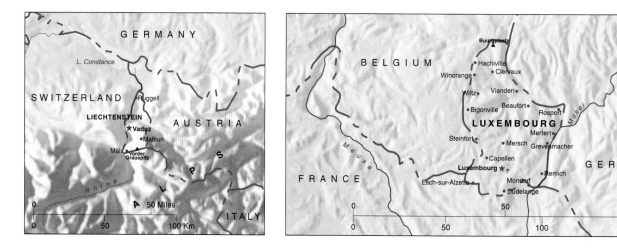

Italy

Italy

Status:	Republic
Area:	116,320 sq. miles
Population:	57.7 million
Capital:	Rome
Language:	Italian
Currency:	Italian lira (100 centesimi)

skiing resorts that support a thriving winter tourist industry. Alpine rivers supply hydroelectric power to the large northwestern industrial centers of Milan, Turin, and Genoa. Just south of the mountains, the land levels out onto the North Italian Plain—Italy's only large lowland area. Farmers in this fertile region grow wheat, barley, rice, vegetables, fruits, and tobacco. The Po River and its **tributaries** provide the extra water needed to irrigate the rice fields in summer. Large numbers of tourists visit Venice and Verona in the northeast and Bologna and Florence farther south in the Apennine foothills.

The Apennine Mountains snake down the peninsula like a backbone, curving from west to east and back again. Italy's highest northern mountains run along the country's Adriatic shore. Broad coastal plains lie to the west. Farther south the mountains hug the Tyrrhenian coast, creating spectacular cliffs and headlands south of Naples. Historic Rome, the ruins of the ancient cities of Pompeii and Herculaneum, the Bay of Naples, and the island of Capri attract thousands of tourists to Italy's western coast. Italy also boasts Europe's only active volcanoes—Vesuvius just inland from Naples, Mount Etna on Sicily, and Stromboli and Vulcano on small islands off the north coast of Sicily.

Southern Italy has a hotter, drier climate than the north. Most of the farmers are smallholders or tenants working

Italy's distinctive long, boot-shaped peninsula stretches 685 miles southward from the Alps to the Mediterranean Sea, reaching almost to the northern coast of Africa. Italy shares borders with France, Switzerland, Austria, and Slovenia and is bound by three seas—the

Tyrrhenian Sea to the west, the Ionian Sea in the south, and the Adriatic Sea on the east. Italy's territory also includes the large islands of Sardinia to the west and Sicily, just off the toe of the boot.

The Alps in the far north provide Italy with magnificent scenery and fine

Italy

farm plots on large estates. They graze sheep and goats on the dry uplands and grow olives, grapes, tomatoes, fruits, vegetables, and flowers—most of which they export to northern Europe.

Italians mine sulfur and mercury, and the quarries at Carrara produce some of the world's finest marble, but the country imports most industrial raw materials, fuel oil, and coal. Italian power is 80 percent thermal and 20 percent hydroelectric. Major iron and steel centers have developed in Taranto, Naples, Piombino, and Genoa. Italians manufacture vehicles, motorcycles, aircraft, ships, military equipment, power tools, electronic goods, household appliances, and textiles—especially fashion and sportswear. Petrochemical plants produce industrial chemicals, fertilizers, plastics, synthetic fibers, and rubber.

Poland

Poland

Status:	Republic
Area:	124,807 sq. miles
Population:	38.7 million
Capital:	Warsaw
Language:	Polish
Currency:	Zloty (100 groszy)

Poland's landscape is dominated by the Great North European Plain, a vast expanse of flat land extending from northern Germany, across Poland, and into neighboring Belarus and Ukraine. Soil quality is poor in northern Poland, and forests cover much of the countryside. Bialowieza National Park on the Polish–Belarussian border protects one of the last undisturbed ancient forests in Europe. Rich soil and the country's major farming regions lie in central and southern Poland. The Sudetic and Carpathian Mountains form Poland's jagged southern border.

Most Polish farms are small family businesses. Not highly mechanized, the farms cover almost two-thirds of the land, producing huge quantities of rye and potatoes. Lesser crops include barley, oats, wheat, sugar beets, and other vegetables. Many farmers also raise pigs, beef and dairy cattle, and sheep.

Poland's only coastline is a short expanse on the Baltic Sea with a well-developed fishing industry. Primary catches are cod and herring, much of which is processed in the ports of Szczecin, Gdańsk, and Gdynia—either frozen or canned for human consumption or turned into animal feed. The ports house ship repair yards, container terminals, and bulk cargo facilities for handling exports of coal, grain, and metal ores.

Southern Poland sits on one of the world's most abundant reserves of hard coal and lignite, a soft brown coal. Polish workers also mine copper, silver, lead, zinc, and nickel. Iron and steel production in Katowice forms the backbone of Poland's industrial sector. Metal-based industries include ships, cars, aircraft, and railroad stock. Lódź is the hub of the country's textile industry, and Plock, near Warsaw, is the center of Poland's petrochemical industry.

The small family farms of central and southern Poland look much as they did a hundred years ago. The owner of this farm is growing grain and root crops, chiefly as feed for pigs and chickens.

Czech Republic, Slovakia, Hungary

Czech Republic

Status:	Republic
Area:	30,448 square miles
Population:	10.3 million
Capital:	Prague
Language:	Czech
Currency:	Koruna (100 haléru)

From 1918 to 1992, the Czech Republic was part of the Communist country of Czechoslovakia. Communist rule ended in 1989 when Václav Havel, a playwright, led the nonviolent Velvet Revolution, which toppled the old regime. In its place the Czech people adopted a democratic system with an elected government. The two factions of the old state—the Czechs and the Slovaks—could not agree on how to proceed, and on January 1, 1993, they separated into two nations called the Czech Republic and Slovakia. Good health and educational services enable the two states to have a higher standard of living than many of the former Communist states.

The Czech Republic is divided into the highland region of Bohemia in the west and the Moravian lowlands in the east. Farmers in both areas produce wheat, sugar beets, rye, hops, potatoes, and other vegetables. Summers are warm, but the winters are long and cold. Bohemian highlanders mine hard coal and lignite. Once the country's primary energy source, lignite is being replaced by cleaner energy forms. Mines in the highlands also produce uranium, lead, zinc, copper, mercury, and tin. Czech factories produce steel, machinery, cars, clothing, and leather goods, much of which is exported to western Europe.

Slovakia

Status:	Republic
Area:	18,923 square miles
Population:	5.4 million
Capital:	Bratislava
Languages:	Slovak, Hungarian, Czech
Currency:	Koruna (100 halierov)

Slovakia comprised the eastern one-third of Czechoslovakia until the two countries gained independence in 1993. The forested Carpathian Mountains dominate northern Slovakia. The rest of the country is mainly lowland, sloping south to east to merge with the Hungarian Plain. Several of Slovakia's rivers flow into the Danube, which marks the country's border with Hungary.

Slovakia's climate is temperate, with cold winters and hot summers, especially in the lowland areas. Farmers tend grains, beets, potatoes, and other vegetables. Pigs are common farm animals, as they are in many eastern European countries, but Slovak farmers also raise beef and dairy cattle, sheep, and poultry. Slovakia's main natural resources are iron ore, copper, lead, zinc, mercury, and perlite—a volcanic rock that is crushed and used to make plaster, cement, and some types of insulation. Factory workers make vehicles, machinery, chemicals, plastics, and paper. Coal-burning and hydroelectric power plants provide the country's energy.

Left: Prague, straddling the Vltava River, is one of Europe's oldest and most beautiful cities. The Charles Bridge, lined with statues of the Christian saints, is a local attraction in this City of a Hundred Spires.

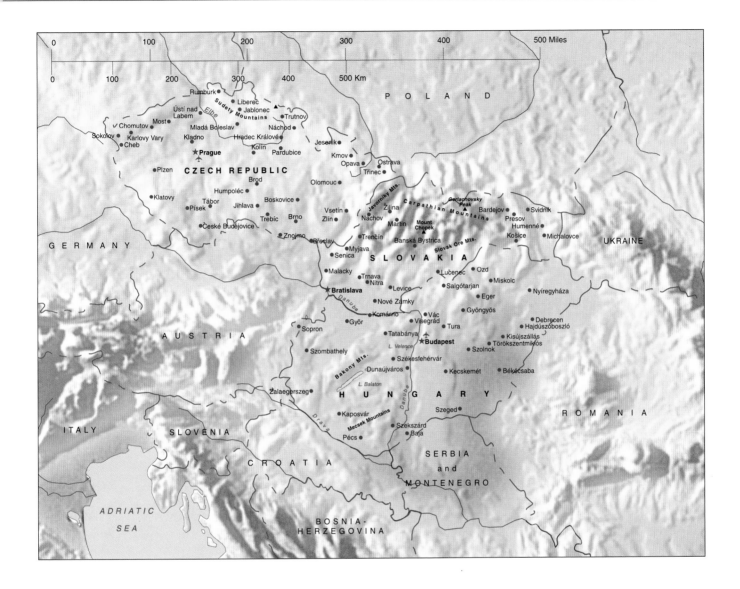

Hungary

Status:	Republic
Area:	35,919 square miles
Population:	10.1 million
Capital:	Budapest
Languages:	Hungarian, German
Currency:	Forint (100 fillér)

Two large lowlands dominate the Hungarian landscape—the Little Plain in the northwest and the Great Plain in the southeast. A line of low hills separates the two plains, stretching from Lake Balaton and the Bakony Forest to the Northern Highlands on the Hungarian-Slovakian border. At 45 miles long, Lake Balaton is central Europe's largest lake and a popular tourist resort.

Some of Europe's most fertile soil covers Hungary's plains, and the country's spring rains and long hot summers are ideal for growing wheat, corn, beets, potatoes and other vegetables. Upland farmers tend grapes for wine. Those in drier, sandy areas raise cattle, pigs, and poultry.

Factories in Hungary's main industrial regions around Budapest and Miskolc produce trucks and buses, machinery, chemicals, textiles, leather goods, and canned foods. Hungary has some natural gas and large deposits of bauxite—the principal ore of aluminum—but has to import most of the fuel and raw materials it needs for industry.

Slovenia, Croatia, Bosnia-Herzegovina

The Former Yugoslavia

Six republics comprised the former Yugoslavia until they split in 1991. Slovenia, Croatia, Macedonia, and Bosnia-Herzegovina quickly declared themselves independent republics. Serbia and Montenegro continued to call themselves Yugoslavia, although this term has only had partial acceptance. Throughout the 1990s, civil wars and ethnic conflicts plagued the region.

Events of the Conflict in the Former Yugoslavia

1990	Slovenia and Croatia hold the first multiparty elections in the Yugoslav republics. Macedonia and Bosnia-Herzegovina hold their own multiparty elections later in the year.
1991	Croatia and Slovenia declare independence. War breaks out between Croats and ethnic Serbs living in Croatian territory.
1992	In January, Macedonia declares independence. Bosnia-Herzegovina declares independence in April. Bosnian Muslims and Bosnian Croats begin fighting. Reports of ethnic cleansing of non-Serbs cause the UN to impose economic sanstions. Serbia and Montenegro form a new Yugoslavia.
1993	International negotiators present the Vance-Owen peace plan, which would divide Bosnia into ethnic provinces. The plan is rejected.
1994	Continued fighting provokes UN and NATO ultimatums; Bosnian Muslims agree to a truce with Bosnian Croats and the Croatian government. A cease-fire is negotiated.
1995	The cease-fire is broken six weeks early. In October, after thousands from both sides have been killed, all parties agree to a truce. The Dayton Peace agreement is signed in November. The United States and NATO agree to supply peacekeeping forces.
1997	Slobodan Milosevic becomes president of the federal republic of Yugoslavia (Serbia and Montenegro).
1998	In Kosovo, a Yugoslav province, Serbian police attempt to crack down on ethnic Albanians. In February, Yugoslav forces enter Kosovo. Under threat of NATO action, Yugoslav troops withdraw in October.
1999	After peace talks between Serbia and Kosovo fail, the UN begins an air strike against Yugoslavia. In May, Milosevic and others are indicted by the International Criminal Tribunal for the Former Yugoslavia (ICTY).

Slovenia

Status:	Parliamentary Democracy
Area:	7,819 square miles
Population:	2 million
Capital:	Ljubljana
Languages:	Slovenian, Serbo-Croatian, Italian
Currency:	Tolar (100 stotins)

Slovenia is a small mountainous country bordered by Italy, Austria, Hungary, and Croatia. It has a short stretch of Adriatic coastline to the southwest. Visitors are attracted to the country's mountain lakes, coastal resorts, limestone caves of Postojna (the largest European caverns), and the medieval capital, Ljubljana.

Slovenes farm about one-quarter of the land, growing grain, potatoes, beets, hops, flax, and fruit trees. Cattle, pigs, sheep, and horses graze on another one-quarter. About 40 percent of the country is covered in trees—conifers on the high ground, with chiefly beech and oak at the lower elevations. Swift rivers contribute hydroelectric power, and large deposits of coal provide fuel for thermal power plants. Slovenia's mines produce mercury, bauxite, copper, antimony, zinc, and iron ore. Manufactured goods include vehicles, chemicals, textiles, and electrical goods.

Croatia

Status:	Parliamentary Democracy
Area:	21,830 sq. miles
Population:	4.6 million
Capital:	Zagreb
Languages:	Slovenian, Serbo-Croatian, Italian
Currency:	Croatian kuna (100 lipes)

Croatia has two distinct climates split east to west along the Dinaric Alps. A large lowland region called the Pannonia Plains extends eastward to the Serbian border, and a contrasting region of limestone mountains extends southward along the coast. The Dinaric Alps and the resorts along the spectacular Dalmatian coast once attracted huge numbers of overseas visitors. Civil war has severely damaged this valuable tourist industry.

Thick black soil on Croatia's lowland plain provides some of the best farmland in Europe, producing large crops of grains, beets, cotton, sunflowers, olives, fruit, hemp, and flax. Local resources include coal, oil, natural gas, and bauxite. Before the civil war, Croatia's well-developed industries produced machinery, chemicals, cement, paper, lumber, electrical goods, and textiles. The people of Croatia are in the process of rebuilding their cities, industries, and **infrastructure**.

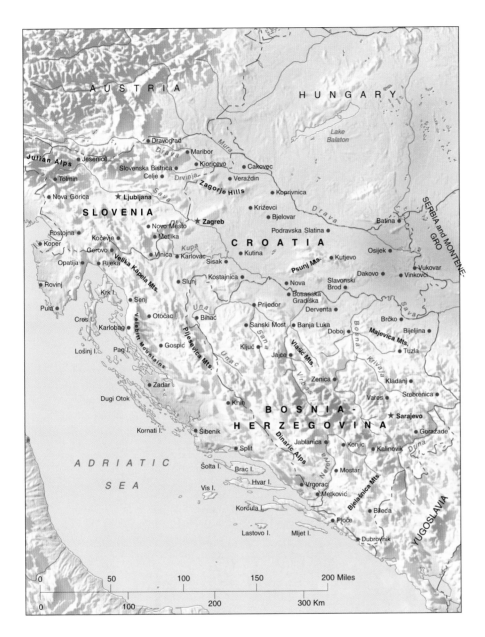

Above: Traditional crafts are still an important part of the local economy in rural parts of Croatia.

Below: A sheltered rocky inlet on Croatia's short Adriatic coastline.

Bosnia-Herzegovina

Status:	Democracy
Area:	19,741 sq. miles
Population:	3.8 million
Capital:	Sarajevo
Language:	Serbo-Croatian
Currency:	Marka (100 pfenniga)

Bosnia-Herzegovina borders Croatia to the west and north. Serbia is to the east, and Montenegro is to the south. The country is nearly landlocked, with just one 12-mile-long stretch of coast near the mouth of the Neretva River. The northern region, Bosnia, is mountainous and thickly forested. Herzegovina, the smaller southern section around the city of Mostar, consists of low hills and flat farmland. The country's coastal climate is mild, but the inland regions have short hot summers and bitterly cold winters with heavy snow.

Before the civil war, Bosnia had a thriving tourist industry of skiing, hunting, fishing, and river kayaking. Vast forests, large reserves of iron ore and coal, and abundant hydro-electric power enabled Bosnian industries to produce vehicles, machinery, textiles, and electrical goods. The country's farmers grew wheat, corn, fruits, vegetables, and tobacco. Much of Bosnia's industry and agriculture were devastated by the war, but efforts are under way to repair the damage.

Serbia, Montenegro, Macedonia

lower pastures, and sheep feed on the higher ground.

Serbian natural resources include oil, gas, coal, copper, lead, and zinc. Montenegrans mine bauxite, coal, and lead. Manufacturing industries are concentrated around Belgrade in the north and Cetinje and Podgorica in the south and output vehicles, military equipment, paper, plastics, cement, textiles, and electrical goods. Civil war and ethnic conflicts have raged since 1992 and have destroyed much of the area's agriculture and industry.

Macedonia

Status:	Republic
Area:	9,927 sq. miles
Population:	2 million
Capital:	Skopje
Language:	Macedonian
Currency:	Macedonian dinar (100 dari)

Serbia and Montenegro (Yugoslavia)

Status:	Republic
Area:	39,448 sq. miles
Population:	10.6 million
Capital:	Belgrade (Serbia) and Podgorica
Languages:	Serbo-Croatian, Albanian, Hungarian
Currency:	New dinar (100 paras)

Serbia and Montenegro are the two former republics of Yugoslavia that act as a joint independent state. The two countries have three contrasting landscapes. Fertile lowlands cover the northern part of Serbia. The plains drain into the Danube River, which flows east into neighboring Romania through a spectacular gorge called the Iron Gate. Central and southern Serbia are mountainous and include parts of the Dinaric Alps and the Balkan Mountains. Roughly one-quarter of Serbia is covered in forest—firs and pines on the mountain slopes, with oak and beech on the lower ground. The third region, Montenegro in the southwest, consists of a limestone plateau with typical **karst** scenery and shrub vegetation. The coastal region has hot, dry summers and cool winters. Inland, the climate is more extreme. The mountains have cool summers and very cold winters, while the northern plains have hot, dry summers and cold winters.

Farmland and pasture cover about half of Serbia and Montenegro. Corn, wheat, potatoes, and tobacco comprise the bulk of the crops, but many farmers grow olives, figs, grapes, pears, plums, and other fruits. Cattle and pigs graze on the

Macedonia is a country of wooded mountains, rising to 9,068 feet in the Korab range on the Albanian border. Most of the land is drained by the south-flowing Vardar River.

Ancient Macedonia included parts of Greece and Bulgaria and was the center of the great Kingdom of Macedonia. Macedonia was in turn part of the Roman, Byzantine, and Ottoman Empires. In 1945 Macedonia one of the six republics of Yugoslavia. Modern Macedonia declared its independence in 1991.

Macedonia's farmers supply most of the country's meat, dairy products, cereals, vegetables, and fruit. They grow cotton and tobacco for home use and for export. Mines produce a wide range of metal ores and some coal, but Macedonia depends on imported oil and gas to fuel its manufacturing industries.

Albania and Greece

Albania

Status:	Republic
Area:	11,100 sq. miles
Population:	3.5 million
Capital:	Tiranë
Language:	Albanian
Currency:	Lek
	(100 qintars)

Greece

Status:	Parliamentary Republic
Area:	50,950 sq. miles
Population:	10.5 million
Capital:	Athens
Language:	Greek
Currency:	Drachma
	(100 leptas)

Mainland Greece occupies the ragged southern end of the Balkan Peninsula, which juts more than 300 miles into the Mediterranean Sea. The country is bordered by Albania, Macedonia, and Bulgaria in the north and by the Ionian Sea to the west. Turkey and the Aegean Sea lie to the east. Greece also includes more than 2,000 islands, most of them scattered across the Aegean side of the mainland. Some islands in the Dodecanese group lie barely 10 miles off the Turkish coast.

Albania is a small country on the Adriatic Sea, cut off from its neighbors by high, rugged, inland mountain ranges. The country has been conquered many times, and for nearly 500 years it was part of the Turkish Ottoman Empire. In 1912 Albania broke free from Turkish rule and declared its independence. From 1928 to 1939, Albania was a monarchy ruled by King Zog. After World War II, it became a Communist republic. In 1992 the Albanian people elected their first non-Communist president.

After years of isolation, Albania is attempting to modernize, but the change from a Communist system to a western-style economy is difficult. Albania is the poorest country in Europe. Most of the people are farmers, growing corn, grapes, sugar beets, olives, potatoes, and grains and raising livestock. Farming methods are often primitive. Few farmers have modern machinery, and many still use horses for plowing and pulling carts. Albania is reasonably rich in resources, yet the country's industries are poorly developed. Albanians mine oil, gas, bitumen (used for surfacing roads), copper, iron, nickel, and large reserves of chrome—the country's most lucrative export.

Fast-flowing mountain rivers generate hydroelectric power, and extensive hardwood and softwood forests supply the raw materials for lumber, plywood, pulp, and paper factories.

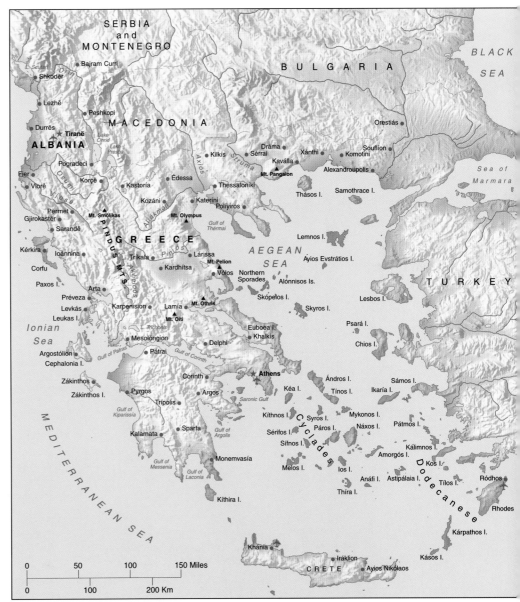

Greece

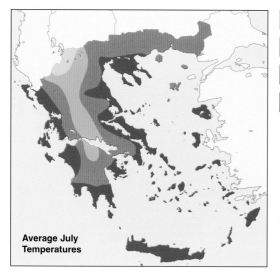

Average July Temperatures

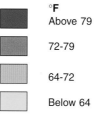

°F
- Above 79
- 72-79
- 64-72
- Below 64

Greece's coastal regions and islands are very hot in summer, although temperatures are lower inland, especially in the mountains. In winter the coastal areas and islands are mild, generally above 40°F, while temperatures in the north central mountains fall to around zero— and often below.

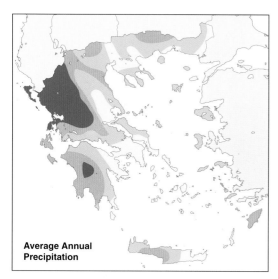

Average Annual Precipitation

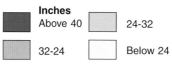

Inches
- Above 40
- 24-32
- 32-24
- Below 24

Left: Prevailing westerly winds ensure that the western side of mainland Greece receives the most rain—40 inches and more compared with a meager 24 inches on the eastern side.

Below: Byzantine buildings overlook the sea at Monemvasia on the Aegean coast—one of the southernmost towns of mainland Greece.

Crete is the largest island, at 3,200 square miles. More than half a million people live on Crete. With their Mediterranean climate, picturesque villages, spring flowers, and beautiful scenery and beaches, the Greek islands attract more than 10 million tourists each year.

Greece is mostly dry, scrub-covered mountains, rising to 8,256 feet in the northwest. Mount Olympus, famous from Greek mythology, towers over the eastern central portion of the country, reaching 9,573 feet. Narrow strips of lowland follow the coast, and several small fertile valleys dot the Macedonia and Thrace regions north of the Aegean Sea. Most Greeks live near the coast and have done so for generations. The country's numerous inlets and bays support Greece's long tradition as a seafaring nation. The country has one of the world's largest merchant fleets, and shipping is a significant source of income.

Greece produces small amounts of bauxite, lead, zinc, chrome, nickel, and silver, but the country does not have the large energy resources needed for **smelting**, so most of the ore is exported. Farming provides the bulk of jobs and income. Farmers grow wheat, corn, tomatoes, olives, grapes, citrus fruits, cotton, and tobacco. Food processing plants create canned olives, olive oil, and dried grapes (sultanas and raisins) for export.

Romania

Romania

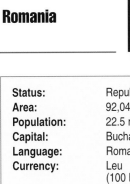

Status:	Republic
Area:	92,042 sq. miles
Population:	22.5 million
Capital:	Bucharest
Language:	Romanian
Currency:	Leu
	(100 bani)

Romania, like many of its neighbors, has recently become a democratic republic after more than 50 years of Communism—24 of them under the rule of Nicolae Ceausescu. In 1989 the Romanian people, backed by the army, overthrew Ceausescu's regime in a short but violent revolution. The people adopted a new constitution in 1991.

Romania is a mountainous country, but the elevations are not so extreme as to inhibit travel. The Transylvanian Plateau in the country's center consists of rolling hills and fertile farmland 1,000 feet to 2,000 feet above sea level. Around it a great arc of mountains,the Moldovian Carpathians and the Transylvanian Alps, snakes south from the Ukrainian border and then goes westward into Serbia. The lower Bihor Mountains in the northwest complete the highland ring encircling the plateau. Outside the mountain ring, lowlands stretch clear to the country's borders. The western lowlands merge with the plains of Serbia and Hungary. The eastern plains slope down to the Black Sea and include the marshes and lakes along the lower Danube River.

The fertile soil of the central plateau and plains provides abundant grains, beets, oilseeds, fruits, and vegetables. Farmers with rich pastures raise pigs, sheep, and dairy cattle. Romania produces enough food for local needs and exports surplus grains, fruits, and wine to neighboring countries. Forests cover

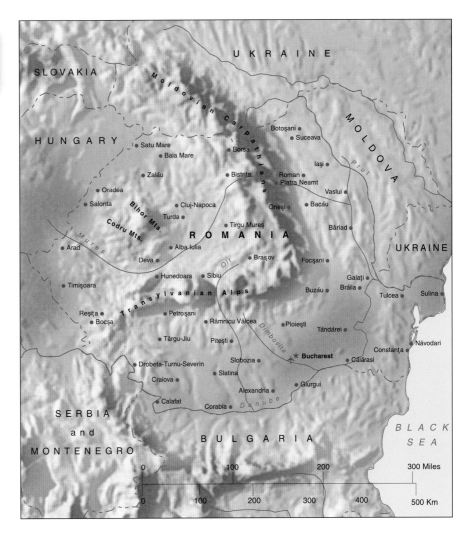

about one-quarter of the land, providing raw materials for house and furniture construction and for the paper industries. Hydroelectric power and natural gas supply much of the nation's energy, but Romania also imports coal and oil. The country's mineral resources include copper, lead, zinc, aluminum ore, and sulfur. Factories concentrated around Bucharest in the south make vehicles, machinery, textiles, furniture, and food products.

Above: One of the many heavy-industry complexes concentrated around the Romanian capital, Bucharest, in the extreme southeast of the country

117

Bulgaria

Bulgaria

Status:	Republic
Area:	42,822 sq. miles
Population:	8.2 million
Capital:	Sofia
Language:	Bulgarian
Currency:	Lev (100 stotinki)

East-west bands of lowlands and mountains separate Bulgaria into four distinct land regions. The fertile Danube Valley stretches across northern Bulgaria. The Balkan Mountains march across the country's middle, rising to about 6,500 feet in the west and gradually descending toward the Black Sea. To the south lies the broad fertile Maritsa River Valley. And south of the Maritsa, the land rises again to the Rhodope Mountains, which separate Bulgaria from Greece and Turkey.

Hot summers and cold winters characterize the Danube Valley, where farmers grow wheat, barley, corn, beets, and vegetables. The Maritsa Valley is milder, with damp winters and warm, dry summers. Farmers in this region cultivate grapes, rice, sunflowers, grains, and tobacco. Bulgarian farmers produce more than just edible crops. The fragrant petals of the country's roses contain a sweet-smelling oil—attar of roses—that is sold to perfumeries all over the world.

Agriculture and tourism drive Bulgaria's economy. Mines in the Rhodope Mountains produce iron, copper, lead, and zinc, but Bulgaria is very short of fuel and has to import energy for its industries. Steel, machinery, cement, and textiles are the country's primary industrial products.

Left: Bright yellow fields of oilseed plants cover much of the Danube lowlands. More than half of Bulgaria's people earn their living from agriculture—one of the highest proportions in Europe.

Below: Workers gather the grape harvest from a hillside vineyard in the Maritsa Valley.

118

Belarus, Moldova, Ukraine

Belarus

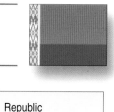

Status:	Republic
Area:	80,154 sq. miles
Population:	10.2 million
Capital:	Minsk
Languages:	Belarussian, Russian
Currency:	Belarussian ruble (100 kopeks)

Belarus has changed hands often. The country was once part of the Mongol Empire, then a portion of Lithuania, then a section of Poland. In 1918 the country achieved its independence but was invaded by Russia the following year, becoming one of the original Soviet Union members. Belarus gained its independence again in 1991 but maintains close ties with Russia.

Most of Belarus is a vast, flat plain. A line of low hills runs through the middle of the country, but the highest point is only 112 feet above sea level.

Above: The main street in Smorgon, in northwestern Belarus

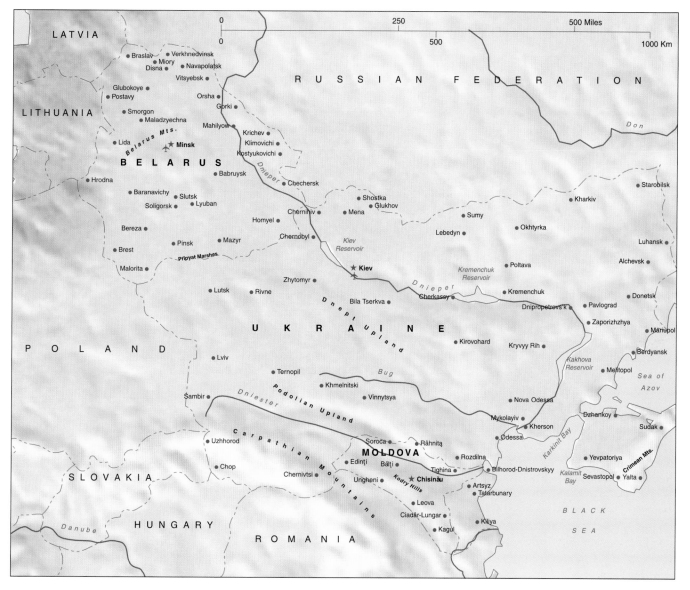

Belarus, Moldova, Ukraine

Southern Belarus contains Europe's largest area of marshes and peat bogs—the famous Pripyat Marshes. Forests cover about one-third of the land—birch and pine in the north, with ash, oak, and hornbeam in the warmer south.

Belarussian factories produce trucks and tractors, machinery, computers, household appliances, pulp, paper, fertilizers, and industrial chemicals. Belarus trades many of its goods to Russia, receiving energy supplies and raw materials in return. Farms cover nearly half of the country. Many farmers concentrate on cattle, pigs, sheep, and goats. The remainder grow grains, beets, potatoes, flax, and hemp.

Moldova

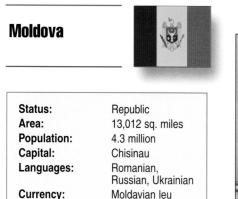

Status:	Republic
Area:	13,012 sq. miles
Population:	4.3 million
Capital:	Chisinau
Languages:	Romanian, Russian, Ukrainian
Currency:	Moldavian leu (100 stotinki)

Moldova is a small republic sandwiched between Ukraine and Romania. Most of the country is hilly, especially in the center where it rises to 1,400 feet. The hills give way to a broad flat plain in the south. Moldova has virtually no mineral resources and no oil or gas, but it has extremely fertile soil and a mild climate. As a result, Moldova's economy depends primarily on agriculture and on industries associated with farming, such as flour milling, food processing, wine making, brewing, and the manufacture of leather goods, ciga-rettes, textiles, soybean products, and sunflower oil.

Ukraine

Status:	Republic
Area:	233,089 sq. miles
Population:	49.9 million
Capital:	Kiev
Languages:	Ukrainian, Russian
Currency:	Hryvnia (100 kopiykas)

Covering more than 230,000 square miles, Ukraine is the largest country lying within Europe. Russia is bigger, but it stretches into northern Asia, so it spans two continents. Ukraine consists mainly of plains, called **steppes,** with low hills separating the major river valleys—the Dniester, the Bug, and the Dnieper, all of which flow into the Black Sea. Ukraine has few mountains. The Carpathians are far to the west, and the Crimean Mountains lie in the south.

Ukraine has abundant peat, coal, and natural gas but has to supplement its meager oil reserves with imports from neighboring countries. Its major industrial regions in the east and south house coal fields and iron ore mines. Ukraine is also one of the world's chief producers of manganese. Like many former states of the Soviet Union, Ukraine's industry was underdeveloped. Modern Ukrainian factories include chemicals, plastics, and food-processing plants. Odessa on the Black Sea is Ukraine's chief port and shipbuilding center.

Above: Ukraine's fertile lowlands produce about 8 percent of the world's barley and 12 percent of the world's sugar beets, but in 1986 huge tracts of farmland were contaminated by the reactor explosion at the Chernobyl nuclear power station.

Above: Modern apartments and offices in the center of Chisinau, Moldova

Above: The Dniester flows from the Carpathians across the lowlands of Ukraine.

Russian Federation (European Russia)

Russian Federation

Status:	Federation
Area:	6,592,819 sq. miles
Population:	146.5 million
Capital:	Moscow
Language:	Russian
Currency:	Russian ruble (100 kopeks)

Russia is the largest country in the world. Even after losing 14 of the 15 republics that comprised the former Soviet Union, Russia is still nearly twice the size of the United States. The Russian Federation stretches 6,000 miles from the borders of Norway, Finland, and the Baltic States in the west to the Pacific Ocean in the east. It extends almost 2,800 miles from the Arctic Ocean to the borders of Kazakhstan, Mongolia, and China.

Russia traces its history to the medieval Slavic state of Kievan Rus, which covered most of modern Ukraine, Belarus, and European Russia. Mongol invaders from central Asia destroyed Kievan Rus in the thirteenth century. In the 1300s, a new state called Muscovy took its place and was succeeded in the 1700s by the Russian Empire. The Russian Revolution of 1917 ended imperial rule, replacing it with a Communist government, which remained in power until 1991.

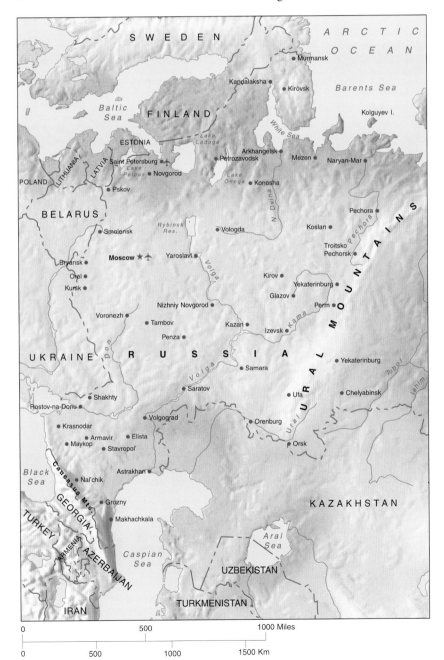

Above: European Russia—west of the Urals—is dwarfed by its eastern (Asian) segment. A train journey from Moscow to Vladivostok takes seven days and passes through eight time zones.

Above center: The cruiser *Aurora* on the Neva River that flows through Saint Petersburg

Above: Russians enjoy a traditional winter pastime—fishing through holes in the ice on a frozen lake at Zagorsk.

Russian Federation (European Russia)

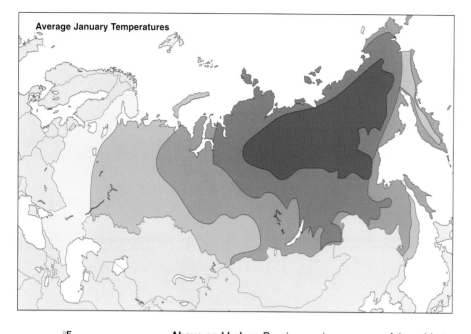

Average January Temperatures

°F
- Above 10
- -4 to 10
- -18 to -4
- -33 to -18
- Below -33

Above and below: Russia experiences some of the coldest weather conditions on earth. In January, temperatures in eastern Siberia plunge as low as -90°F for weeks at a time. Only in the extreme west of the country do average winter temperatures remain above 10°F. Even in summer, the northern half of the country remains below 60°F. The only part of this vast land to receive any real summer warmth is the southwest, bordering the Black Sea and the Caspian Sea—Russia's favorite vacation area.

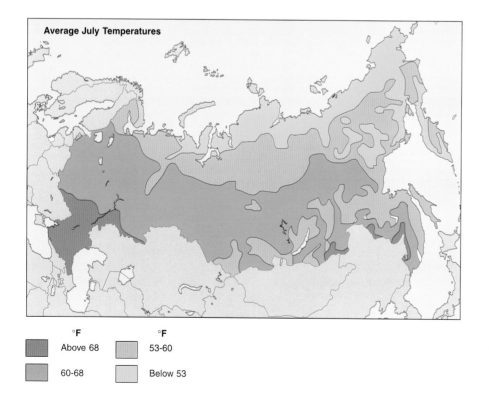

Average July Temperatures

°F
- Above 68
- 60-68

°F
- 53-60
- Below 53

During the 1990s, Russians suffered great hardships. The country tried to change from the Communist system—under which the government controlled everything—to a free-market economy where people can own their own companies and compete with one another for business.

Russia's vast land area consists of four main regions—the European Plain (European Russia), which extends as far as the Ural Mountains; the West Siberian Plain between the Urals and the Yenisey River; the Central Siberian Plateau between the Yenisey and Lena Rivers; and the East Siberian Highlands.

Most of European Russia lies on the European Plain, bounded by the Carpathian and Caucasus Mountains in the south and by the Urals in the east. Mount Elbrus is Russia's highest peak at 18,510 feet. Climate and vegetation vary greatly from north to south. Treeless tundra dominates the Arctic zone. South of the tundra lies a forested belt of pine, spruce, and fir called the **taiga**, which merges southward into mixed forests of birch, oak, elm, and maple. Fishing and herding reindeer are traditional occupations in these harsh northern regions. In the forested zones, farmers grow potatoes and flax and raise livestock. The steppes stretch across the southern part of the country, containing the rich black and brown soil that makes Russia the world's foremost producer of barley, oats, wheat, and rye. Farmers in the warmer southern region bordering Ukraine and the Black Sea grow a variety of vegetables, as well as subtropical crops such as tea and citrus fruits.

Large coal fields operate near the capital city of Moscow, in the northern Urals, and on the Russian-Ukrainian border. Oil fields in the Urals, the Arctic, and the Caucasus Mountains provide fuel and raw materials for Russia's petrochemical industries. Huge iron ore deposits along the Ukrainian border support the country's iron and steel

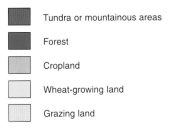

Tundra or mountainous areas

Forest

Cropland

Wheat-growing land

Grazing land

Right: Russia is enormously rich in natural resources. Thousands of square miles of forest yield lumber, pulp, and paper. Fast-flowing rivers provide hydropower. Huge mineral reserves feed the nation's industries. Fertile black soils in the southwest make Russia the world's leading grain producer.

Below: Moscow at midnight. On the left, the clock tower marks one of the main gates in the wall of the Kremlin complex. On the right, spectacular onion domes crown Saint Basil's Cathedral in Red Square. And in the distance, at the far side of Red Square, stands the imposing facade of the State Historical Museum.

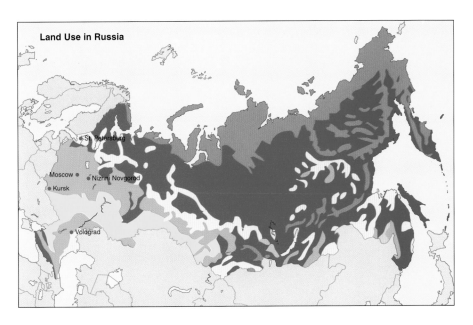

Land Use in Russia

industries. Russia also has vast reserves of most other minerals, but many are located in remote areas, far from European Russia's manufacturing centers, which are located in Saint Petersburg, Moscow, Kursk, Nizhny Novgorod, and Volgograd. To compensate, Russia imports fuel and raw materials from many of the states along its western borders.

Tafraout, an oasis in Morocco

124

AFRICA

20°   10°   0°   10°   20°   30°   40°   50°

40°

30°

Madeira I.

Tropic of
Cancer

Canary Is.

MOROCCO

TUNISIA

MEDITERRANEAN SEA

ALGERIA

LIBYA

EGYPT

RED SEA

Persia

20°

MAURITANIA

WESTERN
SAHARA

MALI

NIGER

CHAD

SUDAN

ERITREA

SENEGAL

GAMBIA

GUINEA-
BISSAU

GUINEA

BURKINA
FASO

DJIBOUTI Gulf of

10°

SIERRA
LEONE

LIBERIA

IVORY
COAST

GHANA

TOGO

BENIN

NIGERIA

CENTRAL
AFRICAN
REPUBLIC

ETHIOPIA

SOMALIA

Gulf of
Guinea

Bioko

CAMEROON

EQUATORIAL
GUINEA

São Tomé
and Principe

GABON

REPUBLIC
OF
THE CONGO

UGANDA

KENYA

INDIA

0°

Cabinda

DEMOCRATIC

REPUBLIC OF

THE CONGO

RWANDA

BURUNDI

TANZANIA

Zanzibar

OCEA

ATLANTIC

SEYCHE

10°

OCEAN

ANGOLA

ZAMBIA

MOZAMBIQUE

Comoros

Mayotte

MADAGASCAR

Mozambique Channel

20°

NAMIBIA

ZIMBABWE

Tropic of
Capricorn

BOTSWANA

SWAZILAND

30°

SOUTH

AFRICA

LESOTHO

0   500   1000   1500   2000 Miles

0   1000   2000   3000 Km

20°   10°   0°   10°   20°   30°   40°   50°

AFRICA

Above: Most North Africans are Muslims, who worship in mosques like the magnificent Koutubia Mosque in Marrakech, Morocco. A muezzin (crier) calls the faithful to prayer from the ornate minaret (tower).

Below: Wildebeest thunder across the open grasslands of South Africa's Rooipoort Game Reserve.

Africa is the second-largest continent by land area (11.7 million square miles) and the third largest by population (771 million people). The continent is a patchwork of more than 50 countries, each with many different people, languages, and customs. Africa's population is spread unevenly across the land. The desert countries of Libya and Mauritania have only about 7 people per square mile, while Nigeria, the most crowded country, supports 319 people per square mile.

The continent stretches 5,000 miles north to south—from the warm shores of the Mediterranean Sea to the cold stormy waters off the Cape of Good Hope—and 4,700 miles west to east, from the Atlantic coast of Senegal to Somalia, which juts into the Indian Ocean. Three major mountain ranges skirt the continent. The Atlas Mountains rise to 13,671 feet in the northwest. Africa's highest peak, Mount Kilimanjaro, at 19,341 feet, towers over East Africa's high plateau. The Drakensberg Mountains rise 11,425 feet above sea level in eastern South Africa and Lesotho.

The Great Rift Valley, Africa's most spectacular landscape feature, is a huge crack in the earth's crust that cuts through the continent for 4,300 miles from the Red Sea to Malawi. Africa embraces some of the world's most noted water features. Lake Victoria, covering 26,828 square miles, is in area the world's second-largest freshwater lake after Lake Superior. The Nile, snaking along for 4,160 miles, is the world's longest river. And Victoria Falls on the Zambia–Zimbabwe border rushes around three islands before plunging 350 feet.

Africa has vast forest resources, as well as huge reserves of copper, diamonds, gold, and petroleum. But most African countries lack the money and skilled workers needed to build and run factories. South Africa, Egypt, Morocco, Algeria, and Nigeria are the only African countries with well-developed industries. Most African families depend on **subsistence agriculture,** growing just enough to feed themselves. Farmers in more fertile areas often grow **cash crops** for export. Large-scale plantations, owned mostly by multinational companies, produce cacao beans, coffee beans, cashews, cloves, bananas, vanilla, tea, cotton, and sugar.

Morocco and Algeria

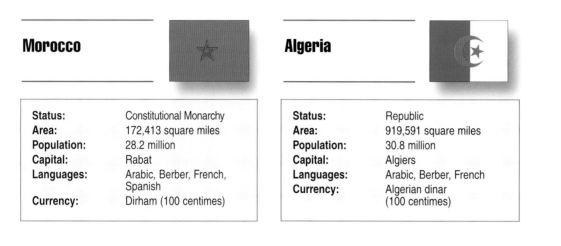

Morocco

Status:	Constitutional Monarchy
Area:	172,413 square miles
Population:	28.2 million
Capital:	Rabat
Languages:	Arabic, Berber, French, Spanish
Currency:	Dirham (100 centimes)

Algeria

Status:	Republic
Area:	919,591 square miles
Population:	30.8 million
Capital:	Algiers
Languages:	Arabic, Berber, French
Currency:	Algerian dinar (100 centimes)

Morocco is bordered by the Atlantic Ocean to the west and the Mediterranean Sea to the north. The two coastlines are separated by a rocky headland that juts toward Spain to form the narrow Strait of Gibraltar. Well-watered fertile plains stretch along the coasts, where farmers produce wheat, barley, corn, sugar beets, beans, fruits, and vegetables. Major landowners control about one-third of the farmland and account for 85 percent of all the crops produced. Most Moroccan farmers get by on a few acres, raising crops and tending sheep, goats, and dairy cattle. Morocco is one of Africa's leading fishing nations. Sardines, mackerel, and tuna are caught and then canned for export or converted into animal feed or fertilizer.

Morocco has about two-thirds of the world's reserves of phosphate rock, which is mined and exported for making fertilizer and other chemical products. The country also has reserves of iron ore, copper, lead, and zinc, but most of the country's energy is based on imported oil.

Casablanca, Morocco's main manu-facturing center, produces cement, chemicals, fertilizers, paper, plastics, leather goods, and processed foods.

Nearly half of Algeria's people live in cities and towns on the narrow coastal plain bordering the Mediterranean Sea. Here the climate is warm, with mild winters and up to 30 inches of rain each year. Farmers in this region grow cereal grains, vines, olives, fruits, and vegetables and raise sheep, goats, and cattle. About 30 percent of Algerians work in factories in Algiers, Annaba, Constantine, Skikda, and other cities on or near the coast. These manufacturing centers produce iron and steel, construction materials, textiles, phosphate fertilizers, and refined petroleum products. The country is rich in oil and natural gas, but political unrest has prevented the government from making full use of these resources. As a result, many thousands of Algerians go abroad, many of them to France, to find work.

The Atlas Mountains rise steeply behind the coastal plain, separating the mild northern region from the hot dry Sahara Desert, which covers 80 percent of the country. The northern Sahara is mainly sand. To the south and east, it is bare rock and boulders. Less than 3 percent of Algerians live in the desert. A few are oil field workers, and some live in scattered oases where dates and cereal grains can be grown. The remainder are nomadic Tuareg people who speak the Berber language and travel between the region's sparse grazing areas with their camels, sheep, and goats.

Right: A natural rock arch in the rugged Tassili Mountains of southern Algeria. Striking landscape features like this are the result of thousands of years of erosion by windblown sand and the flash floods that follow brief but heavy desert rains.

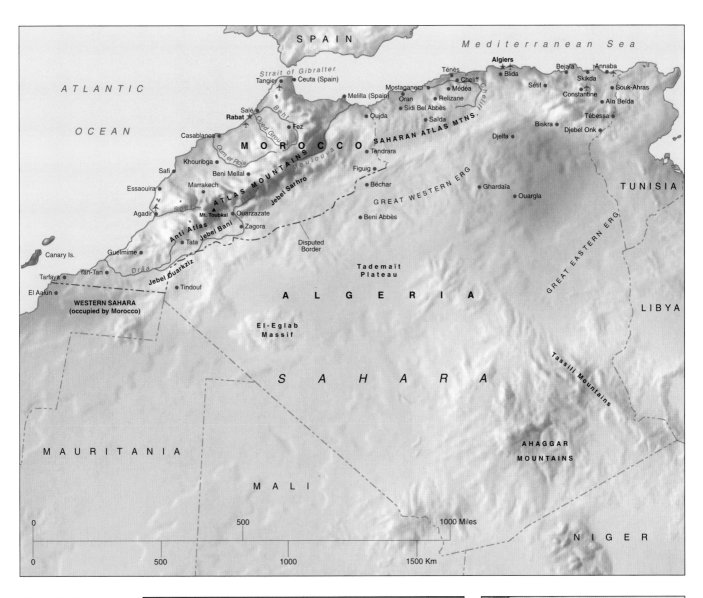

SPAIN

Mediterranean Sea

ATLANTIC

OCEAN

Strait of Gibralter

Tangier · Ceuta (Spain)

Salé · Melilla (Spain)

Rabat ✈

Casablanca ·

Khouribga ·

Safi ·

Essaouira ·

Agadir ·

Canary Is.

Guelmime ·

Tarfaya ·

Tan-Tan ·

El Aaíun ·

WESTERN SAHARA
(occupied by Morocco)

Fez ·

M O R O C C O

Beni Mellal ·

Marrakech ·

Mt. Toubkal ▲ Ouarzazate ·

Anti Atlas Jebel Bani

Tata · Zagora

Jebel Ouarkziz

Tindouf ·

Oujda ·

Tendrara ·

Figuig ·

Béchar ·

Beni Abbès ·

Disputed
Border

A L G E R I A

El-Eglab
Massif

S A H A R A

M A U R I T A N I A

M A L I

Algiers ✈

Ténès · Cheliff
· Blida

Mostaganem · Médéa
Oran · Relizane
Sidi Bel Abbès
Saïda

SAHARAN ATLAS MTNS.

Djelfa ·

Tademaït
Plateau

Ghardaïa ·
· Ouargla

Bejaïa · Annaba
Sétif · Skikda
Constantine · Souk-Ahras
Aïn Beïda

Tébessa ·

Biskra · Djebel Onk ·

T U N I S I A

GREAT EASTERN ERG

L I B Y A

AHAGGAR
MOUNTAINS

Tassili Mountains

0   500   1000 Miles

0   500   1000   1500 Km

N I G E R

Far right: These Moroccan water sellers are a familiar sight in the hot, dry cities. The water is carried in a goatskin bag slung from the shoulder and is served to customers in highly polished cups made of beaten copper.

Right: Farmers' wives wash freshly picked cotton on the banks of the Oued Grou River at Rabat, Morocco.

Tunisia and Libya

Tunisia

Status:	Republic
Area:	63,170 square miles
Population:	9.5 million
Capital:	Tunis
Languages:	Arabic, French, English
Currency:	Tunisian dinar (1,000 millimes)

Tunisia's northern landscape consists of low mountains with patches of cork oak and evergreen woodland. The Atlas Mountains lie near the Mediterranean coast of this North African nation, and the Tabassah Mountains, part of the same Atlas range, lie farther south. Farmers grow wheat and other grains in the Majardah River Valley and in additional fertile lowlands between the two ranges. A vast, dry, grassy plain lies south of the mountains and is dotted with salt lakes and **pans.** Beyond the plain lies the Sahara Desert.

Tunisia's most productive region is the narrow plain along its eastern coast, where fertile soil and winter rains yield excellent crops of grains, citrus fruits, grapes, melons, and olives. Olive groves cover nearly one-third of the country's farmland, making Tunisia the world's fifth-largest producer of olives and olive oil.

Phosphates and oil are Tunisia's major mineral resources. Both are exported in large quantities. The country's manufacturing centers supply textiles, clothing, paper, steel, construction materials, and processed foods to both local and export markets. Tourism is fast becoming one of Tunisia's most important industries. Although Tunisia suffers frequent droughts and dwindling oil reserves, the government devotes nearly half the national budget to education, health care, and other social services.

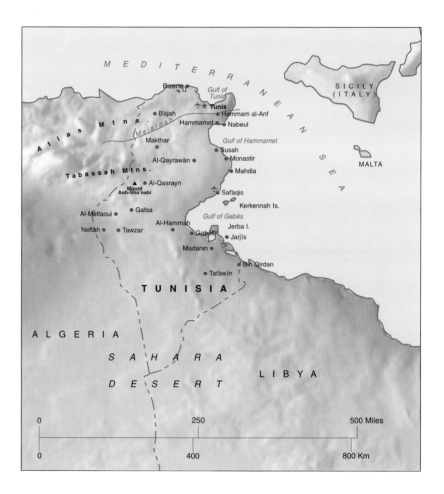

Right: Tunisian elders deep in discussion. The decorative tiled wall mosaics, rush matting, and colorful rugs are typical of the culture.

130

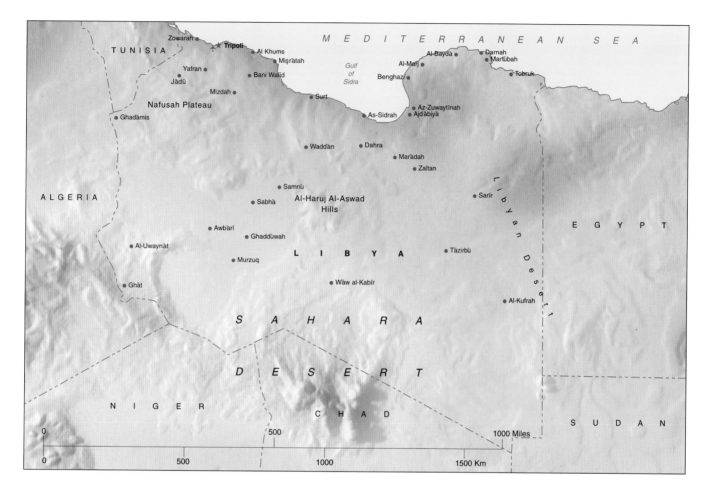

TUNISIA
Zowarah
Tripoli
Al Khums
Mişrātah
Yafran
Jādū
Bani Walīd
Mizdah
Nafusah Plateau
Ghadāmis

MEDITERRANEAN SEA
Gulf of Sidra
Al-Bayda
Darnah
Martūbah
Al-Marj
Benghazi
Tobruk

Surt
As-Sidrah
Az-Zuwaytīnah
Ajdābiyā

ALGERIA

Waddān
Dahra
Marādah
Zaltan

Samnū
Sabhā
Al-Haruj Al-Aswad Hills
Sarīr
Libyan Desert
EGYPT

Awbārī
Ghaddūwah
L I B Y A
Tāzirbū

Al-Uwaynāt
Murzuq
Ghāt
Wāw al-Kabīr
Al-Kufrah

S A H A R A

D E S E R T

NIGER
CHAD
SUDAN

0   500   1000 Miles
0   500   1000   1500 Km

Libya

Status:	Republic
Area:	679,359 square miles
Population:	5.0 million
Capital:	Tripoli
Languages:	Arabic, Berber
Currency:	Libyan dinar (1,000 dirhams)

The Sahara Desert blankets nearly 95 percent of Libya. Vast sand dunes cover much of the country's northern half, gradually giving way to stone-covered desert that rises to a rugged mountain range in the south. Libya's climate is hot and dry, receiving less than two inches of annual rainfall. Of the few Libyans who inhabit this desert area, most live in scattered **oases** and grow dates, grains, and vegetables.

Some work in the desert oil fields. The rest are nomadic herders constantly on the move in search of grazing land for their camels, sheep, and goats.

Most of Libya's people live in towns and villages on the Mediterranean coastal plain, where they enjoy fertile soil, mild temperatures, and up to 16 inches of rain each year. Farmers in this region grow wheat, barley, potatoes, dates, and citrus fruits and raise cattle, sheep, and poultry. Most Libyan farms are small family businesses, so the country imports much of the food it needs to feed its rapidly growing population.

Oil, Libya's principal mineral resource and its most significant export, accounts for about one-quarter of the country's total economic production. Libyans also mine iron ore, lime, gypsum, sulfur, and some natural gas. Oil refineries and factories in the northern cities process foods and produce petroleum and petrochemicals, cement, and some iron and steel.

Above: Sheer rocky cliffs and boulder-strewn plateaus dominate the landscape of southern Libya. To the northeast, in the distance, lie the rolling sand dunes of the Libyan Desert.

Egypt

Egypt
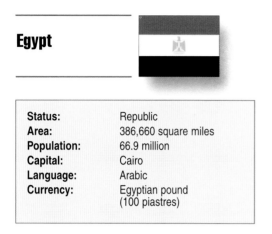

Status:	Republic
Area:	386,660 square miles
Population:	66.9 million
Capital:	Cairo
Language:	Arabic
Currency:	Egyptian pound (100 piastres)

Egypt has the second-largest population in Africa (after Nigeria), and its capital, Cairo, is the continent's most populous city, housing 13 million residents. About 99 percent of Egyptians live on just 4 percent of the land—consisting of the narrow fertile valley of the Nile, the Nile **Delta,** and the banks of the **Suez Canal.**

The Nile River has enabled Egypt to become one of Africa's leading nations. Farmers in the Nile Valley produce nearly all of Egypt's home-grown food including corn, rice, potatoes, wheat, oranges, tomatoes, and sugarcane. These farmers also tend Egypt's most valuable cash crop—high-quality, long-fiber cotton that is exported worldwide. Dams and reservoirs hold back the Nile's waters and provide year-round irrigation.

Sand and rock deserts interspersed with a few salt marshes claim the rest of this North African country. Scattered oases house small communities that grow date palms and vegetables and rear sheep and goats. The deserts are also home to the Bedouin people. Some still follow the traditional nomadic way of life, although many have settled and become farmers.

Egypt is not rich in mineral resources, but petroleum and natural gas, iron ore, manganese, and phosphates are vital exports and provide fuel and raw materials for the country's industries. Cairo and the main port of Alexandria house the country's principal manufacturing centers. Factory goods include petrochemicals, textiles, chemicals, steel, fertilizers, and metal and food products. Cairo is also a major financial center and the launching point for millions of tourists who visit the country's spectacular ancient monuments—the pyramids, the Sphinx, and the Valley of the Kings.

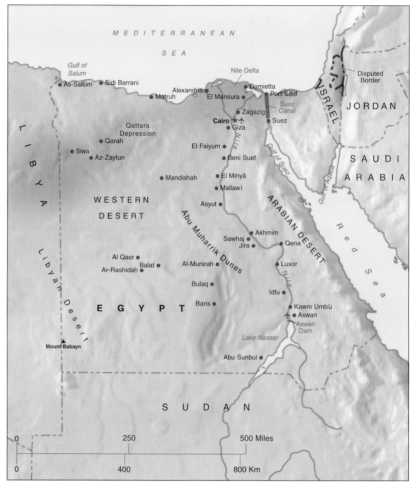

132

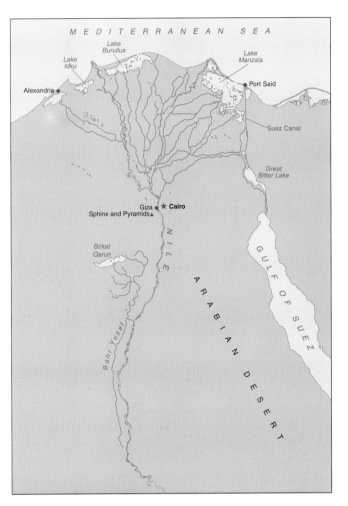

Above: The Nile Valley and its vast river delta are one of the world's most fertile regions. This great river irrigates almost six million acres of farmland in Egypt and three million acres in neighboring Sudan.

Above left: The *felucca* is the traditional boat of Nile fishers and traders.

Left: The Sphinx and the great pyramids at Giza are among the most identifiable sights of the ancient world.

Facing page: The Nile River winds through the center of Cairo—the biggest city in Africa and one of the world's fastest-growing urban centers.

Sudan

Sudan

Status:	Republic
Area:	967,494 square miles
Population:	28.9 million
Capital:	Khartoum
Languages:	Arabic, English
Currency:	Sudanese dinar (100 pounds)

Africa's largest country by area, Sudan is a land of contrasts. Northern Sudan is mainly desert, with less than 4 inches of annual rainfall and daytime temperatures consistently above 100°F. The central region is a vast grassy plain that gets slightly more rain. Southern Sudan is hot and humid with 40 inches of rain each year and temperatures averaging 80°F. This southern region is covered in dense forests and swamps that merge with the tropical rain forests of the Democratic Republic of the Congo and the Central African Republic.

Like Egypt to its north, Sudan depends on the Nile River. About 80 percent of its people live in rural areas, most of them farming the valleys of the Nile and its main tributaries—the White Nile and the Blue Nile. But the valleys are not productive enough to feed everyone. Infertile soil leaves many farmers struggling to grow enough food to feed their families. The remaining 20 percent of the population live in Sudan's major cities—the capital city of Khartoum, Omdurman (the biggest city), Wad Medani, Port Sudan, and Juba. Small factories and service industries provide jobs for a majority of the city dwellers.

Agriculture accounts for 40 percent of Sudan's economy. Cotton and **gum arabic** are the principal exports. Sudanese farmers plant millet, sorghum, sugarcane, and vegetables and produce meat and dairy products for local consumption. Miners extract chromium, gold, gypsum, and oil. Urban factory workers make cement, fertilizers, textiles, and leather products for local and international markets.

Above: A trader sells his goods in a traditional market in Khartoum, Sudan.

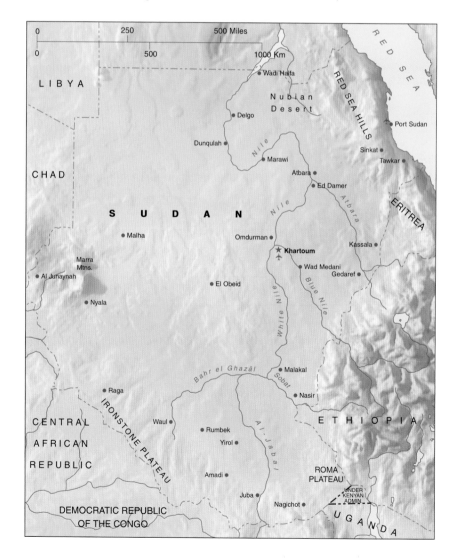

Eritrea and Ethiopia

Eritrea

Status:	Independent State
Area:	45,405 square miles
Population:	4.0 million
Capital:	Asmara
Languages:	Tigrinya, Tigre, Arabic, English
Currency:	Eritrean birr (100 cents)

This former province of Ethiopia has been fought over for centuries. After periods of rule by Italy, Britain, and Ethiopia, Eritrea fell into a bitter civil war in the 1980s and early 1990s. Eritrea formally declared itself, as well as the Dahlak **Archipelago** in the Red Sea, free of Ethiopia in 1993. But the constant conflicts and a succession of severe droughts have devastated this new East African country. Three-quarters of the people depend on foreign food aid, and the country's illiteracy rate is high.

The government in the capital of Asmara is attempting to rebuild Eritrea's economy by supporting traditional textile and leather industries and by developing fishing and tourism. Highland farmers grow sorghum, cotton, **teff**, coffee beans, tobacco, and citrus fruits. The land is not very productive, however, and rainfall is erratic. Eritrea imports food and other goods from neighboring countries. Salt mines in the arid Danakil Depression in the hot, dry eastern region produce the country's most valuable export.

Ethiopia

Status:	Federal Republic
Area:	426,371 square miles
Population:	59.7 million
Capital:	Addis Ababa
Languages:	Amharic, Arabic
Currency:	Ethiopian birr (100 cents)

Rugged mountains and high fertile plateaus veil western Ethiopia, where the highland climate is usually a mild 60°F. Droughts occur and the people are poor, but enough rain falls during most summers for farmers to produce sufficient wheat, corn, sorghum, and teff to feed their families. Most farmers also raise cattle, sheep, goats, and chickens. The richest farmland is in the southwest, where farmers grow commercial crops of oilseed, sugarcane, and coffee beans—the country's biggest export. The Great Rift Valley, which runs north to south through the country, splits the highland region in two. Eastern Ethiopia consists of hot, dry, lowland plains where rainfall seldom exceeds 15 inches, and the temperature averages 80°F. The thermometer can rise to a fierce 120°F in the deserts of the northeast, a largely uninhabited area. Most Ethiopians live in the highlands—85 percent of them in rural villages and scattered farms and the other 15 percent in towns. Addis Ababa, the capital, is home to 2.3 million people.

Ethiopia hosts many different cultures and people, who speak more than 80 languages and 200 dialects. About 40 percent of the people are Ethiopian Orthodox Christians, 40 percent are Muslims, and most of the remainder follow traditional African religions.

Industry is underdeveloped. Ethiopia has few mineral resources, so manufacturing—based mainly in the capital—consists largely of textiles, leather goods, cement, and processed foods. Eritrea's independence left Ethiopia without a coastline, but the two countries reached an agreement allowing Ethiopia to export goods through the Eritrean port of Asseb. Goods are also exported through Djibouti. The long war with Eritrea, a succession of droughts and famines in the 1970s, 1980s, and 1990s, and the effects of deforestation and poor farming methods have left Ethiopia desperately poor and almost completely dependent on international aid.

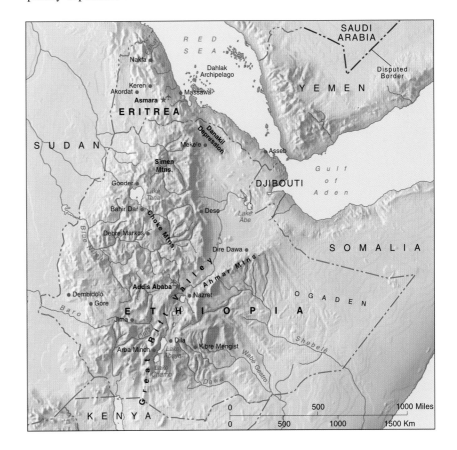

Djibouti and Somalia

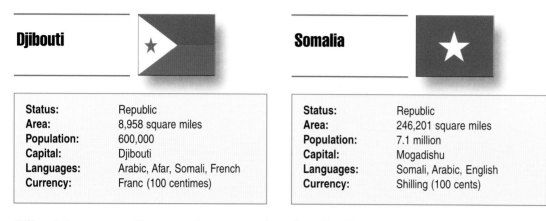

Djibouti

Status:	Republic
Area:	8,958 square miles
Population:	600,000
Capital:	Djibouti
Languages:	Arabic, Afar, Somali, French
Currency:	Franc (100 centimes)

Somalia

Status:	Republic
Area:	246,201 square miles
Population:	7.1 million
Capital:	Mogadishu
Languages:	Somali, Arabic, English
Currency:	Shilling (100 cents)

Djibouti is very small, extremely poor, and depends almost entirely on the fact that it has one of the best harbors on Africa's eastern coast—at the nation's capital, also called Djibouti, on the Gulf of Aden. The port is the end point for a railroad built in 1917 by the government of Ethiopia to link Addis Ababa, Ethiopia's capital, to the coast. A large proportion of Ethiopia's foreign trade passes through the port, providing Djibouti with its primary source of income.

More than 90 percent of Djibouti is desert. Its barren coastal plain suffers one of the hottest, driest climates on earth, with less than five inches of annual rainfall and average temperatures around 90°F. Hilly terrain rises to nearly 5,000 feet in the country's north and west, meeting Ethiopia's highlands at the border.

Most of Djibouti's people belong to two main ethnic groups—the Afar in the north and the Issa in the south. Both groups are traditional nomadic herders of camels, sheep, goats, and cattle, but more and more of them are giving up the struggle to live in the barren countryside and are moving to the capital city and highland towns. This influx of people has put pressure on urban resources already strained by the thousands of refugees who have fled to Djibouti from conflicts in Ethiopia and Somalia. Djibouti is also home to many Arab traders and a large French community—a reminder of the country's 100 years under French rule before it gained independence in 1977. Djibouti exports salt and dates but depends heavily on foreign aid.

Somalia, like so many other African countries, gained independence in 1960 after nearly 100 years of shared **colonial rule** between Britain and Italy. But independence did not bring peace. For the last 30 years, Somalia has been torn apart by civil war, conflict with Ethiopia, and severe droughts that have killed nearly half a million people.

Somalia is a hot, dry East African country, covered almost entirely in dry **savanna** grassland. A low mountain range lies across northern Somalia, where average temperatures reach 100°F and annual rainfall can be as little as 3 or 4 inches. Central and southern Somalia feel almost wet by comparison. Annual rainfall in these low, flat regions can exceed 12 inches, and temperatures range from 64°F to 100°F.

Most of the country is too dry and infertile for farming. Two-thirds of Somalis are nomadic herders—grazing their sheep, goats, cattle, and camels wherever they can find enough pasture. In the south, the Jubba and Shabeelle Rivers provide water for irrigation and enable farmers to grow corn, sorghum, cotton, bananas, citrus fruits, and sugarcane. Somalia's main exports are animal hides and leather goods, bananas, and livestock—most of which Saudi Arabia purchases. The country has to import much of its food, the bulk of its manufactured goods, and all of its oil and petroleum.

After nearly 25 years of intense fighting and severe starvation, Somalia allowed in U.S. forces, which hoped to keep the warring factions apart and to ensure that desperately needed food and supplies would reach the starving people. The following year, the United Nations took over the operation, but in 1995 the peacekeepers withdrew, unable to stop the fighting.

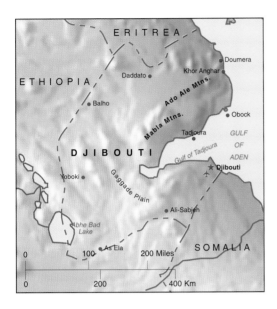

Above: Somali nomads draw water for their camels from a deep well in the Ogaden Desert on the country's border with Ethiopia.

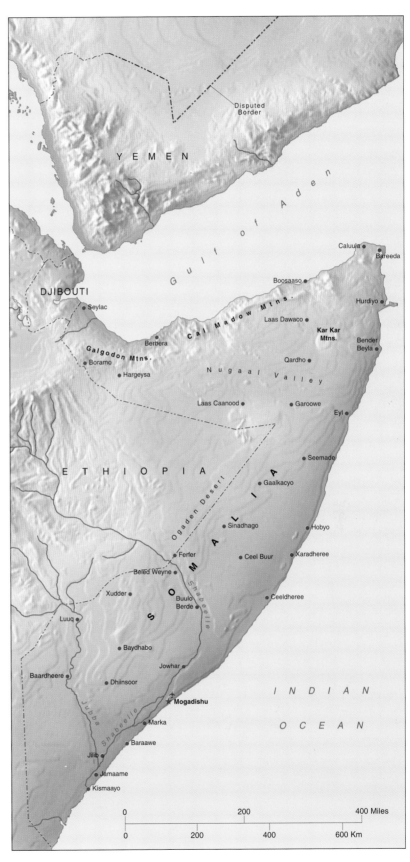

Western Sahara and Mauritania

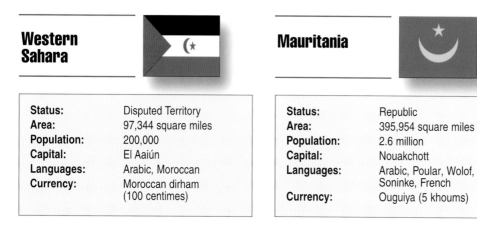

Western Sahara	
Status:	Disputed Territory
Area:	97,344 square miles
Population:	200,000
Capital:	El Aaiún
Languages:	Arabic, Moroccan
Currency:	Moroccan dirham (100 centimes)

Mauritania	
Status:	Republic
Area:	395,954 square miles
Population:	2.6 million
Capital:	Nouakchott
Languages:	Arabic, Poular, Wolof, Soninke, French
Currency:	Ouguiya (5 khoums)

Western Sahara, formerly Spanish Sahara, lies on Africa's northwestern coast. Most of the country is barren desert dotted with wadis (dry streambeds) that fill briefly after occasional rainstorms but dry out almost immediately. The Saharawi people are mostly Arab and Berber nomads who roam the desert with their herds of camels, sheep, and goats. The inland desert soil is too dry and infertile for agriculture, although small farms on the coast manage to grow grains and vegetables. Fishing crews along the coast catch and dry fish for export to the Spanish-owned Canary Islands, 70 miles off the African coast. Western Sahara's one asset is its huge reserves of phosphate rock, an ingredient in fertilizers. The deposits southeast of the capital of El Aaiún are the largest in the world. The valuable minerals are one of the reasons neighboring states have tried to take control of the country.

Spain established a colony in the area in 1884 but gave up its claim in 1976 under pressure from Morocco and Mauritania. Morocco then ruled the northern part of the territory, and Mauritania governed the south. The Polisario Front—a local independence movement—became the third player in a bitter struggle for control. Mauritania pulled out in 1979, but Morocco still holds power. Since 1992 Morocco has been promising a referendum (a public vote) on whether Western Sahara should become independent, but the process has been deadlocked by disagreements over who is eligible to vote.

Mauritania bridges two worlds—the Arab world to the north and black African world to the south. Most of the northerners are of Arab and Berber descent who speak Arabic and follow the Islamic faith. A large proportion of black Africans, many of whom are Christians or followers of traditional religions, inhabit southern Mauritania. The country was a French colony from 1903 until it achieved independence in 1960. Military leaders ruled Mauritania until 1991, when the country adopted a new constitution and democratic elections.

The vast sand plains and rocky highlands of the Sahara Desert dominate most of the country. The **Sahel,** a belt of low, arid plains covered in sparse grass and scrub, stretches across Mauritania's southern border. Most of the people living in the Sahel region are nomadic herders. Black Africans, most of them settled farmers, are concentrated in the southwest where the fertile soil of the Senegal River and its tributaries affords premium crops of millet, corn, beans, rice, and dates. Coastal fisheries provide another important source of food and export income. High-grade iron ore mined near Fdérik is Mauritania's most valuable mineral resource. Most of it is exported to Europe. Fish, iron ore, and copper exports do not earn enough to support the economy, and Mauritania depends heavily on foreign aid, much of it from France.

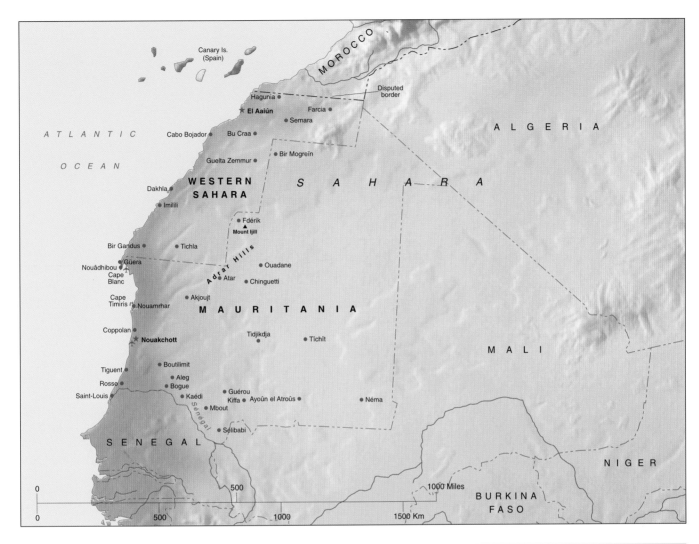

Canary Is.
(Spain)

MOROCCO

ATLANTIC

OCEAN

Disputed
border

Hagunia
El Aaiún
Farcia
Semara

ALGERIA

Cabo Bojador
Bu Craa

Guelta Zemmur
Bir Mogreïn

S A H A R A

Dakhla
WESTERN
SAHARA

Imilili

Fdérik
Mount Ijill

Bir Gandus
Tichla

Adrar Hills

Ouadane

Nouâdhibou
Güera
Cape
Blanc

Atar
Chinguetti

Cape
Timiris
Akjoujt
Nouamrhar

M A U R I T A N I A

MALI

Coppolan
Nouakchott

Tidjikdja
Tichît

Tiguent
Boutilimit

Rosso
Aleg
Bogue

Saint-Louis
Guérou
Kaédi
Ayoûn el Atroûs
Néma

Kiffa
Mbout

Senegal
Sélibabi

S E N E G A L

NIGER

0
500

1000 Miles

BURKINA
FASO

0
500
1000
1500 Km

139

Mali and Burkina Faso

Mali

Status:	Republic
Area:	478,838 square miles
Population:	11 million
Capital:	Bamako
Languages:	French, local languages
Currency:	CFA franc (100 centimes)

Burkina Faso

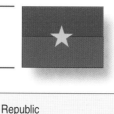

Status:	Republic
Area:	105,792 square miles
Population:	11.6 million
Capital:	Ouagadougou
Language:	French
Currency:	CFA franc (100 centimes)

Mali is a land of plateaus and plains, hot sand, and mild **tropics.** Northern Mali, which the Sahara Desert partly covers, receives very little rain and often reaches temperatures over 110°F at midday. The central region spans the Sahel, which is populated mainly by nomadic herders. Southern Mali enjoys a tropical climate of 80°F temperatures and annual rainfall of about 35 inches—most of it falling between July and October.

Southern Malians farm the land, growing corn, millet, cassava, sorghum, rice, and yams on the fertile soil along the Senegal and Niger Rivers. But even in the south, life is extremely hard. Very few farmers can afford tractors, modern tools, or fertilizers, and most of them struggle to grow enough food for their families.

When there is enough rain, farmers in the south grow peanuts, cotton, and sugarcane for export, and fishing crews catch carp, catfish, and perch from the main rivers for export to neighboring countries. Mali has large reserves of iron ore, gold, copper, bauxite, uranium, manganese, phosphates, and salt, but only salt, phosphates, and a small amount of gold are excavated. Radical investment is needed to develop these resources. Manufacturing provides jobs for about 10 percent of Mali's people, who produce textiles, leather goods, processed foods, and cement. The country depends heavily on foreign aid, especially from France, which ruled Mali until independence in 1960.

Surrounded by Niger, Mali, and the coastal states of Côte d'Ivoire, Ghana, Togo, and Benin, Burkina Faso is one of the poorest and least-developed countries in Africa. Formerly the French colony of Upper Volta, this West African country gained independence in 1960 and later changed its name to Burkina Faso, meaning "land of the honest people."

The landscape consists mostly of wooded grasslands that rise to 2,300 feet above sea level in the west. The soil is poor and the climate is dry, especially in the north where most of the people herd livestock. Cattle, sheep, and goats account for almost half of Burkina Faso's export earnings, and much of the livestock goes to its southern neighbors. River valleys in the south provide the best cropland. Farmers grow millet, corn, sorghum, rice, and beans for their families and cotton, peanuts, and **shea nuts** for export—primarily to France.

Burkina Faso's people belong to many ethnic groups, embrace a wide variety of languages, beliefs, and customs, and live in very distinct homes and villages. Most of the rural people live in extended family groups or clan communities, but as in other poor countries, people are moving away from the country and into the towns in search of jobs. Many young men have found work in factories or on coffee bean and cacao bean plantations in Côte d'Ivoire and Ghana. Poverty and a lack of social services have led to a short **life expectancy,** a high **infant mortality** rate, frequent epidemics, and illiteracy. Less than 30 percent of the children attend primary school, and less than 1 in 10 of the people can read and write.

Right: An aerial view of a village in central Mali. The houses are typically square, with mud-brick walls and flat roofs. Circular mud-brick silos with thatched roofs contain stored grain.

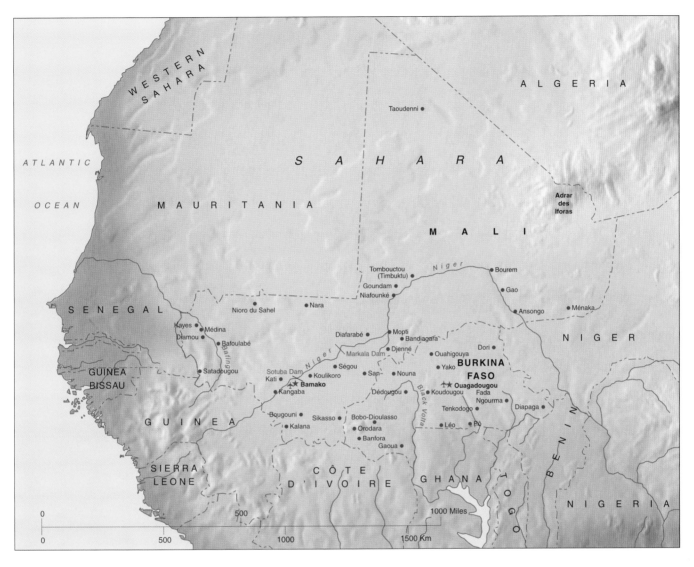

Right: Tombouctou (also spelled Timbuktu) in central Mali is a small trading settlement. But between 1200 and 1500, it was one of the most important commercial centers in Africa—a fact reflected in this old sign indicating that the town is 52 days' travel by camel from Morocco.

Niger and Chad

Niger

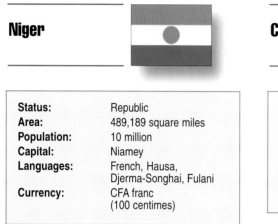

Status:	Republic
Area:	489,189 square miles
Population:	10 million
Capital:	Niamey
Languages:	French, Hausa, Djerma-Songhai, Fulani
Currency:	CFA franc (100 centimes)

The Sahara Desert covers three-quarters of Niger, one of the hottest, driest countries on earth. Sand and stony plateaus blanket most of the land, which rises to a central mountain region with peaks to 6,300 feet. The desert sees little rain, and temperatures often exceed 120°F. Small groups of nomadic Tuareg and Fulani people graze livestock in the desert during the short rainy season from July to September, moving to the thinly wooded savanna in the dry months. The savanna enjoys up to 22 inches of rain annually and is home to the Hausa, Djerma-Songhai, and Kanuri peoples, who are mostly settled farmers. Only 3 percent of the country is cultivated, but nearly 90 percent of the labor force works in agriculture. Farmers grow cassava, millet, sorghum, beans, and rice as food crops and cotton and peanuts for export. Most exported crops are grown in the southwest, on the Niger River's floodplain. Nigerien farmers also export livestock, meat, and animal hides. Repeated droughts in the last few decades have damaged Niger's fragile farming economy and have caused widespread suffering.

Niger's principal industry is uranium mining, but a drop in world demand during the 1980s reduced the resource's value. Nigeriens also mine phosphates, iron ore, and tin. Factory workers in cities such as Niamey, Agadez, Maradi, and Zinder process food and create textiles, leather goods, and cement. But with no railroads, few good roads, and inadequate communication between regions, industrial development is very limited. The country has large foreign debts and depends heavily on foreign aid.

Chad

Status:	Republic
Area:	495,753 square miles
Population:	7.7 million
Capital:	N'Djamena
Languages:	French, Arabic, Sara
Currency:	CFA franc (100 centimes)

Chad is a large landlocked country with few natural resources, a harsh desert climate, and little productive farmland. Ravaged by droughts and famine, it is one of the world's poorest countries. The country is torn by conflicts between the nomadic herders of the northern desert and the many different ethnic groups of the south, most of whom are farmers.

Most of Chad consists of a huge depression edged by mountains in the north, east, and south. Lake Chad, in the west, is all that remains of a huge lake that once filled most of the depression. Lake Chad varies in area from about 4,000 square miles in the dry season to nearly 10,000 square miles during the rainy months from May to October. Farmers around its shores rely on the lake's seasonal flooding to irrigate their rice and corn crops. Fishing on Lake Chad and on the Chari and Logone Rivers is an important source of food and income.

About 80 percent of the people live in the south, where up to 50 inches of annual rain enable farmers to grow millet, rice, sorghum, and cotton—the country's principal export crop. Chad's few mineral resources include oil, uranium, and natron, a sodium carbonate mineral mined near Lake Chad. But development is hampered by a lack of roads, railroads, and equipment. Chad has developed little industry and has to import most of its food and energy. France and the United States provide financial aid, and many international charities have donated food, tents, and medical aid during the worst droughts.

Right: Nomadic Tuareg on camels and on foot make their way through the dusty scrub landscape of a valley in the Air Massif in north central Niger.

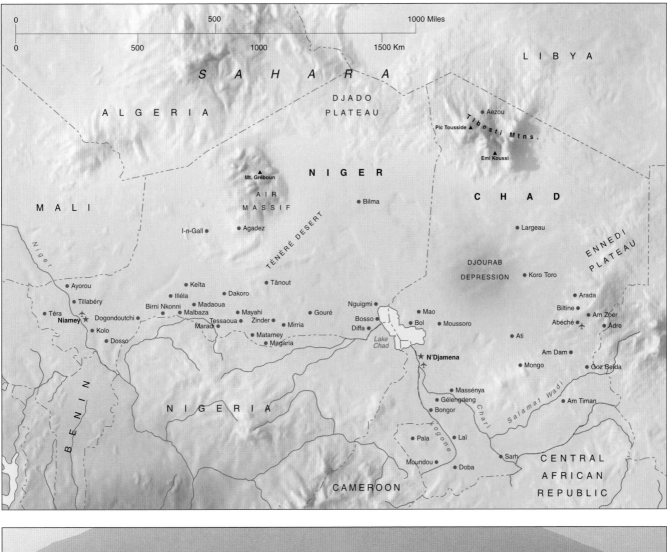

Senegal, Gambia, Guinea-Bissau

Senegal

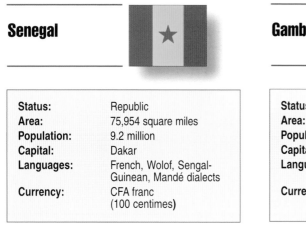

Status:	Republic
Area:	75,954 square miles
Population:	9.2 million
Capital:	Dakar
Languages:	French, Wolof, Sengal-Guinean, Mandé dialects
Currency:	CFA franc (100 centimes)

Gambia

Status:	Republic
Area:	4,363 square miles
Population:	1.3 million
Capital:	Banjul
Languages:	English, Mandinka, Fula, Wolof
Currency:	Dalasi (100 butut)

Senegal, shaped like a lion's head and looking as if it is devouring Gambia, includes the westernmost point on mainland Africa. Low plains dominated by wooded savanna cover most of the land. Rainfall and vegetation vary from north to south. Annual rainfall is about 15 inches in the sparsely wooded grasslands of the north. Southern Senegal is more densely forested and receives as much as 50 inches of rain each year. Northern portions of the country have suffered from erosion, so Senegal's government has enlisted international aid for tree-planting projects to protect these semi-arid areas.

Nearly all of Senegal's people are black Africans, and about 85 percent are Muslims. The largest ethnic groups are the Wolof, Fulani, Serer, Toucouleur, Diola, and Mandingo. Each group has its own language, cultural traditions, and housing and clothing styles. Farmers in the more fertile south grow sorghum, millet, and beans for local use. Nuts are exported whole or to be processed into oil. Farmers along the country's main rivers are able to irrigate their land to produce cotton.

Senegal has a thriving fishing industry, and urban factory workers produce textiles, food products such as peanut oil and processed fish, chemicals, and consumer goods. Golden beaches attract a growing number of tourists each year, but economic benefits are not shared by most of the population. Senegal's people remain poor. Only 10 percent can read and write. There are very few doctors, and epidemics occur frequently.

Buried in Senegal like an earthworm, Gambia is barely 180 miles long east to west and is only 30 miles at its widest, north to south. The capital, Banjul, at the mouth of the Gambia River, is a busy port and the country's only large town. Mangroves and swamps line the coast and the riverbanks. Sparse forest and savanna dot the rest of the landscape.

Gambia is a poor country, with very little fertile land and no mineral resources. Farmers grow tropical fruits in the west and sorghum and rice on the higher ground north and south of the river. Peanuts are Gambia's main cash crop and principal export. The country also derives some income by transporting goods overland from Banjul to Senegal, Mali, and Guinea.

Above: Beautiful beaches of silver sand, backed by palm groves full of colorful birds, are beginning to attract large numbers of international tourists to Gambia—providing this poor country with an important new source of income.

Guinea-Bissau

Status:	Independent State
Area:	13,946 square miles
Population:	1.2 million
Capital:	Bissau
Languages:	Portuguese, Crioulo
Currency:	Guinea-Bissau peso (100 centavos)

Guinea-Bissau is a small, very poor West African country that gained independence from Portugal in 1974 after an 11-year war. In addition to its mainland territory, Guinea-Bissau includes the Bijagós Islands clustered off its coast. The country's capital, Bissau, is the principal port and largest city. Many long inlets along the country's coast allow boats to reach towns and villages miles inland.

Guinea-Bissau is mostly flat. Swamps and mangroves line the coast and inlets, providing fertile soil on which farmers grow rice. Farther inland the land rises to a plateau a few hundred feet above sea level. Farmers grow peanuts and cashews for export. Corn, yams, and beans are cultivated for local markets. Many inland farmers also raise cattle and poultry. Fish is the country's only other export, but nuts and fish cannot support the economy. More than 60 percent of Guinea-Bissau's income is from foreign aid. To restart the economy, Guinea-Bissau's government is encouraging investment in roads and machinery.

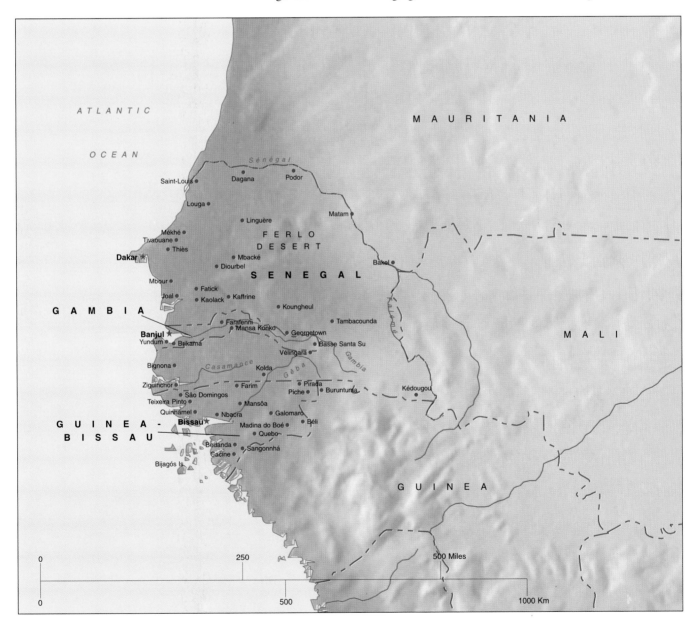

Guinea, Sierra Leone, Liberia

Guinea

Status:	Republic
Area:	94,927 square miles
Population:	7.5 million
Capital:	Conakry
Languages:	French, Fula, Malinké, Susa
Currency:	Guinea franc (100 centimes)

Sierra Leone

Status:	Republic
Area:	27,699 square miles
Population:	5.3 million
Capital:	Freetown
Languages:	English, French, Mende, Temne, Krio
Currency:	Leone (100 cents)

Guinea looks like a boomerang, extending inland from its short West African coastline in a wide arc that supports many landscapes. The coastal strip is marshy, backed by a narrow plain that rises to a central plateau called the Fouta Djalon. Upper Guinea, an area of grassy savanna, stretches across the country's northern edge. The forested hills of the Guinea Highlands dominate the southeast.

Despite its many resources, Guinea is a poor country that has suffered from inadequate government since gaining independence from France in 1958. It has a rich cultural tradition, but education and health services suffer from lack of funding, and economic improvements have been slow.

Lowland crops include rice, cassava, and bananas. Farmers in the savanna grow coffee beans, cacao beans, corn, and millet and raise cattle. Guinea's commercial growers produce bananas, coffee beans, cacao beans, palm oil, and peanuts. Guinea has about one-third of the world's bauxite reserves and pulls enough ore from the earth to comprise nearly 95 percent of the country's export earnings. But bauxite mining is hampered by inadequate roads, railroads, and equipment.

The country takes its name from Sierra Lyoa, or the Lion Mountains, the name that fifteenth-century Portuguese seafarers gave to the country's mountainous headland. The outcropping shelters the capital city of Freetown and forms the world's third-largest natural harbor. British **abolitionist** Granville Sharp founded Freetown in 1787 to provide a home for freed slaves.

Sierra Leone's coast is a 25-mile-wide bed of swamps that rise gently to a grassy savanna with scattered trees. Hills and plateaus cover the country's eastern region. The temperature averages 80°F, and rainfall varies from 150 inches at the coast to 80 inches in the highlands. Even with abundant rain, the gravelly, sandy soil is not very fertile, but farmers manage to grow rice, cassava, sorghum, and millet for their own tables and coffee beans, cacao beans, peanuts, and ginger for export. Forest hardwoods and Atlantic fish round out the country's vital resources. Mineral exports dominate the economy, accounting for 80 percent of the country's income. Sierra Leone is one of the world's leading diamond producers and exports bauxite and rutile—an important source of titanium.

Liberia

Status:	Republic
Area:	43,000 square miles
Population:	2.9 million
Capital:	Monrovia
Languages:	English, local languages
Currency:	Liberian dollar (100 cents)

Liberia, from the Latin for "free land," was founded in 1816 by the American Colonization Society as a settlement for freed U.S. slaves whom the society had returned to Africa. Gaining independence in 1847, Liberia is the only country in black Africa that has never been under colonial rule. Slave descendants comprise just 5 percent of the population. The other 95 percent consists of many local African ethnic groups—the Kpelle, Bassa, and a dozen smaller groups—each with its own language, culture, and traditional territory.

Swamps and mangroves fringe the coast. Inland are grassy plains and the highlands that border Guinea and Côte d'Ivoire. Liberia's climate is hot and humid, with marked wet and dry seasons. About 75 percent of the people work in agriculture, growing cassava, rice, sugarcane, and fruit and raising sheep, goats, pigs, and poultry. Most of the produce is used rurally, so Liberia must import food to feed its city dwellers. Large estates, mostly foreign-owned, cultivate the export crops—coffee beans, cacao beans, and rubber. Liberia's miners dig large quantities of iron ore for export. Shipping, insurance, and other financial services help support the economy. Education and health services are better than in most West African countries, but there are shortages of teachers and doctors, especially in rural areas.

Right: Rubber trees in Liberia. Plantation workers cut a V-shaped groove into the bark, and the milky latex from which rubber is made oozes into a cup fixed below the cut. The trees are "tapped" in rotation, and each new cut is made just below the previous one, leaving a herringbone pattern.

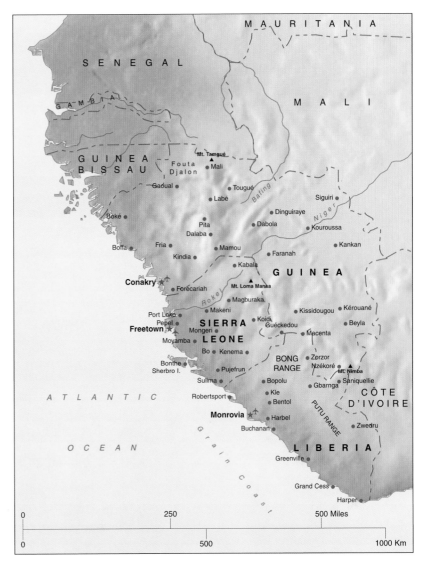

Côte d'Ivoire, Ghana, Togo

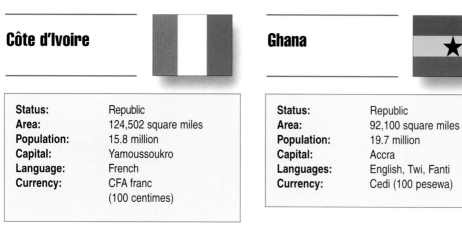

Côte d'Ivoire

Status:	Republic
Area:	124,502 square miles
Population:	15.8 million
Capital:	Yamoussoukro
Language:	French
Currency:	CFA franc (100 centimes)

Ghana

Status:	Republic
Area:	92,100 square miles
Population:	19.7 million
Capital:	Accra
Languages:	English, Twi, Fanti
Currency:	Cedi (100 pesewa)

Côte d'Ivoire—the Ivory Coast—was named by fifteenth-century French seafarers who traded for ivory in the plentiful jungles of West Africa. The territory was a French colony from 1893 until it gained independence in 1960. Côte d'Ivoire has been the country's official name since 1986.

The land has four distinct regions—a coastal strip of sandbars and lagoons, a belt of tropical rain forest 95 to 185 miles wide, a broad wooded savanna in the north, and highlands in the west. The country's climate ranges from hot, wet, and humid near the coast to mild, dry, and variable in the hills.

More than 60 ethnic groups, practicing an abundance of languages and cultures, inhabit Côte d'Ivoire. Most of the people are farmers who live in small villages and produce cassava, corn, rice, and yams for home use and coffee beans, cacao beans, sugarcane, palm oil, cotton, pineapples, and rubber for export. Industries include oil refining, textiles, timber, fishing, and processing of sugar, palm oil, and fish products. After 1960 Côte d'Ivoire built on the French legacy of roads, railways, industrialization, and strong educational and health services, becoming one of West Africa's strongest economies. Even so, falling world prices and reduced financial aid from France have caused economic difficulties. Although the official capital since 1983, Yamoussoukro shares some governmental functions with the former capital of Abidjan.

Fifteenth-century Portuguese explorers found this West African country so rich in gold that they dubbed it the Gold Coast. After periods as a Portuguese, a Dutch, and a British colony, Ghana became in 1957 the first black African colony to achieve independence.

Ghana's altitude changes very little from its coast to its northern border with Burkina Faso. Dense rain forests cover the southwestern region and provide valuable tropical hardwoods such as mahogany for export. Grassy savanna covers much of rest of the country. Confined by the Akosombo Dam, Lake Volta in east central Ghana is one of the largest artificial lakes in the world. The dam provides hydroelectric power for Ghana's towns and a large aluminum smelting plant at Tema. Ghana also exports electricity to Togo and Benin.

Ghana, like Côte d'Ivoire, went through a period of prosperity, but political changes and falling prices for cacao beans—the country's principal export—and other agricultural products have left the country with huge debts. Ghana must continue to develop industries such as food processing, textiles, timber and furniture making, cement, and mineral exports.

Ghana's education system is one of the best in black Africa, and state-funded health services keep life expectancy and infant mortality rates close to the average for the continent.

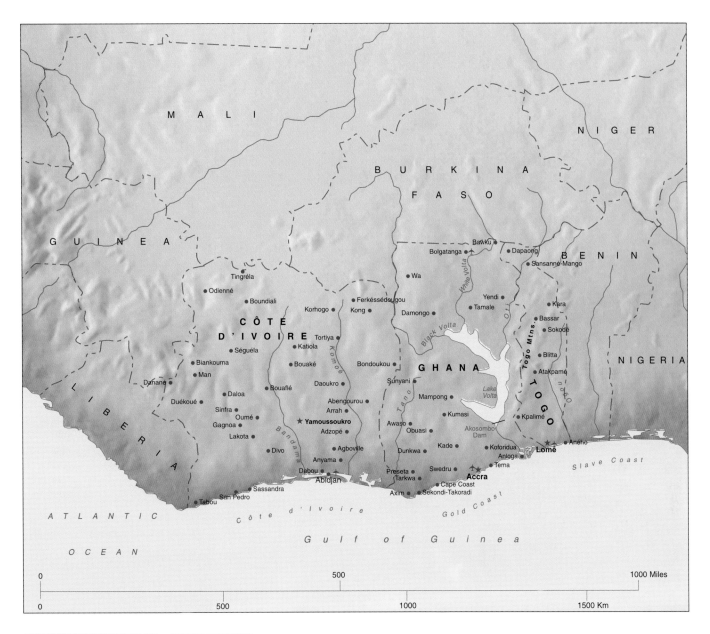

M A L I

N I G E R

B U R K I N A

F A S O

G U I N E A

Bawku

Bolgatanga

Dapaong

B E N I N

Sansanne-Mango

Tingréla

Wa

Odienné

Yendi

Kara

Boundiali

Ferkéssédougou

Damongo

Tamale

Bassar

Korhogo

Kong

Sokodé

CÔTE

Tortiya

D'IVOIRE

Blitta

Séguéla

Katiola

Atakpamé

N I G E R I A

Biankouma

Bouaké

Bondoukou

G H A N A

Man

Togo Mtns.

Danané

Daoukro

Sunyani

Lake

T O G O

Daloa

Bouaflé

Volta

Duékoué

Abengourou

Mampong

Kpalimé

Sinfra

Arrah

Kumasi

Oumé

★ Yamoussoukro

Awaso

Gagnoa

Adzopé

Obuasi

Akosombo

Lakota

Dam

Aného

Divo

Agboville

Dunkwa

Kade

Koforidua

Lomé

Anyama

Anloga

Dabou

Preseta

Swedru

Tema

Slave Coast

Abidjan

Tarkwa

Accra

L I B E R I A

Sassandra

Cape Coast

San Pedro

Axim

Sekondi-Takoradi

Gold Coast

Tabou

Côte d'Ivoire

A T L A N T I C

Gulf of Guinea

O C E A N

White Volta

Black Volta

Komoé

Tano

Bandama

0		500		1000 Miles
0	500	1000	1500 Km	

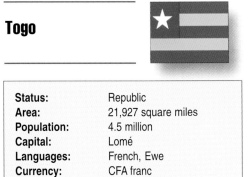

Togo

Status:	Republic
Area:	21,927 square miles
Population:	4.5 million
Capital:	Lomé
Languages:	French, Ewe
Currency:	CFA franc
	(100 centimes)

Just 365 miles north to south and less than 90 miles across at its widest, Togo is one of Africa's smallest countries. Formerly part of German Togoland and once a United Nations **trusteeship** administered by France, Togo gained independence in 1960.

The Togo Mountains dominate the country's western edge then angle across the center, dividing the country in two. South of the hills, a plateau covered in grasslands and hardwoods slopes down to a coastal plain dotted with swamps and palm forests. To the north, rolling savanna and thorny scrub extend to the Burkina Faso border.

Most of the people are small-scale farmers who grow cassava, millet, corn, rice, yams, and beans to feed their families. Larger farms produce coffee beans, cacao beans, peanuts, palm oil, and cotton for export. Livestock and fishing contribute to the food supply. Phosphates, mined in the southeast, are Togo's principal mineral export.

Benin and Nigeria

Benin

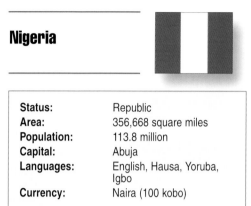

Status:	Republic
Area:	43,483 square miles
Population:	6.2 million
Capital:	Porto-Novo
Language:	French
Currency:	CFA franc (100 centimes)

Nigeria

Status:	Republic
Area:	356,668 square miles
Population:	113.8 million
Capital:	Abuja
Languages:	English, Hausa, Yoruba, Igbo
Currency:	Naira (100 kobo)

Looking somewhat like a turkey drumstick, this former French colony in West Africa gained its independence in 1960 and changed its name from Dahomey to Benin in 1975. Porto-Novo is the capital city, but Cotonou, the largest city and principal port, is the main business, cultural, and administrative center.

Sandy beaches and lagoons extend along the short coastline. No natural harbors exist, so ships must anchor offshore or alongside two long jetties built out to sea at Cotonou. Most of southern Benin is flat and forested, with areas of marshland. Savanna grasslands in the north rise to hills 2,000 feet above sea level in the northwest. The south is hot and humid throughout the year, while northern Benin enjoys a seasonal climate with a cooler, drier winter.

The Beninese are descended from a variety of ethnic backgrounds, and many follow traditional **animist** religions. About half the population works in agriculture. Farmers in the sparsely populated north herd livestock or grow cotton—the country's most significant export. Some southern farmers grow just enough to feed their families, but others produce palm kernels—the country's most valuable food export—as well as coffee beans, cacao beans, tobacco, and shea nuts. Benin produces some gold, oil, and limestone but has little industry and depends largely on foreign aid, principally from France.

Nearly 114 million people live in Nigeria, making it Africa's most populous country. Abuja, in the country's center, was chosen as the new capital in 1991, but the former capital city of Lagos—the largest city south of the Sahara—is Nigeria's commercial and industrial hub.

The Niger and Benue Rivers cut this West African country into three triangles. High grassy plains fill the upper triangle, dropping to the flat, fertile lowlands of the Sokoto River in the northwest and the dry, sandy Chad Basin in the northeast. Highlands south of the Niger and Benue rise to about 1,900 feet in the west and to more than 5,000 feet on Nigeria's eastern border. Forested lowlands extend about 100 miles inland from coastal swamps and lagoons and from the huge fan-shaped delta of the Niger. Nigeria's rainy season extends from April to October. The remainder of the year is considered the dry season. Rainfall and temperature vary considerably, from 150 inches of rain and 80°F at the coast to less than 30 inches and 105°F in the north.

Nigeria is home to more than 250 ethnic groups, the largest of which are the Hausa and Fulani in the north, the Yoruba in the southwest, and the Igbo in the southeast. About 75 percent of Nigerians live in rural areas and depend on agriculture, but Nigeria also has a large urban population living in cities such as Lagos, Ibadan, Kano, Enugu, Kaduna, Zaria (home of the country's largest university), and Port Harcourt—the country's second port after Lagos.

Petroleum is Nigeria's principal resource and the economy's mainstay. Most of the oil fields are in the southwest and in offshore waters. Tin and columbite (used in steel making) are mined in the central highlands. Miners also extract coal, gas, iron ore, lead, and zinc. Nigeria's coastal waters, lakes, and rivers produce an abundance of fish, and the lowland forests yield valuable timbers. These resources support a range of industries including oil refining, food processing, and the production of cement, chemicals, fertilizers, textiles, and steel. Most farms in Nigeria are small family businesses that raise crops and livestock for local use. Larger farms concentrate on export crops—the most important being cacao beans, palm oil, peanuts, and rubber.

Right: With her baby tied securely to her back, a Nigerian woman sweeps up corn. Her brightly colored wraparound skirt and loose turban are traditional women's dress in rural areas. Rural men wear loose robes or loose-fitting jackets with short or long trousers.

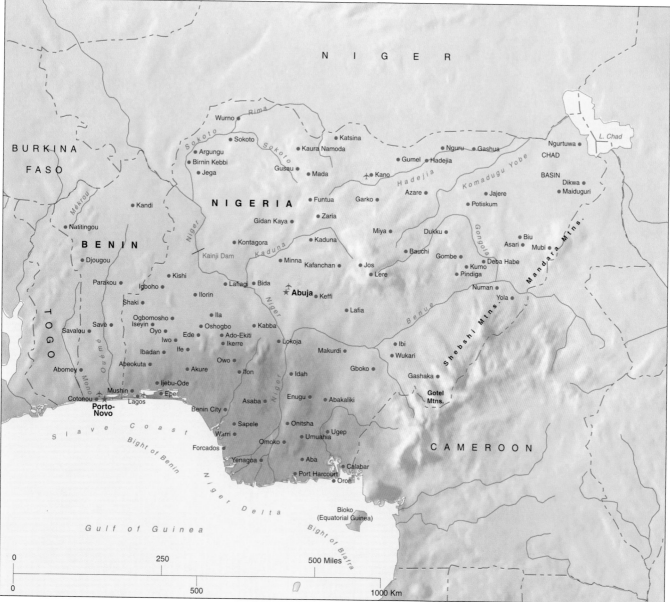

Cameroon and the Central African Republic

Cameroon

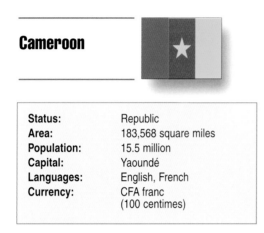

Status:	Republic
Area:	183,568 square miles
Population:	15.5 million
Capital:	Yaoundé
Languages:	English, French
Currency:	CFA franc (100 centimes)

After World War I (1914-1918), the **League of Nations** declared the former German **protectorate** of Cameroon a trusteeship that France and Britain would govern. In 1960 French Cameroon achieved independence. A year later, the southern portion of British Cameroon voted to join the new republic, while the northern section became affiliated with Nigeria.

A range of hills and mountains runs along Cameroon's western edge, from Lake Chad in the north to Mount Cameroon, the country's highest point at 13,353 feet above sea level. A forested plateau in the country's middle drops to dry savanna in the north, tropical rain forest in the south, and a coastal plain in the southwest. Annual rainfall ranges from 400 inches in the west to 15 inches in the north.

Climate and terrain determine how people live. People on the savanna—Hausa, Fulani, and related groups, most of whom are Muslim—herd livestock and grow grain. The Bamileke inhabit the western highlands, while the Doula, Ewondo, and Fang occupy the central and southern areas. Most are settled farmers, growing cassava, corn, and yams for their families and bananas, coffee beans, cacao beans, cotton, rubber, and peanuts for export. Petroleum for oil processing and bauxite for making aluminum are important mineral exports and drive two of Cameroon's major industries. Good transportation systems, hydropower from the Sanaga River, a deepwater port at Douala, and a broad range of manufacturing industries contribute to the country's economic health. As one of the more developed African nations, Cameroon offers its people advanced health and educational services.

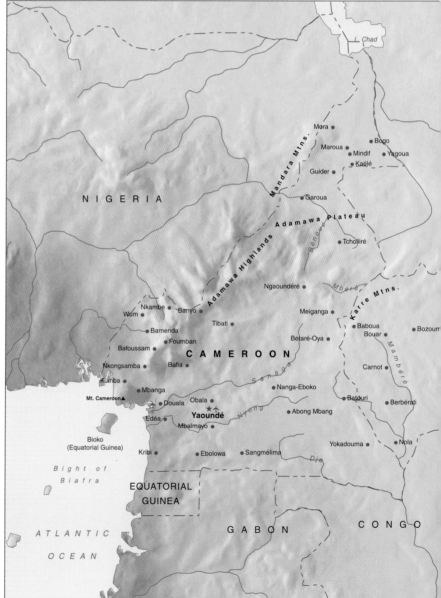

Left: Beehive-shaped granaries in a village in the Mandara Mountains of northern Cameroon are used to store millet. The intricately woven caps of the granaries can be lifted off to pour in the grain.

Right: Hardwoods are one of the Central African Republic's few natural resources.

Central African Republic

Status:	Republic
Area:	240,533 square miles
Population:	3.4 million
Capital:	Bangui
Language:	French, Sango
Currency:	CFA franc (100 centimes)

This landlocked country in Africa's middle was formerly a French colony. It achieved independence in 1960, but the following years were turbulent. David Dacko, the country's first elected president, was forced from office in 1966 by Jean-Bedel Bokassa. Bokassa ruled for more than a decade as a self-crowned emperor but was deposed in 1979 by Dacko's supporters, who put Dacko back in charge. Several years later, Dacko was overthrown by the military. The Central African Republic has returned to democratic rule under a new constitution. But with few roads, no seaport, and very little industry, the country is one of the poorest and least developed in Africa. It still relies heavily on financial aid from France.

Tropical savanna grasslands, 2,000 to 3,000 feet above sea level, cover most of the country. Rain forests lie in the south, and dry savanna is on the country's borders with Chad and Sudan. The country's low altitude keeps the average temperature near 80°F and annual rainfall at about 54 inches.

Most Central Africans are farmers who take advantage of the mild climate to grow enough food for themselves. People only keep cattle in areas where there are no **tsetse flies**, because the flies transmit deadly diseases to cattle, horses, and humans. Coffee beans, cotton, and **sisal**—the principal cash crops—are exported by ship through Bangui, the capital and principal river port. The country also exports tropical hardwoods, diamonds, and some gold, but most of the country's mineral resources lie untouched.

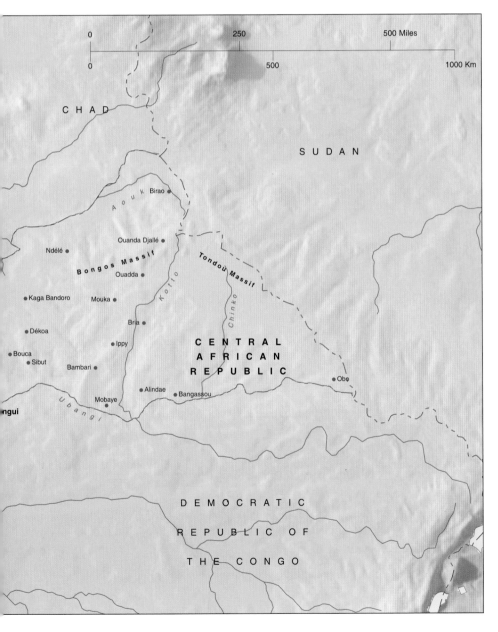

Equatorial Guinea, São Tomé and Príncipe, Gabon

Equatorial Guinea

Status:	Republic
Area:	10,830 square miles
Population:	400,000
Capital:	Malabo
Languages:	Spanish, Fang
Currency:	CFA franc (100 centimes)

São Tomé and Príncipe

Status:	Independent State
Area:	371 square miles
Population:	200,000
Capital:	São Tomé
Language:	Portuguese
Currency:	Dobra (100 centavos)

Gabon

Status:	Republic
Area:	103,347 square miles
Population:	1.2 million
Capital:	Libreville
Languages:	French, Fang, Eshira
Currency:	CFA franc (100 centimes)

Equatorial Guinea consists of two sections—a small territory called Mbini (formerly Río Muni) on the West African mainland and five offshore islands. The capital and largest city, Malabo, is on the biggest island, Bioko. Portugal claimed the territory in 1472 but gave it to Spain in 1778. Equatorial Guinea gained its full independence in 1968.

On the mainland, a narrow coastal plain covered in mangroves bounds a dense tropical rain forest. The soil is poor, and the mainland population of about 320,000 survives by subsistence farming, by growing coffee beans, and by harvesting tropical hardwoods, notably okoumé.

The islands are made of volcanic rock, which provides fertile soil. Farmers on the islands grow cassava, yams, and bananas as food crops and bananas, coffee beans, and cacao beans for export. Fishing and forestry contribute to the economy.

The tiny country of São Tomé and Príncipe consists of two main islands and several smaller ones in the Gulf of Guinea, about 180 miles west of Gabon and Mbini. São Tomé accounts for nearly 85 percent of the country's land area and is home to 95 percent of the population. Most of the remaining 5 percent live on Príncipe, 80 miles to the northeast. The country gained its independence in 1975, after 500 years of Portuguese rule. About 70 percent of the people are Creoles—people of mixed black African and European ancestry. Mainland Africans, Cape Verdians, and Europeans comprise the remainder.

The capital city of São Tomé is the largest urban area, the principal port, and the country's center for trade. A hot, humid climate and rich volcanic soil provide an excellent agricultural base. Cacao beans, coffee beans, coconuts, copra, and bananas are the major export crops.

Gabon in West Africa is one of six African countries that straddle the equator. Libreville—the capital and main port—lies just north of this imaginary line. Libreville, meaning "free town," was named by French missionaries who settled freed slaves there in 1849. Gabon achieved independence in 1960, after 50 years as a French colony.

Sandy beaches, lagoons, and swamps line the 550-mile coast. Inland, dense tropical rain forests blanket the land, rising to rolling plateaus and hills. Gabon's principal river—the Ogooué—and its tributaries cut deep valleys through the highlands. The climate is hot and wet, with average temperatures around 80°F and about 100 inches of annual precipitation.

Gabon is one of Africa's least populated countries. People are unevenly distributed, mainly inhabiting villages along the coast and river valleys, where they grow cassava, yams, bananas, and mangoes. Many also fish the rivers and coastal waters and hunt in the forests. The land is not very fertile, so Gabon must import most of its food. The country is one of Africa's richest in terms of natural resources. Its many forests yield high-quality woods such as mahogany, ebony, and okoumé. Oil fields in the south also garner foreign income, and Gabon is a major producer of manganese, uranium, and iron. Despite a large foreign debt, the government is investing in education and health services.

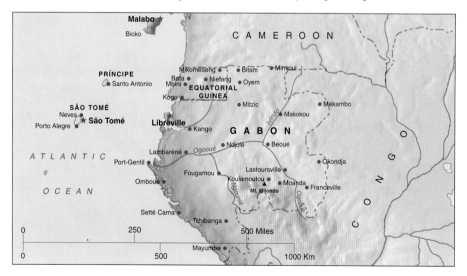

Republic of the Congo

Status:	Republic
Area:	132,046 square miles
Population:	2.7 million
Capital:	Brazzaville
Languages:	French, Lingala, Kilkongo
Currency:	CFA franc (100 centimes)

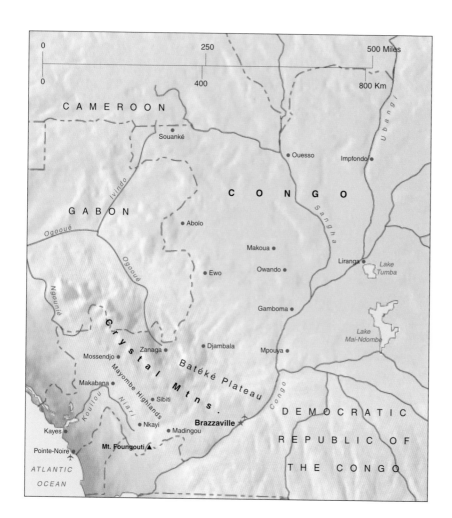

For centuries the Republic of the Congo's coastline was an abundant source of slaves and ivory for European traders. In 1883 the territory became a French protectorate, and in 1910 it joined Chad, the Central African Republic, and Gabon as part of French Equatorial Africa. Congo achieved indepen-dence in 1960 and, after four decades of political turmoil, is developing into a modern multiparty state in central Africa.

The country's narrow coastal plain backs up to the 2,500-foot high Mayombe Highlands. Beyond the highlands lies the broad, fertile Niari River Valley. Grassy upland plains fill the center of the country, and dense forests and swamps cover much of the north. Congo's climate is hot and humid.

The country's principal ethnic groups include the Kongo, who are mostly farmers living in the south and west; the hunting and fishing Batekes of the highlands; the Sangha, who live in the country's northern forests; and the M'Bochi—a group once devoted to fishing. An unusually high proportion of the population are urban dwellers—nearly half the people live in Brazzaville, Pointe-Noire, and other southern and coastal towns.

Congo's farmers grow cassava, corn, rice, plantains, and other crops for personal consumption. Larger farms, mostly state owned, produce coffee beans, cacao beans, and sugarcane for export. Tropical timbers contribute to the economy, but petroleum is the principal commercial export, followed by lead, potash, and zinc. The country is more industrialized than most of its neighbors. Congolese factory workers produce textiles, chemicals, paper, wood products, palm oil, and sugar.

Left: The dense rain forests that cover much of Congo are a source of some of the world's finest tropical hardwood timbers. They are used worldwide for making high-quality furniture and internal fittings such as stairs and paneled walls.

The Democratic Republic of the Congo and Uganda

The Democratic Republic of the Congo (Zaire)

Status:	Republic
Area:	905,351 square miles
Population:	50.5 million
Capital:	Kinshasa
Languages:	Swahili, Lingala, Kikongo, French
Currency:	Congolese franc

The Democratic Republic of the Congo—formerly Zaire—is a vast country in central Africa that is joined to the coast by Cabinda, a narrow land corridor between Angola and the Republic of the Congo. Belgium ruled the country from 1885 until it gained independence in 1960. Since then ethnic violence, army mutinies, attempts by the mineral-rich Shaba region (formerly Katanga) to break away, and political and economic crises have plagued the country.

One of the world's largest tropical rain forests covers most of the northern part of the country. Conditions are hot and humid year-round, averaging 90°F and more than 80 inches of annual rain. Warm, dry savanna stretches across the country north and south of the rain forest. High plateaus and mountains dominate the east and southeast, rising to 16,763 feet atop Margherita Peak in the Ruwenzori Mountains. The 2,900-mile Congo River and its tributaries—together forming more than 7,000 navigable miles—provide the principal transportation routes for most of the country. Railways in the south link mining areas to the river ports and to the seaport at Matadi.

The country's people speak more than 200 languages. About 80 percent of the people belong to one of the main Bantu-language groups—the Luba and Kongo in the south and the Mongo who dwell in the rain forests. The north is sparsely populated. Most of the people live in the southern savanna, the eastern highlands, and the lower Congo River Valley. Each year thousands of rural Congolese move into the cities of Kinshasa, Kananga, Mbuji-Mayi, Lubumbashi, Kisangani and Bukavu. This migration not only increases urban overcrowding but also stretches already lean resources.

The country's poverty springs from political chaos, not from a lack of resources. It produces half the world's cobalt, ranks sixth in copper production, and is the leading producer of industrial diamonds. Congolese miners excavate tin, zinc, manganese, gold, and silver. Offshore oil fields and hydroelectric power plants provide ample energy resources, and the forests yield high-value timbers, palm oil, and rubber. Farming is done mostly on a small scale for local consumption, but larger farms grow cacao beans, coffee beans, cotton, and tea for export.

Uganda

Status:	Republic
Area:	93,066 square miles
Population:	22.8 million
Capital:	Kampala
Languages:	English, Swahili
Currency:	Ugandan shilling

Europeans arriving in this small, landlocked country in the 1850s found one of the richest kingdoms in Africa. Made a protectorate of Britain in 1894, Uganda gained its independence in 1962. Until 1986 civil unrest and military uprisings caused great hardship and economic strife, the worst of which occurred under Idi Amin Dada from 1971 to 1979. In the early 1990s, a stable government supported by the people enabled Uganda to start rebuilding its economy and to attract foreign investment.

Most of Uganda is a high plateau that lies 3,000 feet above sea level, with thick forests in the south and savanna in the drier north. The extreme northeast is semi-desert. The Virunga and Ruwenzori ranges in the southwest provide spectacular scenery, with Mount Stanley's snow-capped peak rising to 16,763 feet. Lakes Victoria, Albert, Kyoga, and many others cover nearly one-fifth of the country.

The decades of conflict have severely damaged Uganda's health and educational services—a problem intensified by rapid population growth and the highest incidence of AIDS in Africa. Agriculture dominates the economy. Farmers grow cassava, corn, beans, yams, and bananas as food crops. Larger farms and plantations grow coffee beans (the principal cash crop), tea, cotton, and sugarcane for export. Mines near Kasese in the southwest produce copper, Uganda's main mineral resource. The ore is sent by rail to Jinja for **smelting** and on through Kenya to the port of Mombasa. The Owen Falls Dam at Jinja provides hydropower for the town's manufacturing industries.

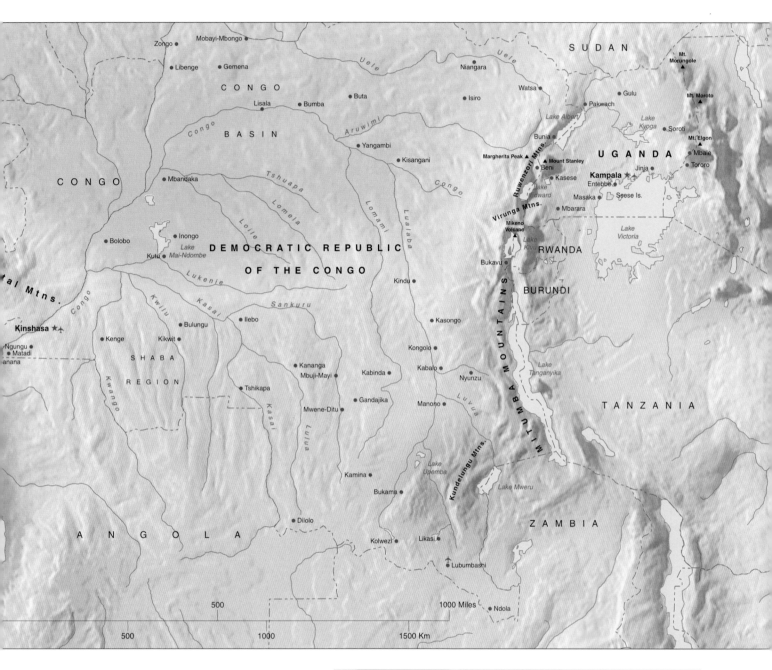

Right: The forests of central Africa are home to the largest and rarest of all primates—the gorilla. Lowland gorillas are found in several of the dense rain forests, but the rarest species of all—the mountain gorilla—is found only in the mountain forests where the borders of the Democratic Republic of the Congo meet those of Uganda, Rwanda, and Burundi.

Kenya

The former colony of Kenya gained independence in 1963 after 20 years of violent opposition to British rule. Since independence, internal conflicts have continued to damage the country's economy. In 1992 the government allowed multiparty elections for the first time in 25 years. Population growth and droughts have also increased Kenya's problems.

From a narrow coastal plain, Kenya's landscape rises quickly to the 4,000-foot plateau that covers much of the country. In the west, the land rises even higher, to the 13,000-foot Kenya Highlands, which the Great Rift Valley splits in two. Mount Kenya, 17,058 feet high, dominates the south central highlands. Along Kenya's borders with Ethiopia and Somalia is a dry semi-desert region that supports very few people—mostly wandering livestock herders. More than 85 percent of Kenyans live in the southwestern highlands, where the altitude and a cool, moist, sunny climate combine with fertile volcanic soil to provide good growing conditions for both tropical and **temperate** crops. Farmland is split just about evenly between subsistence crops, such as corn and wheat, and cash crops, such as coffee beans and tea, which account for nearly half the country's export earnings. Farms on the tropical coastal strip produce sisal, cashews, sugarcane, and cotton for export. Kenya used to grow enough food to feed all its people, but the population has grown so fast that large amounts of food must be imported.

Kenya's industrial products are processed foods, paper, textiles, chemicals, and cement. Imported oil is processed at a refinery at Mombasa, and there are several vehicle assembly plants. Energy for the cities and for industry comes from imported oil, from hydroelectric plants on the Taro River, and from Africa's first **geothermal power** station near Lake Naivasha. World-famous national parks and a magnificent coast support a thriving tourist industry.

Top: The Masai are a nomadic, livestock-herding people with a rich culture of song, dance, and storytelling.

Above center: Nairobi, Kenya's national capital, is a sprawling city of almost 850,000 people. This view shows the modern office blocks along Government Road, one of the city's principal thoroughfares.

Above: The twin peaks of Mount Kilimanjaro, just over the border in Tanzania, dominate the scenery of Kenya's southern border region.

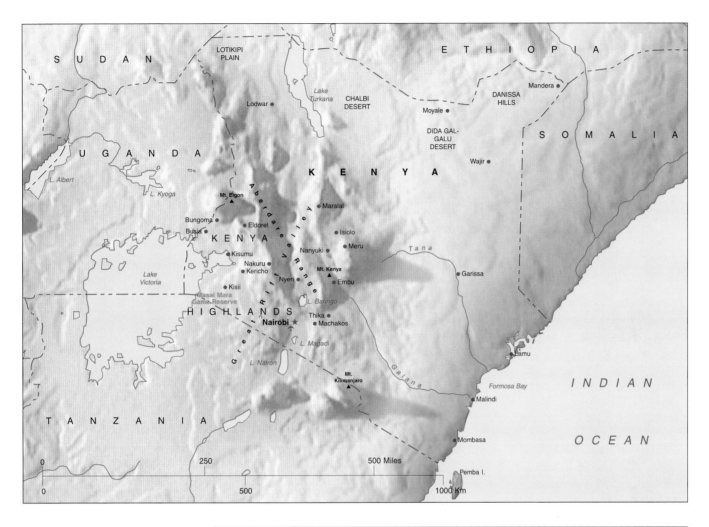

Right: Eager tourists get their first close-up view of elephants in the Masai Mara Game Reserve in southwestern Kenya. Tourism provides employment for 40,000 Kenyans and is an important source of income for the country.

Tanzania, Rwanda, Burundi

Tanzania

Status:	Republic
Area:	364,900 square miles
Population:	31.3 million
Capital:	Dar es Salaam
Languages:	Swahili, English
Currency:	Tanzanian shilling (100 cents)

Tanzania formed in 1964 when the mainland state of Tanganyika banded politically with the East African island of Zanzibar. A rolling plateau of savanna grassland, 3,500 feet above sea level, covers most of mainland Tanzania. Mangroves fringe a narrow coastal plain in the east. Northern Tanzania is hilly and home to Mount Kilimanjaro, Africa's highest peak, which rises to 19,341 feet on the border of Tanzania and Kenya. Lake Victoria dips into the country's northwestern corner, and Lake Tanganyika—the world's longest freshwater lake—forms part of the western border. Zanzibar, 23 miles offshore, is the largest **coral island** off the coast of Africa. Tanzania's climate ranges from 70°F and 24 inches of rain in the central highlands to 90°F and 58 inches annually at the coast.

Agriculture accounts for about two-thirds of Tanzania's income. Rural farmers raise cassava, corn, bananas, and vegetables, often having just enough to feed their families. Larger farms, mostly government owned, produce coffee beans, tea, cotton, cashews, and tobacco for export. Cloves are Zanzibar's most important export.

Tanzania's miners excavate small amounts of diamonds, gold, tin, iron ore, and coal, but the country is not highly industrialized. Factories produce processed food, textiles, fertilizers, paper, cement, and other goods, mostly for local markets. Spectacular wildlife, beautiful scenery, and unspoiled beaches attract growing numbers of tourists.

Rwanda

Status:	Republic
Area:	10,170 square miles
Population:	8.2 million
Capital:	Kigali
Languages:	Kinyarwanda, French, English
Currency:	Rwanda franc (100 centimes)

Rwanda's history and politics are closely linked with those of its central African neighbor, Burundi. After World War I ended, the League of Nations placed this former German colony under Belgian control. At that time, it formed the northern half of the Ruanda-Urundi territory. But the country was bitterly divided by ethnic conflict between the small but dominant Tutsi people and the much larger Hutu group—subsistence farmers with no political or economic power.

In 1962 the two parts of Ruanda-Urundi separated into independent nations—Rwanda and Burundi—but the conflict continued. In the mid-1990s, 500,000 Rwandans were massacred. Hundreds of thousands of refugees fled first to Burundi, then into neighboring Tanzania and the Democratic Republic of the Congo as Burundi also collapsed into civil war.

Rwanda is small and very poor, and it is home to many more people than the land can support. But Rwandans continue to develop their country. Tin and wolframite—the principal ore of tungsten—account for one-quarter of Rwanda's exports. Coffee beans, tea, and pyrethrum, an insecticide made from chrysanthemums, comprise the rest. The valleys are fertile, even though the higher land is badly eroded, and the country has great potential to attract tourists—especially to Volcanoes National Park in the Virunga Mountains, where rare mountain gorillas can still be seen.

Left: Covering an area of 26,828 square miles, Lake Victoria is second only in area to Lake Superior in the United States and Canada.

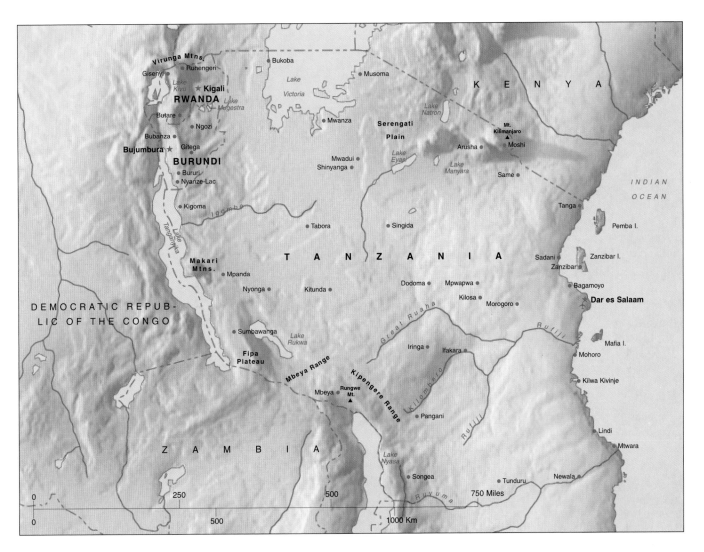

Burundi

Status:	Republic
Area:	10,745 square miles
Population:	5.7 million
Capital:	Bujumbura
Languages:	Kirundi, French, English
Currency:	Burundi franc (100 centimes)

Burundi, like its northern neighbor Rwanda, has been devastated by civil war for several decades. Hundreds of thousands of Tutsis and Hutus have been killed, wounded, or driven from their homeland in outbreaks of ethnic violence.

Most of Burundi's people are poor subsistence farmers who grow cassava, corn, beans, and yams and raise cattle for milk and meat. Farmers on more fertile land grow coffee beans, tea, and cotton for export. Robusta coffee beans, used to make instant coffee, are grown on land up to 4,500 feet above sea level. The more valuable arabica coffee beans, sold as whole beans or ground coffee, are grown at higher elevations. Fishing on Lake Tanganyika provides an important source of food for local markets.

Burundi's mines produce small quantities of tungsten, gold, and cassiterite—the chief source of metallic tin—but the country has developed very little manufacturing.

161

Angola and Namibia

Angola

Status:	Independent State
Area:	481,351 square miles
Population:	12.5 million
Capital:	Luanda
Language:	Portuguese
Currency:	Kwanza (100 lwei)

Namibia

Status:	Independent State
Area:	318,259 square miles
Population:	1.6 million
Capital:	Windhoek
Languages:	English, Afrikaans, German
Currency:	Namibian dollar (100 cents)

Angola is a large, sparsely populated country on the western coast of southern Africa. Its territory includes the tiny province of Cabinda in the northwest, which is separated from the rest of the country by the Congo River and the Republic of the Congo's narrow land corridor to the coast.

Portuguese slave traders established colonies on Angola's coast in the sixteenth century, and later colonists cultivated sugarcane and tobacco for the European market. Angola won its independence from Portugal in 1975 after a long and bloody war, but the principal rebel armies continued fighting until the early 1990s.

Grass-covered plateaus, 4,000 to 6,000 feet above sea level, cover most of the country, with a range of hills in the west dropping sharply to a narrow coastal plain. In the hotter, wetter north, thick forests merge with those of the Democratic Republic of the Congo. In the south, the savanna gives way to stony desert and scrub.

Decades of war have left Angola's railroads and mines in ruins and the country poor and heavily in debt. But a stable government has many resources with which to jumpstart the economy. Most of Angola has ample water and fertile soil, especially in the river valleys. The coastal waters teem with fish. The mining regions hold huge reserves of iron ore and some of the world's richest diamond deposits, and Cabinda is rich in oil. Most of Angola's farmers grow cassava, corn, bananas, and sugarcane as food crops, but a rejuvenated economy could restore the country's once-strong exports of coffee beans, cotton, sugarcane, corn, and fruits.

Above: Windhoek, the capital of Namibia, has a population of just over 104,000. The styles of its older buildings reflect the country's history of German and later South African control.

Below: Seafarers had good cause to name this the Skeleton Coast. There was little hope of survival for anyone shipwrecked here.

Namibia, formerly called South-West Africa, won independence in 1990 after 75 controversial years under South African control. Before South Africa controlled it, Germany had ruled the territory as a protectorate for 31 years.

With only five people per square mile, Namibia is one of the most sparsely populated countries in Africa. Dry rolling grasslands, 3,000 to 6,000 feet above sea level, blanket most of the country's interior. The Namib Desert—home to the world's largest sand dunes, some of which stand more than 1,200 feet high—covers the 80-mile-wide coastal strip, while the Kalahari Desert dominates the country's southeast. The narrow Caprivi Strip in the extreme northeast, ceded to Germany by Britain in 1893, provides Namibia with a land corridor to the Zambezi River.

Namibia is not fertile, but farmers in the central uplands and northern areas are able to grow corn, millet, and vegetables, and there is sufficient grass for grazing cattle and sheep. Coastal fisheries provide employment and an important source of food, but excessive fishing has caused catches to diminish. Mining dominates Namibia's economy, with gem-quality diamonds, copper, zinc, lead, silver, gold, and the world's most productive uranium mine providing much of the country's export income. Tourism is a growing industry with great potential for future development. Etosha Game Park in the northwest contains all the principal big game species and attracts many visitors each year.

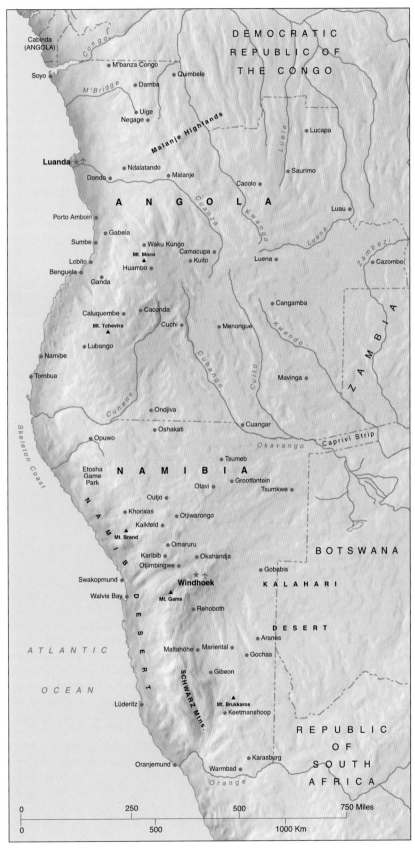

Zambia and Malawi

Zambia

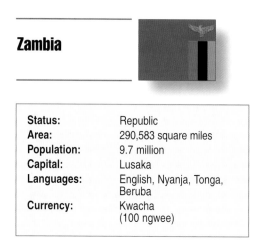

Status:	Republic
Area:	290,583 square miles
Population:	9.7 million
Capital:	Lusaka
Languages:	English, Nyanja, Tonga, Beruba
Currency:	Kwacha (100 ngwee)

Zambia in south central Africa became an independent nation in 1964. From 1924 to 1953, it was the British colony of Northern Rhodesia, and from 1953 until 1963 it formed part of the Federation of Rhodesia and Nyasaland, along with Southern Rhodesia (Zimbabwe) and Nyasaland (Malawi).

A vast undulating plateau that lies 4,000 feet above sea level covers most of Zambia. The southern part is drained by the Zambezi River and its principal tributaries, the Kafue and the Luangwa. Lake Kariba, formed by the Kariba Dam on the Zambezi, is Africa's second-largest artificial lake. Generators in the dam supply power to both Zambia and its southern neighbor Zimbabwe. Victoria Falls, upstream of the dam, is one of the world's great tourist attractions. The Chambeshi River, which flows into the marshlands around Lake Bangweulu, and the Luapula River, which flows north from the lake and then joins the Congo, drain Zambia's northern region. Most of the plateau is savanna grassland, with forested valleys full of mopani trees. The Muchinga Mountains rise to 7,000 feet near the border with Malawi.

Zambia's economy is almost completely dependent on one commodity—copper—which accounts for nearly 90 percent of the country's income. Exports of lead, zinc, cobalt, and other minerals account for most of the rest. Zimbabwe, Mozambique, and South Africa provide rail access to seaports. Kitwe in north central Zambia is the country's mining center and, like the capital city of Lusaka, is attracting many poor rural

people in search of work. Rapid urban population growth is straining the country's inadequate educational and health systems.

Zambia's farmers grow corn, millet, sorghum, cassava, and beans as staple food crops, while some of the larger farms on fertile valley soil produce tobacco, fruit, cotton, and sugarcane commercially. Some farmers raise cattle in the south, but tsetse flies prevent livestock raising in the north.

Right: Baobab trees—one of the most distinctive and typical trees of Africa—stand like sentries on the flat savanna plains of Zambia.

Malawi

Status:	Republic
Area:	45,745 square miles
Population:	10 million
Capital:	Lilongwe
Languages:	Chichewa, English
Currency:	Kwacha (100 tambala)

About 520 miles long and 100 miles wide, Malawi sits at the southern end of Africa's Great Rift Valley on the western and southern shores of Lake Nyasa. Rich volcanic soil and lake sediment provide some of the most fertile farmland in Africa, but only one-third of the land is suitable for farming. To the west and south, the land rises steeply to about 4,000 feet. Mount Mulanje, Malawi's highest peak, reaches 9,843 feet in the south.

The climate in the valley bottom is hot and humid, averaging about 75°F. Malawi's highlands are cooler at 55° to 65°F. Annual rainfall ranges from 60 inches in the north to 33 inches in the south. A warm, wet season occurs from December to March. Malawi's cool, dry season extends from May to October.

More than half the country's people live in the south, primarily in the capital city of Lilongwe and in Blantyre—the country's principal business and industrial center. Both cities are overcrowded, having seen rapid growth in the 1980s, with the influx of more than one million refugees from Mozambique's civil war.

Despite its fertile land, Malawi remains very poor. Government policies favor large commercial farms that produce tea—the predominant cash crop—and cotton, tobacco, sugarcane, and peanuts for export. Most farmers have only a few acres of land and struggle to raise enough food for their families. Factories in Blantyre and crews that fish Lake Nyasa provide important sources of food and employment. The country's lack of roads and machinery has kept it from developing a timber industry—another possible source of income.

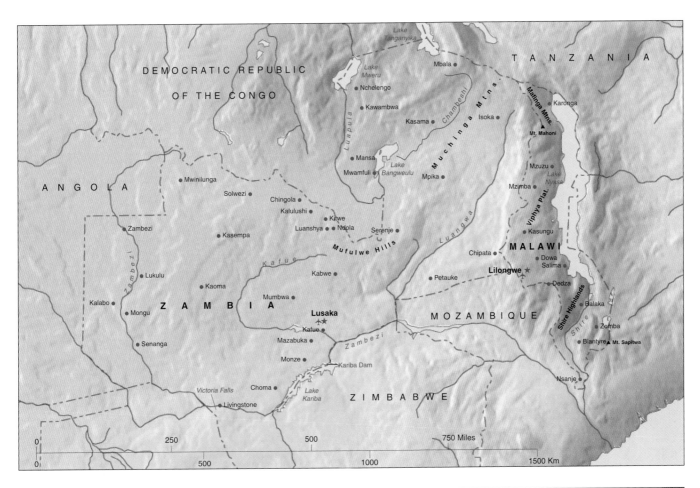

Right: Victoria Falls, named for Queen Victoria by the British explorer David Livingstone who discovered them in 1855, plunge more than 300 feet into a narrow gorge on the Zambezi River in southern Zambia. The constant roar and clouds of spray earned the falls their local name—Mosi-oa-Tunya—"the smoke that thunders."

Mozambique, Seychelles, Comoros, Réunion

Mozambique

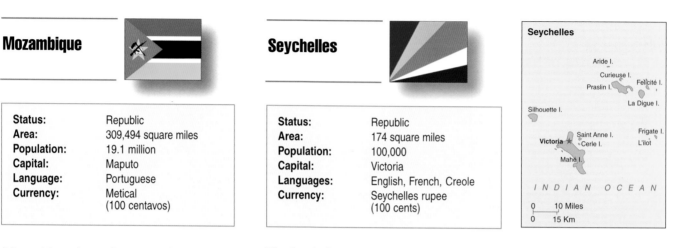

Status:	Republic
Area:	309,494 square miles
Population:	19.1 million
Capital:	Maputo
Language:	Portuguese
Currency:	Metical (100 centavos)

Mozambique, in southeastern Africa, has fertile land, minerals, forests, and hydroelectric power. Yet life expectancy there is among the shortest in Africa, infant mortality is among the highest, malnutrition is widespread, and in many areas health and medical services are nonexistent. The causes lie in the country's recent history. Mozambique gained independence in 1975 after 400 years as a Portuguese colony and after a bloody 10-year war. A civil war that continued until the mid-1990s added to the devastation and left half the population dependent on foreign aid.

A wide coastal plain with many port cities covers half the country, rising inland to low plateaus and then to highlands and mountains on the borders. Most of the land is savanna grassland, but forests in the north contain ebony, ironwood, and other valuable timbers. Lowland plantations produce cashews, coconuts, cotton, and sugarcane for export. Inland farmers harvest cassava, corn, and vegetables for their dinner tables.

Mozambique's natural resources include gold, diamonds, uranium, iron ore, copper, bauxite, coal, and offshore gas. The economy also depends on foreign aid and on payments from neighboring countries for railroad access to the harbors at Maputo, Beira, Quelimane, and Pemba.

Seychelles

Status:	Republic
Area:	174 square miles
Population:	100,000
Capital:	Victoria
Languages:	English, French, Creole
Currency:	Seychelles rupee (100 cents)

The Seychelles comprise about 115 islands. The larger ones are granite and are mountainous. The smaller ones are low and made of coral. Almost 90 percent of the people live on the main island, Mahé. The economy depends mainly on tourism. Small farms produce some food for local use, but most of the islands' food is imported. Tea growing and tuna fishing also contribute to the economy.

Comoros

Status:	Republic
Area:	861 square miles
Population:	600,000
Capital:	Moroni
Languages:	French, Arabic
Currency:	CFA franc (100 centimes)

The Comoros Islands became independent from France in 1975, following a referendum (a vote of the people). The country is poor, with most of the people dependent on subsistence farming. Vanilla, cloves, and ylang-ylang—a perfumery essence obtained from the flowers of a native tree—are the islands' only significant exports.

Réunion

Status:	Overseas Department of France
Area:	969 square miles
Population:	700,000
Capital:	Saint Denis
Languages:	French
Currency:	French franc (100 centimes)

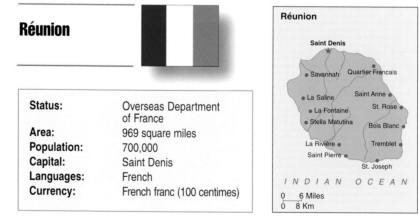

Réunion has been an Overseas Department of France since 1946. Before that it was a French colony for 300 years. The island's principal exports are vanilla, tobacco, tea, and perfumes.

Madagascar and Mauritius

Madagascar

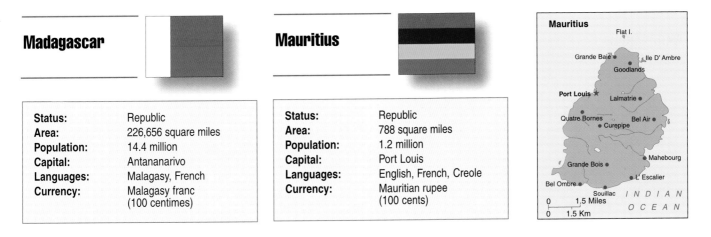

Status:	Republic
Area:	226,656 square miles
Population:	14.4 million
Capital:	Antananarivo
Languages:	Malagasy, French
Currency:	Malagasy franc (100 centimes)

Mauritius

Status:	Republic
Area:	788 square miles
Population:	1.2 million
Capital:	Port Louis
Languages:	English, French, Creole
Currency:	Mauritian rupee (100 cents)

Madagascar is actually one large island and many tiny islands separated from the southern African mainland by the Mozambique Channel. The main island lies about 250 miles off the coast and was a French colony, until it gained independence in 1960. A high rugged plateau divided by river gorges dominates the island's center. Most of the people live in this region, where temperatures average a pleasant 65°F and where 55 inches of rain fall annually. Timber cutting and **slash-and-burn** agriculture have stripped bare many of the central hills, creating extreme soil erosion. The government and international aid agencies are implementing reforestation programs to stop the destruction.

To the west the land slopes steadily to the coast—a much drier region with a smaller population that lives in the fertile river valleys. Desert scrub and patches of dry forest dominate the southwest—an area that contains some of the world's most ancient and unusual plants, half the world's chameleon species, and the unique monkeylike lemurs. In the east, the land drops steeply to a narrow coastal plain, where the main port of Toamasina is located.

The Malagasy population is comprised of many ethnic groups, mostly of mixed black African and Indonesian ancestry. The vast majority are farmers who raise cattle on the drier grassland areas and cultivate rice—the principal staple food—cassava, yams, and other crops in the fertile valleys and coastal areas. Coffee beans are Madagascar's chief export, followed by vanilla and cloves. Miners excavate chromite, graphite, gold, and semiprecious stones, but industry is under-developed and consists chiefly of processing agricultural products for export.

This remote country is in the Indian Ocean consisting of one large island and about 20 smaller ones. It gained independence from Britain in 1968 and declared itself a republic in 1992. Sugarcane plantations long ago replaced all the native vegetation. Sugarcane is still an important export crop, but the island economy has diversified to include tourism, fishing, tea growing, manufacturing of clothing, and banking.

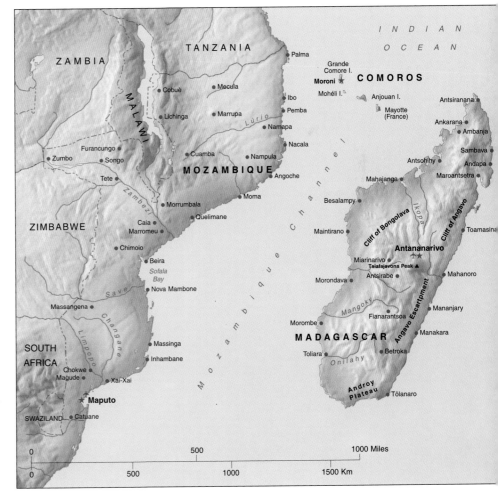

Botswana and Zimbabwe

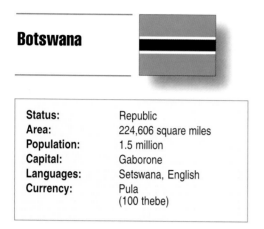

Botswana

Status:	Republic
Area:	224,606 square miles
Population:	1.5 million
Capital:	Gaborone
Languages:	Setswana, English
Currency:	Pula
	(100 thebe)

This large, landlocked country in the center of southern Africa achieved independence in 1966 after 71 years as the British protectorate of Bechuanaland. It is one of Africa's most thinly populated countries, with just seven people per square mile. Dry rolling plateaus about 3,000 feet above sea level cover much of the country. Low hills rise in the east and northwest. A huge depression in the north receives the waters of the Okavango River, which flows south from the Angolan Highlands. In the rainy season, the waters spread out to form the vast Okavango Swamps that teem with wildlife. Tiny Lake Ngami is all that remains in the dry season. Streams flowing eastward from the marshes evaporate in a large salt basin called the Makgadikgadi Pans. The Kalahari Desert covers much of central and southwestern Botswana.

Most of Botswana's people live in small rural villages in the eastern half of the country, where they farm and raise cattle. Corn, sorghum, and millet are the principal food crops, but the land is not very fertile, so Botswana imports food from its neighbors. Livestock comprises the core of Botswana's agricultural economy. The country exports beef and leather, and the production of leather goods is one of the few manufacturing industries.

The discovery of minerals in the 1970s enabled Botswana to grow from one of Africa's poorest nations to one showing rapid economic improvement. Diamonds from the mines at Orapa and Jwaneng account for 80 percent of export earnings. The remainder is mostly copper from Selebi-Phikwe and coal from the east. Botswana's principal economic partner is South Africa. Botswanan exports headed to sea travel by rail through South Africa, and South African investments have long supported Botswana's mining industries. South Africa also provides jobs for thousands of Botswanans.

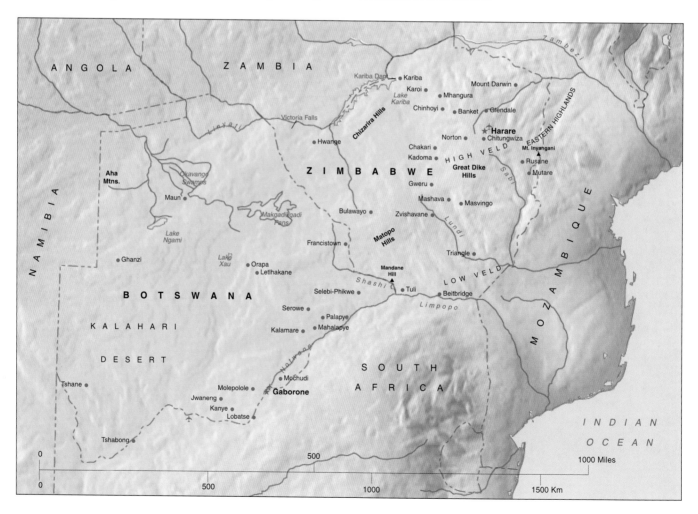

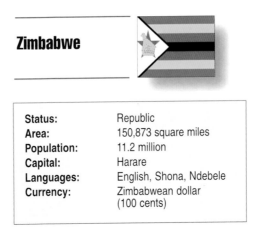

Zimbabwe

Status:	Republic
Area:	150,873 square miles
Population:	11.2 million
Capital:	Harare
Languages:	English, Shona, Ndebele
Currency:	Zimbabwean dollar (100 cents)

Above: Traditional Zimbabwean houses are often decorated with bold geometric patterns in contrasting colors.

Below: The Okavango Swamps in northern Botswana attract ecotourists and birdwatchers from all over the world.

Zimbabwe's journey to independence began in 1965, when the ruling white minority unilaterally declared independence from Britain rather than accept black majority rule. International political pressure, **trade sanctions**, and a long guerrilla war finally forced the white minority to concede. Zimbabwe gained independence under black majority rule in 1980.

Located in southern Africa, Zimbabwe has four natural regions. The High **Veld,** a 4,000-foot rolling plateau, runs southwest to northeast across the country. Large farms in this area, many of them still owned by white farmers, produce Zimbabwe's principal export crops—tobacco, cotton, sugarcane, and tea. A narrow ridge called the Great Dike stretches for 300 miles across the highlands. The dike consists of **igneous rocks** that were forced up through the surrounding rocks as molten magma. These rocks contain platinum, nickel, chromite, and other minerals, which account for about 20 percent of the country's exports. The Low Veld consists of sandy plains in the valleys of the Lundi, Sabi, and Limpopo Rivers. The Eastern Highlands rise to 8,507 feet at Mount Inyangani near the Mozambican border. Hot, wet summers and cool dry winters make some of the High Veld farms very productive, but most black Zimbabwean farmers work small plots on the less fertile Low Veld and manage to grow just enough corn and millet to feed their families.

Coal from the Hwange region and hydroelectric power from the Kariba Dam provide ample energy for Zimbabwe's well-developed industrial districts in Harare and Bulawayo. Iron and steel, automobile assembly, textiles, chemicals, and the processing of agricultural products such as leather, tobacco, soybeans, and sunflower seeds drive the country's industrial sector. Zimbabwe exports goods by rail through South Africa and Mozambique. Tourism also contributes to a balanced economy that supports efficient educational and health systems.

Lesotho and Swaziland

Lesotho

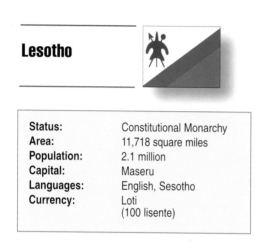

Status:	Constitutional Monarchy
Area:	11,718 square miles
Population:	2.1 million
Capital:	Maseru
Languages:	English, Sesotho
Currency:	Loti (100 lisente)

Swaziland

Status:	Monarchy
Area:	6,703 square miles
Population:	1.0 million
Capital:	Mbabane
Languages:	Siswati, English
Currency:	Lilangeni (100 cents)

This small mountainous country—until 1966 the British protectorate of Basutoland—is completely surrounded by South Africa and depends on that country for most of its food, manufactured goods, energy, and employment.

Dominating much of the country are the high plateaus and peaks of the Moloti and Drakensberg ranges that rise to 11,425 feet at the summit of Mount Ntlenyana on Lesotho's eastern border. Flat plains at about 5,500 feet encompass western Lesotho. The country's altitude affords Lesotho a mild, damp climate, with temperatures around 70°F in January—the heart of summer—and 35°F in the winter month of July. The country averages 28 inches of rain annually, the bulk of it falling between October and April.

Most of Lesotho's people live in small villages in the western plains region, with each family group of thatched dwellings built around a central kraal, or cattle enclosure. Farmers tend corn, sorghum, barley, beans, peas, and other vegetables. Cattle, sheep, and goats supply milk and meat for the table and provide wool for export. Lesotho's eastern highlanders are less settled. Men and young boys spend months in the hills riding on ponies as they move their livestock from place to place in search of grazing land.

Local factories employ Lesotho's citizens in textiles, meat canning, brewing, and furniture making, but jobs are scarce and roughly half the working-age men cross the border to work in South Africa's factories, farms, mines, and service industries. Lesotho has no mineral wealth, but its spectacular mountain scenery is attracting growing numbers of tourists.

The tiny kingdom of Swaziland is bordered on three sides by South Africa and on the fourth by Mozambique. Mountains clad in dense pine forests cover much of the country's western edge. To the east, the land drops through rolling grassy savanna to a flat, rather dry lowland plain. Several large rivers flow across the plain, providing ample water for irrigating farmland and for generating hydroelectricity.

Swaziland has abundant resources. The western highlands contain one of the world's largest asbestos mines, huge reserves of iron ore, and deposits of tin and gold. Swaziland's miners also excavate barite, kaolin, and coal. Natural forests and some of the largest plantation forests in Africa supply the raw material for wood-pulp factories and sawmills, most of them owned by Europeans. Large farms on the fertile savanna and on irrigated land in the lowland plains—also predominantly owned by Europeans—grow sugarcane, rice, cotton, tobacco, and citrus fruits for foreign markets. Meat and animal hides are also significant exports. Manufacturing—mainly processing agricultural and forest products—comprises nearly 25 percent of total productivity.

South African and European companies own many of the large commercial enterprises. Traditional Swazi farmers in rural areas grow corn, millet, beans, and other crops and raise livestock. Cattle, representing wealth and status, have a special importance in Swazi culture and are rarely killed. Rural culture and social traditions remain strong even though many Swazi people live in the urban centers and work in offices and factories.

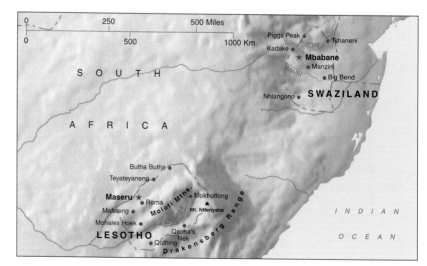

South Africa

South Africa

Status:	Republic
Area:	471,444 square miles
Population:	42.6 million
Capital:	Pretoria (administrative), Cape Town (legislative), Bloemfontein (judicial)
Languages:	English, Afrikaans, Zulu, Xhosa, Ndebele, Sesotho, Tswana
Currency:	Rand (100 cents)

South Africa is the richest, most highly developed country in Africa. It covers barely 4 percent of the continent's land area and is home to only 6 percent of its people, yet it produces 50 percent of Africa's minerals and 40 percent of its manufactured goods. It also generates about 70 percent of the continent's electricity.

The country's history has been one of conflict—from the first wars between Dutch settlers and the Xhosa people, through the Boer War (1899–1902) between Britain and the Afrikaner Orange Free State and Transvaal. In 1948 the white majority introduced **apartheid**, a policy of segregation that fueled a long struggle for black majority rule. The struggle culminated in the election of the nation's first black president, Nelson Mandela, in 1994.

South Africa's landscape is as diverse as its history. Most of the interior consists of an undulating plateau called the veld. The High Veld contains Africa's richest goldfields and much of its best farmland, where farmers cultivate corn, wheat, potatoes, and fruit.

Top right: In Swaziland, the huge reeds that grow along riverbanks and in marshes are made into thatching, baskets, and many other goods.

Center right: Cape Town is one of the world's most beautiful cities, with fine avenues, elegant shops, and parks. Its thriving waterfront serves cargo ships that arrive from all over the world.

Right: On a calm day, the Cape of Good Hope looks tranquil, but it was earlier called the Cape of Storms.

South Africa

In western South Africa lies the lower Middle Veld—cattle-ranching country. The northern Transvaal region consists of rolling grasslands where farmers grow corn, tobacco, and fruit. The Great Karroo Mountains in the south and the Drakensberg Mountains to the east separate South Africa's veld from its narrow coast. The Namib Desert borders the Atlantic coast in the extreme west, and the Kalahari Desert takes up the northwestern corner along the border with Botswana. South Africa's spectacular scenery, 16 national parks, and hundreds of game reserves attract millions of tourists each year.

Much of South Africa's prosperity comes from the country's wealth of minerals, particularly diamonds, gold, silver, platinum, iron ore, copper, manganese, and uranium. Gold earns the most export money, accounting for nearly one-third of the country's income. Oil is the only major mineral resource the country lacks, but South Africa has vast coalfields and has developed the process of creating fuel oil from coal. Coal provides 80 percent of the country's energy. The remainder is hydroelectric and nuclear power.

South Africa's exports consist primarily of minerals and agricultural products such as wool and wine. Manufacturing industries—concentrated in the Witwatersrand region and around the chief ports of Cape Town, Port Elizabeth, East London, and Durban—produce goods mainly for the domestic market. These goods include processed foods, textiles, iron and steel, paper, chemicals, automobiles, furniture, and domestic appliances. South Africa also plays a major role in the trading activities of neighboring countries. Most of the imports and exports of Lesotho, Botswana, and Swaziland and about half the goods traveling to and from Malawi, Zimbabwe, and the Democratic Republic of the Congo cross South Africa by rail and pass through South Africa's seaports.

Top left: Gold has long been one of South Africa's many valuable mineral exports.

Center left: Black rhinos in Kruger National Park are among the great sights for visiting tourists.

Left: With a total population of more than 1.7 million, Johannesburg and its surrounding suburbs and townships form the largest metropolitan area in South Africa.

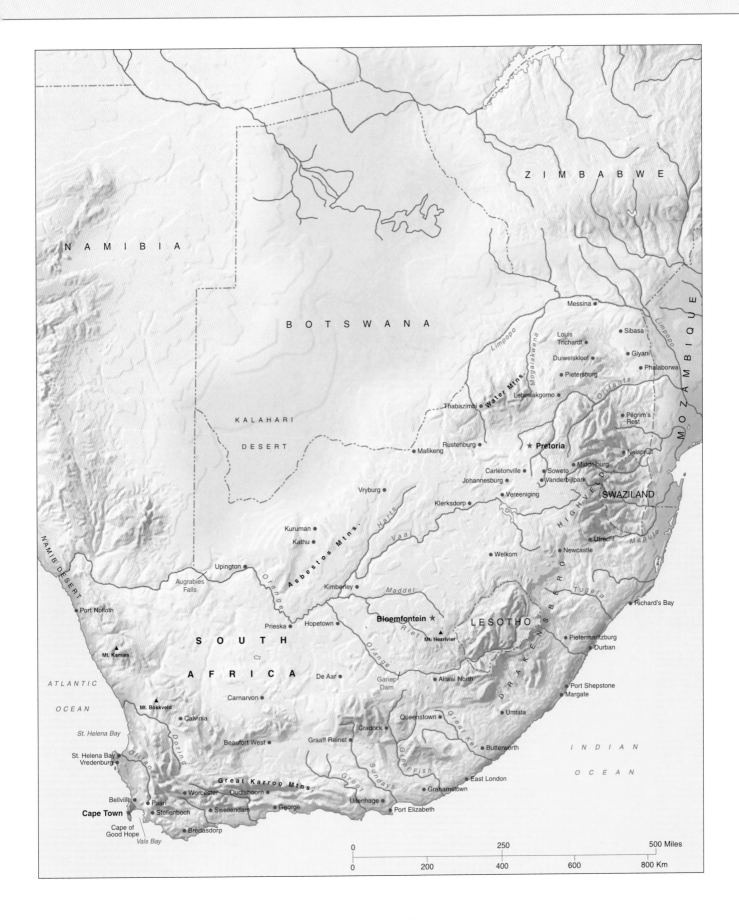

NAMIBIA

ZIMBABWE

BOTSWANA

KALAHARI

DESERT

Messina
Louis
Trichardt   Sibasa
Duiwelskloof   Giyani
Pietersburg   Phalaborwa
Lebowakgomo
Thabazimbi   Water Mtns.   Pilgrim's
                                    Rest
Mafikeng   Rustenburg   ★ Pretoria   Nelspruit
        Carletonville   Soweto   Middelburg
        Johannesburg   Vanderbijlpark
Vryburg   Vereeniging   SWAZILAND
        Klerksdorp
Kuruman   Utrecht
Kathu   Welkom   Newcastle
                            Richard's Bay
Upington   Asbestos Mtns.   Tugela
Augrabies   Kimberley   Madder
Falls
Port Nolloth   Bloemfontein ★   LESOTHO   Pietermaritzburg
        Prieska   Hopetown   Durban
                    Mt. Hexrivier
SOUTH   De Aar   Gariep   Aliwal North   Port Shepstone
Mt. Kamies   Dam   Margate
AFRICA
ATLANTIC   Carnarvon
OCEAN   Mt. Bokkveld   Queenstown   Umtata
St. Helena Bay   Calvinia   Cradock   Butterworth   INDIAN
St. Helena Bay   Beaufort West   Graaff Reinet   OCEAN
Vredenburg   Great Karroo Mtns.   Grahamstown   East London
Bellville   Worcester   Oudtshoorn   Uitenhage
Cape Town ★   Paarl   George   Port Elizabeth
        Stellenboch   Swellendam
Cape of   Bredasdorp
Good Hope
Vals Bay

MOZAMBIQUE
DRAKENSBERG
HIGHVELD

0   250   500 Miles
0   200   400   600   800 Km

The Sea of Galilee, Israel

NORTHERN and WESTERN ASIA

NORTHERN and WESTERN ASIA

The northern and western sections of the Asian continent comprise a vast region that covers 6,800 miles of territory. This part of Asia stretches from the deserts of the **Arabian Peninsula** in the extreme southwest across the snow-covered mountains of Kyrgyzstan and Tajikistan in western central Asia. The region includes the grassy **steppes** of Asian Russia and the ancient forests of Siberia (part of Russia). In the far Russian north lies the frozen **tundra** of the Chukchi Peninsula, which is lashed by the icy waters of the Arctic Ocean and the Bering Sea.

Northern and western Asia also exhibit some of the world's most extreme climatic conditions. For example, the desert interior of Oman in the **Middle East** is one of the hottest places on earth, with temperatures often exceeding 120°F and sometimes soaring well above 130°F. At the other extreme lies the Central Siberian Plateau, where, far from the moderating effects of the oceans, winter temperatures average -50°F and often plunge to -85°F and below.

The northern and western sections of Asia are also sparsely populated. Deserts dominate the Middle Eastern countries of the west, where populations tend to congregate in the coastal regions, in the cooler highlands farther inland, and in the main river valleys. The deserts of the Middle East are largely uninhabited, except for small groups of nomadic **Bedouin.**

The landscapes of western central Asia rise from the dry grasslands bordering the Caspian Sea to the windswept **glaciers** and peaks of the Pamir Mountains and the Tian Shan (mountains). Most of the people live near the shores of the Caspian Sea or in the foothills of the mountains, where rivers provide water for homes and for irrigating fields.

The least populated parts of northern Asia are in Asian Russia. Most of the people live in mining and industrial areas near various cities— Yekaterinburg and Chelyabinsk at the southern end of the Ural Mountains, Novosibirsk and Irkutsk in southern Siberia, and Vladivostok along the coast of the Sea of Japan. The people of the far northern forests and tundra are mainly reindeer herders, trappers, and fishers.

Farmers in the more fertile areas of northern and western Asia produce a variety of grain crops, vegetables, and fruit. Some regions grow vines for wine making, while others raise mulberry trees to provide food for silkworms. Cotton and flax are important nonfood crops in some areas, and the great forests of northern Asia produce vast quantities of lumber, plywood, pulp, and paper products. Rivers are an important source of hydroelectric power.

Oil and natural gas are the principal natural resources of the Middle East—one of the world's leading oil-producing regions. Russia also has vast reserves of both oil and gas and also extensive coalfields. Northern Asia probably has more untapped reserves of minerals that any other region in the world. Miners in the Pamir Mountains, the Tian Shan, the Ural Mountains, and the upland zones of southern Siberia produce iron, copper, lead, zinc, tungsten, tin, gold, and many other minerals. These deposits feed the region's heavy industry and manufacturing centers.

176

ARCTIC OCEAN

0°
20°
Norwegian
Sea
Svalbard
40°
60°
Franz Josef
Land
80°
100°
Severnaya
Zemlya
120°
140°
160°
180°
Bering
Sea
East
Siberian
Sea
New Siberian Is.
Laptev
Sea
Barents
Sea
Kara
Sea
Novaya Zemlya

Kolyma
Lowland

Kamchatka Peninsula

Sea of Okhotsk

URAL MOUNTAINS

West Siberian

Central
Siberian
Plateau

Lower Tunguska

R   U   S   S   I   A

Plain

Ob

Yenisey

Angara

Amur

L. Baikal

Manchurian
Plain

40°

Tobol

Ishim

Irtysh

KAZAKHSTAN

Aral
Sea

Turanian
Plateau

Syr Darya

L. Balkhash

Sayan Mts.

Altai

Gobi
Desert

Sea of
Japan

TURKMENISTAN

UZBEKISTAN

KYRGYZSTAN

Tien Shan

Chukchi Peninsula

Yellow
Sea

Amu Darya

TAJIKISTAN

Tarim Basin

Great
Basin

AFGHANISTAN

Hindu Kush

Kunlun Shan

East China
Sea

Indus

H I M A L A Y A

Ganges

20°

0   1000   2000 Miles

0   1000   2000   3000 Km

South China
Sea

Arabian
Sea

177

Turkey and Cyprus

Turkey

Status:	Republic
Area:	299,158 square miles
Population:	65.9 million
Capital:	Ankara
Language:	Turkish
Currency:	Turkish lira (100 kurus)

Turkey, one of the few countries that spans continents, forms a bridge between Europe and Asia. The European portion of the country, called Thrace, comprises just 3 percent of Turkey's total landmass and sits on the southeastern tip of the continent. The remainder of the country covers a broad peninsula known as Anatolia or Asia Minor. The Straits—the Dardanelles, the Sea of Marmara, and the narrow Bosporus, all of which lead to the Black Sea—separate Turkey's two sections.

Mountain ranges along the country's northern and southern shores border Turkey's two **plateaus.** The Taurus Mountains dominate the south and almost completely hide the western plateau from the sea. The Pontic and Küre Mountains lie along the shore of the Black Sea. The country's coastal regions enjoy hot summers and mild winters, but inland Turkey is a land of extremes, with very hot, dry summers and bitterly cold winters. Less than 10 inches of rain falls each year, and parts of the land are semidesert.

Farmers on the plateaus and in the southern mountains raise sheep and goats. Those in the more fertile western valleys and northern plains grow cotton, tobacco, and olives for export and wheat, fruits, and vegetables for local markets.

Turkey's economy, long reliant on agriculture, is developing around other means of revenue. Miners in eastern Turkey excavate chromite—the country's most valuable mineral export—as well as copper, borax, and coal. Factory workers manufacture motor vehicles, chemicals, and metal, wood, and leather goods. Textiles and clothing account for about one-third of all manufactured exports. Tourism is Turkey's fastest-growing industry, enticing visitors to the historic city of Istanbul, to a wealth of ancient monuments, and to the sunny resorts along the southern coast.

Left: Ancient and modern ways of life exist side by side in rural townships like Sanliurfa in southern Turkey, near the Syrian border.

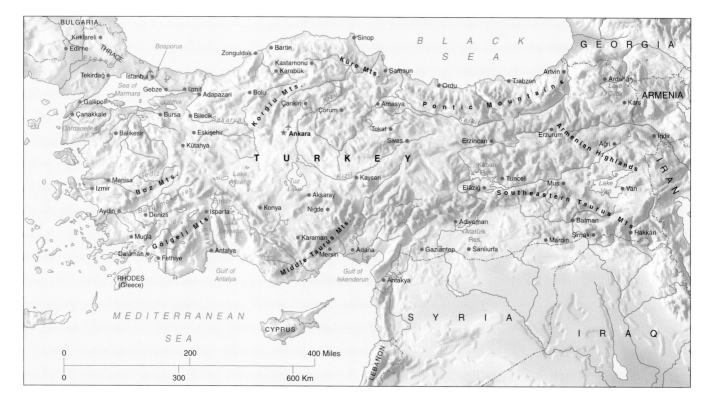

178

Cyprus

Status:	Republic
Area:	3,572 square miles
Population:	0.9 million
Capital:	Nicosia
Languages:	Greek, Turkish
Currency:	Cypriot pound (100 cents) Turkish lira (100 cents)

A small island in the eastern Mediterranean Sea, Cyprus has been divided since 1974, when Turkish forces took command of the island's northern section. The intervening years have been harsh, and the relatively poor inhabitants of the Turkish sector rely heavily on aid from Turkey. Cypriots of Greek origin remain in control of the more prosperous south, where the economy thrives despite the conflict. Repeated United Nations (UN) efforts have failed to bring about a settlement, although an uneasy standoff has replaced the bitter fighting. Only Turkey recognizes the northern section as a separate country.

Cyprus is a scenic land with a pleasant climate. Mount Olympus, the highest peak, rises to 6,403 feet in the center of the Troodos Mountains, which dominate central and western Cyprus, while the rugged limestone mountains of Kyrenia parallel the northern coast. The broad fertile Mesaoria Plain lies between the two ranges, spanning the country from Morphou in the west to Famagusta in the east.

Farmers in the north raise sheep and grow grains, grapes, olives, vegetables, and citrus fruits. Southern farmers benefit from better soil and ample water for irrigation. Their crops include fruits, salad crops, early vegetables, and flowers for export to mainland Europe.

Above: The rocky shoreline near Paphos on the southwestern coast of Cyprus is associated with Aphrodite, the Greek goddess of love and beauty.

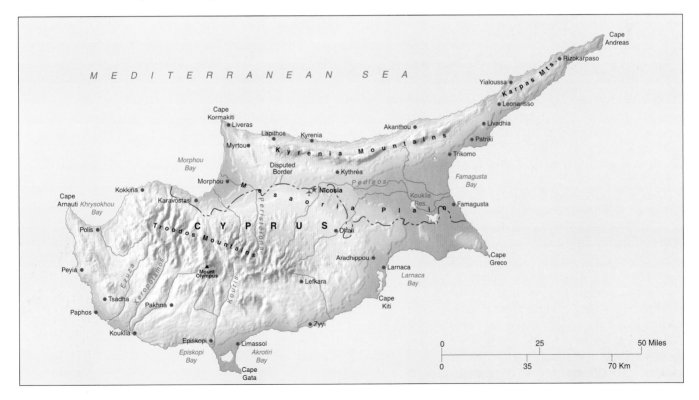

Syria

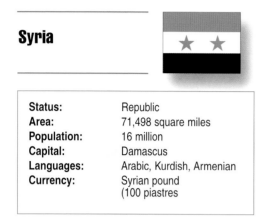

Status:	Republic
Area:	71,498 square miles
Population:	16 million
Capital:	Damascus
Languages:	Arabic, Kurdish, Armenian
Currency:	Syrian pound (100 piastres

Syria boasts a long history and a rich culture. Some of the world's earliest farming methods developed in the fertile valleys of the Euphrates and Tigris Rivers almost 10,000 years ago. A people called the **Semites** were living in the region by about 1500 B.C. They adapted part of the Egyptian writing system to create their own alphabet. Poetry and crafts, such as weaving, glassmaking, and metalworking, flourished. More than 2,000 years ago, ancient cities such as Palmyra were important trading centers on the caravan routes linking Asia, Africa, and Europe.

Western and central Syria can be divided into three principal land regions. A narrow coastal plain along the Mediterranean Sea has rich soil and a mild, moist climate. Winds blowing in across the water provide about 40 inches of annual rain, allowing coastal farmers to grow a variety of crops without the need for irrigation. Inland from this plain and running south to the Jordanian border lie the rugged Anti-Lebanon and Jebel Druz Mountains, whose west-facing slopes catch the moisture carried by the **prevailing winds.**

To the east of the mountains lies another, less-fertile plain. Farmers here rely for irrigation on the mountain streams and the Orontes River, which flows northward through a series of gorges and broad valleys. Most Syrians live in the plains regions bordering the mountains. The capital city of Damascus, near the country's southeastern border, houses more than one million residents, and the populations in Aleppo, Homs, Hamah, and the coastal city of Latakia each exceed 150,000. Much of the remaining population live in small towns and villages that dot the countryside.

Northeast of the plains lies a vast inland plateau covered in scrub and dry grassland. Southward the land becomes more barren until it merges with the scorching sands of the Syrian Desert. The broad Euphrates River Valley winds across the plateau, providing the only fertile land in this vast, sparsely populated landscape. Farmers in scattered villages manage to grow enough food for their own needs, and small groups of nomadic Bedouin–with their camels, sheep, and goats–eke out a living in the driest desert regions.

Cotton and wheat dominate Syria's cropland, supplemented by barley, sugar beets, olives, other fruits and vegetables, and tobacco. Most farms are small family businesses and are not highly mechanized. In the poorer rural areas, many farmers still use wooden plows and hand tools to cultivate their land.

Oil wells clustered in the northeast provide Syria's chief mineral resource. Miners also extract phosphates to make fertilizer and mine gypsum and limestone for the plaster and cement used in local construction projects. Syria's chief manufacturing industries—textiles, glass, and processed foods—are concentrated in the country's large western towns.

Below: A baker in Tall Abyad in northern Syria works late into the night baking bread for the villagers' evening meal. During the Islamic month of **Ramadan,** Muslims (followers of Islam) take neither food nor drink during the hours of daylight.

Right: A Syrian woman draws water from a well in the northern city of Aleppo. This large city is a mixture of old and new. Many residents wear modern clothes and live in modern houses and apartments, but the city also has extensive older quarters with traditional houses and old marketplaces.

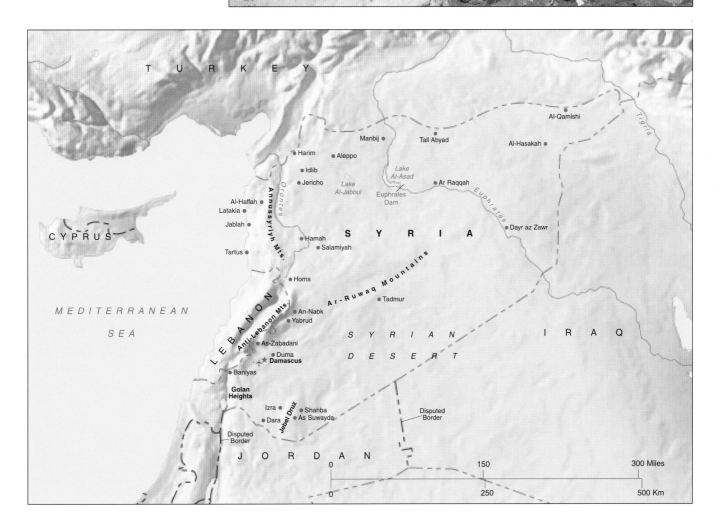

Lebanon

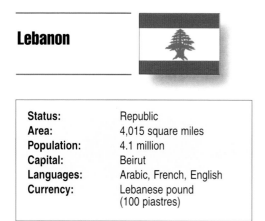

Lebanon

Status:	Republic
Area:	4,015 square miles
Population:	4.1 million
Capital:	Beirut
Languages:	Arabic, French, English
Currency:	Lebanese pound (100 piastres)

This small Arab country at the eastern end of the Mediterranean Sea has long sandy beaches backed by a narrow coastal plain. Beyond the plain, the land rises steeply to a double range of rugged mountains running north to south, parallel to the coast. The Lebanon Mountains form the first range, rising to 10,131 feet above sea level. The land then dips into the deep Bekáa Valley before rising again to the Anti-Lebanon Mountains on the border with Syria.

Hot dry summers, mild wet winters, and rich soil provide favorable farming conditions on the coastal plain. Winter rains falling on the Bekáa Valley support a second fertile farming region. Apples, peaches, oranges, lemons, grapes, and cherries are Lebanon's most valuable crops. Farmers also grow tobacco, potatoes, sugar beets, and many other vegetables for both local use and export. Lebanon's mountain regions once were famous for their cedar forests. Clear-cutting has left only sparse areas of coarse grasses and scrub for grazing sheep and goats. Factory workers in the capital city of Beirut and in Tripoli process foods and manufacture textiles, electrical goods, furniture, and chemicals.

From the 1820s to the 1970s, Beirut was one of the Middle East's leading commercial centers. Imports and exports passed regularly through Lebanon's ports. Trade flourished among Middle Eastern countries and trading partners on several continents. That prosperous era ended in the early 1970s, when civil war tore apart the country. Muslim and Christian communities clashed over the presence in Lebanon of members of the Palestine

Liberation Organization (PLO), which raided Israeli targets from base camps in Lebanon. Continued internal hostilities and retaliatory attacks by Israel against PLO bases in Lebanon caused widespread damage to Lebanon's cities—especially Beirut—and to the country's economy. Israel withdrew its forces from southern Lebanon in 2000. Despite the problems of the past, many of Lebanon's banks and businesses have survived, and the government is working to rebuild homes, factories, and roads damaged by the wars.

Above: Good soils, water from the hills, and an industrious workforce have made the narrow Bekáa Valley one of Lebanon's principal vegetable and fruit growing regions.

Right: The Lebanese capital of Beirut, on the eastern coast of the Mediterranean Sea, has a population of over 700,000. In the past, it was one of the leading cultural and commercial centers of the Middle East, and even after years of conflict it remains a significant trade and business center.

Israel and Jordan

Israel

Status:	Republic
Area:	8,130 square miles
Population:	6.1 million
Capital:	Jerusalem
Languages:	Hebrew, Arabic, English, Yiddish
Currency:	Shekel (100 agorot)

Four contrasting regions comprise Israel's landscape. A narrow fertile coastal plain fronts the Mediterranean Sea. Its northern section broadens around the Qishon River in the Plain of Esdraelon, where farmers grow grain, cotton, and vegetables. South of the Qishon, the drier Plain of Sharon supports the country's citrus farmers but must be irrigated.

The rolling hills of Galilee dominate north central Israel. Rich dark soils and plentiful rainfall sustain highly productive commercial gardens, where farmers grow vegetables and flowers for both local use and export.

The Jordan River Valley, running north to south from the Sea of Galilee to the Dead Sea, marks much of Israel's border with Jordan. Lying 1,300 feet below sea level, the Dead Sea is the lowest point on the earth's surface. It has no outlet and is the world's saltiest inland sea, providing Israel with a source of bromine, potash, and salt. The Jordan Valley is dry and not naturally fertile. Irrigating near the river and draining the marshy area north of the Sea of Galilee have created more fertile agricultural land.

The arid plateau of the Negev Desert covers southern Israel. Very little rain falls in this triangular-shaped region. Farmers in the desert's north raise fruits, vegetables, tomatoes, and **fodder crops** for dairy herds. Their fields are irrigated with water drawn from the Jordan River and from the streams that drain the southern coastal plain.

Almost 90 percent of Israelis live in urban areas, nearly a quarter of them in the three largest cities—Jerusalem, Tel Aviv-Jaffa, and Haifa. Factory workers in the industrial areas around Tel Aviv-Jaffa, Haifa, and the deepwater port of Ashdod produce chemicals, household goods, electronic equipment, scientific instruments,

paper, plastics, fertilizers, and textiles. Miners in the Negev Desert extract oil, copper, and phosphates, and a pipeline carries imported oil from Elat on the Gulf of Aqaba to a refinery at Haifa. Despite having to import most of its fuel and raw materials, Israel is the most industrialized country in the Middle East.

The State of Israel was created in 1948 from part of the former territory of Palestine. Neighboring Arab countries and displaced Palestinians opposed the new state, and Israel's short history has been one of constant wars. Signs of a negotiated peace only began to emerge in the late 1990s. Since 1967 Israel has occupied the West Bank (an area west of the Jordan River), the Gaza Strip (Egyptian territory), and the Golan Heights (Syrian territory). Israel removed its troops from a defensive buffer zone inside the southern border of Lebanon in 2000.

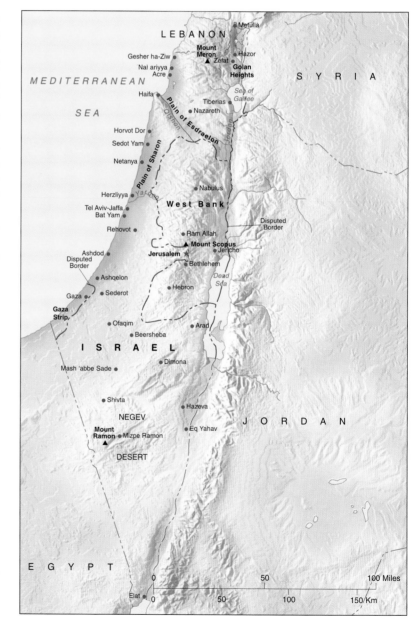

Above: Jerusalem, Israel, is a holy city to Jews, Christians, and Muslims alike. The beautiful Dome of the Rock (foreground) is the city's holiest Muslim shrine.

Above: The barren wilderness of the desert surrounds Mount Ramm (5,755 feet) in southwestern Jordan.

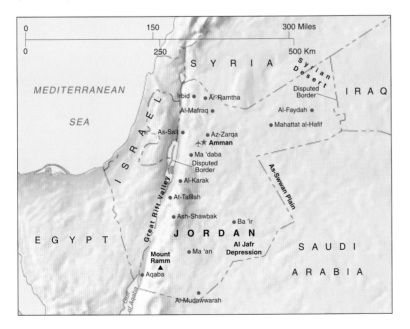

Jordan

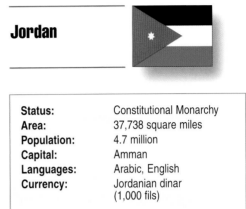

Status:	Constitutional Monarchy
Area:	37,738 square miles
Population:	4.7 million
Capital:	Amman
Languages:	Arabic, English
Currency:	Jordanian dinar (1,000 fils)

The Hashemite Kingdom of Jordan does not have the oil wealth enjoyed by some neighboring Arab states. Its developing economy is based on the service industry, agriculture, and mining and is also supported by foreign aid.

The country has three principal land regions. In the west lies the Jordan River Valley. The land is not very fertile, but farmers are able to grow fruits and vegetables on fields irrigated by river water. To the south, the land rises to the Transjordan Plateau, a rolling upland region containing many of Jordan's largest cities and towns and most of its best farmland. Barley, wheat, citrus fruits, olives, and vegetables are the principal crops covering the northern plateau. The southern plateau region is very dry, supporting only small crops of wheat and olives. Northeastern Jordan lies on the Syrian Desert, which sees less than 10 inches of rain annually, and summer temperatures soar to 120°F. Few people live here apart from small groups of nomadic goat and sheep herders.

Many Jordanians work in neighboring countries. About 70 percent of those who remain in Jordan work for the government, for the military, or in various service industries such as education, banking, or the hotels and restaurants that support the growing numbers of tourists visiting the country's ancient sites.

Mines in the plateau region produce potash and phosphates, which are turned into fertilizers for export. Fertilizers, cement, and refining of imported oil comprise Jordan's only large-scale industries. Smaller factories in the plateau towns produce leather goods and textiles, processed food, pharmaceuticals, and some chemicals. Power for these industries comes from imported oil.

Iraq

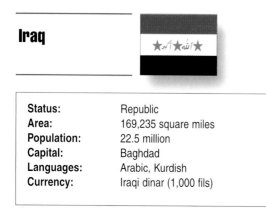

Status:	Republic
Area:	169,235 square miles
Population:	22.5 million
Capital:	Baghdad
Languages:	Arabic, Kurdish
Currency:	Iraqi dinar (1,000 fils)

Iraq is split in three by the Euphrates and Tigris Rivers—waterways that once supported the world's oldest known civilization. Farming communities occupied Sumer, in what would become southeastern Iraq, about 3500 B.C. The great city of Babylon—at the heart of the Babylonian Empire— flourished on the Euphrates's fertile banks from about 2200 B.C. until 539 B.C., when it was overthrown by Persian invaders.

The Zagros Mountains dominate northeastern Iraq, rising to more than 10,000 feet above sea level as they extend toward northern Iran and southeastern Turkey. Bitterly cold winters and just 15 inches of annual rainfall create a harsh environment for the local people.

Dry, rolling hills cover the northern plains between the Tigris and Euphrates Rivers. Farmers in the small, scattered villages grow wheat and barley on the productive soil that collects in the hollows and valleys. Sheep and goats graze on the surrounding dry grasslands. Southward from the capital city of Baghdad is an area between the two great rivers that provides Iraq's most fertile farmland. Farmers on the great southern plain grow grains, rice, fruit, and vegetables, irrigating their fields with water from the Tigris and Euphrates through a complex system of dams, channels, and control sluices. The two rivers meet at Al Qurnah, forming the Shatt al Arab. This channel flows southward to the Persian Gulf, where its delta forms Iraq's only stretch of coastline. Some of Iraq's most productive oil fields lie in this region, between the city of Basra and Iraq's border with Kuwait. Southeastern Iraq is a vast area of marshland and swamps.

Desert covers most of southwestern and western Iraq in a wilderness of sand dunes and bare limestone rock that stretches deep into Syria,

Jordan, and Saudi Arabia. As in most deserts, there are no permanent rivers, just *wadis* (dry river channels) that briefly fill after a rainfall but dry out again almost immediately. The land is empty except for groups of Bedouin nomads and their camels, sheep, and goats.

Iraqis manufacture natural gas, phosphates, sulfur, cement, iron and steel, textiles, ceramics, chemicals, and household goods, but oil has been the country's economic mainstay for many years. Oil revenues helped improve schools, hospitals, roads, and the irrigation systems used to water the farms of Iraq's southern plains.

Much of that progress, however, was destroyed by war. A conflict with neighboring Iran, from 1980 until 1988, and the Gulf War, which followed Iraq's invasion of Kuwait in 1990, left Iraq's roads, bridges, oil refineries, factories, phone system, and parts of the main cities in ruins. Recovery has been hampered by international **trade sanctions** that were imposed when Iraq refused to cooperate with UN arms inspectors sent in under a cease-fire agreement.

Right: Traditional reed dwellings of the Marsh Arabs of southeastern Iraq

Opposite top: Kazimiya, Shrine of the Seventh and Ninth Imams, in Baghdad. With a population of almost six million, Baghdad is one of the largest cities in the Middle East. As far back as A.D. 800, it had over a million residents and was a world center of learning, culture, and religion. It contains some of the most beautiful mosques in the Islamic world.

Above: Muslim pilgrims sit in the quiet shade of the ornately decorated Pilgrimage Shrine in Karbala.

Opposite bottom: One of the many hundreds of oil pumping stations that dot the deserts of Iraq

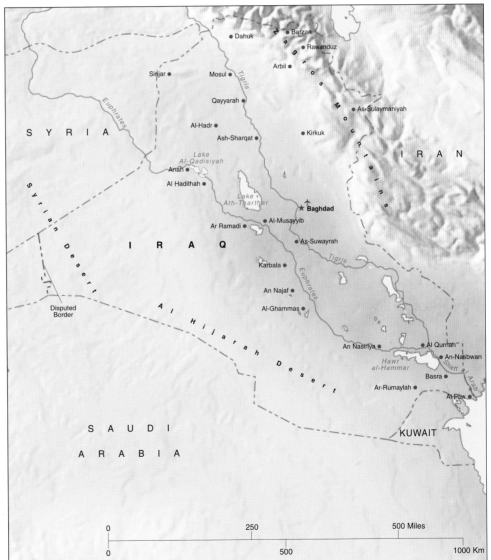

Iran

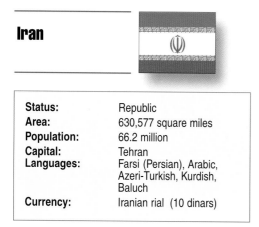

Iran	
Status:	Republic
Area:	630,577 square miles
Population:	66.2 million
Capital:	Tehran
Languages:	Farsi (Persian), Arabic, Azeri-Turkish, Kurdish, Baluch
Currency:	Iranian rial (10 dinars)

Iran is an ancient land with a history dating back 5,000 years. Around 550 B.C., Iran (then known as Persia) was the center of an empire stretching across southwestern Asia, southern Europe, and part of North Africa. For much of the twentieth century, powerful shahs (kings) ruled the country. The last shah, Mohammad Reza Pahlavi, was forced into exile in 1979 by an Islamic revolution that brought to power the religious leader **Ayatollah** Ruhollah Khomeini. The ayatollah died in 1989, and more moderate politicians took charge of the government.

Fundamentalist clerics still have enormous influence in Iran's affairs. Women in particular have felt the effect. The rise of fundamentalism swept away all signs of modernization, such as free speech, relaxing of traditional dress codes, and relaxing of the strict rules governing women's lives. While Iran's large cities have schools, hospitals, and other amenities, most small rural communities have few of these benefits, and most houses do not have running water or electricity.

A desert plateau, 3,000 feet above sea level, dominates central and eastern Iran. North of the plateau, the rugged Elburz Mountains tower over a narrow coastal plain bordering the Caspian Sea. Mount Damavand, Iran's highest peak, rises to 18,984 feet in this range. West of the plateau, the broad Zagros range forms a mountainous barrier between Iran and Iraq. Lesser mountain ranges ring the eastern and southern margins of the plateau. Iran's central desert area is one of the driest, most barren places on earth. Few people live there. A narrow coastal plain on the shores of the Caspian Sea and a small fertile lowland area at the head of the Persian Gulf provide Iran's only good agricultural land. Farmers supplement the principal crops of wheat and barley with lentils, cotton, sugar beets, fruits, vegetables, and tea. Farmers use less fertile land to raise cattle, sheep, and goats. Water is always in short supply in the south. The Caspian coastal plain is the only region that enjoys plentiful rain and a mild climate. Many of Iran's cities depend for their water on a labyrinth of tunnels and reservoirs that tap underground water supplies and catch what little rain falls inland.

Oil and gas are Iran's most important natural resources. The country is one of the world's top ten oil producers, and its gas reserves are second only to those of Russia. But Iran's war with Iraq from 1980 to 1988 and continuing internal political instability have greatly reduced its oil exports. The country supplements its economy by mining copper, chromite, iron ore, lead, and zinc. Factory workers manufacture machines, cement, chemicals, petroleum products, processed foods, textiles, and leather goods. Fishing fleets roam the Persian Gulf and the Caspian Sea in search of tuna, sardines, shrimp, carp, salmon, and sturgeon—a huge fish whose eggs yield the tiny, crunchy delicacy called **caviar.** Most of the fish is consumed locally, but the caviar is a valuable export.

Right: Two worlds meet in the Iranian desert—with oil wells of the industrial age towering over a livestock herder whose way of life goes back thousands of years.

Far right: Wool dyers in Esfahan prepare sheep and goat wool for the country's textile industries.

Left: Worshipers and visitors gather outside the magnificent Shrine of Fatimeh in Qom.

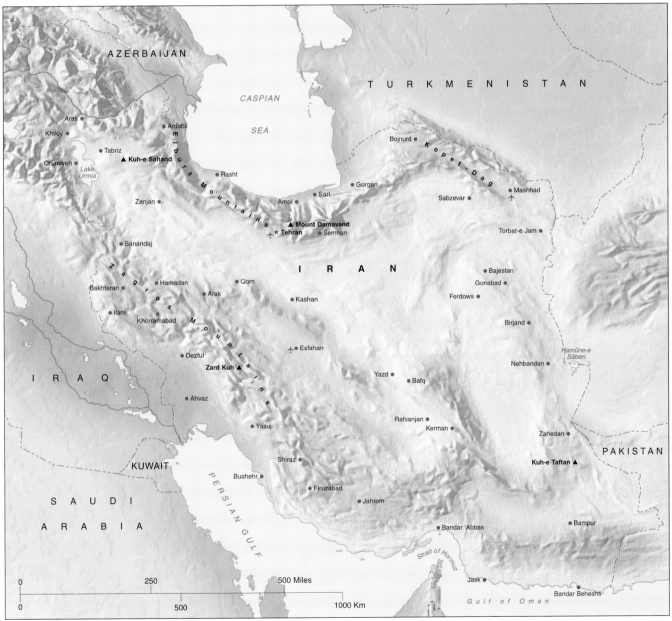

AZERBAIJAN

CASPIAN

SEA

TURKMENISTAN

Aras

Khvoy

Ardabil

Bojnurd

Kopet-Dag

Tabriz

Kuh-e Sahand

Rasht

Mashhad

Orumiyeh

Lake
Urmia

Zanjan

Amol

Sari

Gorgan

Sabzevar

Mount Damavand

Tehran

Semnan

Torbat-e Jam

Sanandaj

IRAN

Bajestan

Zagros

Hamadan

Qom

Gonabad

Bakhtaran

Arak

Kashan

Ferdows

Ilam

Khorramabad

Mountains

Esfahan

Birjand

Dezful

Hamûne-e
Sâberi

Zard Kuh

Yazd

Nehbandan

IRAQ

Ahvaz

Bafq

Yasuj

Rafsanjan

Kerman

Zahedan

PAKISTAN

KUWAIT

Shiraz

Kuh-e Taftan

PERSIAN GULF

Bushehr

Firuzabad

SAUDI

Jahrom

ARABIA

Bandar 'Abbas

Bampur

Strait of Hormuz

Jask

0   250   500 Miles

Gulf of Oman

Bandar Beheshti

0   500   1000 Km

Saudi Arabia and Kuwait

Saudi Arabia

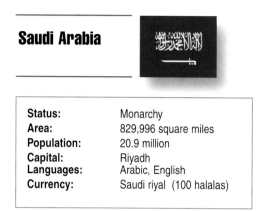

Status:	Monarchy
Area:	829,996 square miles
Population:	20.9 million
Capital:	Riyadh
Languages:	Arabic, English
Currency:	Saudi riyal (100 halalas)

Saudi Arabia is the largest country in the Middle East, but more than 95 percent of its land is desert. A vast rocky plateau stretches across the country's middle. This area is dotted with **oases**—the most fertile of which support farming communities that grow dates, melons, vegetables, wheat, and other crops.

A broad area of sand dunes called An-Nafud lies north of the plateau, merging with the stony Syrian Desert on Saudi Arabia's borders with Jordan and Iraq. South of the plateau, bare rock and patchy vegetation meet a seemingly endless sea of sand dunes. Some of the mounds reach almost 1,000 feet in height. This is the Rub al-Khali (Empty Quarter)—the largest unbroken expanse of sand on earth. The only settlements are a few scattered oases. Most of the desert's inhabitants are nomadic Bedouin herders who travel constantly with their camels, goats, and sheep to find grazing land.

Mountains dominate western Saudi Arabia. They rise sharply from the northern Red Sea, dip slightly as they go south, and rise again to more than 10,000 feet near the border with Yemen. A narrow coastal plain lies between the mountains and the warm waters of the Red Sea. Asir—the southern part of the plain—is the most fertile region in Saudi Arabia.

Roughly three-quarters of the population live in urban areas, such as the capital city of Riyadh in east central Saudi Arabia and in Jidda, Al-Maqnah, and the Islamic holy cities of Mecca and Medina. More than 1.5 million pilgrims make the journey to Mecca every year. Nearly all Saudis are Muslims and are expected to make the *hajj,* or pilgrimage to Mecca, at least once in their life. The country's only non-Muslim residents are foreign-born people who work mostly in the oil fields and in communications, in construction, and in financial industries.

Saudi Arabia is the world's leading oil producer. Thirty years of multibillion-dollar oil revenues have allowed the government to fund a massive modernization program—building schools, colleges, hospitals, airports, and seaports and investing heavily in new industries and agricultural improvements.

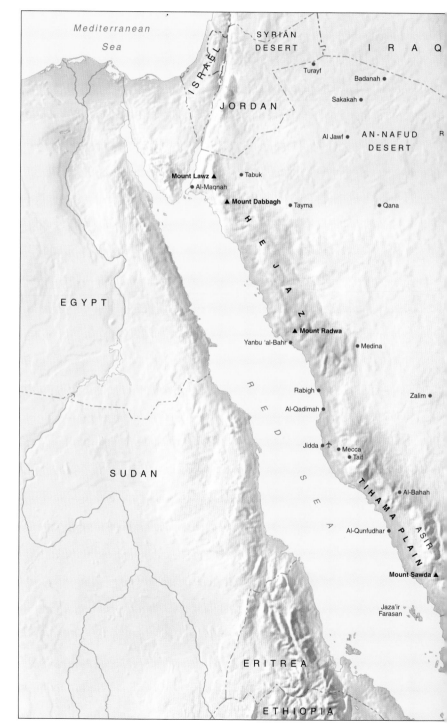

Kuwait

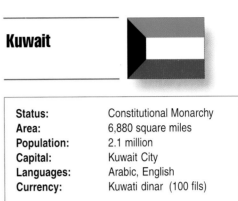

Status:	Constitutional Monarchy
Area:	6,880 square miles
Population:	2.1 million
Capital:	Kuwait City
Languages:	Arabic, English
Currency:	Kuwati dinar (100 fils)

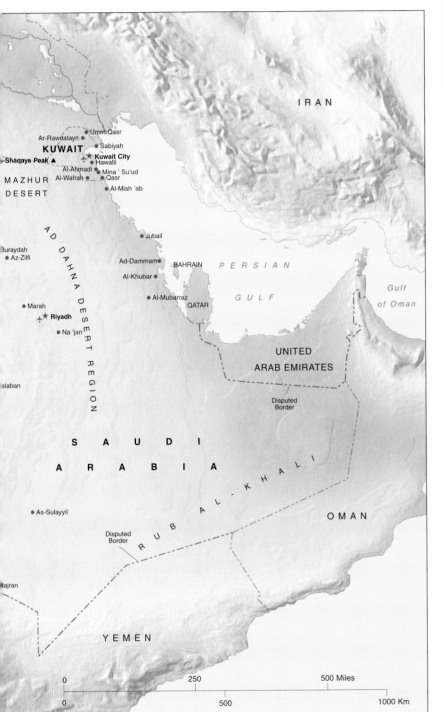

Tiny Kuwait is dwarfed by its enormous neighbors, Iraq and Saudi Arabia, but this small wedge of land on the northwestern shore of the Persian Gulf accounts for about one-tenth of the world's known oil reserves.

Kuwait's oil-related wealth has caused conflict. In response to an oil-pricing dispute, Iraq invaded Kuwait in 1990. Saudi Arabia, fearing an Iraqi invasion on its own territory, assisted Kuwait in forcing out Iraq. A UN-sponsored force eventually freed Kuwait. Although Iraq formally abandoned its claims to Kuwaiti territory in 1994, relations between the two countries have remained strained. Saudi Arabia and Kuwait, on the other hand, have grown closer.

Rainfall is sparse, and most of Kuwait consists of flat, stony desert, where temperatures rise to 104°F in summer. Farmers are able to take advantage of a small coastal strip with milder conditions and a little more rain, but much of the country's food must be imported.

Kuwaitis benefit from free education and health services and no taxes. Women enjoy more freedom and opportunity than they do in many neighboring Arab states. A serious lack of water was eased when the government used oil export revenues to install desalination plants, which turn seawater into fresh water. In 1960 further sources of fresh water were discovered deep underground.

Kuwait is a Muslim country, but laws forbid discrimination against non-Muslims. The country has an unusually varied population for an Islamic state. Arabs from several other Middle East countries live in Kuwait, alongside large numbers of Pakistanis and Indians, many of whom work on the country's numerous big construction projects.

191

Bahrain, Qatar, United Arab Emirates

Bahrain

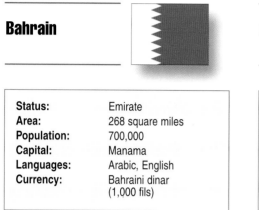

Status:	Emirate
Area:	268 square miles
Population:	700,000
Capital:	Manama
Languages:	Arabic, English
Currency:	Bahraini dinar (1,000 fils)

Qatar

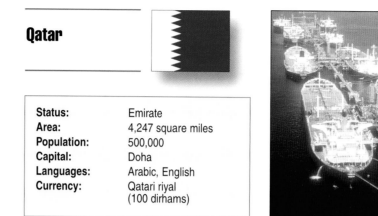

Status:	Emirate
Area:	4,247 square miles
Population:	500,000
Capital:	Doha
Languages:	Arabic, English
Currency:	Qatari riyal (100 dirhams)

Bahrain is a cluster of more than 30 islands in the Persian Gulf, about 20 miles off the eastern tip of Saudi Arabia. The country's capital city, Manama, sits at the northern end of Bahrain Island—the largest and most populated island of the group. A paved causeway provides a direct link to the Saudi Arabian mainland.

Desert covers most of the islands. Before the discovery of petroleum in 1932, Bahrain was poor and underdeveloped. Oil revenues have turned the country into one of the richest in the world. Bahrainis have a very high standard of living. Most people live in comfortable apartments with air conditioning and refrigerators. Education is free, and the country has hundreds of schools, including two universities. Health services are excellent, and the people enjoy a healthy diet of fish, rice, vegetables, and fruit—especially dates.

Rainfall is sparse, averaging just three inches annually, but numerous freshwater springs and wells provide plenty of water for domestic use and for irrigation of the fertile farmland found on northern Bahrain Island. Oil refining is the main industrial activity. The huge refinery on Sitrah Island keeps busy processing the country's petroleum as well as oil delivered by pipeline from Saudi Arabia. Other industries include ship repair, chemicals, and aluminum products, and Bahrain is the major banking center for the Persian Gulf region.

The tiny Arab nation of Qatar occupies a rocky desert peninsula that juts into the Persian Gulf. Saudi Arabia and the United Arab Emirates are Qatar's mainland neighbors. Discovery of oil in the 1940s transformed Qatar from a poor nation of camel herders, **subsistence farmers,** and pearl divers into a wealthy urbanized nation with free education and health services and a very high standard of living.

Oil revenues paid for desalination plants to provide fresh water for homes, hotels, offices, and industrial areas and enabled the government to sink many deep wells to provide water for irrigation. Qatari farmers meet most of the country's vegetable needs and provide some of its grain and fruit, but meat, dairy products, and many manufactured goods are imported. The government owns most of Qatar's industries, which range from oil refining and petrochemicals to commercial fishing, fertilizer production, and plastics.

Above left: Oil tankers are being loaded at a deepwater jetty in Qatar.

Above: One of the many large oil storage facilities in the United Arab Emirates

Right: A traditional bazaar (market) in Abu Dhabi

United Arab Emirates

Status:	Federation of Seven Emirates
Area:	32,278 square miles
Population:	2.8 million
Capital:	Abu Dhabi
Languages:	Arabic, English
Currency:	UAE dirham (100 fils)

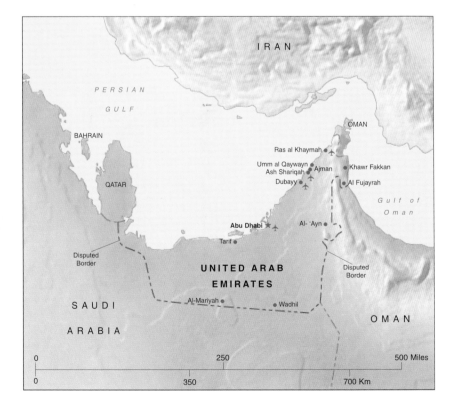

The United Arab **Emirates** is a **federation** of seven independent states bordering the southern shore of the Persian Gulf. The member-states and their capital cities, from west to east, are Abu Dhabi, Dubayy, Ash Shariqah, Ajman, Umm al Qaywayn, Ras al Khaymah, and Al Fujayrah. Abu Dhabi is the federation's capital and second largest city. Dubayy is the largest urban area and the federation's principal port and business center. Formerly a British **protectorate,** the seven countries were once called the Trucial States. Six of the states gained independence in 1971 and were joined by the seventh, Ras al Khaymah, the following year.

The countries that formed the United Arab Emirates, like its neighbor Qatar, used to be dependent on camel herding, fishing, trading, and subsistence farming. Life for its people changed dramatically with the discovery of oil in the 1950s. The modern federation has one of the world's highest standards of living.

Yemen and Oman

Yemen

Status:	Republic
Area:	203,850 square miles
Population:	16.4 million
Capital:	Sana'a
Language:	Arabic
Currency:	Yemeni rial (100 fils)

Shaped like a fat check mark cradling the southern edge of Saudi Arabia, Yemen occupies the southwestern corner of the Arabian Peninsula. Yemen's territory includes the Red Sea islands of Kamaran and Perim and Socotra Island in the Arabian Sea. Modern Yemen was formed in 1990 by the joining of two separate nations—South Yemen and North Yemen. South Yemen tried to pull out in 1994, and bitter fighting erupted. Peace was restored, with UN help, but relations between the south and the dominant north remain strained.

Yemen consists of rugged mountains in the west and a desert in the east that spreads northward into Saudi Arabia's Rub al-Khali. Temperatures are very hot and humid along the narrow coastal plain, but the country enjoys cooler, milder conditions in the highlands, where fertile valleys provide Yemen's best farmland. Yemenis cultivate crops in the highlands and on scattered desert oases, and they graze sheep, goats, and camels in the drier desert areas. Fishing crews ply the abundant waters along the coastline.

A large oil refinery at Aden processes oil from Yemeni fields in the northwest, as well as oil from other Persian Gulf states. The government has used oil revenues to boost agriculture—building dams and irrigation projects—and to provide the population with improved schools, medical facilities, and housing. Aden is home to one of the region's main trading ports, providing repair yards and other services for ship operators. Construction projects are the other main employer, but hundreds of small factories and local craftspeople produce handmade brass and copper goods, saddles and harnesses, pottery, jewelry, and the ornate daggers (*jambiyas*) that form part of traditional Arab dress.

Left: The minaret of a mosque overlooks the town of Raydah in the western part of Yemen.

Oman

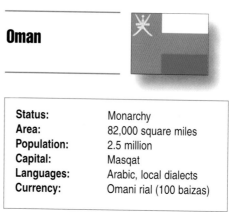

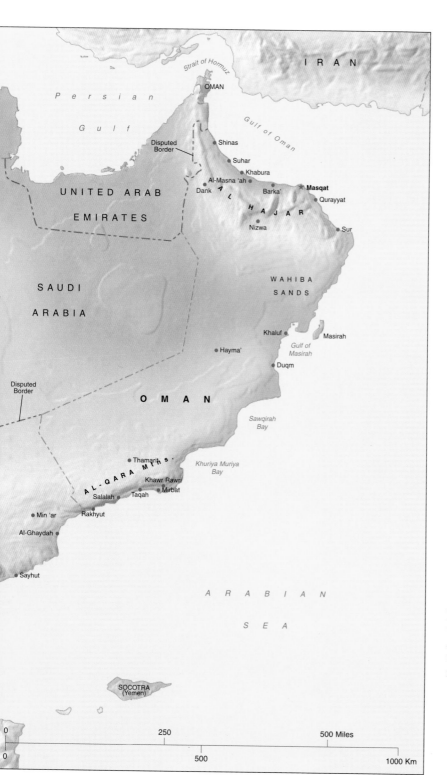

Status:	Monarchy
Area:	82,000 square miles
Population:	2.5 million
Capital:	Masqat
Languages:	Arabic, local dialects
Currency:	Omani rial (100 baizas)

Oman curves around the southeastern corner of the Arabian Peninsula, exposing a long coastline on the Arabian Sea and a short stretch of coastline facing Iran across the Gulf of Oman. The narrow **Strait of Hormuz,** off Oman's northernmost tip, guards the entrance to the Persian Gulf. Much of the world's oil is shipped through this narrow seaway.

Oman shares its borders with Yemen, Saudi Arabia, and the United Arab Emirates. Similar to its neighbors, Oman is mostly desert. One of the earth's hottest areas, the country often sees temperatures rise to 120°F, sometimes soaring above 130°F. Rainfall is meager. Most villages draw their water from deep wells, some of them part of a canal system from ancient times. The land is very dry, and farmers in small, scattered villages struggle to grow enough grain, vegetables, and fruit to meet their needs. Camels, goats, and sheep provide meat, milk, and hides for leather. Along the coast, most Omanis work in fisheries or on large date palm plantations. Alfalfa, coconuts, onions, tomatoes, and wheat prosper in the most fertile areas.

Oman embraces its history and cultural ways. Most of the people wear traditional dress and nearly all are devout Muslims. Money from oil exports funds an ongoing program to build schools and adult education centers, but literacy levels lag behind those of many Persian Gulf states.

Russian Federation (Asian Russia)

Russian Federation

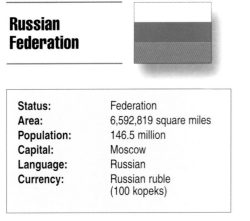

Status:	Federation
Area:	6,592,819 square miles
Population:	146.5 million
Capital:	Moscow
Language:	Russian
Currency:	Russian ruble (100 kopeks)

Climate and vegetation define four broad zones that stretch west to east across Asian Russia. The extreme northern reaches support a bleak landscape of mosses, shrubs, and dwarf trees called tundra. The soil is permanently frozen, and winters are long and harsh. Summers offer a brief respite, during which the soil's surface thaws and some vegetation grows—enough to feed

Above: Asian Russia—east of the Urals—is almost three times the size of the country's European segment. Russia is a sparsely populated land of plains, plateaus, and forests. A train journey from Moscow to Vladivostok takes seven days and passes through eight time zones.

Right: Vladivostok, on the southeastern coast of Siberia, is Russia's most important Pacific seaport. Shipyards, fish canneries, and factories producing mining equipment and other heavy machinery are the principal employers.

ARCTIC OCEAN

Saint Lawrence I.
(U.S.)

Wrangel I.

Bering Strait

B e r i n g

Mys Shmidta

Chukchi Peninsula

Gulf of
Anadyr

S e a

Franz
Josef Land

E a s t

Pevek
Ayon I.

Anadyr

*Barents
Sea*

Komsomolets I.

S i b e r i a n

Bilibino

Koryak Mountains

New Siberia I.

S e a

Nizhnekolymsk

Novaya Zemlya

October
Revolution I.

Bol'shevik I.

Kotel'nyy I.

New Siberian Is.
Lyakhovskiye
Ostrova

Srednekolymsk

Korf

Karagin I.

*Kara
Sea*

L a p t e v

Novosibirsk

Kolyma

Palana

Belyy I.

Byrranga Mtns.

Bol'shoy
Begichev I.

S e a

Kolyma Mountains

Kamchatka Peninsula

Tiksi

Cherskiy Range

Kuril Islands

North Siberian

E a s t

Oimyakon

Magadan

Petropavlovsk-
Kamchatskiy

Ural Mtns.

Lowland

Verkhoyanskiy Khrebet

Noril'sk

Central

S i b e r i a n

Okhotsk

Gulf of Ob

Udachnyy

Sangar

S e a   o f

Igarka

Siberian

Yakutsk

O k h o t s k

Nadym

Lena

Nyurba

H i g h l a n d s

Dzhugdzhur Range

Mimyy

Lower Tunguska

Tura

Lensk

Surgut

W e s t

P l a t e a u

Yenisey

Aldan

Sakhalin I.

S i b e r i a n

R U S S I A

Neryungri

Badzhal'skiy Mtns.

Komsomol'sk
na-Amure

Nizhnevartovsk

Bodaybo

Tynda

Amur

Sikhote-alin Mtns.

Plain

Angara

Ust'-Ilimsk

Zeya

Tatar Strait

Krasnoyarsk

Ust'-Kut

Shimanovsk

Yuzhno-
Sakhalinsk

Tomsk

Bratsk
Reservoir

Khabarovsk

Ob

Bratsk

Lake
Baikal

Kemerovo

Yenisey

Shimanovsk
Blagoveshchensk

Vyazemskiy

Soya Strait

Omsk

Novosibirsk

Yablonovyy Range

Nerchinsk

Barnaul

Novokuznetsk

Ust-Ordinskiy

Chita

Baley

J A P A N

Abakan

Angarsk
Irkutsk

Ulan Ude

Borzya

Prokopyevsk

Sayan Mtns.

▲ Munku-Sardyk

Aginskoyo

Spassk-Dal'niy

Kyzyl

Kyakhta

Ussurlysk

KAZAKHSTAN

Vladivostok

Nakhodka

Sea of

M O N G O L I A

Japan

**NORTH
KOREA**

**SOUTH
KOREA**

C H I N A

0   500   1000   1500 Miles

0   500   1000   1500   2000   2500 Km

Russian Federation (Asian Russia)

reindeer, hares, lemmings, and ptarmigan and the wolves, foxes, stoats, owls, and hawks that hunt them.

Dark **coniferous** forests of pine, fir, and spruce lie south of the tundra, merging into **deciduous** forests of birch, oak, aspen, and maple. Deer, elk, beavers, brown bears, and squirrels are typical forest animals. Rolling grassy plains called the steppes stretch across Russia south of the forests. Thick dark soils in this region provide Russia's best farmland. The steppes offer little cover from predators. Animals able to survive here are those that burrow—hamsters, susliks, lemmings, and marmots—and the eagles and buzzards that patrol the skies. Deserts and mountains dominate Russia's southern edge, forming natural borders with its huge southern neighbors—Kazakhstan, Mongolia, and China.

Asian Russia has three major land divisions—the West Siberian Plain, the Central Siberian Plateau, and the East Siberian Highlands. The Urals form a long, narrow

Left: Oil pipelines run for hundreds of miles across the forested landscape, carrying crude oil from the Siberian oil fields to European Russia, where demand for energy is greatest and where the largest refineries are located. The zigzag construction allows the pipeline to expand and contract without cracking as temperatures rise and fall.

north-south barrier between European Russia and the westernmost Asian Russian landform—the West Siberian Plain. East of the mountains, the West Siberian Plain stretches for nearly 1,000 miles. The northern section of the plain is low and marshy. In the southern section, farmers use the fertile soil to raise barley, oats, rye, potatoes, sugar beets, fruits and vegetables, and fodder crops for beef and dairy cattle. The plain also contains rich oil and gas fields, and miners take out coal, iron ore, lead, and zinc from deposits along the mountainous southern edge. Omsk, Novosibirsk, Tomsk, and Novokuznetsk are the main manufacturing centers of the West Siberian Plain.

The Central Siberian Plateau lies east of the Yenisey River. The topography ranges from 2,000 feet above sea level to 11,451 at the top of Munku-Sardyk, the tallest peak in the Sayan Mountains. Forests cover much of the land. The plateau lies in the heart of the huge Asian landmass, far from any moderating effects of the ocean. In winter it is one of the coldest places on earth. January temperatures in northeastern Siberia average below -50°F and can plunge to -90°F. Few people live in this region's far north, but industrial cities such as Krasnoyarsk and Irkutsk have developed in the south, where miners extract gold, nickel, tungsten, tin, and other minerals.

Beyond the Lena River, the land rises to the East Siberian Highlands—a vast empty wilderness of pine forests and mountain ranges. The highlands stretch unbroken to the Chukchi Peninsula, which faces the United States across the narrow Bering Strait, and to the leaf-shaped and volcanic Kamchatka Peninsula that partly encloses the Sea of Okhotsk. Inhabitants of this region cluster around the inland city of Yakutsk, around Khabarovsk on the Amur River, and around the industrial city and seaport of Vladivostok on the Sea of Japan's northwestern coast.

Below: A huge roll of heavy packaging paper is hoisted off the production machine at a paper mill in Siberia.

Kazakhstan

Kazakhstan

Status:	Republic
Area:	1.05 million square miles
Population:	15.4 million
Capital:	Astana
Languages:	Kazakh, Russian
Currency:	Tenge (100 tiyn)

One of western Asia's largest countries, Kazakhstan ranks ninth in the world in land area. In 1991 Kazakhstan gained its freedom from the Soviet Union after 70 years under Communist rule. Since becoming an independent **republic,** Kazakhstan's government has built a new capital, Astana, near the center of the country. Almaty, the former capital, lies close to the border with China and remains Kazakhstan's largest city and principal commercial and cultural center.

Kazakhstan extends almost 1,800 miles east to west, up to 900 miles north to south, and boasts a variety of landscapes. Dry lowland plains wrap around the northern tip of the Caspian Sea. The Karagiye Basin, between the coastal town of Aqtau and the Turkmenistan border, is the lowest point in the country at 433 feet below sea level. Rolling steppes cover much of northern Kazakhstan, and sandy deserts dominate the country's southern region. The rugged Altai Shan (mountains) rise on the country's northeastern border with Russia, and the Tian Shan form the southeastern border with Kyrgyzstan and China. Rivers rising in the mountains feed Lake Balkhash, the largest lake in the country at 6,670 square miles.

The dry grassy plains that cover much of the country are not well suited to farming. Most Kazakhs were traditionally nomads, traveling with the sheep, goats, camels, cattle, and horses that provided their transportation, food, and materials for clothing and shelter. The traditional Kazakh home was a portable tentlike structure, called a yurt, made of thick felt mats covering a frame of bent poles. The yurt provided a warm, windproof shelter in the bitterly cold winter and cool shade in the hot summer months. Some Kazakhs still live as their ancestors did, but most rural villagers live in houses.

Prime farmland lies in northeastern Kazakhstan where farmers sow barley, wheat, cotton, and vegetables and graze sheep, and beef and dairy herds. During the Communist era, Kazakhstan's government greatly expanded agricultural production by irrigating dry western lands with water from feeder rivers to the Aral Sea. While this enabled some farmers to grow rice, grain crops, and vegetables, the Aral Sea shrank by 70 percent. These irrigation projects left much of the former sea glistening with salt pans and littered with the rotting hulks of stranded fishing boats.

Kazakhstan is rich in mineral resources. Miners in the northeast extract coal, while those in the central and eastern regions mine copper, zinc, iron, lead, tin, titanium, vanadium, thallium, and other valuable minerals. Oil and gas are pumped from fields beneath the Caspian Sea.

Factories in the principal industrial towns of Almaty and Shymkent in the southeast and Karaganda and Pavlodar in the northeast provide textiles, chemicals, leather goods, machinery, electrical goods, and food products.

Right: A Kazakh horseman looks across the rolling forests and grasslands that supported his nomadic ancestors and their livestock for thousands of years.

Below left: Kazakhstan has a long tradition of creating fine buildings from its principal natural construction material—wood. This magnificent example stands in Almaty, the historic former capital and principal cultural center.

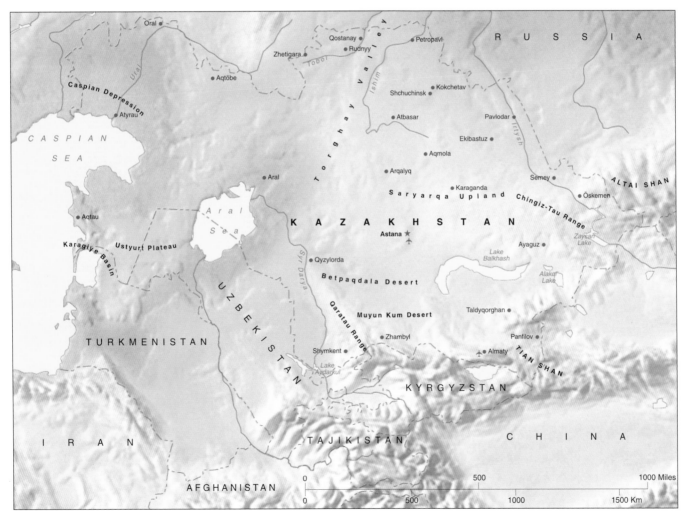

Uzbekistan and Turkmenistan

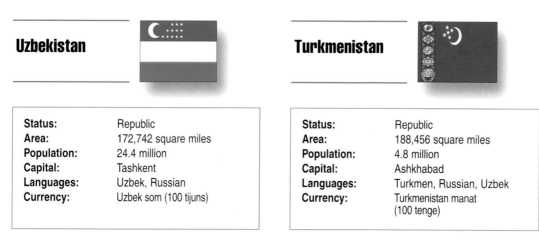

Uzbekistan

Status:	Republic
Area:	172,742 square miles
Population:	24.4 million
Capital:	Tashkent
Languages:	Uzbek, Russian
Currency:	Uzbek som (100 tijuns)

Turkmenistan

Status:	Republic
Area:	188,456 square miles
Population:	4.8 million
Capital:	Ashkhabad
Languages:	Turkmen, Russian, Uzbek
Currency:	Turkmenistan manat (100 tenge)

Uzbekistan lies in western central Asia and shares borders with Kazakhstan, Kyrgyzstan, Tajikistan, Turkmenistan, and Afghanistan. The latter is the only one of Uzbekistan's neighbors that wasn't a former Soviet republic.

The vast barren wilderness of the Kyzyl Kum Desert fills the country's center. Few people, apart from workers in scattered mining settlements, live in this region. Farther west, dry grasslands and deserts border the Aral Sea, merging with the arid plains and plateaus of Kazakhstan and Turkmenistan. Most inhabitants of western Uzbekistan live in small towns and villages clustered along the banks of the Amu Darya (River) and its tributaries.

About 80 percent of the Uzbeks are farmers, a fact that concentrates the population in southern and eastern Uzbekistan. The land in these areas rises to meet the Tian Shan and the Pamir Mountains. The region's rich soil and mountain streams support fertile crops such as rice, grains, vegetables, melons, and cotton—the country's principal export crop. Sheep and dairy cattle are significant livestock, supplying mutton and milk for the country's traditional dishes. The high-quality wool of the Karakul sheep is another important export.

Uzbekistan's miners extract coal, copper, gold, petroleum, and natural gas. Industrial contributions include textiles, chemicals, farm machinery, and fertilizers. Traditional craft workers in rural areas create carpets, shawls, jewelry, ceramics, wood products, and metal goods.

Dominated by the large, central Kara-Kum Desert, Turkmenistan is ringed by Kazakhstan, Uzbekistan, Afghanistan, Iran, and the Caspian Sea. The country's landscapes include low coastal plains hugging the Caspian Sea, mountains along the border with Iran, and the broad Amu Darya Valley forming the northern boundary with Uzbekistan. The Kara-Bogaz Gol, a deep gulf near the Caspian shore, is the country's lowest point at 102 feet below sea level. Summers are very hot, with temperatures reaching 120°F. Winters are bitterly cold. Thermometers hover near zero for many weeks. Rainfall is scarce, providing just a few inches annually to most of the country.

Small settlements are located at desert oases, but most Turkmen live by water—near the coast of the Caspian Sea, beside the 750-mile long Kara-Kum Canal, or in the irrigated highland river valleys. Farmers in these regions grow grains, vegetables, and grapes for local consumption, but more than half the cultivated land in Turkmenistan is committed to cotton, the country's principal crop. Many farmers supplement their crops by raising sheep, camels, pigs, and horses.

Turkmenistan's chief natural resources are oil and gas. The mining industry provides copper, lead, mercury, gold, and other minerals, including limestone and sand for Turkmen homes. Factories—concentrated around the capital city of Ashkhabad and in the city of Chardzhou—produce textiles, glassware, petrochemical products, and cement.

Right: A Turkmen woman wears a traditional costume of brightly patterned fabrics, a headdress, and handmade jewelry.

Far right: An Uzbek miner tends a large coal-cutting machine in one of the country's modern mines.

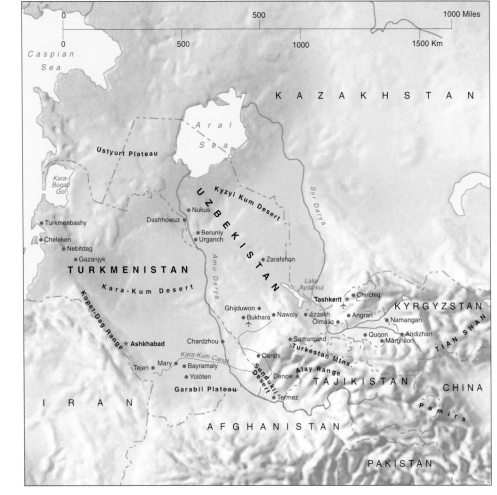

Below: An Uzbek elder wears the traditional wound cloth headdress known as a *termez*.

Kyrgyzstan and Tajikistan

Kyrgyzstan

Status:	Republic
Area:	76,641 square miles
Population:	4.7 million
Capital:	Bishkek
Languages:	Kyrgyz, Russian
Currency:	Kyrgyz som (100 tyin)

Tajikistan

Status:	Republic
Area:	55,251 square miles
Population:	6.2 million
Capital:	Dushanbe
Languages:	Tajik, Uzbek, Russian
Currency:	Tajik ruble (100 tanga)

Kyrgyzstan is a small, landlocked country high in the Tian Shan and the Alai Mountains of western central Asia. Rugged and inhospitable, three-quarters of the country sit more than 5,000 feet above sea level—most of it covered in glaciers and snowfields. Pobedy Peak, Kyrgyzstan's highest summit, towers 24,406 feet over the eastern border with China. Winter temperatures often fall to -20°F in the mountains. Sheltered valleys and lowlands experience warm, dry summers and cold winters. Rainfall is minimal, so the country taps mountain rivers for water to use on crops, in homes, and by the industrial sector.

The people of Kyrgyzstan once wandered across the lowlands and foothills, grazing their sheep, goats, pigs, cattle, and horses. Few people still follow the traditional nomadic ways, but livestock continues to be vital to the economy. Farmers grow cotton, rice, fruits, sugar beets and other vegetables, and mulberry—a tree whose leaves feed silkworms.

Kyrgyz miners extract the country's reserves of coal and minerals such as uranium, mercury, lead, gold, and zinc. The country also holds untapped oil reserves. Manufacturing industries, concentrated mostly around the capital city of Bishkek, use these resources to produce textiles, machinery, domestic appliances, and electronics. The government is expanding the industrial sector and attracting foreign investors, making Kyrgyzstan one of the fastest-growing economies among former Soviet republics.

Tajikistan, like its neighbor Kyrgyzstan to the north, is a rugged, mountainous country. Half of its land reaches 10,000 feet above sea level. The Pamir Mountains to the southeast form a border with Pakistan. The Zeravshan, Turkestan, and Alai Mountains dominate central and northern Tajikistan. The country's valleys and lowlands experience long, hot, dry summers and cool winters. Both urban and rural populations rely for water on the country's rivers. Irrigation projects in eastern and northern Tajikistan support the country's agriculture.

Cotton is Tajikistan's most significant commercial crop, but farmers also grow many fruits, vegetables, and grains. Cattle, chickens, and sheep provide meat, milk, eggs, wool, and leather, and domesticated yaks graze on the high mountain slopes. Some farms specialize in growing mulberry trees for silkworm farms, while others harvest eucalyptus, geraniums, and other plants whose oils and fragrances are used to make perfumes.

A huge dam at Nurek on the Vakhsh River supplies hydroelectric power to a large aluminum refinery and to other industries concentrated around the capital city of Dushanbe. The Nurek Reservoir provides water for the cities and farms of western Tajikistan. Tajik miners extract antimony, lead, tungsten, uranium, and zinc, and the country possesses large gold and silver reserves. Unlike neighboring Kyrgyzstan, economic develop-ment in Tajikistan has suffered throughout the 1990s from internal conflict and civil war.

Right: A few Kyrgyz families still follow the traditional ways, living in tentlike yurts and constantly moving from pasture to pasture with their livestock. The yurt, made of felt, is warm, comfortable, and immensely practical in the rugged conditions.

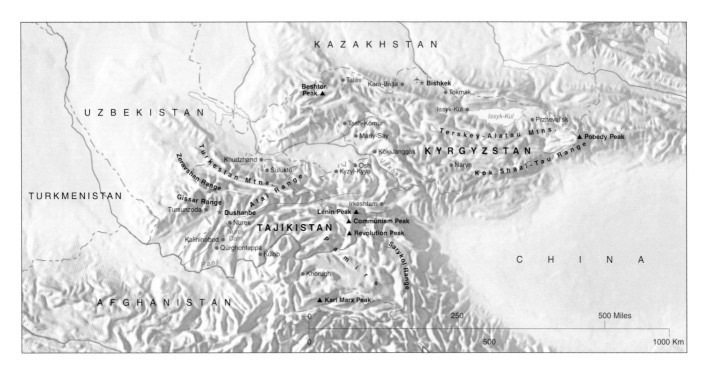

Georgia, Armenia, Azerbaijan

Georgia

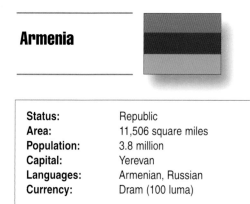

Status:	Republic
Area:	26,911 square miles
Population:	5.4 million
Capital:	Tbilisi
Languages:	Georgian, Russian, Armenian
Currency:	Lari (100 tetri)

Georgia broke away from the former Soviet Union in 1991. The country's independence has been marred by ethnic conflicts between the dominant Georgians, who comprise 70 percent of the population, and the peoples of South Ossetia, Abkhazia, and Adjaria who demand self-government for their regions. Years of unrest have damaged the country's economy and have slowed development.

Mountains dominate northern and southern Georgia. The broad, fertile Kura River Valley in central Georgia and the western lowland plains bordering the Black Sea provide excellent farmland. These areas have hot summers and mild winters and receive ample rainfall.

Farmers in the western plains grow citrus fruits, tea, and **tung trees,** whose seeds yield valuable oil used in paints and varnishes. Wheat, barley, and vegetables are the main crops farther inland. Many farmers also cultivate flowers and herbs for the perfume industry. Mulberry trees support a thriving silk industry. The soil on sunny hillsides produces grapes for making wine. Large forests in the mountainous regions provide raw materials for lumber and plywood factories.

Georgia's miners excavate many minerals, but food processing remains the country's primary industry, and food products are its main export. Coastal resorts along the Black Sea attract large numbers of tourists, many of them from neighboring Russia.

Right: Turkish-style bathhouses nestle among modern apartment blocks in the old sector of the Georgian capital of Tbilisi.

Armenia

Status:	Republic
Area:	11,506 square miles
Population:	3.8 million
Capital:	Yerevan
Languages:	Armenian, Russian
Currency:	Dram (100 luma)

Nestled between Georgia, Azerbaijan, Iran, and Turkey, this tiny state is the smallest of the 15 former Soviet republics and one of five that declared independence in 1991. A mountainous plateau, 5,000 feet above sea level, covers most of the country. The plateau is dissected by deep river gorges and is dotted with towering peaks reaching higher than 12,000 feet above sea level. Armenia also boasts more than 100 lakes. Forests of beech, oak, and **hornbeam** blanket parts of Armenia's eastern mountains. Short grasses and scrub cover much of the rest.

Low rainfall in the valleys combined with short hot summers, very cold winters, and a lack of investment have kept agricultural productivity quite low. Farmers grow wheat, barley, potatoes, walnuts, and quinces and other fruits on fertile black soil in the valleys, but farming is most productive on irrigated land in the Araks River Valley on Armenia's borders with Turkey and Iran.

Vanadzor, Gyumri, and Yerevan in the northwest and Kapan in the southeast are important manufacturing centers. Hydroelectric power stations on fast-flowing rivers such as the Hrazdan provide power for the country's main industries—machinery, chemicals, electronics, and textiles. These industries, along with the copper, lead, and zinc produced by Armenia's miners, account for about two-thirds of Armenia's economic production.

Above: Roadside vendors sell fruit at Garni in Armenia.

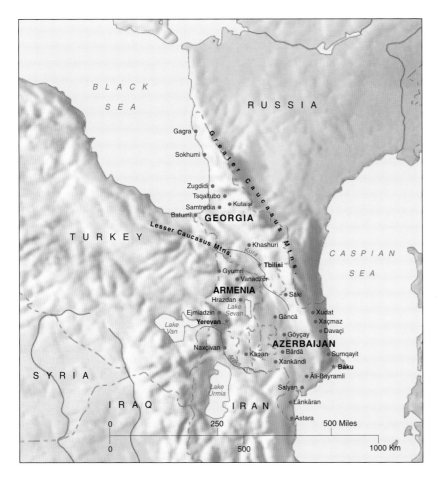

Azerbaijan

Status:	Republic
Area:	33,436 square miles
Population:	7.7 million
Capital:	Baku
Language:	Azeri Turkish
Currency:	Azeri manat (100 qepik)

Azerbaijan is divided into three distinct land regions. The Greater Caucasus Mountains run east to west near the country's northern edge, separating Azerbaijan from Georgia and Russia and marking a line between the continents of Europe and Asia. Rocky highlands rise in the west and southwest. Between the two highland regions, a broad, lowland plain slopes down to the Caspian Sea. The small autonomous republic of Naxçivan, which is geographically separate but still belongs politically to Azerbaijan, lies beyond Azerbaijan's southwestern border and is surrounded by Armenia.

Oil fields near the capital city of Baku and beneath the Caspian Sea provide Azerbaijan's principal source of income. The country also extracts aluminum, copper, iron, and salt. Factories in the main industrial centers of Baku, Gäncä, Säki, Xankändi, and Naxçivan produce aluminum, machinery, chemicals, textiles, cement, and timber products.

Azerbaijan depends heavily on its waterways. Hydroelectric stations use river water flowing from the surrounding mountains to power much of the country's industrial sector. Rivers also irrigate farms on the dry central plain, where rainfall is generally minimal. Lowland farmers grow grains, cotton, vegetables, fruits, and tea. Those in the upland regions raise sheep, goats, and cattle and grow fodder crops for winter animal feed.

The Great Wall of China at Shanxi, China.

SOUTHERN and EASTERN ASIA

SOUTHERN and EASTERN ASIA

The southern and eastern sections of the huge Asian continent comprise a land area that contains almost every kind of landscape imaginable, every climatic extreme on earth, and a kaleidoscope of peoples with widely different languages, religions, lifestyles, and economic conditions.

Southern and eastern Asia stretches west to east for more than 3,700 miles from Pakistan to the Pacific coast of China. North to south covers 4,000 miles from China's northern border with Russia to the tropical islands of Indonesia. Mount Everest, the world's highest mountain, towers 29,028 feet above sea level in the eastern Himalayas, while some of the world's deepest ocean trenches plunge six and a half miles below sea level off Japan and the Philippines.

Vast rolling steppes, high plateaus, and huge deserts dominate the western and northern parts of the region. To the south and east, densely forested mountains and hills cover much of the land. Some of the world's mightiest rivers—the Ganges, the Brahmaputra, the Mekong, the Chang (Yangtze), and the Huang He (Yellow)—pass powerfully through the region, crossing fertile coastal plains and broad deltas to reach the ocean.

The peoples and lifestyles of southern and eastern Asia are as varied as their landscapes. Mongolia's livestock farmers graze their sheep and cattle on vast plains. Rice farmers in the mountains of the Philippines plant their crops on small steep hillside terraces constructed 2,000 years ago. Factory workers in many southern Asian countries work from dawn till dusk for very low wages. And hunger, water shortages, and inadequate health and educational services are a fact of life for millions. But alongside the nations with less in the way of services are some of the world's most powerful and dynamic economies. Japan is one of the world's leading manufacturers of cars, electronic goods, textiles, and household appliances. Farther south are other world-ranking industrial and commercial centers, including Taiwan, Singapore, and Hong Kong (part of China).

In addition to economic powerhouses, there are population powerhouses in southern and eastern Asia, too. India and China together are home to 37 percent of the world's population. With the populations of Indonesia and Bangladesh added in, these four nations alone account for 43 percent of the world's people—but they all inhabit a combined land area that represents just 8 percent of the earth's total. These sorts of contrasts make southern and eastern Asia among the most complex areas of the world.

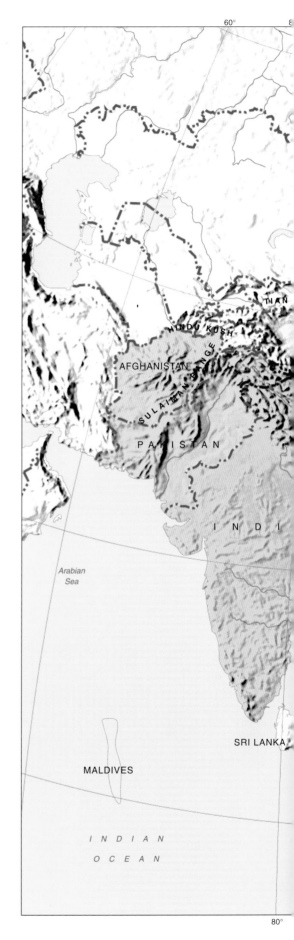

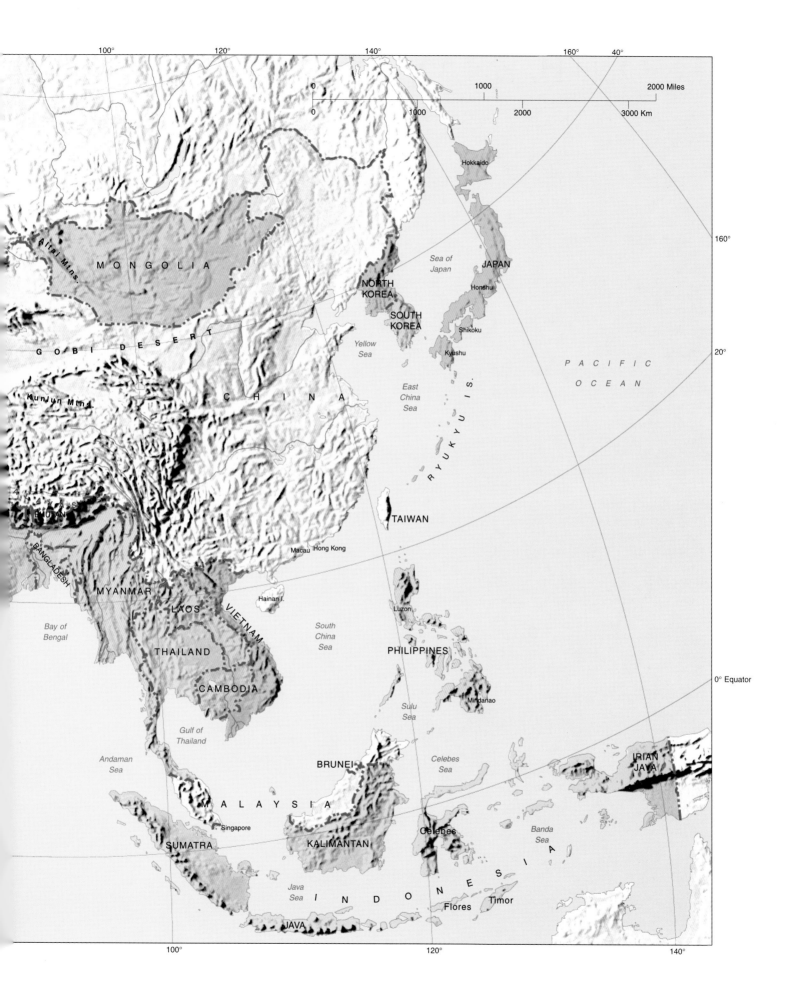

100°   120°   140°   160°   40°

0   1000   2000 Miles

0   1000   2000   3000 Km

Altai Mtns.

MONGOLIA

Hokkaido

160°

Sea of
Japan

JAPAN

NORTH
KOREA

SOUTH
KOREA

Honshu

GOBI DESERT

20°

Yellow
Sea

Shikoku

Kyushu

Kun Jun Mtns.

CHINA

East
China
Sea

PACIFIC
OCEAN

R Y U K Y U   I S.

BHUTAN

TAIWAN

BANGLADESH

Macau Hong Kong

MYANMAR

Hainan I.

LAOS

VIETNAM

Luzon

Bay of
Bengal

THAILAND

South
China
Sea

PHILIPPINES

0° Equator

CAMBODIA

Mindanao

Andaman
Sea

Gulf of
Thailand

Sulu
Sea

Celebes
Sea

IRIAN
JAVA

BRUNEI

MALAYSIA

Singapore

Celebes

Banda
Sea

SUMATRA

KALIMANTAN

I   N   D   O   N   E   S   I   A

Java
Sea

Flores

Timor

JAVA

211

China

China

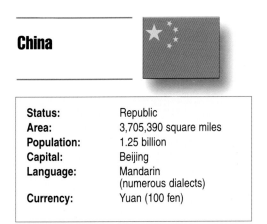

Status:	Republic
Area:	3,705,390 square miles
Population:	1.25 billion
Capital:	Beijing
Language:	Mandarin (numerous dialects)
Currency:	Yuan (100 fen)

China has by far the largest population of any nation in the world, with more than 1,250 million people. It is also one of the world's largest countries by land area. China's vast territory is also enormously varied in topography and climate. The rugged Tian Shan, the Pamir Mountains, and the Karakoram Mountains rise in the west, forming a high, cold, rocky barrier between China and Kazakhstan, Kyrgyzstan, Tajikistan, and Pakistan. The eastern part of the Tian Shan range extends across northwestern China becoming the Mongolian Uplands—a dry, high desert region with few inhabitants. The Gobi Desert's stony expanse forms part of this arid plateau. Daytime temperatures in the deserts can soar past 100°F in summer, plunging to -30°F during the icy winter nights.

North and east of the highlands lie large areas of loess—fine, yellowish soil formed from the clay deposits left behind by glaciers, then blown around and dumped in thick layers by the wind. The soils, though fertile, are soft and easily eroded. One of China's great rivers, the Huang He (Yellow River) flows across this region. The river takes its name from the huge amounts of yellow mud that stain its waters. Little rain falls in northern China, and the winters are long and very cold. Average January temperatures drop well below freezing. Farmers in the north concentrate on hardy crops like winter wheat, corn, and millet.

The towering Himalayas and the lofty Plateau of Tibet dominate southwestern China. The Himalayas contain the world's highest peak, Mount Everest, which at 29,028 feet is a legendary mountain to climb. Most of the plateau consists of bare rock, gravel, and snow fields, but farmers are able to graze hardy yaks on the sparse mountain pastures and to grow vegetables and grains in some of the sheltered valleys and low-lying areas.

China's Eastern Lowlands form a long narrow north-south belt of hilly country dissected by broad river valleys such as the Chang (Yangtze). The lowlands support much of China's most productive crop-

Below: A goatherd tends his flock near Yang-chou in China's Eastern Lowlands, with the hills of the Mongolian Uplands rising in the distance.

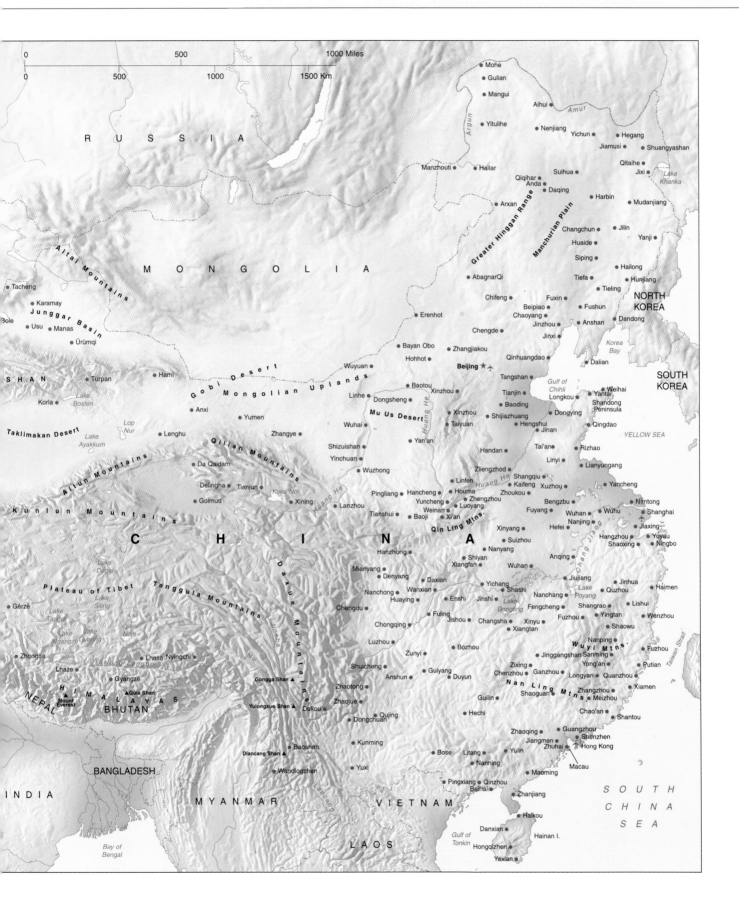

land. Farmers grow wheat, rice, and vegetables, and raise cattle, pigs, and poultry. These lowlands also contain some of China's largest coalfields and iron ore deposits. Extensive forests wedged between the lowlands and the Pacific Coast supply premium timber for construction projects. Just beyond the trees, the coast is dotted with several natural deepwater harbors.

A small, circular lowland called the Sichuan Basin, on the eastern edge of the Plateau of Tibet, provides a second important agricultural region. The climate here is mild, and the hilly land is broken up with fertile valleys. Most farmers cultivate terraced fields to make the best use of every available acre. Primary crops are rice, corn, potatoes, cabbage, apples and pears, sugar beets, soybeans, and tea. Nonfood crops include rubber, cotton, and tobacco.

Steep wooded hills and rocky mountains cover most of southeastern China. Much of

Below: Flooded rice fields, known as rice paddies, cover much of the Xi Jiang river valley in the Guangxi region in southeastern China.

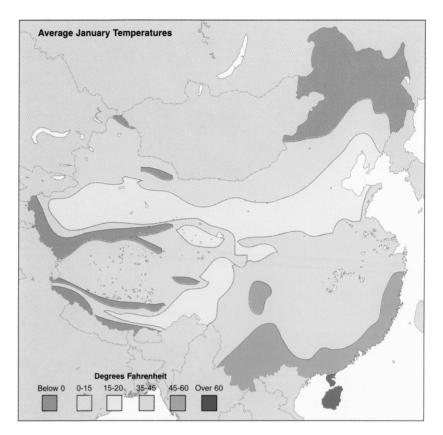

Average January Temperatures

Degrees Fahrenheit

Below 0   0-15   15-20   35-45   45-60   Over 60

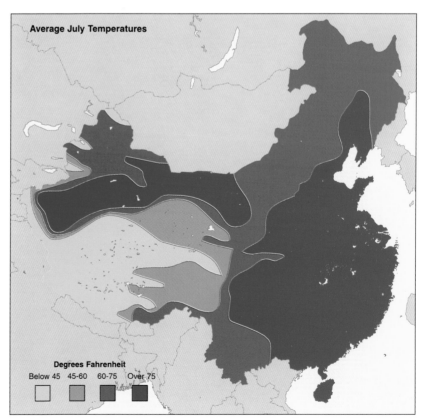

Average July Temperatures

Degrees Fahrenheit

Below 45   45-60   60-75   Over 75

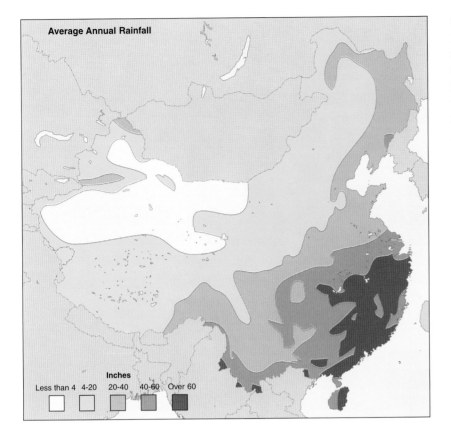

Average Annual Rainfall

Inches

Less than 4 | 4-20 | 20-40 | 40-60 | Over 60

the land is too steep for farming, but the valleys contain good cropland, and the wide delta of the Xi Jiang (West River)—southern China's principal waterway—supports deep, fertile soil. Southeastern China enjoys a tropical climate with mild winters, hot summers, and plentiful rainfall. Farmers here grow many varieties of grains, vegetables, and fruits and tend large herds of cattle, sheep, goats, pigs, chickens and ducks. China's farmers raise about one-third of the world's pigs, using them not only for their meat but also for their manure, which is an excellent fertilizer.

Roughly one-fifth of the world's population lives in China, but the people are distributed unevenly. Only about 10 percent of the population live in western China, settling in the valleys and foothills that ring the mountainous western and southern borders. The deserts and plateaus of west central China appear even emptier, with less than

Below: The Palace of Heavenly Purity, built in 1420 and now a museum, is one of the finest buildings in the Forbidden City, in Beijing.

China

five people per square mile. People along these borderlands—subsistence farmers and livestock herders—include a mix of ethnic Chinese and several minority ethnic groups such as Kazakhs, Mongols, Uygurs, Manchus, and Tibetans.

Eastern China is much more densely populated, with up to 1,000 people per square mile. About 80 percent of the eastern inhabitants live in small farming villages scattered across the land. Many of these farming communities belong to a cooperative system, in which a large group of members decides which crops and livestock each family farm will produce. After the harvest, part of the crop is sold to the government, and part of it goes to the community for sale or distribution. Any surplus can be eaten by the family or sold in the local market. Farming is not highly mechanized, and the people work long hours, often using simple hand tools. Horses, oxen, handcarts, and bicycles are common transportation options. Most rural families live in single-story houses of mud or clay brick, with a thatch or tile roof. There are few luxuries, but most homes have electricity, and most villages have schools, libraries, and community centers.

China also has some of the world's largest and most crowded cities. Shanghai has nearly 12 million people, Beijing supports 10 million, and more than 30 other cities house at least one million people each. Most major Chinese cities have built large, new apartment complexes alongside the older houses. Living units are small, but most people have enough income to meet their needs, and all have access to education, health care, and community services. City dwellers work in manufacturing, in shops, in service industries, in transportation, in education, and in government administration. Shanghai is the principal manufacturing center, followed by Beijing, Tianjin, and Shenyang in the north; Guangahou, Hangzhou, and Wuhan in the south; and Chongqing and Chengdu in east central China. Factory workers produce industrial and farm machinery, vehicles, textiles, fertilizer, cement, chemicals, and household goods such as sewing machines, televisions, and furniture. China has developed many hydroelectric plants that provide 20 percent of its power needs. The remainder comes from vast coalfields in the north and northeast and large oil fields in Manchuria, near Tianjin, and on the Shandong Peninsula. Miners also extract huge quantities of iron ore, tungsten, antimony, lead, and tin.

Throughout most of its long history, China remained isolated from the rest of the world. The mountain ranges, forests, and deserts that

encircle most of its western and southern borders cut off China from western Asia and Europe. The Pacific Ocean formed a natural barrier between China and the developing world of North America. This geographical separation combined with an ancient Chinese policy of discouraging contact with other countries, meant that the country's culture, traditions, and internal politics remained unaffected by world events well into the nineteenth century.

Powerful dynasties (ruling families) governed the Chinese Empire from the third century B.C. until the eighteenth century when a dramatic rise in the population and a succession of failed harvests led to widespread suffering and political unrest. The great empire began to crumble and fall apart. Wars with Britain and Japan in the nineteenth century hastened the empire's collapse, and in 1912 China's last emperor abdicated. China became a chaotic republic, ruled by army generals, powerful regional governors, and local warlords. After almost 40 years of civil hostilities and a long war with Japan, the Communist leader Mao Zedong took control in 1949, founding the People's Republic of China.

Since Mao's death in 1976, his successors have continued to insist on total government control, but they have also recognized the need for economic growth. They have encouraged foreign investment and have increased trade with Japan, the United States, and Germany. The government has set up special economic zones where foreign firms can establish businesses in China. The government also continues the staggering task of modernizing China's agriculture, industry, infrastructure, and urban areas.

Above: Few rural farms are mechanized. These farmers are threshing their rice crop with traditional hand tools.

Below: Peasant communities depend almost entirely on wood for fuel. Gathering the day's supply is hard work.

Hong Kong and Macau

Below: Sampans (traditional Chinese craft) provide homes for many thousands of Hong Kong's residents.

Bottom: The view across Hong Kong's busy harbor, from Hong Kong island to Kowloon on the mainland.

Hong Kong lies at the mouth of the Zhu Jiang (Pearl River) about 90 miles southeast of Guangzhou. It comprises a mountainous peninsula jutting from mainland China, and 235 islands—the largest of which is Hong Kong Island, the territory's capital and commercial center.

Leased to Britain in 1898, Hong Kong was returned to Chinese rule with great ceremony in 1997. It forms an important part of modern China's expanding economy. Most of its people work in banking and financial services, tourism, international trade, and manufacturing—sending watches, textiles and clothing, electronic equipment, and plastic goods all over the world.

The tiny territory of Macao, including the nearby islands of Coloane and Taipa, lies about 40 miles west of Hong Kong. Portuguese traders settled in Macao in 1557, and for the next 200 years the city and its port dominated the international trade in silk, spices, and other goods. A treaty with china recognized the settlement as Portuguese territory in 1887. Portugal returned Macao to Chinese rule in 1997. More than 90 percent of Macao's people are Chinese. Most of the rest are Portuguese.

Macao's thriving capitalist economy benefits China, which supplies virtually all Macao's food, fresh water, and energy needs and buys manufactured goods from the region. Tourism and light industry are Macao's main economic activities. Factory workers produce textiles and fireworks, which are exported to China and countries all over the world. Hotel staff, restaurant workers, and taxi drivers support a successful tourist industry. Around six million tourists visit Macao each year—almost 80 percent of them from Hong Kong.

Tawan

Taiwan

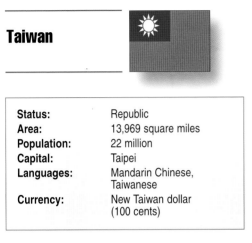

Status:	Republic
Area:	13,969 square miles
Population:	22 million
Capital:	Taipei
Languages:	Mandarin Chinese, Taiwanese
Currency:	New Taiwan dollar (100 cents)

The 250-mile-long island of Taiwan lies astride the Tropic of Cancer, about 90 miles off the Chinese coast. It has a warm, moist climate through most of the year, with heavy monsoon rains between June and August. The highest mountains receive snow in the winter. Mountains extend along the whole length of Taiwan, dominating the central and eastern parts rising to 12,000 feet in places. Evergreen forests of camphor, hemlock, and cork oak cover the lower slopes of the mountains, with cedar, larch, and pine forests taking over higher up.

Along the eastern coast, the mountains slope down steeply to the sea, creating a rugged coastline with a very narrow coastal plain. By contrast, along the western coast, low rolling hills slope down to a broad, fertile plain and provide Taiwan's only large area of lowland. Most of the population live in the towns and cities of the west, where most of the island's agriculture also takes place. A bit farther inland are fertile valleys, where farmers build terraces into the hillsides to create more land for cultivation. Taiwan's principal crops are rice, maize, bananas, citrus fruits, asparagus, sweet potatoes, and other vegetables, sugar cane, and tea. Chickens, ducks, and pigs are the most common livestock. Coastal fishing crews bring in shrimp, tuna, and other fish for the local markets.

Taiwan is not rich in mineral resources, but the island's miners produce modest quantities of coal, copper, gold, silver, sulfur, and salt. Limestone quarries produce hard stone for building houses and roads, and oil and gas wells contribute to the country's energy needs. Most raw materials, however, are imported. Manufacturing industries in the larger towns produce electronic goods such as calculators, television sets, and radios. They also make textiles and clothing, plastics, toys, and a wide range of forest products—bamboo, lumber, plywood, paper, and wooden furniture.

Above: Salt is separated from sea water in large evaporation ponds, and then scraped into piles to await transportation to the packing factory.

219

Mongolia

Mongolia

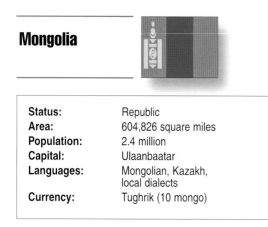

Status:	Republic
Area:	604,826 square miles
Population:	2.4 million
Capital:	Ulaanbaatar
Languages:	Mongolian, Kazakh, local dialects
Currency:	Tughrik (10 mongo)

Mongolia, sandwiched between Russia and China in eastern central Asia, is the world's largest land-locked country. Spanning 1,500 miles from east to west and nearly 800 miles from north to south, it is larger than Alaska. Yet Mongolia is one of the world's most sparsely populated countries, with an average of less than four people per square mile. It is a harsh, rugged country of mountain ranges, upland plateaus, windswept plains, and deserts. Mongolia's climate is typical of a highland region far from the softening influence of the sea. Summers are short and often hot, with temperatures up to 100°F. Winters are long, windy, and bitterly cold, with temperatures dropping to 55°F. Heavy snowfalls are common in the mountainous regions.

Mountains and high steppes dominate northern Mongolia. The Altai Shan (mountains) rise above 14,000 feet on Mongolia's border with China, the Hangayn Mountains stretch across the country's middle. The densely forested Hentiyn Nuruu extends northeast from the capital city of Ulaanbaatar to the Russian border. A high undulating plateau dotted with lakes and forests covers northwestern Mongolia. The country's largest body of water, Uvs Nuur, has an area of more than 1,300 square miles. Lower plains of semi-arid grassland cover the east, gradually becoming more arid as they merge with the barren expanse of the Gobi Desert, which stretches across much of Mongolia's border with China.

The country's people boast a long history of herding livestock. Traditionally nomadic, they constantly shifted their cattle, horses, sheep, goats, and camels from one grazing area to another. Their homes were circular tentlike structures, called yurts, that were made of thick felt mats fixed over a frame of bent poles. Yurts could be dismantled for transportation, but some early pictures show them being carried on large carts pulled by oxen.

The ancient people of Mongolia, the Mongols, possessed unmatched skill with horses and bows and arrows. Their warlike character made them a major force in the Mongol Empire of Genghis Khan, which dominated Asia through the Middle Ages (A.D. 500 to A.D. 1500). Herding livestock has replaced both the warring skills and the nomadic lifestyle, as the principal farming activity in Mongolia and a mainstay of the economy. Most of the population has settled in small villages that dot the vast grazing lands. Mongolians raise more than 20 million head of livestock—about half of them sheep. Cattle, wool, hides, and dairy products comprise the country's principal exports. Mutton, beef, milk, and cheese form the

Below: Mongolian men sitting outside a traditional yurt making felt from sheep's wool.

basis of the national diet. In the country's hilly north, farmers plant grains and vegetables in the fertile black soil.

From 1921 to 1990, Mongolia was a Communist state dependent on the Soviet Union for financial assistance. Mining and manufacturing grew rapidly during this period, eventually contributing as much to the country's economy as agriculture did. When the Soviet Union broke apart, Mongolia's financial aid dried up. The country continued to develop its mining interests, producing coal, oil, iron ore, copper, molybdenum, tin, gold, lead, and other minerals. Factory workers made textiles, glass, ceramics, timber products, and other goods. But economic growth has faltered and the country has been unable to continue modernizing its industries and transportation systems without the additional funding.

Above: The magnificent walled temple of Karakoroum Erdeni Dzu, set against the vast landscape of the Mongolian Plain..

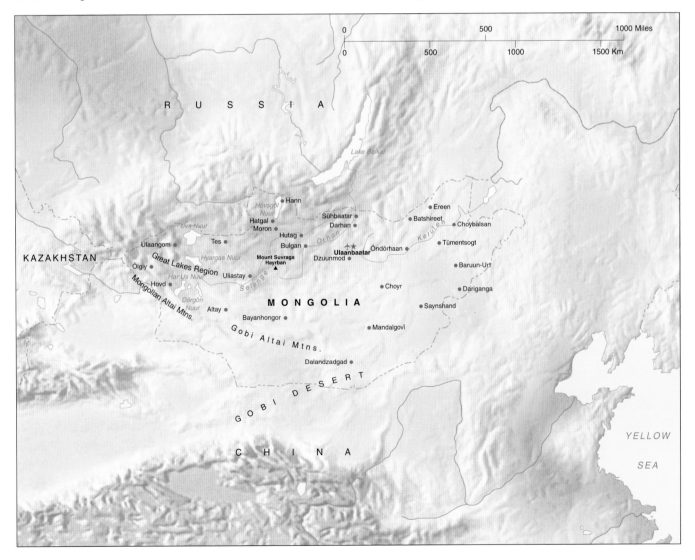

North Korea and South Korea

Two nations—North Korea and South Korea—occupy the mountainous 670-mile-long Korean Peninsula, which juts southward from the coast of eastern Asia. The Sea of Japan lies to the east of the peninsula. To the west extend Korea Bay and the Yellow Sea. The Korea Strait, south of the peninsula, separates South Korea from the northern tip of Japan. About 3,000 islands, most of them dotting the waters west and south of the peninsula, belong to the two countries. North Korea shares its northern border almost entirely with China. Just one short section in the extreme northeast is shared with Russia.

Before World War II (1939-1945), Korea was one nation but had been occupied by Japan since 1910. By the war's end, Japan had relinquished control, and Korea had separated into two nations. North Korea adopted a Communist regime, while South Korea was strongly anti-Communist. Friction between the two followed, and in 1950 North Korea invaded South Korea, igniting the Korean War. China and the Soviet Union supported North Korea. The United States and other non-Communist countries assisted South Korea. The war ended in 1953, but a permanent peace treaty has not been signed. In the spring of 2000, the first direct meeting between the leaders of the two Koreas signaled a possible end to the stalemate.

Above: The "Bridge of No Return" border crossing, near Panmunjom in North Korea.

222

Democratic People's Republic of Korea
(North Korea)

Status:	Republic
Area:	46,541 square miles
Population:	21.4 million
Capital:	Pyongyang
Language:	Korean
Currency:	North Korean won (100 zeuns)

Republic of Korea
(South Korea)

Status:	Republic
Area:	38,324 square miles
Population:	46.9 million
Capital:	Seoul
Language:	Korean
Currency:	South Korean won (100 chon)

Three distinct land regions divide North Korea. A broad plain subdivided by low hills parallels the western coast, providing most of North Korea's best farmland. Government-organized co-operatives divide the land into farming communities of up to 300 families. Each family works a section of the land, earning a portion of the harvest and a small income. The bulk of the produce is given to the government for distribution to the cities. Principal cooperative crops include rice, corn, millet, potatoes, and other vegetables. Most farmers also raise chickens and pigs.

Monsoon rains and winter snows provide 30 to 60 inches of precipitation each year, enough to meet the needs of both rural and urban populations. Roughly half the North Koreans reside in this western region—about two million of them in the capital city of Pyongyang. The country's industrial strength is based on mining, iron and steel, machinery, chemicals, and textiles. Miners dig copper, iron ore, lead, zinc, and tungsten, much of it for export to China, Japan, and Russia.

Forested mountains cover central North Korea. The country's largest region has a small population and virtually no agriculture. Residents support their families by mining many of the country's raw materials and by cutting timber for construction, furniture, and plywood and paper production.

A narrow band of coastal lowlands face the Sea of Japan. About one-quarter of the country's people live in the area, farming North Korea's second most productive farmland area.

South Korea has two principal land regions. Wide flat plains separated by ribbons of rolling hills form a broad band around the western and southern coasts. Central and eastern South Korea is covered in densely forested mountains. The fertile, well-irrigated coastal plains support most of South Korea's agriculture. In sharp contrast to state-run North Korea, southern farms are almost entirely small, privately owned family businesses. The farmers supplement the primary crop of rice with barley and a great variety of vegetables, including white radishes, onions, cabbages, sweet potatoes, and fruits such as apples and oranges. Farmers in the mountain regions cultivate every spare foot of land possible. They terrace the hillsides, farm the valley floors, and plant crops in the few small areas of lowland along the eastern coast. South Korea's large fishing fleet catches a variety of seafood for local and international markets.

About three-quarters of South Koreans inhabit the coastal plains, where manufacturing and service industries provide about 75 percent of the country's jobs. In the 1950s, North Korea dominated the peninsula's industrial force. South Korea invested heavily in both traditional and high-tech industries, overtaking North Korea as a major producer and worldwide exporter of iron and steel, ships, cars, machinery, chemicals, and tires. The country also manufactures and exports computers, audio and video equipment, cameras, household electrical goods, textiles, and clothing.

Right: Pusan—one of the principal cities on the southeast coast of South Korea.

Japan

Japan

Status:	Constitutional Monarchy
Area:	145,869 square miles
Population:	126.7 million
Capital:	Tokyo
Language:	Japanese
Currency:	Yen (100 sen)

Four large islands—Hokkaido, Honshu, Shikoku, and Kyushu—account for nearly 98 percent of Japan's land area. These islands lie in a 1,180-mile-long arc off the Asian mainland, facing Russia, North and South Korea, and China across the Sea of Japan and the East China Sea. Japan's remaining 2 percent of land includes about 4,000 smaller islands. Some nestle near the coasts of the main islands. Others, such as the Izu, Daito,

Bonin, and Volcano Islands, reach far into the Pacific Ocean. And the Ryukyu Islands extend like a string of pearls from Kyushu Island southwest almost to Taiwan.

Japan's islands lie above one of the most geologically active sections of the earth's crust. Far beneath the island chains, a section of seabed is dragging another down and beneath it. As the seabed grinds, earthquakes—1,500 each year—jolt Japan's landscape and people. Most quakes are minor tremors, causing little or no damage, but every few years a large earthquake strikes, causing extensive damage and casualties. The earthquake of January 17, 1995, rocked the industrial city of Kobe at the southern tip of Honshu Island. The quake destroyed at least 103,000 homes, killed more than 5,000 people, injured 27,000, and left one-fifth of the city's population homeless.

Volcanoes are another geologic component of Japanese life. The islands are actually the tops of a huge range of volcanic mountains rising from the Pacific seabed. More than 150 large volca-

Below: Bridges, water, cherry blossom, and varicolored foliage are the classic components of traditional Japanese formal gardens.

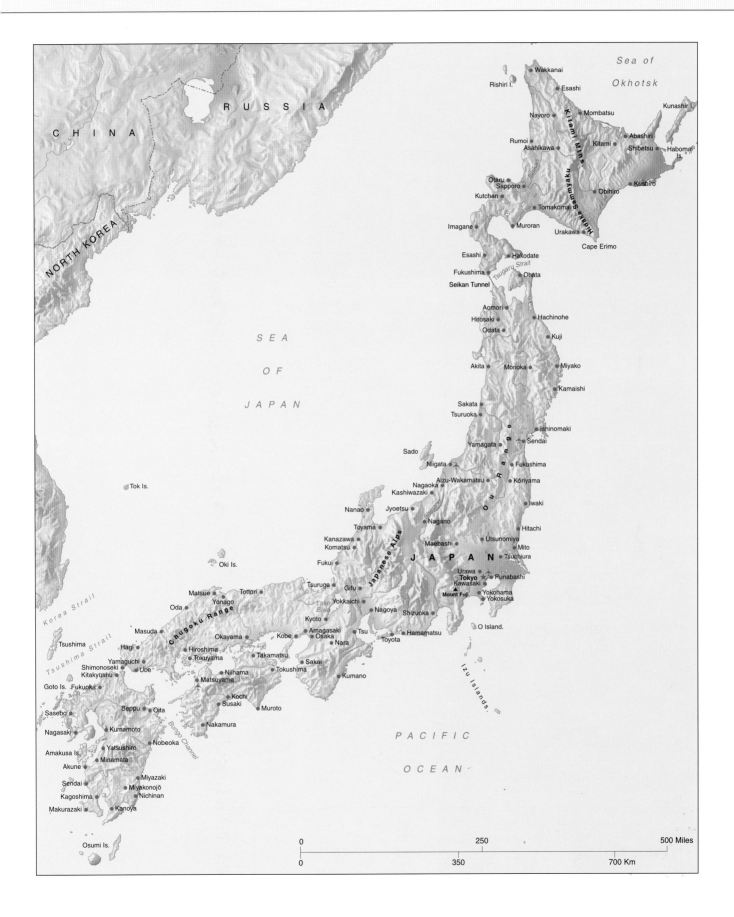

Sea of
Okhotsk

Wakkanai
Rishiri I. Esashi
Nayoro Mombatsu
Kunashir I.
Kitami Mtns.
Rumoi Abashiri
Asahikawa Kitami
Shibetsu
Habomai
Is.
Otaru Kushiro
Sapporo Obihiro
Kutchan
Tomakomai Hidaka Summits
Imagane Muroran
Urakawa
Cape Erimo

Esashi Hakodate
Fukushima Tsugaru Strait
Seikan Tunnel Ohata

Aomori
Hirosaki Hachinohe
Odata Kuji

Akita Morioka Miyako
Kamaishi

Sakata
Tsuruoka Ishinomaki
Yamagata Sendai
Sado
Niigata Fukushima
Aizu-Wakamatsu Kōriyama
Nagaoka
Kashiwazaki Iwaki
Nanao Jyoetsu
Toyama Nagano Hitachi
Kanazawa Utsunomiya
Komatsu Maebashi Mito
Fukui JAPAN Tsuchiura
Urawa
Tokyo Punabashi
Tsuruga Gifu Kawasaki
Matsue Tottori Yokohama
Yonago Yokkaichi Mount Fuji Yokosuka
Oda Chugoku Range Kyoto Nagoya
Masuda Lake Shizuoka O Island.
Okayama Biwa
Hagi Kobe Tsu Hamamatsu
Yamaguchi Hiroshima Amagasaki Toyota
Shimonoseki Tokuyama Osaka Nara
Kitakyushu Ube Takamatsu Sakai
Goto Is. Fukuoka Nihama Tokushima Kumano
Matsuyama
Sasebo Kochi
Beppu Oita Susaki Muroto
Nagasaki Kumamoto Nakamura
Amakusa Is. Yatsushiro Nobeoka
Akune Minamata
Sendai Miyazaki
Kagoshima Miyakonojō
Makurazaki Kanoya Nichinan

Osumi Is.

SEA

OF

JAPAN

Tok Is.

Oki Is.

Korea Strait

Tsushima

Tsushima Strait

Bungo Channel

Izu Islands.

PACIFIC

OCEAN

CHINA

RUSSIA

NORTH KOREA

Japanese Alps

Ou Range

0		250		500 Miles

0		350		700 Km

Japan

noes peek above the ocean's surface, and about half of them are still active (capable of erupting). Mount Fuji, an inactive volcano, forms Japan's highest summit, rising to 12,388 feet above sea level on Honshu Island.

Spectacular mountains, rolling hills, and precious forests cover much of Japan, providing stunning scenery for the country's many visitors. Nearly 70 percent of the land is mountainous, so Japan's 126 million people tend to concentrate near the coasts, where narrow plains provide space for urban development. Flat land is so scarce that many of Japan's large industrial cities sit on shore land that has been pumped dry. The most heavily inhabited areas lie along the Pacific coast of Honshu Island, where major cities, industrial centers, and ports have developed around deep sheltered bays. Tokyo's metropolitan area houses more than 12 million people, and the surrounding area holds another 6 million. Osaka's residents number nearly 10 million. Other major urban areas include Yokohama, Nagoya, Osaka, and Kyoto—each home to several million people.

Despite its small size, Japan has one of the world's strongest economies. The country's gross domestic product (GDP)—the total value of all the goods and services produced within the country in a year—is second only to that of the United States. Japan has achieved this rank with relatively few natural resources. Japanese miners extract small quantities of coal, lead, tin, zinc, manganese, silver, and other minerals, but Japan imports most of its copper and aluminum and nearly all the coking coal and iron ore used in its huge iron and steel industry. Japan produces steel for its own use as well as manufacturing steel sheets, rolls, pipes, and wire for export. The country's powerful industrial economy is built on three crucial steps—import raw materials; turn them into high-value, high quality products using modern technology and the skills of a industrious

Center: Tokyo shoppers examine the latest goods on display in a downtown electronics store.

Left: Japan's famous "Bullet trains" are part of a rail transport system the operators proudly claim is the most reliable and punctual in the world.

labor force; and export those goods all over the world. This approach has moved Japan to the forefront of the world's trading nations.

About one-quarter of Japan's workforce is employed in manufacturing industries. Automobiles are among the country's principal exports. More than eight million of them are produced annually. Japan is also the world's leading shipbuilder and a major supplier of heavy machinery, such as cranes, turbines, machine tools, and electrical equipment. Factory workers create cameras, watches, scientific instruments, audio and video equipment, computers, calculators, washing machines, and many other household goods. Textiles, ceramics, paper, and wood products are also exported, and the country's petrochemical industries—using oil and natural gas as raw materials—produce a wide range of plastics, and synthetic fibers for the textile trade. The five principal manufacturing regions are Tokyo–Yokohama; Nagoya–Yokkaichi; Kobe–Kyoto–Osaka; and Niihama–Hiroshima–Fukuyama–Okayama, all on the Pacific coast, and Komatsu–Toyama–Niigata on the Sea of Japan coast.

More than half the Japanese are employed in one of the service industries—working as health-care providers, teachers, bank tellers, insurance agents, telephone operators, and hotel and restaurant workers. Many work as tour guides for the country's thriving tourist industry.

Japan's climate varies a great deal from north to south. Residents of Hokkaido experience cool summers and bitterly cold winters, often with thick snowfalls. Honshu has warm, humid summers and winters that get more mild the farther south on the island one travels. As the southernmost large island, Kyushu enjoys a warm, temperate climate, with hot summers and mild winters. Most of Japan receives ample rainfall to meet the needs of both city dwellers and farmers. Only Hokkaido's eastern side has a markedly dry climate.

Japan makes productive use of its relatively sparse farmland. Farmers have boosted productivity by irrigating, by terracing the hillsides, by choosing high-yield crop strains, and by using large amounts of fertilizer. Rice is the country's most significant crop and the basis of its national diet. Japanese farmers grow many varieties of vegetables and fruits, and many raise poultry, pigs, and cattle. Some farmers specialize in

nonfood crops such as tobacco, and mulberry trees, whose leaves are used to feed silkworms. Japan's agriculture sector produces almost 70 percent of the country's food needs. The remainder is imported.

With a long coastline and hundreds of bays and inlets, Japan has a long tradition of fishing and the largest fishing fleet in the world—estimated at more than 400,000 vessels. Traditional fishers with small boats work the coastal waters, while the large modern deepsea trawlers, seiners, and squid-catchers roam the oceans. Fish has long been Japan's principal source of animal protein, and nutritionists believe that the combination of rice, fish, and vegetables in the Japanese diet has long protected the population from the high incidence of heart disease seen in other developed countries.

Above: Japan has a rich and complex theatrical tradition dating back many centuries.

Left: High-class Japanese cuisine combines fresh ingredients and perfect presentation. Peasants are more likely to dine on boiled rice and a few vegetables.

Pakistan and Afghanistan

Pakistan

Status:	Federal Republic
Area:	307,375 square miles
Population:	146.5 million
Capital:	Islamabad
Languages:	Punjabi, Urdu, Sindhi, Pashtun, Baluchi, English
Currency:	Pakistan rupee (100 paisa)

Pakistan emerged as a country in 1947, when India gained its independence from Britain. A large section of the Indian subcontinent became the predominantly Hindu state of India. The other, smaller section became the Islamic state of Pakistan, home to a population that was 95 percent Muslim. Pakistan then consisted of West Pakistan and East Pakistan, two Muslim territories located nearly 1,000 miles apart. Civil war led to a breakup in 1971, and East Pakistan gained independence as Bangladesh. West Pakistan became simply Pakistan.

The dry, barren Baluchistan Plateau blankets most of southwestern Pakistan. With less than five inches of annual rainfall, the area supports little vegetation. Few people inhabit the region apart from scattered settlements of sheep and goat herders. In northern Pakistan, the land rises to the rugged mountains of the North-West Frontier province, where the Khyber Pass links Pakistan with neighboring Afghanistan. Farther east rises the world's second-highest peak, K2 (also known as Godwin Austen), which towers 28,250 feet on the Himalayan border with China.

Stretching northward and eastward from the Arabian Sea, the Thar Desert reaches deep into India along several river valleys. Farmers have been able to tap into the area's rivers to irrigate parts of the desert for cultivation. The lowlands of the Indus River and its principal tributaries dominate the Punjab and Sind provinces of eastern Pakistan. Over millions of years, these rivers have deposited thick layers of silt, forming a broad, fertile alluvial plain. Even here, in Pakistan's wettest region, annual rainfall rarely exceeds 20 inches. The farmers of these plains channel the rivers into extensive irrigation systems, which allow the farmers to grow wheat, rice, chickpeas, vegetables, and fruits. Cotton and sugarcane are the country's primary nonfood crops.

Most of Pakistan is underdeveloped. Two-thirds of the people live in farming villages with few modern amenities. The country is short on schools and teachers as well as on hospitals and medical staff. Despite government efforts to improve educational standards, less than 50 percent of school-age children attend classes and only about one in four Pakistanis can read and write.

Manufacturing employs about 15 percent of the population, mostly in the urban centers of Karachi, Hyderabad, Lahore, Multan, Rawalpindi, and Peshawar. Factory workers produce textiles and clothing, processed foods, fertilizers, and cement. Along the coast, many Pakistanis work in the fishing industry, catching shrimp, sardines, shark, and other fish for local and foreign markets.

Below: Not for the faint-hearted. A swaying suspension bridge spans a mountain river at Gilgit in the wild terrain of northeastern Pakistan

228

Afghanistan

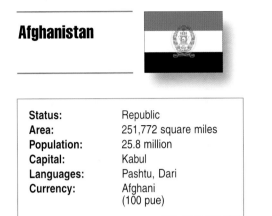

Status:	Republic
Area:	251,772 square miles
Population:	25.8 million
Capital:	Kabul
Languages:	Pashtu, Dari
Currency:	Afghani (100 pue)

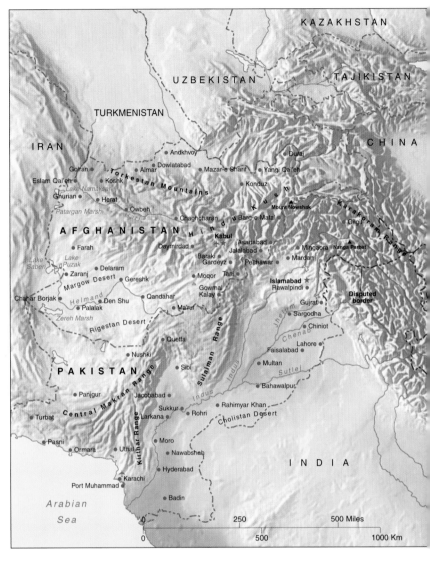

Afghanistan is a rugged, mountainous, landlocked country ringed by Iran, Turkmenistan, Uzbekistan, Tajikistan, China, and Pakistan. Its people belong to more than 20 ethnic groups, and power struggles among them have led to constant political unrest. A military coup in 1973 replaced Afghanistan's monarchy with a republic, but further unrest led to occupation by Soviet troops. Since the Soviet withdrawal, internal conflicts have continued, and some have been extremely violent and disruptive.

Rolling plains and plateaus stretch across northern Afghanistan, supporting sheep and goat herders on sparse grasslands. The soil is fertile, but annual rainfall rarely exceeds seven inches. Farmers cultivate the river valleys, diverting water to their fields through irrigation channels. To assist the agricultural sector, the government has built large irrigation systems along some of the major rivers—the Helmand, the Qonduz, and the Harirud.

The high mountains of the Hindu Kush fill central Afghanistan, rising to more than 20,000 feet near the Pakistani border. Many Afghanis live in the high, cold valleys of this region. The farmers grow grain and vegetables using hand tools and centuries-old farming methods and graze livestock on the sparse hillside pastures.

Arid plains and deserts cover southwestern Afghanistan. Rivers crossing this desolate western region flow into the Sistān Basin—an area of shallow salty lakes and marshlands. Farmers redirect the waters of the Helmand River to irrigate their fields of wheat, corn, and barley.

Afghanistan has little industry, and most of its rich mineral deposits lie undeveloped because of their remote locations. The country has developed two valuable minerals for export—natural gas and the stone lapis lazuli. Other exports include cotton, nuts, leather goods, silverware, jewelry, and the fine wool of the Karakul sheep.

Above: Magnificent scenery of Mount Nowshak, Northeast Afghanistan.

229

Nepal and Bhutan

Nepal

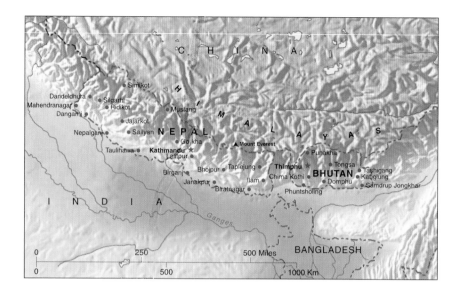

Status:	Constitutional Monarchy
Area:	56,826 square miles
Population:	24.3 million
Capital:	Kathmandu
Languages:	Nepali, many local dialects
Currency:	Nepalese rupee (100 paisa)

The remote mountain kingdom of Nepal lies in the Himalayas, sandwiched between China and India. More than 80 percent of the country is covered by these towering mountains and by the hills and valleys of a lesser range, the Mahabharat Mountains, that lies to the south. The broad fertile Tarai Plain stretches west to east across the southern edge of the country, along the border with India.

Nepal's mountainous terrain and lack of roads make communication difficult, especially for the 55 percent of the population that lives in the mountain regions. The economy is underdeveloped, and there are few schools or hospitals. A government program begun in the 1950s to improve health and educational services has raised the country's literacy rate from 5 percent to about 20 percent of the population, but lack of education remains one of Nepal's greatest barriers to progress.

Nearly all of the Nepalese depend on agriculture for their income. People in the high mountains raise sheep and longhaired yaks. The animals' milk is a fundamental part of the local diet, and their wool is woven to make clothes and blankets. Some crops in this area cling to the terraced hillsides, but much of the original forest has been cut for firewood causing the hillsides to wash away. Farmers at the lower elevations benefit from better soils, a mild, cool climate, and summer rains. They harvest rice, corn, millet, wheat, and vegetables and herd cattle, oxen,

Above: The magnificent ramparts of Mount Everest.

sheep, and goats. Most Nepalese farmers work small family plots and manage to produce just enough food for their own needs, with a small surplus to sell or trade. Popular imports include kerosene and salt.

The Tarai enjoys a hot, wet climate, with ample moisture and fertile soil. Farmers in the plain grow grains, vegetables, sugarcane, and nonfood crops such as jute and tobacco. Some sections of the Tarai are covered in jungle and swamp, teeming with wildlife such as crocodiles, elephants, leopards, rhinoceroses, and tigers.

Nepal's mineral resources—coal, iron, copper, and gold—are undeveloped because of their remote locations. The country has little industry apart from craftwork, but countries such as the United States, Britain, Switzerland, and China are providing aid to create more industry and jobs. Nepal's hope for the future lies in its huge potential for hydroelectric power from Himalayan rivers. With international funding Nepal will be able to build several giant power stations and to sell the electricity to the industrial regions of northern India.

Bhutan

Status:	Absolute Monarchy
Area:	18,147 square miles
Population:	800,000
Capital:	Thimphu
Languages:	Dzongkha, English
Currency:	Ngultrum
	(100 chetrum)

The tiny mountain kingdom of Bhutan lies between India and Tibet—formerly an independent country but since the 1950s an autonomous (self-governing) region of China. Like neighboring Nepal, Bhutan has three major land regions. The high Himalayas dominate the north—cold, windy, with ice-covered peaks and large areas of bare rock. Herders raise goats and yaks on the rough, windswept mountain pastures. South of the main Himalayas the land consists of low mountains and rolling hills, densely covered with ash, oak, and poplars. Good soils and the milder, damper climate of the sheltered valleys allow farmers there to grow wheat, barley, rice, and vegetables. Some of the lower south-facing hills are hot and humid, and that same climate extends across the rolling plains and broad river valleys that cover the south of the country. Farmers in this fertile tropical area grow rice, bananas, and citrus fruits, and miners in the south produce coal, much of which Bhutan exports to India.

With aid from India, Bhutan is modernizing its road system, improving its agriculture, and developing industries such as food processing for export. A hydroelectric power station has been built to supply the capital, Thimphu, and others are planned.

Top: Nepalese men drinking tea at the local store — often a favorite place to meet and talk.

Above: Terraced rice paddies at Kanglung in eastern Bhutan.

Right: A young Buddhist monk collects alms (donations, usually of food or drink) in the streets of his village. Most young Bhutanese men spend at least two years in a monastery.

231

Bangladesh, Sri Lanka, Maldives

Bangladesh

Status:	Republic
Area:	55,598 square miles
Population:	125.7 million
Capital:	Dhaka
Languages:	Bengali, English
Currency:	Taka
	(100 poisha)

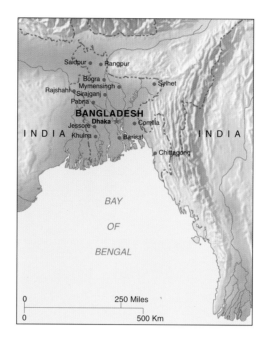

Bangladesh consists almost entirely of a flat alluvial plain, formed over millions of years by the meandering and frequent flooding of the country's three major rivers—the Ganges, the Brahmaputra, and the Meghna. They flow through Bangladesh to the Bay of Bengal. Most of the country lies less than 50 feet above sea level, making Bangladesh the world's most flood-prone country. Heavy monsoon rains from May to October often cause the rivers to burst their banks, and cyclones sweeping in from the Bay of Bengal can drive inland enormous volumes of water. These awesome storms have devastated entire villages and left hundreds of square miles of crops rotting under several feet of muddy, salty water.

Bangladesh is one of the world's most heavily populated countries, with more than 2,200 people per square mile. It is also a very poor country. More than 80 percent of Bangladeshis live in rural areas and grow rice, wheat, beans, vegetables, and jute—the primary nonfood crop. The soil is fertile and the government has made efforts to improve farm yields with fertilizers, better varieties of seed, and more modern farming methods. But with so many mouths to feed, most Bangladeshis do not have enough to eat.

Typical rural homes are built of bamboo and thatch. Only a third have electricity, running water, or sanitation. The cities are bursting, with millions of people living in makeshift homes in sprawling shantytowns. Health and education services do not begin to meet the country's needs.

Jute factories—Bangladesh's only large-scale industrial employers—process the plant's fiber into ropes and sacking. Workers in small factories fabricate leather goods, textiles, pottery, and metal goods. Fishing boats that ply the coasts and rivers provide an important source of food, allowing Bangladesh to export large quantities of shrimp and prawns.

Below: Elephants are still widely used to haul logs in the forests. Handlers reward these strong, intelligent animals with a refreshing scrub in the river after a hard day.

Sri Lanka

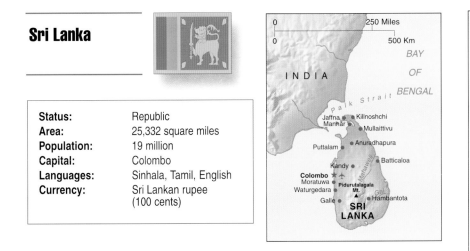

Status:	Republic
Area:	25,332 square miles
Population:	19 million
Capital:	Colombo
Languages:	Sinhala, Tamil, English
Currency:	Sri Lankan rupee (100 cents)

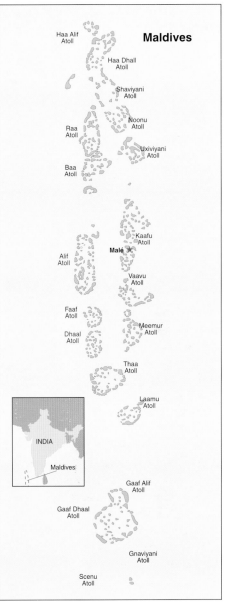

Droplet-shaped Sri Lanka is a beautiful island of wild animals, coastal plains, and forested mountains reaching to 8,000 feet in the south. Once a British colony named Ceylon, the island is famous for its Ceylon tea, which it exports and consumes locally in great quantities.

Two major ethnic groups dominate life and politics in Sri Lanka. The mostly Buddhist Sinhalese comprise 74 percent of the population and largely control the government. The predominantly Hindu Tamil make up 18 percent of the country's inhabitants and feel their lack of political power has led to fewer educational and employment opportunities. Outbreaks of fighting between the rivals have torn the island for nearly 50 years.

Sri Lanka's economy is based on farming. About half the labor force works the land, growing rice, rubber, tobacco, coconuts, and tea—Sri Lanka's most valuable export. Another 10 percent work in processing plants or textile factories. And the country's service industries—government offices, communications, and transportation—employ 35 percent. Colombo, on the southwestern coast, is the island's capital, largest city, and principal seaport.

Maldives

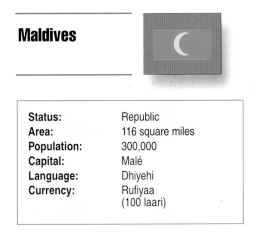

Status:	Republic
Area:	116 square miles
Population:	300,000
Capital:	Malé
Language:	Dhiyehi
Currency:	Rufiyaa (100 laari)

More than 1,000 coral islands make up the Maldives. They stretch in a 475-mile-long chain in the Indian Ocean. One of the world's smallest countries, the island group sits off India's southwestern tip, covering little more than 100 square miles. Just over 200 of the islands are inhabited. Many are tiny atolls that barely break the ocean surface. Some of the islands lie so low in the water that ocean experts fear they eventually may submerge altogether.

Maldivian livelihoods depend on fishing, tourism, and farming. Thousands of boats head to sea each day, pulling in bonito and tuna for local consumption and for export—primarily to Sri Lanka and Japan. Glistening white beaches and a hot, sunny tropical climate attract large numbers of visitors each year. Tourism is responsible for about 20 percent of the country's economy. Farmers on the islands grow crops—primarily millet, sweet potatoes, peppers, breadfruit, and other fruits—for local dinner tables and for the island's hotels.

233

India

Status:	Federal Republic
Area:	1,269,340 square miles
Population:	986.6 million
Capital:	New Delhi
Languages:	Hindi, English, Telugu, Bengali, Marathi, Urdu, other regional dialects
Currency:	Rupee (100 paisa)

India is the world's seventh-largest country but is second only to China in population. Nearly one billion people—one-sixth of the world's people—live in India.

Long before humans lived there, the Indian subcontinent had a remarkable and spectacular history. Along with South America, Africa, Antarctica, and Australia, India once formed part of a vast supercontinent, called Gondwana, that was situated far south of its current location. When Gondwana broke apart more than 200 million years ago, India drifted northward, crossed the equator, and crashed into the landmass that would become Asia. The collision didn't happen quickly, like a car wreck. It took millions of years. But India plowed so hard into Asia that it buckled and crushed a 1,500-mile long, 200-mile-wide section of the earth's crust, pushing it five miles into the sky. The result of that geological collision is the Himalayas—the world's tallest mountain range, which marks India's borders with China, Nepal, and Bhutan.

The huge diamond-shaped subcontinent —2,000 miles from north to south and 1,000 miles across at its widest—contains enough variety of landscapes and people to be several countries. Snow-covered mountain peaks and vast open plains meet deserts, high plateaus, and dense rain forests. India's people speak 14 major languages and more than 1,000 additional lan-

Left: Houses, temples, boats, and people crowd every inch of the Ganges riverfront at Varanasi, in the north-central Indian state of Uttar Pradesh. To Hindus, the Ganges is the most sacred river in India.

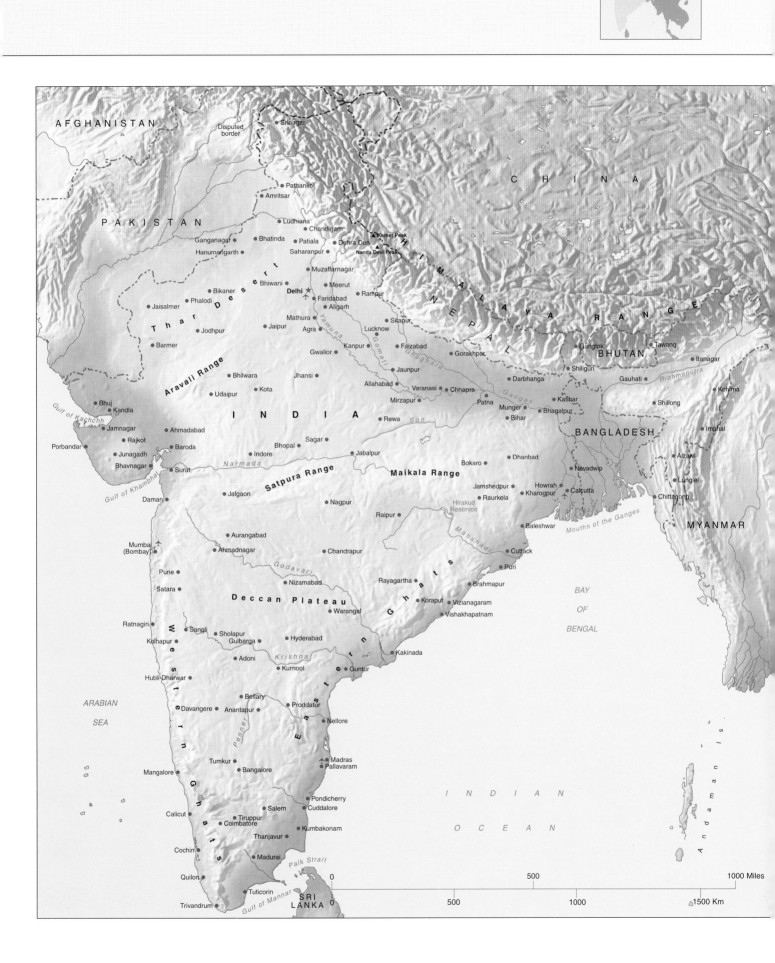

AFGHANISTAN

PAKISTAN

Disputed border

Srinagar

CHINA

Pathankot
Amritsar
Ludhiana
Chandigarh
Ganganagar
Bhatinda
Patiala
Dehra Dun
Kamet Peak
Hanumangarth
Saharanpur
Nanda Devi Peak
Muzaffarnagar
Bikaner
Bhiwani
Meerut
Delhi
Faridabad
Rampur
Phalodi
Jaisalmer
Mathura
Aligarh
Sitapur
Jodhpur
Jaipur
Agra
Lucknow
Faizabad
Barmer
Kanpur
Gorakhpor
Gangtok
Tawang
Itanagar
Bhilwara
Jhansi
Jaunpur
Darbhanga
Shiliguri
Gauhati
Kohima
Udaipur
Kota
Allahabad
Varanasi
Chhapra
Shillong
Mirzapur
Patna
Katihar
Bhuj
Kandla
Rewa
Son
Munger
Bihar
Bhagalpur
Imphal
Jamnagar
Ahmadabad
BANGLADESH
Porbandar
Rajkot
Baroda
Bhopal
Sagar
Aizawl
Junagadh
Indore
Bokaro
Dhanbad
Navadwip
Bhavnagar
Surat
Narmada
Jabalpur
Lunglei
Daman
Satpura Range
Maikala Range
Howrah
Jamshedpur
Chittagong
Jalgaon
Nagpur
Kharogpur
Calcutta
Raurkela
Raipur
Hirakud Reservoir
MYANMAR
Mumbai (Bombay)
Aurangabad
Chandrapur
Baleshwar
Mouths of the Ganges
Ahmadnagar
Cuttack
Pune
Godavari
Puri
Satara
Nizamabad
Rayagartha
BAY
Ratnagiri
Deccan Plateau
Warangal
Koraput
Brahmapur
OF
Sangli
Sholapur
Gulbarga
Hyderabad
Vizianagaram
BENGAL
Kolhapur
Adoni
Krishna
Vishakhapatnam
Hubli-Dharwar
Kurnool
Guntur
Kakinada
Bellary
ARABIAN
Davangere
Anantapur
Proddatur
SEA
Nellore
Tumkur
Madras
Mangalore
Bangalore
Pallavaram
INDIAN
Andaman Is.
Calicut
Pondicherry
OCEAN
Tiruppur
Salem
Cuddalore
Coimbatore
Kumbakonam
Thanjavur
Cochin
Madurai
Quilon
Palk Strait
Tuticorin
SRI
Trivandrum
LANKA
Gulf of Mannar

Gulf of Kachchh
Gulf of Khambhat

Thar Desert

Aravali Range

INDIA

Yamuna
Gomati
Ghaghara
Ganges
Brahmaputra

NEPAL

HIMALAYA RANGE

BHUTAN

Western Ghats
Eastern Ghats

Penner

Mahanadi

0   500   1000 Miles

0   500   1000   1500 Km

India

guages and dialects. About one-third of the population principally speaks Hindi—one of India's 14 official languages. Millions more use it as their second language. English, a reminder of India's colonial connection to Britain, is still widely used in government circles and by the legal, academic, and scientific communities.

India was home to two very early civilizations—one centered in the Indus Valley around 2600 B.C., the other in the Ganges Valley around 1500 B.C. Over the centuries, India has been both a large sprawling empire and a collection of separate states. Colonists from Portugal, Britain, France, and the Netherlands arrived in the fifteenth and sixteenth centuries, but the British East India Company steadily established itself as the dominant power. The British government formally colonized India in 1805, and it remained under British rule until 1947. At that time, India was divided, or partitioned, into modern India, which is predominantly Hindu, and the primarily Muslim state of Pakistan. Border conflicts between the two states and religious conflicts both between the states and within each state have plagued the subcontinent ever since.

India itself can be divided into three major land regions. A northern strip of foothills and towering peaks in the Himalayas supports India's highest summit, Kanchenjunga, which rises to 28,208 feet on the border with Nepal. Few people live in the high mountains, but villagers in the foothills graze sheep and goats on the mountain pastures and grow rice, wheat, and vegetables. Farmers in northern India grow rice on the fertile soil of the terraced foothills and cultivate fruit and nut trees. Above the terraces, the dry, rugged hills are crossed by ancient tracks that lead northward into China and westward into Pakistan. Far to the east, where India borders Myanmar (formerly Burma), greater rainfall allows upland farmers to raise wheat, barley, and rice. Parts of this region enjoy more than 300 inches of annual rain. The village of Cherrapunji holds the world record for a single year's rainfall—1,042 inches. Forests throughout the foothills provide construction timber and fuel for homes, but in many areas too much wood has been cut and the hillsides are badly eroded.

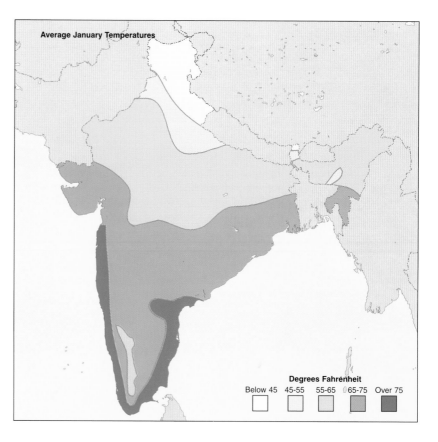

Average January Temperatures

Degrees Fahrenheit
Below 45 45-55 55-65 65-75 Over 75

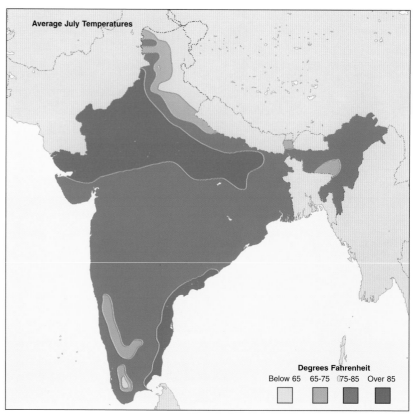

Average July Temperatures

Degrees Fahrenheit
Below 65 65-75 75-85 Over 85

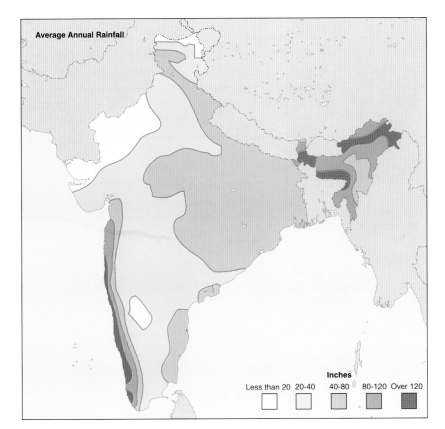

Average Annual Rainfall

Inches
Less than 20 | 20-40 | 40-80 | 80-120 | Over 120

South of the mountains, a broad plain stretches from east to west across the continent ending in the hot and dusty Thar Desert. Only small groups of sheep and goat herders roamed the desert until 1986, when a new canal provided irrigation for crops and farmers were encouraged to settle there. The desert also contains one of India's nuclear power stations, and the country's nuclear test site.

The tropical state of Gujarat, south of the desert and bordering the Arabian Sea, is one of India's principal cotton-growing regions. The country's great rivers—the Ganges and the Brahmaputra—dominate the central and eastern plains. Fed by runoff from Himalayan glaciers and snowfields, the rivers and their tributaries flow across broad fertile plains, meeting in Bangladesh before emptying into the Bay of Bengal. The rivers provide ample irrigation, allowing the plains' farmers to grow much of India's food. Rice covers the greatest percentage of India's cultivated land, but farmers also grow wheat, millet, sorghum, and many varieties of peas and beans. Local markets also brim with onions, cauliflower, eggplant, potatoes, apples, and bananas. Many farmers grow

and sell tea, sugarcane, cotton, jute, tobacco, and rubber.

Farther south lies India's great triangular Deccan Peninsula, a huge plateau sloping gently from west to east. Rocky mountain ranges mark the plateau's edge. The steep, 5,000-foot Western Ghats overlook a narrow coastal plain on the Arabian Sea, while the 2,000-foot Eastern Ghats slope to a broader coastal plain facing the Bay of Bengal. On most of the Deccan, farmers grow grains and vegetables and raise large herds of cattle and buffalo for their milk and for their strength in pulling carts and plows. Western Deccan farmers take advantage of their wetter soil to grow mainly cotton and sorghum. Farmers in the drier eastern sector harvest millet, beans, sugarcane, and spices. India's southwestern coast enjoys a hot tropical climate with more than 120 inches of annual rain and abundant crops of peppers, mangoes, bananas, and coconuts.

Coastal inhabitants eat a great deal of fish, supporting a large portion of India's fishing industry. Vessels chug home at the end of the day bursting with prawns, mackerel, herring, sardines, shark, and Bombay duck—a small fish that is dried and used in many curried dishes.

About 70 percent of India's people reside in small rural farming communities, often numbering no more than 1,000 people. The remaining 30 percent live in towns and small cities. Only about 250 urban areas house more than 100,000 people, and just ten of them have more than a million people—the three largest being Calcutta (11 million), Mumbai (formerly Bombay) (10 million), and Delhi (7 million). But the urban population is growing quickly. Improved health care has allowed people to live much longer, and the rural poor are flocking to urban areas in search of jobs. Many are disappointed and end up in overcrowded slums or on the streets.

Although India's major cities are among the most crowded urban environments in the world, recent government health and education programs have had considerable success. Since the 1950s, life expectancy has increased by 25 years, as new hospitals and clinics have been built. Teams of health workers have visited thousands of rural communities giving

India

Above: Throughout rural India, oxen, bullocks, and buffalo provide most of the power for carts, plows, water pumps, and threshing grain.

Below: Dramatic scenery in one of the many mountain passes in Kashmir.

advice on childcare, nutrition, hygiene, and sanitation. The government has also invested in schools, teachers, books, and public television services, all of which have led to a dramatic rise in India's literacy rate. About half the population can read and write—more than twice as many as in the 1950s, when these programs began.

Agricultural progress has not been as dramatic. Parts of the northwest are very dry and have suffered severe droughts. The rest of the country lies at the heart of the Asian monsoon region. From June to September, warm winds blow in from the southwest carrying moisture from the Indian Ocean. This moisture falls as torrential rain and often causes flooding in low-lying areas like the Ganges Delta. The Bay of Bengal is also prone to hurricanes. These devastating storms have destroyed coastal villages, have killed livestock, and have buried precious crops under several feet of muddy saltwater.

India's industries have grown rapidly since independence. More people are employed in the textile industries than in any other sector. Mumbai and Ahmadabad in the west are the principal cotton centers,

Above: Camel driver, Rajasthan, western India.

Above right: Decorative boats on Dal Lake near Srinagar in northern Kashmir.

Right: A farmer heads for the local market in Tamil Nadu state in southeast India.

wool processing is based in Punjab in the far northwest, and jute factories are concentrated around Calcutta. Textiles and clothing are among India's principal exports. Iron and steel plants at Bhilai, Bokaro, Durgapur, and Raurkela in the eastern Deccan process local iron ore with locally mined coal to supply steel for factory-made cars, bicycles, railroad parts, household appliances, and other metal goods. Factory workers in cities such as Delhi, Ahmadabad, and Hyderabad manufacture electrical goods, lace, decorative wood and leather goods, fine brassware, and food products for both local and overseas markets. India's chemical plants produce pharmaceuticals, dyes, fertilizers, and industrial chemicals. India meets more than half its energy needs with local resources. Power stations burn Deccan coal and use oil from wells off the coast near Mumbai and onshore in Assam. Another 35 percent is hydroelectric power from major river stations, and the remainder is nuclear power.

Myanmar and Thailand

Myanmar

Status:	Republic
Area:	261,228 square miles
Population:	48.1 million
Capital:	Yangon
Languages:	Burmese, English, several local dialects
Currency:	Kyat (100 pyas)

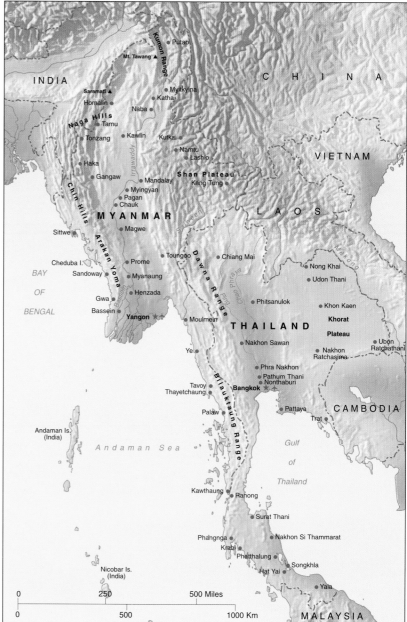

Myanmar has a 1,650-mile-long coastline on the Bay of Bengal and shares its land borders with Bangladesh, India, China, Laos, and Thailand. The country changed its name from Burma in 1989, but many Burmese, who oppose the government, still use the old name.

Myanmar is a land of mountains, dense tropical rain forests, and great river valleys. The low-lying Arakan Yoma range in the west overlooks a narrow fertile plain fronting the Bay of Bengal. This highland region runs north through the Chin and Naga Hills along Myanmar's border with India. Clothed in dense tropical forests, the hills hold much of the world's teak—one of Myanmar's most valuable exports. The high peaks of the Kumon range—rising to 19,296-foot Hkakabo Razi in the far north—and the Shan Plateau's wooded hills separate Myanmar from China. To the east, the Tanen and Dawna Mountains dominate the country's borders with Thailand and Laos.

Three great rivers—the Irrawaddy, the Sittang, and the Salween—and their tributaries flow from north to south through Myanmar's middle. Low-lying hills separate the rivers from one another. Their broad, fertile valleys support the country's most productive farmland. The many mouths of the Irrawaddy spill into the Bay of Bengal through a huge delta. To the east of the delta, the Sittang and the Salween empty into the Andaman Sea. The capital city of Yangon (formerly called Rangoon) and several other towns and cities are built in the delta area. Other towns lie along the coast or inland in the principal river valleys.

About 75 percent of the Burmese live in small villages of thatched bamboo houses. Some of the homes sit on stilts to protect against river floods brought on by the monsoon rains. Myanmar's economy is still developing, but nearly 80 percent of Burmese can read and write, many attend college, and most have better health care than people do in other developing Asian countries.

More than 60 percent of Myanmar's workforce tends the soil. Rice is the principal crop—covering more than half the cultivated land—supplemented by fruits and vegetables, sugarcane, wheat, tobacco, cotton, and rubber. Factories concentrated in Yangon manufacture textiles, metal wares, and processed foods. Forestry and fishing are also significant employers. Myanmar has large reserves of undeveloped mineral wealth and is a major producer of jade, rubies, and sapphires, which are exported worldwide.

Thailand

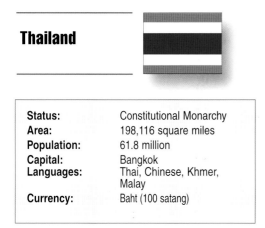

Status:	Constitutional Monarchy
Area:	198,116 square miles
Population:	61.8 million
Capital:	Bangkok
Languages:	Thai, Chinese, Khmer, Malay
Currency:	Baht (100 satang)

Thailand is a tropical Southeast Asian country of forests, mountains, lakes, and rivers. Winters are mild, springtime is hot and dry, and summers are long, hot, and very humid. The climate is generally hot and sticky along the coasts but cooler and drier in the northern highlands.

About 75 percent of Thailand's people live in rural areas. Farming is the principal occupation, and rice is the dominant crop. Farmers also cultivate cassava, corn, soybeans, sugarcane, bananas, coconuts, and pineapples. Cotton, jute, and rubber are the chief non-food crops.

Thailand also has considerable mineral wealth. Miners dig up zinc, copper, feldspar, kaolin, lead, limestone, and lignite. Buried in the sandbars of Thailand's shallow coastal waters are some of the world's richest tin deposits—making Thailand one of the world's leading suppliers of that valuable mineral. The country extracts natural gas from offshore wells in the Gulf of Thailand but otherwise is short of fuel and has to import most of the oil it needs.

Tropical hardwoods—especially teak—were one of Thailand's chief exports until unregulated cutting created mudslides, rock falls, and massive soil erosion. Enormous environmental damage and destruction of entire villages led the Thai government to halt hardwood cutting in 1988. The country focused on developing other industries, especially tourism and manufacturing. The capital city of Bangkok has become a major manufacturing center, producing textiles, automobiles, electronic goods, cement, pharmaceuticals, paper, plywood, and agricultural chemicals.

Thailand's growing economy supports free primary schools and a large number of secondary schools and colleges. Nearly 90 percent of the population can read and write. But the drift of poor rural people to the cities and the continued presence of many Vietnamese refugees have placed great pressure on housing and other services.

Top: More than 400 temples grace Thailand's capital, Bangkok, on the delta of the Chao Phraya River. Their intricately decorated walls and ornate spires are a major tourist attraction.

Above left: Figures of the Buddha, usually covered in gold leaf, are the focal point of Buddhist temples.

Above right: Traders and shoppers throng the floating markets of Bangkok's rivers and canals.

Vietnam, Laos, and Cambodia

Vietnam

Status:	Republic
Area:	128,066 square miles
Population:	79.5 million
Capital:	Hanoi
Languages:	Vietnamese, French, English
Currency:	Dông (100 xu)

Vietnam is a long, narrow, S-shaped country with a 2,140-mile-long coastline on the South China Sea. The country stretches 1,030 miles north to south and 380 miles west to east at its widest, although the central section is barely 30 miles wide.

France controlled Vietnam before World War II (1939-1945), but Japan occupied the country during the war. France's efforts to regain control after the war were defeated in 1954 by the Communist army of the Vietminh. Peace negotiators divided the country into Communist North and non-Communist South, but fighting soon broke out between the two nations and escalated into a full-scale civil war. The United States was deeply involved in support of South Vietnam but withdrew when the two Vietnams declared a cease-fire in 1973. In 1975 the Communist regime unified the country.

Densely forested mountains cover northwestern Vietnam, continuing in a narrow mountain chain along the borders with Laos and Cambodia. Most Vietnamese live in two large river deltas that dominate eastern Vietnam. The Red River Delta in the north and the Mekong Delta in the south provide fertile farmland where Vietnamese farmers grow rice, maize, cassava, soybeans, vegetables, peanuts, coconuts, coffee beans, and cacao beans. Cotton, jute, rubber, and tobacco are the main nonfood crops. Fishing crews catch crabs, lobsters, shrimp, and squid off the coast. Apart from coal in the north, Vietnam has few mineral resources. Factory workers produce farm machinery, bicycles, cement, fertilizers, and textiles.

Laos

Status:	Republic
Area:	91,429 square miles
Population:	5.0 million
Capital:	Vientiane
Languages:	Lao, French, Vietnamese
Currency:	Kip (100 at)

Laos, like its neighbor Vietnam, was formerly a French-controlled territory. The country threw off foreign control in 1954 but then suffered a long period of civil war before it emerged as an independent Communist state in 1975.

Mountains blanketed in dense, humid tropical rain forest cover the north of the country, while broad, fertile lowlands along the Mekong River and its many tributaries dominate the south. Farmers in the highlands grow maize, rice, tobacco, and cotton. Lowland farmers harvest rice as their principal crop, along with vegetables, fruit, maize, and coffee beans. Most farmers also raise pigs, cattle, and poultry.

Laos is rich in natural resources but poor in infrastructure—the roads, refineries, and other operations that help export the resources. As a result, its deposits of gold, lead, silver, tin, zinc, and other minerals and its valuable stand of tropical hardwoods, gums, and resins have yet to be tapped.

Left: Youngsters have fun wherever they live, and Vietnam's rivers provide a natural playground.

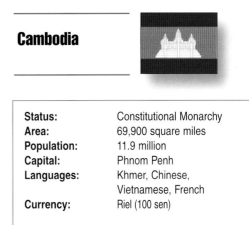

Status:	Constitutional Monarchy
Area:	69,900 square miles
Population:	11.9 million
Capital:	Phnom Penh
Languages:	Khmer, Chinese, Vietnamese, French
Currency:	Riel (100 sen)

Cambodia is a mainly lowland country in Southeast Asia, ringed by low forested hills along its borders with Thailand, Laos, and Vietnam. In the south, Cambodia has a short coast on the Gulf of Thailand. The country's principal port, Kompong Som, lies on the south side of a large enclosed bay, just over 100 miles southwest of the capital city of Phnom Penh.

The largest ethnic group in Cambodia are the Khmer, whose ancestors ruled a vast empire in Southeast Asia about a thousand years ago. The magnificent ruined temples of Angkor, capital of the Khmer Empire, are among the most spectacular ancient monuments in southern Asia.

The tradition of royal rule gave way in 1863 to French control as part of French Indochina. Cambodia became fully independent in 1954 but then suffered years of civil war. For nearly 20 years, it was ruled harshly by the Communist Khmer Rouge. In 1993 Cambodia's monarchy was reinstated.

Most of Cambodia's people are farmers, living in small lowland villages. With fertile soils, plentiful rain, and numerous rivers to provide water, most farmers grow two or even three crops of rice a year. Rivers, lakes, and warm offshore waters yield Cambodia's other main food—fish. Cotton and rubber are important commercial crops. Factory workers produce textiles, plywood, cement, and tires.

Left: Water buffaloes are the "living tractors" of rural Asia, pulling carts and plows, hauling logs in the forests, and driving threshing machines, water pumps, sugar cane presses, and other machines.

Malaysia, Singapore, and Brunei

Malaysia

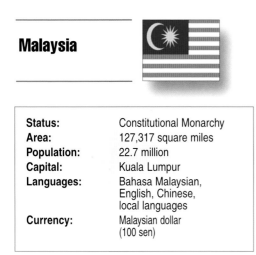

Status:	Constitutional Monarchy
Area:	127,317 square miles
Population:	22.7 million
Capital:	Kuala Lumpur
Languages:	Bahasa Malaysian, English, Chinese, local languages
Currency:	Malaysian dollar (100 sen)

Malaysia has two large but widely separated land areas. West Malaysia consists of the southern end of the long, paddle-shaped Malay Peninsula which also holds Thailand. East Malaysia, 400 miles away across the South China Sea, consists of the territories of Sarawak and Sabah on the northern side of the island of Borneo. (The other parts of Borneo belong to Indonesia or form the independent country of Brunei.)

The modern state of Malaysia was formed in 1963, when the Federation of Malaya and the British colonies of Singapore, Sarawak, and Sabah joined together. Singapore left the federation in 1965 to become an independent country.

Roughly 50 percent of the people of Malaysia are Malay, 35 percent are Chinese, and 10 percent are Indian. The rest, especially people in Sarawak and Sabah, belong to many smaller ethnic groups. This ethnic diversity gives Malaysia a rich and varied culture in which art, music, dance, drama, and sports play a part. Islam, Hinduism, Buddhism, Christianity exist side by side without conflict.

Much of Malaysia is covered in dense tropical forests. From the Thai border, a ridge of mountains runs down the Malay Peninsula, where 80 percent of the Malaysians live. The ridge forms a thinly populated inland zone that is separated from the densely populated coastal areas where the principal cities are located.

Rugged mountains dominate the interior of Sarawak and Sabah, while fertile plains line parts of the coast. The highlands of East Malaysia are famous for their dramatic limestone scenery.

Above: Old architecture of the secretariat buildings contrast with the modern city in Kuala Lumpur.

Towering rock outcrops loom out of the forest, and huge cave systems run for miles beneath the surface.

Malaysia's economy, one of the strongest economies in Asia, is based on agriculture, industry, and trade. The country produces half the world's palm oil and one-third of the world's rubber, as well as being a major producer of cacao beans, tobacco, coconuts, tea, peppers, pineapples, and other fruits. Malaysia's forests produce valuable hardwoods that are shipped worldwide as logs, boards, veneers, plywood, and furniture. Malaysia is the world's third-largest producer of tin and ranks as a major producer of oil and gas. Long-established industries produce textiles, rubber goods, timber products, and foodstuffs, while a host of new high-tech industries export electronic equipment, industrial chemicals, pharmaceuticals, and plastics, chiefly to Japan, Singapore, the United States, and Europe. This strong economic base gives most of Malaysia's people access to good educational and health-care services.

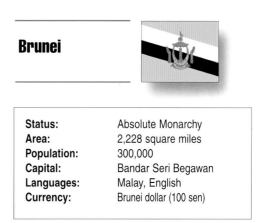

Singapore

Status:	Republic
Area:	239 square miles
Population:	4 million
Capital:	Singapore
Languages:	Malay, Mandarin Chinese, English, Tamil
Currency:	Singapore dollar (100 cents)

Singapore is a small country by area, but it is one of the economic power-houses of Southeast Asia. The country consists of one main island (Singapore Island) and about 50 smaller ones that are clustered at the tip of the Malay Peninsula. The city of Singapore is the capital and one of the world's busiest seaports.

The skyline of the crowded, bustling capital is dominated by the high-rise towers of its commercial district. These structures rise above traditional shop-houses, elegant apartment buildings, shopping malls, industrial districts, and the container terminals, warehouses, and repair yards that service the endless flow of ships.

Forests once covered Singapore's low-lying land, but most of the trees were cut down in colonial days to make way for groves of nutmeg, cloves, rubber, and coconuts. Almost half the land is built on, and most of the rest consists of parks and other public spaces. Singapore's small amount of farmland produces fruit and vegetables for local use, but most of the island's food has to be imported. Water is piped in from Malaysia to meet the city's needs.

Like Malaysia, Singapore has a diverse population. About 78 percent are Chinese, 14 percent Malay, and 7 percent Indian. A small number of Europeans and Americans live in Singapore, where hundreds of international companies have offices.

Singapore's wealth comes from importing and exporting goods from all over the world. It also has a thriving manufacturing sector making electrical and electronic goods, textiles, clothing, cameras, scientific instruments, chemicals, plastics, and food products. Heavy industry consists of ship repairs and oil refining.

The wealth generated by Singapore's economy provides the people with some of the highest living standards in Asia, including high wages, free schools, modern health-care services, and a rich cultural life. More than 90 percent of the people can read and write, one of the highest literacy rates in Asia.

Right: Modern office blocks tower over Singapore's waterfront.

Brunei

Status:	Absolute Monarchy
Area:	2,228 square miles
Population:	300,000
Capital:	Bandar Seri Begawan
Languages:	Malay, English
Currency:	Brunei dollar (100 sen)

Brunei is a small W-shaped country on the northern coast of the island of Borneo, facing the South China Sea. Most of the country consists of a broad coastal plain, rising inland to wooded hills.

Formerly a British protectorate, Brunei achieved independence in 1984 and is ruled by a sultan (king) who is elected for life by a council of senior politicians. About 65 percent of the people are Malay and predominantly Muslim. Another 25 percent are Chinese and Christian. More than 70 percent of the population live in the towns and cities.

The mainstays of Brunei's economy are the oil and gas fields that lie beneath its coastal waters. Money from the sale of oil and gas has made Brunei wealthy. The people enjoy a high standard of living, with free education and health care. The government is the country's largest employer, providing jobs for more than half the nation's workforce. The remainder work on small farms, in the coastal fisheries, and in small factories making consumer goods, chiefly for local use.

Philippines

Status:	Republic
Area:	115,830 square miles
Population:	74.7 million
Capital:	Manila
Languages:	Tagalog, English, Spanish, Cebuano
Currency:	Filipino peso (100 centavos)

Above: Modern buildings dominate the center of Manila.

The Republic of the Philippines consists of more than 7,100 islands, set in the western Pacific Ocean between Taiwan to the north and Indonesia to the south. The island group extends 1,150 miles north to south, nearly 700 miles west to east, and has almost 11,000 miles of coastline. About 1,000 of the islands are inhabited. Most Filipinos live on the two largest islands—Luzon at the northern end and Mindanao in the south—and on the cluster of medium-sized islands called the Visayas that lie between them. About half the total population lives on Luzon, with the greatest concentration in and around the capital city of Manila.

Mountains dominate the interior of most of the larger islands, with lowland plains fringing the coasts. The only large inland plains are on Luzon and Panay, where fertile soils support the islands' most productive rice farms. The Philippine islands were formed by volcanoes, and more than 20 of them are still active. Mount Pinatubo, northwest of Manila Bay, erupted in 1991 in one of the most violent volcanic eruptions of the past century. Forests cover about half the total land area, providing the islands with a valuable resource. Philippine mahogany is exported worldwide, pine and bamboo are used for large- and small-scale construction projects. The cottonlike fiber that covers the seed pods of the kapok tree is harvested and exported for use as an insulation material and for stuffing furniture.

Spain founded a colony in the Philippines (named for King Philip II of Spain) in 1566 and governed the islands for the next 300 years. The United States took control in 1898, and made the islands a self-governing commonwealth in 1935. The Philippines became fully independent in 1946.

The Philippines population contains many different ethnic groups. Most Filipinos are descended from early immigrants from Indonesia and Malaya. Others are descended from more recent arrivals from China, India, Japan, Europe, and North America. A few large groups dominate the lowlands and cities of the main islands, but the mountainous regions are home to many smaller groups who speak more than 100 local languages and dialects and have their own distinctive traditions and cultures.

The islands' fertile volcanic soils and a hot, damp, tropical climate make the land very productive. Filipino farmers grow most of the food the country needs. Rice and maize are the staple food crops. Others include cassava, sweet potatoes, mangoes, and bananas. Cacao beans, coffee beans, pineapples, sugarcane, hemp, and tobacco are grown for use within the Philippines and also for export. Farmers also raise large numbers of cattle, water buffalo, pigs, goats, and hens. Most of the crops are grown on the plains, but the northern part of Luzon also contains some of Asia's most spectacular hillside rice terraces some of them built more than 2,000 years ago. As well as producing food, these remarkable fields are a major tourist attraction, along with the islands' stunning scenery, wild flowers and birds, and beautiful beaches.

Fishing is a major industry in this island nation. Fishing crews catch sardines, mackerel, tuna, and many other fish offshore, and crabs, shellfish, and sponges are harvested from the shallow coastal waters. Fish farmers raise shrimp and tilapia, a popular food fish, in artificial ponds constructed along the shores.

Mining and manufacturing are the fastest-growing sectors of the economy. Miners produce copper, nickel, and gold for export, but the islands also contain large reserves of chromite, lead, silver, manganese, and zinc that have yet to be exploited. Food processing is the largest industry. Newer industries include textiles, clothing and shoes, electrical and electronic goods, and furniture.

The economy of the Philippines is still developing, but government projects over the past 20 years have improved housing, health care, water supplies, and sanitation. Almost 90 percent of the population can read and write, and nearly all school-age children attend school.

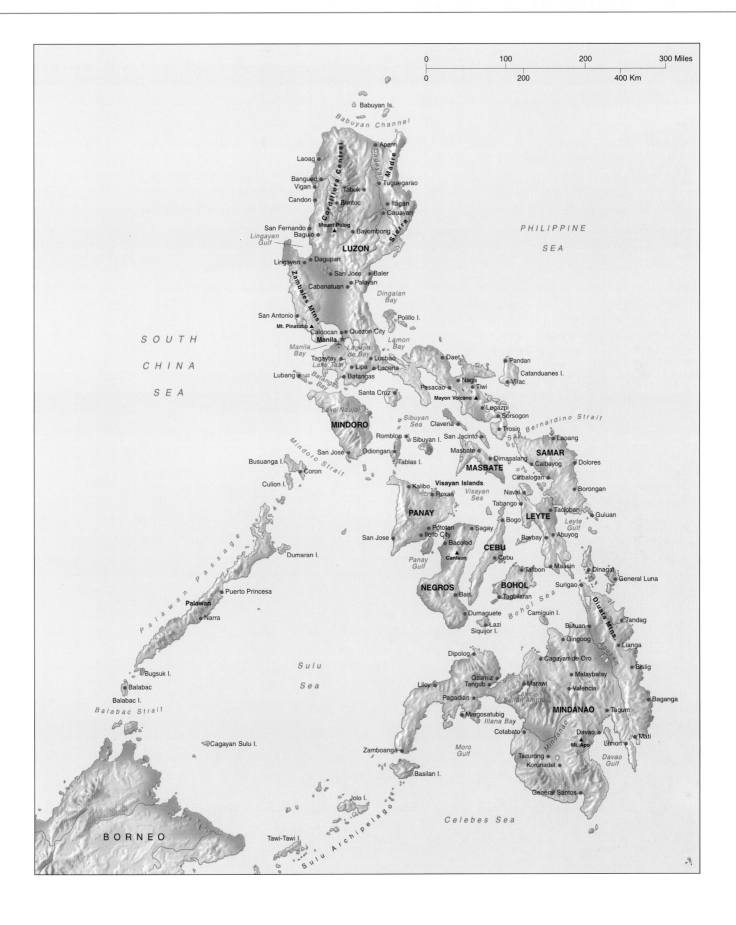

0   100   200   300 Miles
0   200   400 Km

Babuyan Is.

Babuyan Channel

Laoag
Aparri
Cordillera Central
Cagayan
Madre
Bangued
Tuguegarao
Vigan
Tabuk
Bontoc
Candon
Ilagan
Cauayan
San Fernando
Mount Pulog ▲
Baguio
Bayombong
Lingayen Gulf
LUZON
Sierra
Lingayen
Dagupan
San Jose
Baler
Cabanatuan
Palayan
Dingalan Bay
Zambales Mtns.
San Antonio
Polillo I.
Mt. Pinatubo ▲
Caloocan
Quezon City
Manila ★
Lamon Bay
Manila Bay
Laguna de Bay
Tagaytay
Lucbao
Daet
Pandan
Lake Taal
Lipa
Lucena
Naga
Catanduanes I.
Lubang
Batangas
Tiwi
Virac
Batangas Bay
Santa Cruz
Pasacao
Mayon Volcano ▲
Lake Naujan
Sibuyan Sea
Legazpi
Sorsogon
MINDORO
Claveria
Trosin
San Bernardino Strait
San Jose
Romblon
Sibuyan I.
San Jacinto
Laoang
Mindoro Strait
Odiongan
Masbate
Dimasalang
SAMAR
Busuanga I.
Tablas I.
MASBATE
Calbayog
Dolores
Coron
Catbalogan
Borongan
Culion I.
Kalibo
Visayan Islands
Naval
Dumaran I.
Roxas
Visayan Sea
Tabango
Tacloban
Guiuan
PANAY
Bogo
LEYTE
Leyte Gulf
San Jose
Pototan
Sagay
Baybay
Abuyog
Iloilo City
Bacolod
CEBU
Cebu
Panay Gulf
Canlaon ▲
Dinagat
NEGROS
Tañbon
Maasin
General Luna
Bais
BOHOL
Surigao
Puerto Princesa
Tagbilaran
Bohol Sea
Camiguin I.
Diuata Mtns.
Tandag
Palawan
Dumaguete
Butuan
Lianga
Narra
Lazi
Gingoog
Siquijor I.
Dipolog
Cagayan de Oro
Bislig
Palawan Passage
Ozamiz
Malaybalay
Liloy
Tangub
Marawi
Valencia
Baganga
Bugsuk I.
Pagadian
Lake Sultan Alonto
Tagum
Balabac
Margosatubig
MINDANAO
Balabac I.
Illana Bay
Davao
Balabac Strait
Cotabato
Mt. Apo ▲
Lunon
Mati
Cagayan Sulu I.
Tacurong
Davao Gulf
Zamboanga
Moro Gulf
Koronadel
Basilan I.
General Santos

SOUTH CHINA SEA

PHILIPPINE SEA

Sulu Sea

BORNEO

Jolo I.

Tawi-Tawi I.

Sulu Archipelago

Celebes Sea

Indelesia

Indonesia

Status:	Republic
Area:	741,097 square miles
Population:	212 million
Capital:	Jakarta
Languages:	Bahasa Indonesian, Dutch, English
Currency:	Rupiah (100 sen)

Indonesia consists of more than 13,600 islands strung out in a 3,100-mile chain across a vast expanse of tropical sea between the eastern Indian Ocean and the western Pacific Ocean. Many of the islands cover only a few square miles, but Indonesia also includes some of the world's largest islands. Sumatra, for example, is nearly 1,060 miles long, and Java is more than 620 miles long. Indonesia also includes the western half of the world's second-largest island, New Guinea, called Irian Jaya, and more than three-quarters of the world's third-largest island, Borneo, which makes up the province of

Kalimantan. People inhabit about half the islands, but 80 per cent of the population live on Sumatra, Java, Kalimantan, Sulawesi, and Irian Jaya, with almost half the total population crowded onto Java.

Most of Indonesia's people are of Malay descent, but the population also includes Chinese, Papuans, Arabs, and Polynesians. Islam is the dominant religion, but millions of people on the smaller islands and in remote inland regions also follow ancient traditional beliefs. The largest cities are Jakarta, Surabaya, and Bandung (all on Java) and Medan on Sumatra. The majority of the nation's people, however, live in small rural communities.

The Indonesian islands are dotted with hundreds of active volcanoes. Mountains covered in dense rainforest dominate the interior regions, while broad fertile plains fringe the coasts. Forestry workers extract teak, ebony, and other valuable hardwoods from the forests—chiefly on Borneo and Sumatra. Rattan and bamboo are also harvested for making mats and furniture. Most village houses are made of these versatile materials.

Agriculture is the backbone of Indonesia's economy. The country's farmers benefit from rich volcanic soil, plentiful rain, and year-round sunshine, all of which allows them to grow a wide variety of crops. Large plantations on the main islands produce coffee beans, tea, sugarcane, palm oil, rubber, and tobacco

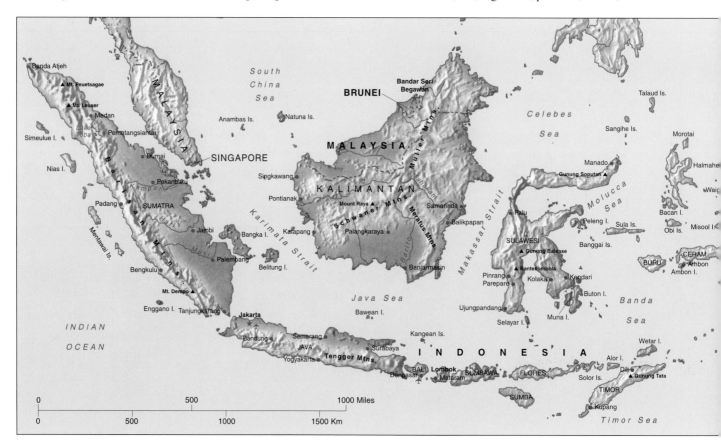

Above: Indonesian houses are built to several striking traditional designs. This style, built by the Minangkabau people of Sumatra, has roof-ends that sweep upward like the horns of a water buffalo.

Below: A young Indonesian villager heads for the paddy fields, protected from the hot sun by a wide hat made of woven bamboo.

as cash crops. Smaller farms grow rice as their main food crop, along with maize, sweet potatoes, cassava, bananas, and other fruits and vegetables. Rural farms are not highly mechanized. Most farmers use traditional hand tools, and plows and carts are pulled by oxen and water buffalo. Many farmers also raise pigs, goats, and poultry for the table. In coastal areas, sardines, anchovies, tuna, prawns, and shellfish provide the protein in people's diets.

Oil and natural gas fields on Java and Sumatra supply fuel to the islands and are also Indonesia's principal export. Tin, from islands off the northern coast of Sumatra, is the country's second major mineral export. Miners also extract smaller amounts of coal, copper, manganese, and nickel. Manufacturing is a relatively small part of the economy, and is concentrated almost entirely on Java. Factory workers process food products for export and make textiles, glassware, rubber products such as car tires, furniture, paper, and other wood products. Newer industries include car and truck assembly plants and petrochemical plants fed by the country's oil fields.

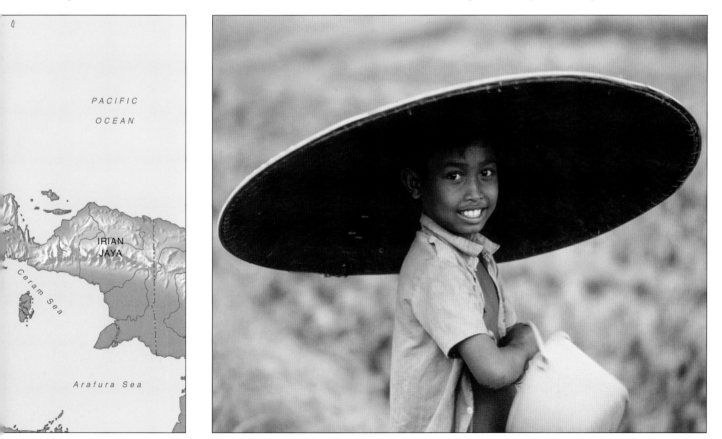

Vanua Levu Island, Fiji

AUSTRALIA, the PACIFIC, and ANTARCTICA

AUSTRALASIA, the PACIFIC, and ANTARCTICA

Three enormous and hugely contrasting regions—Australia, the islands of the Pacific Ocean, and the great southern continent of Antarctica—lie in the Southern Hemisphere. Together they cover 40 percent of the earth's surface, yet between them they have a total population of barely 30 million people.

Australia is the only country to have an entire continent to itself. Separated from other land areas 200 million years ago, Australia became home to a unique collection of animals and plants, many of them found nowhere else on earth. Its original people, the Aborigines, arrived by canoe from Southeast Asia more than 40,000 years ago. These

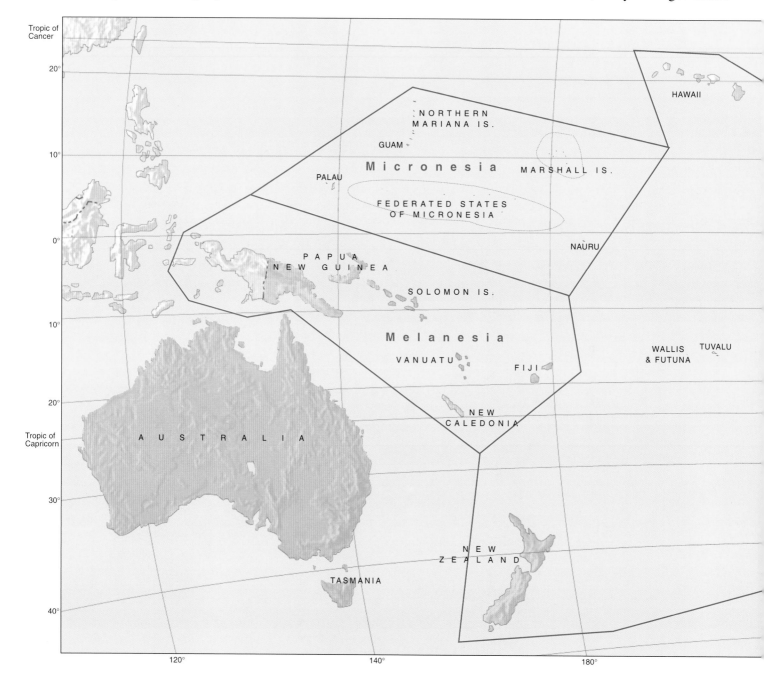

early peoples lived by hunting and gathering. In the 1600s, when Europeans first began to explore the Southern Hemisphere, about 300,000 Aborigines lived in Australia. Britain took control of the continent in the late 1700s, using it first as a place to send convicted criminals. It was not until the 1800s that the British began to explore the country, setting Australia on the road to become a leading industrialized nation.

The Pacific Ocean covers more of the earth's surface than all the world's land areas combined. It stretches more than 14,500 miles, from the islands of Malaysia in the west to the coast of Colombia in the east and from the Bering Sea off Alaska's shores in the north to the icy waters of Antarctica in the south. Almost lost within this vast expanse are between 20,000 and 30,000 islands—the exact number is unknown. Thousands are tiny coral islands and reefs that hardly break the ocean surface. Others, such as New Guinea and New Zealand, are among the world's largest islands. Scattered across the ocean—alone or in clusters or in beadlike chains—the Pacific islands are home to a remarkable variety of peoples. Geographers divide the islands into three groups. Melanesia, meaning "black islands," includes New Guinea, the Solomons, New Caledonia, and Vanuatu. To the north lies Micronesia (small islands), including Guam, the Marshall Islands, the Caroline Islands, Nauru, and others. And to the east stretches Polynesia (many islands), a group that extends north to south from Hawaii to New Zealand and west to east from Tuvalu to Easter Island.

Antarctica has no people, apart from a few thousand visiting scientists, and no year-round animal residents. In summer its shores and offshore islands teem with breeding seabirds, penguins, and seals, but in winter it is almost deserted—a vast, high, windswept plateau of snow and ice, broken in places by the jagged peaks of mountain ranges jutting up through ice up to two miles thick.

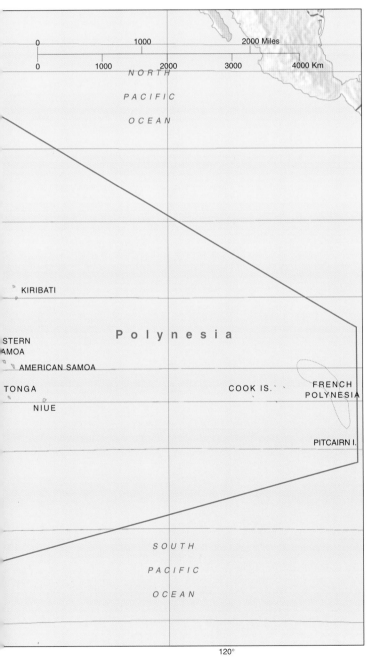

Above: Floodwaters frequently cover the swamp-lined banks of Papua-New Guinea's Sepik River, so the local people build their houses on stilts.

Papua New Guinea

Papua New Guinea

Status:	Constitutional Monarchy
Area:	178,703 square miles
Population:	4.7 million
Capital:	Port Moresby
Languages:	English, Pidgin English, Motu
Currency:	Kina (100 toea)

Papua New Guinea consists of the eastern half of the island of New Guinea and more than 600 smaller islands, including New Britain, the Bismarck Archipelago, Bougainville Island, the Louisiade Archipelago, and the D'Entrecasteaux Islands. Papua New Guinea's nearest neighbors are Indonesia, Malaysia, and the Philippines to the west and northwest and Australia to the south. In the late nineteenth century, parts of the region were controlled by Germany and later Britain. After World War I (1914-1918), the island became a mandated territory under the League of Nations. By the end of World War II (1939-1945), the United Nations (the league's successor) had declared it a trust territory to be administered by Australia. Papua New Guinea became independent in 1975 but maintains close ties to Australia.

Mountains that reach 8,000 to 14,000 feet above sea level dominate the interior of the main island. In between the mountains are steep river gorges. Tropical rain forests cover most of the land, but broad valleys and basins within the mountains provide large areas of rich soil that support most of the country's agriculture. Most of Papua New Guinea's people live in these highland valleys and basins, where the climate is cooler and healthier than it is on the coast.

Papua New Guinea's hot, humid coastal plains support a number of large towns—Wewak, Madang, Lae, and Popondetta on the north coast and Kerema, Kupiano, and the capital of Port Moresby in the south. However, swamps cover large parts of the coast, and few people live in these areas.

Left: Mount Hagen tribesmen gather in full ceremonial costume for a singsing (feast). Shells and wild boar tusks decorate their belts and necklaces, and bird of paradise feathers adorn their magnificent headdresses. A bird of paradise also features on the country's flag.

Most of Papua New Guinea's people live in small villages, where hundreds of dialects are spoken and where there is a huge variety of traditions and customs. Farmers on most of the islands grow taro, yams, and bananas in the wetter areas and sweet potatoes, coconuts, and other vegetables and fruits on the drier soils. Pigs and chickens provide meat for most families. Farmers on small holdings and on large plantations produce cash crops for export. The principal commercial crops are coffee beans, cacao beans, copra, and tea, with smaller amounts of peanuts, tobacco, rubber, and pyrethrum (used to make insecticides).

The farmers who live in the forested regions of the mountainous interior follow an age-old farming practice called shifting cultivation. According to this practice, farmers clear the land of trees and undergrowth, which are then burned. The resulting ash fertilizes the soil, allowing crops to be grown for two or three years. The farmers move on, clearing a new patch and enabling the forest to regenerate trees and undergrowth in the old plot.

Forestry workers extract hardwoods for export as logs, sawn lumber, plywood, and veneers. These goods are destined mainly for Australia, Asia, and Europe. Fishers catch many species for the home and export markets, the most valuable export being skipjack tuna.

Factories in Port Moresby, Lae, Madang, Bulolo, and Goroka on the main island, in Kieta on Bougainville Island, and in Rabaul on New Britain process farm and forest produce and manufacture furniture, textiles, clothing, cement, and chemicals. Papua New Guinea has many large mineral deposits, but many are in inaccessible regions and so far have not been exploited. Natural gas fields around the Gulf of Papua produce energy for the country. The chief mineral exports are copper and gold from the world's biggest copper mine, which is located at Panguna on Bougainville Island. Japan, Germany, and Spain buy the bulk of the copper exports. Papua New Guinea is not wealthy, but its government is using the profits of its developing economy to improve access to health-care and educational services.

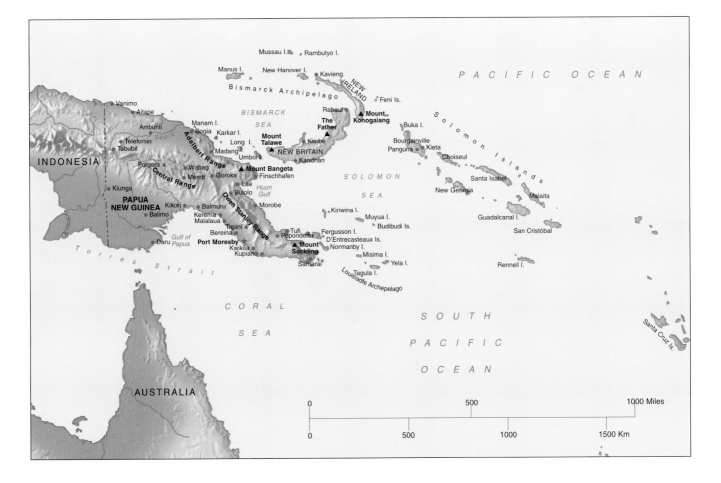

Australia

Australia

Status:	Constitutional Monarchy and Federation of States
Area:	2.98 million square miles
Population:	19.0 million
Capital:	Canberra
Languages:	English
Currency:	Australian dollar (100 cents)

Australia—the world's sixth largest country—is the only country to occupy an entire continent. It is also one of the most thinly populated countries in the world, with an average of only six people per square mile. But even that figure is misleading. Deserts, scrub, and dry grasslands cover nearly all of western and central Australia, and these arid and semi-arid regions support an average of only one or two people per square mile.

Most of Australia's 19 million people are concentrated along the southern and eastern coasts, where there is enough rainfall to support intensive agriculture and large urban areas. In fact, more than 80 percent of Australians live in cities and towns. Some of the largest cities are Perth in the southwest, Adelaide, Melbourne, and Sydney in the southeast, and Brisbane in the east.

Agriculture and mining are the mainstays of Australia's economy. They employ relatively few people but produce virtually all Australia's export goods. The two sectors are also the source of raw materials for many of Australia's industries.

About 65 percent of Australia's land is available for farming, but climate and terrain determine how farmers use the land. The western two-thirds of Australia consist of a vast, dry plateau. Deserts, unsuitable for any kind of farming, fill the central region and are surrounded by dry grasslands that extend to the coast. Livestock farmers raise sheep on these grasslands, primarily for their wool, which is one of Australia's principal exports. Rainfall increases toward the southwest, allowing farmers to grow wheat, another important export. A small region south of Perth is wet enough to nurture crops of fruits and vegetables and to support dairy herds. In the northern part of the state of Western Australia, farmers graze herds of beef cattle.

The eastern one-third of Australia divides into two subregions—a central lowland region and the eastern highlands, which parallel the coast from Cape York to Melbourne. Farmers in the southern part of the lowlands raise cattle and sheep and grow wheat, barley, and vegetables. The Great Dividing Range dominates the eastern highlands. This region of hills and plateaus is not very high—the highest point is Mount

Right: Ayers Rock— Uluru in the native Aboriginal language —rises to 2,844 feet in central Australia. Caves along its flanks contain hundreds of ancient Aboriginal rock paintings.

Kosciuszko at 7,310 feet—but it separates rivers flowing into the hot interior from those that flow to the Pacific coast. More rain falls on the highlands than on any other part of Australia, and the region's fertile soil supports Australia's most productive farms. Farmers in the states of New South Wales and Victoria grow rice, wheat, barley, vegetables, sugarcane, oranges and other fruits, and grapes for making wine. Others specialize in beef and dairy produce. Farmers farther north, along the coast of the state of Queensland, concentrate on raising sugarcane and tropical fruits such as bananas and grapefruit.

Australia is one of the world's leading exporters of diamonds, lead, and bauxite (the principal ore of aluminum) and is a major supplier of iron ore, nickel, silver, tin, copper, gold, tungsten, and zinc. Australian miners also produce gypsum and asbestos, which are used for making construction materials, and uranium, which powers nuclear plants. Coal, oil, and gas fields provide much of Australia's energy needs and are supplemented by some of the world's biggest solar energy complexes.

Manufacturing and service industries provide more than three-quarters of the country's jobs. Many workers process farm products such as meat, dairy products, wool, sugarcane, and fruit for export. Factories produce furniture, textiles, clothing, shoes, household appliances and other consumer goods, while heavier industries include iron and steel, car manufacture, chemicals, and paper. Tourism is another important industry. Attractions like the Great Barrier Reef and Ayers Rock provide thousands of jobs and attract more than one million visitors every year.

Because of the country's successful economy, most Australians enjoy a high standard of living, with comfortable housing, well-developed social amenities, and excellent educational and health systems. In addition to supporting sports facilities of nearly every kind, the cities also cater to a wide variety of cultural tastes, with some of the world's finest opera houses, concert halls, theaters, and art galleries. Medical and

Below: Sydney Harbor, with downtown office blocks forming a backdrop to the city's spectacular modern Opera House.

Above: An Aboriginal elder. In recent years, Aboriginal claims to ownership of their traditional lands and sacred places has been a big issue in Australian politics. The Aborigines are an ancient people with a rich and complex culture based on their close relationship with the animals, plants, and landscapes of their tribal territories.

Above: The main road from Western Australia to the cities of south-east Australia runs close to the south coast, across the dry, flat expanse of the Nullarbor Plain. The plain is well named. Nullarbor comes from the Latin words *nullus* and *arbor*—"no tree".

educational support is also available to the 13 percent of tha population who live in the widely scattered mining settlements and sheep stations (ranches) of the interior, commonly called the outback. Members of Australia's famous Royal Flying Doctor Service are always ready to go to the outback to give urgent medical assistance. Teachers use two-way radios to reach young people studying at home.

More than 40,000 years ago, Australia's indigenous people, the Aborigines, arrived from Southeast Asia. They traveled by raft or canoe across the shallow seas that separated Asia and Australia at that time. Numbering more than 200,000, they live mainly in rural areas of the states of New South Wales, Queensland, and Northern Territory. In recent decades, many young Aborigines have moved to the towns, but most are disadvantaged in terms of education, employment, and living standards. Many Aborigines feel a great sense of injustice at the treatment of their people, their ancient culture, and their ancestral lands by the overwhelmingly dominant European-descended population.

European settlement began with a British penal colony in New South Wales in 1788. But exploration and voluntary settlement developed rapidly through the nineteenth century, based principally on mining and sheep farming. The fledgling states of Australia joined together under a federal constitution in 1901. The British monarch is head of state and is represented in Australia by a governor-general.

Australia still has close links with Britain, but since the 1960s trade has become more and more focused on Asia, especially Japan and China, and on the United States. Partly as a result of this shift, many Australians believe the time has come for the country to break its historic ties with Britain and to become a republic. Another factor has been the change in Australia's population mixture. Historically, England, Scotland, Ireland, Germany, and the Netherlands supplied most of Australia's immigrants, but the country relaxed its immigration laws in the 1960s, and since then new waves of immigrants have arrived from Greece, Italy, eastern Europe, the Middle East, and Asia.

New Zealand

New Zealand

Status:	Constitutional Monarchy
Area:	104,452 square miles
Population:	3.8 million
Capital:	Wellington
Languages:	English, Maori
Currency:	New Zealand dollar (100 cents)

Above: Lush grazing land in the east of New Zealand's North Island.

New Zealand, separated from Australia by the Tasman Sea, lies almost 1,000 miles southeast of its giant neighbor. New Zealand's two main islands—North and South—and a scattering of smaller ones form the southernmost islands of Polynesia. Geological activity thrust the islands above sea level recently—at least in geologic time. South Island broke the surface 10 to 15 million years ago, and parts of North Island pushed upward within the past 5 million years.

Volcanic mountains cover the central and western portions of North Island. The tallest peak is Mount Ruapehu, which rises to 9,175 feet above sea level. Thick layers of volcanic lava extend over much of the land, creating fertile soil. Geysers and bubbling mud pools attract millions of tourists and provide New Zealand with a valuable energy source. Holes drilled deep into the ground tap superheated steam, which is used to drive the turbines of geothermal power stations. Low hills in eastern North Island offer grazing for beef cattle, dairy herds, and sheep, while farmers in the region's coastal lowlands grow fruits and vegetables. Forests, sandy beaches, and sheltered inlets make the ragged northern peninsula a popular vacation area.

The larger South Island is dominated by the Southern Alps, which angle across the country from northeast to southwest. Snowfields and glaciers cover Mount Cook (12,349 feet) and other neighboring peaks, which tower above forested slopes and beautiful lakes. Stunning mountain scenery attracts walkers and climbers from all over the world. Dense forests cover the western slopes of the Alps, which drop steeply to a narrow coastal plain. To the east, the mountains slope more gently to the broad, flat Canterbury Plains and to the rolling hills of Otago in the south. The Canterbury Plains provide New Zealand's only extensive lowland area, where farmers grow wheat, barley, oats, and fodder crops.

Cropland and pasture are New Zealand's greatest assets, supporting nearly 60 million sheep and about 8 million cattle. Mutton, lamb, beef, dairy produce, and wool are exported to Australia, Britain, Europe, Japan, and the United States and make up about half the country's export earnings. New Zealand farmers are also the world's principal suppliers of kiwi fruit. A thriving fishing industry hauls in crabs, lobsters, and shellfish for the home market and for export. New Zealand's forestry industry supports lumber, plywood, and paper factories. More than 90 percent of the wood comes from plantations of pine.

Hydroelectric stations on rivers supply about 75 percent of New Zealand's energy needs. Geothermal energy, coal, oil, and natural gas provide the rest. New Zealand's modest reserves of iron ore, gold, silver, and tungsten are insufficient to support heavy industry, so iron and steel, industrial machinery, cars, buses and trucks, and oil are the country's principal imports. Factories concentrated around Dunedin and Christchurch on South Island and around Wellington (the nation's capital) and Auckland on North Island produce textiles, clothing, food products, furniture, metal goods, chemicals, and petroleum products.

New Zealand's mixed economy supports a high standard of living. Most people live in comfortable, well-equipped homes. Excellent health-care and educational services are available to everyone. The cities provide theaters, galleries, and other cultural attractions, and most towns have a wide range of sports facilities. The countryside caters to nearly every outdoor activity from skiing to sailing.

The first settlers in New Zealand were the Maori, who arrived from islands elsewhere in Polynesia more than 1,000 years ago. The Maori make up about 15 percent of the population, with the remaining 85 percent being the descendants of British immigrants who began to arrive in the 1800s. Equal opportunity is a hallmark of the New Zealand way of life, and many Maori have achieved prominence in business and public office. The national government is still trying to resolve long-standing disputes over land rights. It is also attempting to improve educational and job opportunities for low-income Maori.

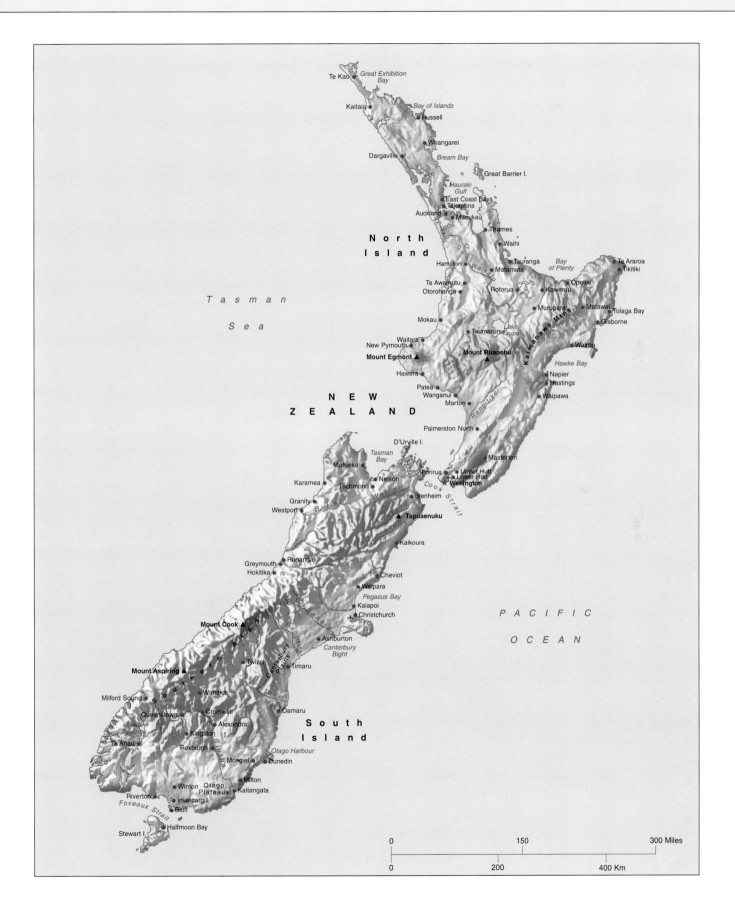

Te Kao
Great Exhibition Bay

Kaitaia
Bay of Islands
Russell

Whangarei

Dargaville
Bream Bay

Great Barrier I.

Hauraki Gulf

East Coast Bays
Takapuna
Auckland ● Manukau

Thames

**N o r t h
I s l a n d**

Waihi

Hamilton
Waikato
Tauranga
Bay of Plenty
Matamata
Te Araroa
Tikitiki

T a s m a n

Te Awamutu
Otorohanga
Rotorua
Kawerau
Opotiki

Mokau
Murupara
Matawai
Tolaga Bay

S e a
Lake Taupo
Gisborne

Waitara
Taumarunui
New Pymouth
Wairoa

Mount Egmont ▲
Mount Ruapehu ▲

Hawera
Hawke Bay

Patea
Napier
Wanganui
Hastings

N E W
Marton
Waipawa

Z E A L A N D

Palmerston North

D'Urville I.
Masterton

Tasman Bay
Motueka
Porirua
Upper Hutt
Lower Hutt
Wellington

Karamea
Richmond
Nelson

Granity
Blenheim

Westport
Butler

Tapuaenuku
▲ Tapuaenuku

Kaikoura

Greymouth
Runanga

Hokitika
Cheviot

Waipara
Pegasus Bay

Kaiapoi
Christchurch

Mount Cook ▲

Ashburton
Canterbury Bight

Twizel
Timaru

Mount Aspiring ▲
Canterbury Plains

Milford Sound
Wanaka

Queenstown
Cromwell
Oamaru

Lake Wanaka

Alexandra
S o u t h

Kingston
I s l a n d

Te Anau
Roxburgh

Otago Harbour

Mosgiel ● Dunedin

Winton
Milton
*Otago
Plateaus*
Kaitangata

Riverton
Invercargill

Foveaux Strait
Bluff

Stewart I.
Halfmoon Bay

*P A C I F I C

O C E A N*

0		150		300 Miles

0	200	400 Km

Northern Marianas, Guam, Marshall Islands

Northern Marianas

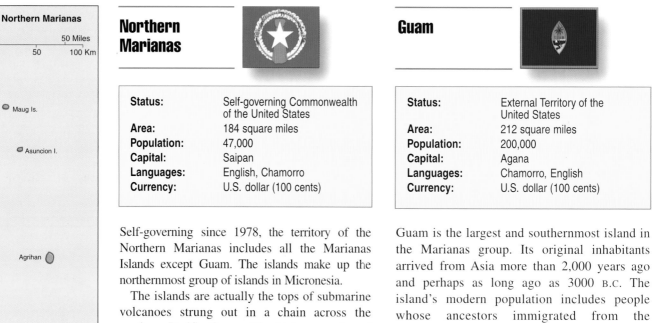

Status:	Self-governing Commonwealth of the United States
Area:	184 square miles
Population:	47,000
Capital:	Saipan
Languages:	English, Chamorro
Currency:	U.S. dollar (100 cents)

Self-governing since 1978, the territory of the Northern Marianas includes all the Marianas Islands except Guam. The islands make up the northernmost group of islands in Micronesia.

The islands are actually the tops of submarine volcanoes strung out in a chain across the northern Pacific Ocean. The high, rugged, and youngest islands are at the northern end of the chain and still experience volcanic eruptions. Pagan, Agrihan, and Anatahan are the three largest islands in this group. The southern islands in the Marianas are older. Erosion has worn down their volcanic peaks, and coral reefs have grown up around their shores. Saipan, Tinian, and Rota are the largest in this group.

Native islanders—who are called Chamorros—are descended from settlers who came to the islands from the Asian mainland thousands of years ago. Since then, Europeans, Filipinos, and others have joined the population. The commonwealth status of the Marianas confers U.S. citizenship on the people who live there. Fishing and farming provide some of the food required, but additional supplies are imported from the United States. Tourism is the principal economic activity.

Above: Dramatic cliffs line parts of the coast of Saipan Island in the Northern Marianas.

Guam

Status:	External Territory of the United States
Area:	212 square miles
Population:	200,000
Capital:	Agana
Languages:	Chamorro, English
Currency:	U.S. dollar (100 cents)

Guam is the largest and southernmost island in the Marianas group. Its original inhabitants arrived from Asia more than 2,000 years ago and perhaps as long ago as 3000 B.C. The island's modern population includes people whose ancestors immigrated from the Philippines, Japan, China, Indonesia, the United States, and Europe.

Densely forested volcanic mountains dominate the south of the island, while the north consists of a limestone plateau edged by coastal plains. Workers cleared most of the forests that once covered the north of the island to make way for the large U.S. naval and air force facilities that provide jobs for many of the local people.

White sandy beaches fringe most of the coast, with coral reefs offshore, and these natural attractions support tourism, another major source

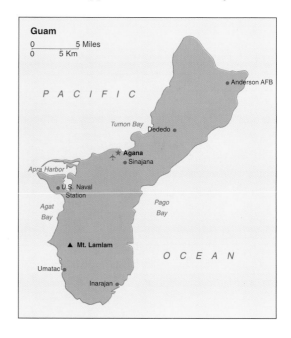

of income. Thousands of tourists, mainly from Japan, visit Guam each year. Local farmers grow sweet potatoes, taro, coconuts, and fruits, and fishers catch tuna and other fish in the surrounding waters. But most of the island's food supplies are imported from the United States. Small businesses on Guam make textiles and process tobacco and copra (dried coconut meat) for export.

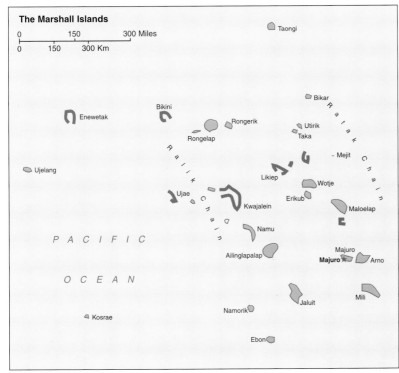

Left: A nineteenth-century lookout post guards one of Guam's many bays. The War in the Pacific National Historical Park on Guam commemorates U.S. troops who fought in the Pacific in World War II (1939-1945).

Marshall Islands

Status:	Republic in Free Association with the United States
Area:	69 square miles
Population:	100,000
Capital:	Majuro
Languages:	English, Marshallese dialects
Currency:	U.S. dollar (100 cents)

The Marshall Islands

The Marshall Islands total more than 1,000 coral islands, tiny islets, atolls, and reefs in eastern Micronesia. The islands form two parallel chains that are 125 miles apart and about 620 miles long. The eastern chain is called the Ratak (Sunrise) Chain. The western one is the Ralik (Sunset) Chain. American military scientists carried out nuclear tests on two of the northernmost islands—Enewetak and Bikini—between 1946 and 1958. Radioactive contamination has meant those islands have remained uninhabited since that time. The United States still maintains a large military base on Kwajalein Atoll.

The fine coral sand that covers the islands is unsuited to agriculture, but local farmers manage to grow the few crops—coconut palms, bananas, papayas, and breadfruit trees—that can tolerate the conditions. Copra, from which coconut oil is extracted, is the main agricultural export. But the economy depends largely on tourism and on money paid by the United States for its use of the islands as military bases.

Federated States of Micronesia, and Palau

Federated States of Micronesia

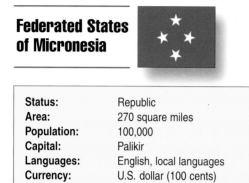

Status:	Republic
Area:	270 square miles
Population:	100,000
Capital:	Palikir
Languages:	English, local languages
Currency:	U.S. dollar (100 cents)

The Federated States of Micronesia consist of more than 600 islands and tiny coral islets in the Caroline Islands archipelago, scattered across 1,500 miles of the North Pacific Ocean. The islands are clustered into four groups, which are also administrative units, or states—Yap, Chuuk, Pohnpei, and Kosrae. Each of the states has a dominant local language that is used alongside English, the official language. More than one-fourth of Micronesia's people live in the capital, Palikir, on the main island of Pohnpei. After wartime occupation by the Japanese, the islands were a UN Trust Territory from 1947 and gained full independence in 1986.

The United States ensures the islands' defense under a special agreement.

Tropical rain forests cover much of the land of the larger, higher islands, with mangrove forests fringing the coasts. The thin sandy soil of the smaller coral islands cannot support such dense vegetation, so their main vegetation consists of sparse grasses and stands of coconut trees, breadfruit trees, and pandanus palms. Most of the people live in small village communities and make their living from subsistence farming and fishing. Farmers raise breadfruit, taro, bananas, and coconuts for food and prepare copra for export. The copra (dried coconut meat) is processed abroad to yield coconut oil. Micronesia's fishers catch a variety of fish and shellfish for local use. The islands also receive payments from U.S., Japanese, and Korean fishing fleets in return for permission to catch tuna in the islands' territorial waters. Miners extract small amounts of phosphate, which is exported for making fertilizer. These sources of income, however, do not earn enough to pay for all the goods Micronesia needs to import, and the islands' economy depends heavily on grants from the United States.

Below: Traditional dances, songs, and stories play a large part in Pacific Island cultures. Here, dancers perform at a cultural center at Palikir, Micronesia's capital city, on Pohnpei Island.

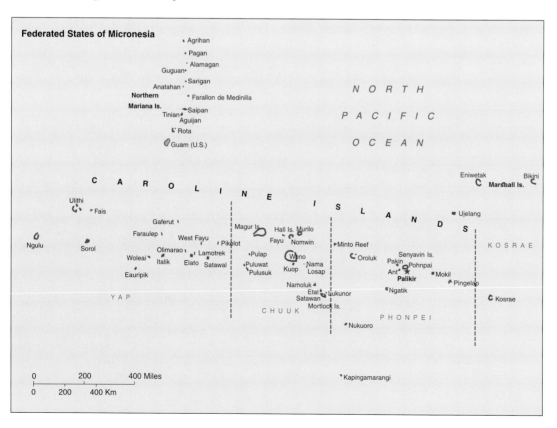

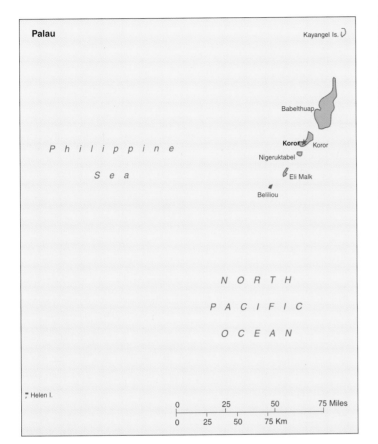

Palau

Above: Spectacular limestone caverns at Babelthuap, Palau.

Palau

Status:	Republic
Area:	178 square miles
Population:	17,000
Capital:	Koror
Languages:	Palauan, English
Currency:	U.S. dollar (100 cents)

Palau consists of a cluster of more than 200 islands and small coral islets. The group sits to the west of the Caroline Islands. Most of Palau's inhabitants live on the small island of Koror, which lies in the middle of the group. The rest of the population is spread over seven other nearby islands. The present capital, built on Koror and sharing the same name, grew up around the island's fine deepwater harbor. But the city has no room to expand, and a new administrative center is being built on the much larger island of Babelthuap to the north, where broad coastal plains surround a mountainous interior.

Palau gained independence in 1994—the last of the U.S. administered Pacific Trust Territories to do so. Like Micronesia, Palau has a special agreement under which the United States is responsible for the islands' security and defense.

Most of the people of Palau are subsistence farmers or fishers or are employed by the government or in the islands' growing tourist industry. Farmers grow taro, cassava, sweet potatoes, coconuts, and other fruits and vegetables and export copra as their main cash crop. Fishers concentrate chiefly on high-value tuna for export. Scuba diving, snorkeling, sailing, and sport fishing attract large numbers of visitors each year, principally from the United States, Japan, Taiwan, and Hong Kong.

265

Nauru and the Solomon Islands

Nauru

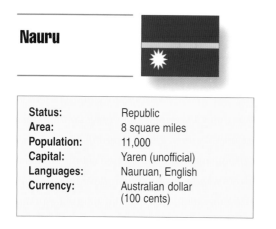

Status:	Republic
Area:	8 square miles
Population:	11,000
Capital:	Yaren (unofficial)
Languages:	Nauruan, English
Currency:	Australian dollar (100 cents)

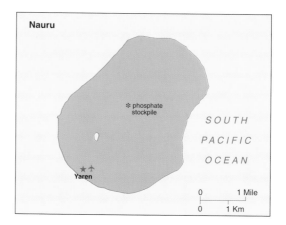

Nauru

phosphate stockpile

SOUTH PACIFIC OCEAN

Yaren

0   1 Mile
0   1 Km

Right: Children enjoy a traditional game on Malaita Island in the Solomon Islands. Their tightly curled hair is a characteristic of the Melanesian people.

Nauru, a tiny speck of land in the west central Pacific Ocean just south of the equator, is the third-smallest country in the world. Only Vatican City and Monaco are smaller in land area. The country consists of a single oval coral island, three miles wide and three-and-a-half miles long. A narrow fertile coastal plain encircles a dry central plateau that rises to 225 feet above sea level. Most Nauruans live in small settlements that dot the coast. There is no official capital, but the largest settlement, Yaren, on the southern coast, serves as the country's administrative center.

Native islanders of Polynesian, Micronesian, and Melanesian descent make up about two-thirds of Nauru's population. The remaining one-third are nearly all contract workers from neighboring Pacific islands, from Hong Kong in China, and from Australia. These workers labor in the island's phosphate-mining industry.

High-grade phosphate rock is Nauru's sole valuable natural resource and is exported all around the Pacific as a raw material for making fertilizer. For the past 30 years, income from phosphate exports has provided the islanders with a high standard of living, free schools, free medical services, and government-subsidized housing. But there has been a high price to pay. Mining has left the island's interior a desolate wasteland of bare rock and spoil heaps, and the phosphate reserves are almost exhausted. Britain and Australia—partners in the exploitation of the phosphates—have paid large sums in compensation, but the Nauruan government is looking for new sources of income and employment. Options include expanding the country's fishing industry, promoting tourism, expanding the airport at Yaren as a hub for Pacific air traffic, and developing the island's financial services as a tax haven for businesses and wealthy individuals.

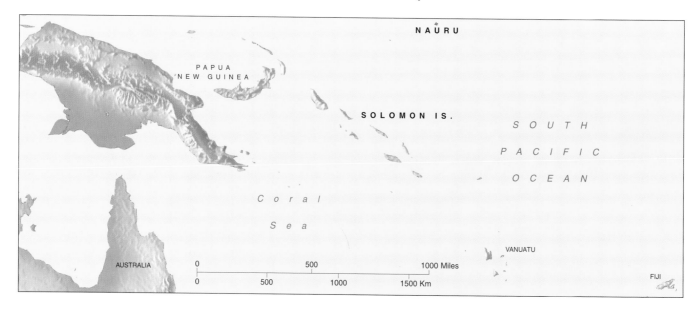

NAURU

PAPUA NEW GUINEA

SOLOMON IS.

SOUTH PACIFIC OCEAN

Coral Sea

VANUATU

AUSTRALIA

0   500   1000 Miles
0   500   1000   1500 Km

FIJI

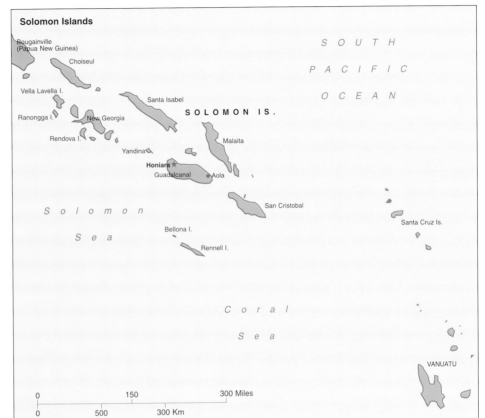

Solomon Islands

Solomon Islands

Status:	Constitutional Monarchy
Area:	11,158 square miles
Population:	400,000
Capital:	Honiara
Language:	English
Currency:	Solomon Islands dollar (100 cents)

The Solomon Islands are located in the southwestern Pacific Ocean, about 1,000 miles northeast of Australia. Six main islands account for most of the country's land area—Choiseul, Santa Isabel, New Georgia, Guadalcanal, Malaita, and San Cristobal. The Solomons also include many smaller islands. Guadalcanal is the largest island and contains the capital, Honiara, home to about 10 percent of the population. Britain ruled the Solomon Islands as a protectorate from 1893 until the country became fully independent in 1978 as a member of the British Commonwealth.

Steep, rugged, densely forested volcanic mountains dominate the interior of the principal islands, rising to about 4,000 feet in places. Narrow coastal plains fringe the shores, providing fertile soils for the country's farmers. Climate varies from year-round heat and humidity in the north to a milder, more seasonal climate in the south.

Almost 90 percent of the islanders make their living from farming. They grow a variety of fruits and vegetables as food crops and raise cacao beans, palms (for oil), and coconut trees (for copra) as export crops. Fishing—especially for tuna—and timber from the rich hardwood forests provide the biggest share of the islands' export earnings. Miners on Bellona Island, south of the main group, produce phosphates for export.

Japan is the country's biggest customer for all these commodities. Exports are essential to the islands, because most manufactured goods and energy supplies have to be imported. The country has few industries. The difficult terrain, which makes road building almost impossible, restricts development.

267

Vanuatu and New Caledonia

Vanuatu

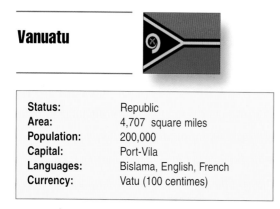

Status:	Republic
Area:	4,707 square miles
Population:	200,000
Capital:	Port-Vila
Languages:	Bislama, English, French
Currency:	Vatu (100 centimes)

Thirteen large islands and 70 smaller ones make up the territory of Vanuatu in the southwestern Pacific. Britain and France governed the islands, then known as the New Hebrides, from 1906 to 1980, when Vanuatu became an independent country.

Volcanic eruptions on the Pacific seabed created the Y-shaped island chain of Vanuatu, and several of the islands still have active volcanoes. Because the islands are geologically young, their interiors are still rugged and mountainous, with forested hills sloping steeply down to narrow coastal plains where fertile soil supports farming. Most of the people live in small villages in houses made of bamboo and thatched with palm fronds. The farmers grow a variety of fruits and vegetables and raise chickens, cattle, and pigs. Much of the food is used locally, although many farmers also produce copra and cacao beans as a cash crops for export. Like many island nations, Vanuatu has a tradition of fishing, and fish and shellfish are an important part of the diet. The capital of Port-Vila on Éfaté Island and Santo on Espiritu Santo are the only urban centers of any size.

With no industry, no mineral resources, and terrain that makes road building extremely difficult, Vanuatu makes full use of its internal air transport system and its coastal freight and passenger boats. Tourism is the fastest-growing industry and an important provider of jobs. The islands' hot climate, spectacular mountain scenery, exotic flowers and birds, and extensive reefs attract large numbers of visitors, principally from Japan and Australia.

Above: An outdoor food market at Port Vila, Vanuatu.

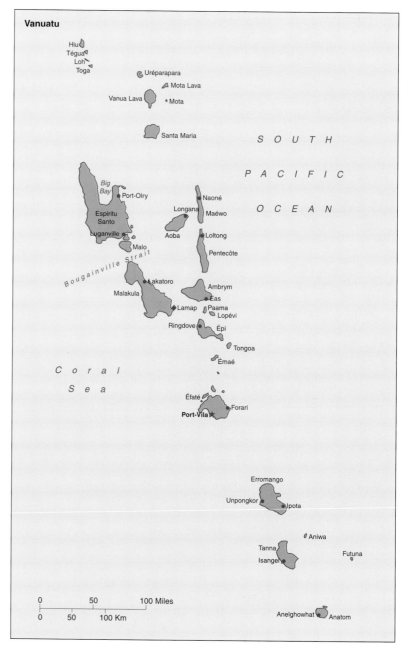

268

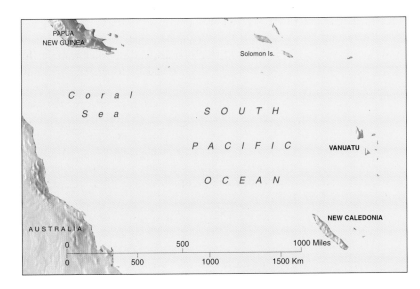

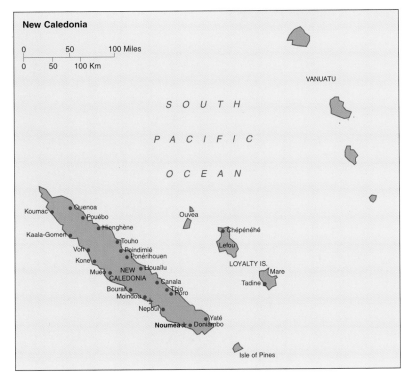

New Caledonia

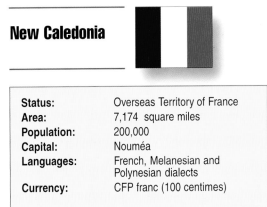

Status:	Overseas Territory of France
Area:	7,174 square miles
Population:	200,000
Capital:	Nouméa
Languages:	French, Melanesian and Polynesian dialects
Currency:	CFP franc (100 centimes)

New Caledonia, an Overseas Territory of France, is one of the most southwesterly of the Melanesian islands and lies about 820 miles northeast of Brisbane, Australia. The main island is 250 miles long and 30 miles wide and is completely ringed by coral reefs. The Loyalty Islands and the Isle of Pines and Bélép Islands are dependencies of New Caledonia.

Native Melanesians make up 43 percent of the population, Europeans account for 37 percent, with Polynesians and Indonesians making up most of the remainder. One commodity—nickel—dominates New Caledonia's economy. The country is one of the world's leading suppliers. Miners extract the ore from large open-pit mines at Poro and Thio on New Caledonia's northern coast and at Nepoui on the southern coast. The ore is purified for export at a huge smelting plant at Doniambo, near the capital.

Tourism is New Caledonia's second-biggest source of income. The islands lie about 1,500 miles south of the equator and have a pleasant climate with well-marked seasons. Clear waters and extensive reefs attract divers and snorkelers, while the scenery, beaches, and old colonial architecture draw visitors from many parts of the world. Unfortunately, political unrest has damaged the tourist industry in recent years, but the islands' natural resources—combined with finan cial support from France—still ensure good living standards, educational opportunities, and health-care services for New Caledonia's people.

Kiribati and Tuvalu

Kiribati

Status:	Republic
Area:	280 square miles
Population:	79,000
Capital:	Tarawa
Languages:	Kiribati, English
Currency:	Australian dollar (100 cents)

Kiribati is the most widely spread island nation on earth. Its 33 islands are strung out across almost two million square miles of the central and western Pacific Ocean. Kiribati straddles both the equator and the international date line. Its territory consists of the volcanic island of Banaba (formerly called Ocean Island) and three groups of coral islands and atolls—the 16 islands of the Gilbert Islands group, the eight Phoenix Islands, and eight of the Line Islands. One island—Kiritimati (Christmas Island)—accounts for almost half the nation's total land area. The highest point above sea level is a mere 265 feet on Banaba. Many of Kiribati's smaller islands and atolls stand only 10 to 15 feet above sea level and are at risk of disappearing forever if global warming does result in a significant rise in world sea levels.

Kiribati was formerly part of the British protectorate of the Gilbert and Ellice Islands. The Ellice Islands separated in 1975 and became the independent nation of Tuvalu in 1978. In 1979 the Gilbert Islands achieved independence as Kiribati.

Mines on Banaba once produced phosphate, but the reserves ran out in 1980, causing severe economic problems. The islanders mainly work in agriculture and fishing and receive foreign aid to supplement their incomes. Most of the people live in small villages, where houses are made of wood with thatched palm roofs. They grow bananas, papayas, breadfruit, sweet potatoes, and taro as their main food crops. Many also grow coconuts to produce copra, which is the principal agricultural export. Fish exports, especially of tuna, account for one-third of the country's income. More money comes from selling fishing licenses to U.S., Japanese, Taiwanese and Korean fleets.

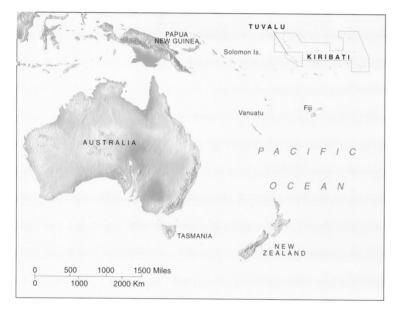

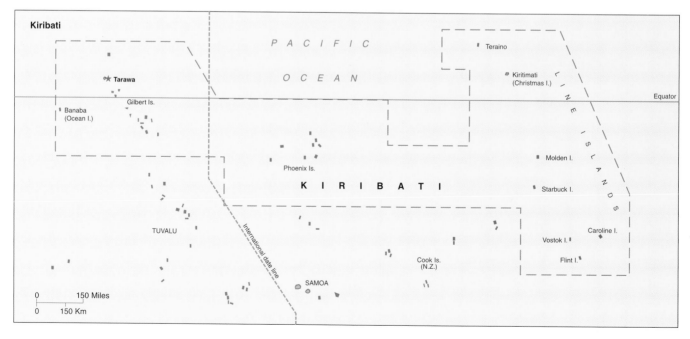

Above: Preparing breadfruit, on North Tarawa Island, Kiribati.

Tuvalu

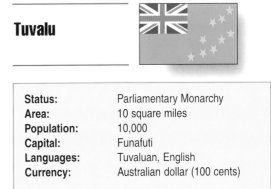

Status:	Parliamentary Monarchy
Area:	10 square miles
Population:	10,000
Capital:	Funafuti
Languages:	Tuvaluan, English
Currency:	Australian dollar (100 cents)

The nine coral islands that make up Tuvalu have a total land area that ranks them as the fourth-smallest country in the world after Vatican City, Monaco, and Nauru. Nowhere does the land rise more than 15 feet above sea level. Almost one-third of the Tuvaluan people live on Funafuti Atoll, home of the national capital (also called Funafuti) and the country's airport.

Most Tuvaluan people live in small communities and make their living by farming and fishing. The islands' poor soil consists almost entirely of coral sand and is unsuitable for most plants. Farmers rely on species like coconut palms, pandanus palms, bananas, and taro that can tolerate the harsh conditions. Most islanders also raise pigs and chickens for food. Copra is the only significant farm export. Fish are an important part of the local diet and are also a source of income—both from selling fish and from selling fishing licenses to boat operators from Japan and the United States. Apart from artisans making mats, baskets, and carvings, there is no manufacturing, and many Tuvaluans seek jobs abroad or on cruise ships. Britain, Australia, New Zealand, and Japan help to support the Tuvaluan economy with financial grants.

Tuvalu

Nanumea
Lolua

Niutao

Nanumanga

S O U T H

P A C I F I C

O C E A N

Nui

Vaitupu

Funafuti
Nukufetau

Funafuti
Nukulaelae

Nukulaelae

0   75   150 Miles
0   75   150 Km

Fiji, Wallis and Futuna

Fiji

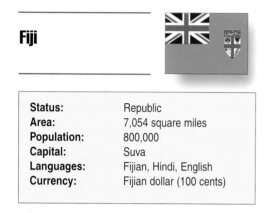

Status:	Republic
Area:	7,054 square miles
Population:	800,000
Capital:	Suva
Languages:	Fijian, Hindi, English
Currency:	Fijian dollar (100 cents)

With 800,000 people inhabiting about 100 of the country's more than 300 islands, Fiji has the largest population of any of the Pacific island countries with the exception of Papua New Guinea. Two ethnic groups dominate life in Fiji. Native Fijians—Melanesians who have populated the islands for thousands of years—make up 46 percent of the population. The Fijians own most of the land and control the government and administration. Another 49 percent consists of Indians who are the descendents of workers brought in by the British in the 1800s. The Indian community dominates the professional and business life of the islands. Fijians fear losing control, and Indians resent being treated as second-class citizens. These conflicting interests have troubled the islands since Fiji ceased to be a British colony and became independent in 1970.

Fiji's two largest islands, Vanua Levu and Viti Levu, account for most of the country's land area. Volcanic eruptions created the islands, and their interiors are still mountainous, rising to 4,341 feet at Mount Tomanivi on Viti Levu. About 30 other peaks exceed 3,000 feet above sea level. Coral reefs ring the main islands. The smaller islands consist almost entirely of coral.

Fertile volcanic soils on the coastal lowlands of the main islands support most of Fiji's agriculture. Fijian farmers grow rice, fruits, and vegetables for local use, and many also raise pigs and chickens. Processed sugar is Fiji's principal export, and Indian tenant farmers grow most of the sugarcane on small holdings leased from Fijian landowners. Factory workers in large sugar mills at Lautoka, Labasa, and Bua process the cane into sugar. Coconuts are the second most valuable crop. The copra is transported to factories at Suva, where it is pressed to produce coconut oil for export. In recent years, Fiji's farmers have started growing cacao beans and ginger to broaden the range of agricultural exports. Fiji's main customers are Britain and Europe, Malaysia, China, Australia, New Zealand, and the United States.

Miners on Viti Levu extract gold for export, and manufacturing plants in the main towns produce textiles, clothing, furniture, farm machinery, and other goods, mainly for local use. Fiji's beautiful beaches and scenery, pleasant climate, clear waters, and countless reefs support a thriving tourist industry that provides many jobs in hotels, in restaurants, in transportation, and in other services.

Below: Colonial style buildings at Nadi, on Viti Levu, Fiji.

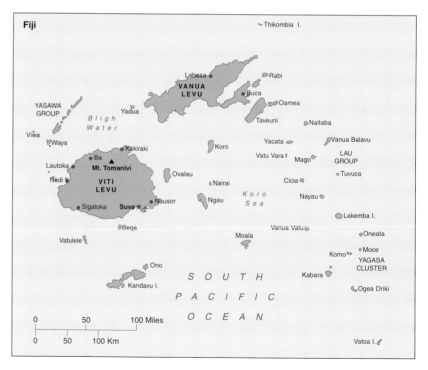

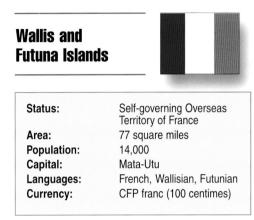

Wallis and Futuna Islands

Status:	Self-governing Overseas Territory of France
Area:	77 square miles
Population:	14,000
Capital:	Mata-Utu
Languages:	French, Wallisian, Futunian
Currency:	CFP franc (100 centimes)

The Wallis and Futuna Islands lie about 300 miles northeast of Fiji and consist of three main islands—Futuna, Alofi, and Uvea—plus a scattering of smaller islands, reefs, and atolls. Uvea, the principal island of the Wallis group, is by far the largest and is home to about 60 percent of the country's people. It also contains the largest settlement—the capital Mata-Utu, with a population of about 850. Hills cover the interior of the island, with low plains around the coast and fringing coral reefs offshore. Futuna and Alofi are higher, with more rugged, mountainous interiors and narrower coastal plains.

The islands have no natural resources, and most of the islanders make their living by subsistence farming and fishing. Most grow cassava, sweet potatoes, and bananas as their main food crops and coconut trees as a source of copra, which is sold for processing to yield coconut oil. The economy of the islands depends greatly on financial aid from France.

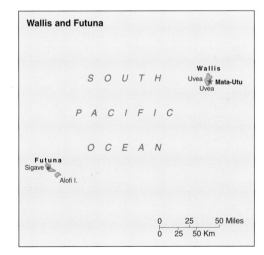

Above: Mountain peaks rise dramatically in the northwest of Viti Levu, Fiji.

Western Samoa, American Samoa, Tonga

Western Samoa

Status:	Constitutional Monarchy
Area:	1,097 square miles
Population:	200,000
Capital:	Apia
Languages:	Samoan, English
Currency:	Tala (100 sene)

Western Samoa's people inhabit two large islands, Savai'i and Upolu, and two smaller islands, Apolima and Manono, which lie in the Apolima Strait between the main islands. Five other islands are uninhabited. Two-thirds of the Samoan people live on Upolu, the smaller, lower, and more fertile of the main islands. Volcanic mountains dominate the interior of Savai'i and Upolu, dropping steeply to narrow fertile plains around the coasts. Dense tropical rain forests cover the interior regions.

Most of the people live in village communities and make their living by farming and fishing. The climate is warm and tropical, and typical Samoan houses have thick thatched roofs to provide shade and open sides to let in cool breezes. In wet, windy weather, the owners let down woven palm-leaf curtains to keep their homes warm and dry. Samoan farmers grow bananas, breadfruit, taro, and other fruits and vegetables for their own use, and many also keep pigs and chickens. Coconuts (for producing copra), taro, and cacao beans are the principal commercial crops. New Zealand buys most of Western Samoa's farm exports.

Western Samoa is not a rich country, but its people enjoy a good standard of living. The government, small businesses, and a thriving tourist industry provide employment. The government also supplies free health-care services and free schooling.

American Samoa

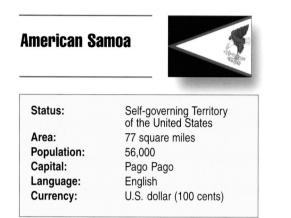

Status:	Self-governing Territory of the United States
Area:	77 square miles
Population:	56,000
Capital:	Pago Pago
Language:	English
Currency:	U.S. dollar (100 cents)

Six of American Samoa's seven islands are part of the island chain that also includes Western Samoa. The seventh island, Swains Island, lies 200 miles away to the north. American Samoa's capital and only large town, Pago Pago, is located on the largest island of Tutuila and is built around one of the finest natural harbors in the Pacific.

Densely forested mountains cover much of the land, with fertile soils in some of the valleys and on the flat coastal plains. Farmers grow taro, coconuts, bananas and other fruit and vegetables, chiefly for local use. Fishing is one of the principal employers. Tuna meat accounts for more than 95 percent of the country's exports. Some is exported fresh, but most of it is canned in local factories. Virtually the entire catch goes to the United States. The government, tourism, and small factories provide employment for those not engaged in farming and fishing.

With hardly any natural resources, American Samoa would be a poor country were it not for huge financial support from the U.S. government, which pays for health care, schools, and other social services. American Samoa is a self-governing U.S. territory. Its people have right of entry to the United States, and more American Samoans live in Hawaii and the mainland United States than live on the islands. The money they send back to their families provides further help to the local economy.

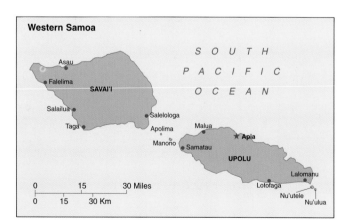

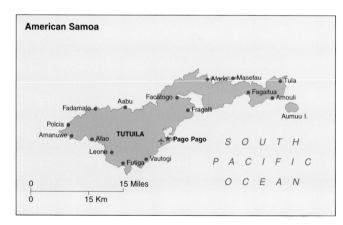

Tonga

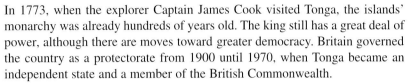

Status:	Constitutional Monarchy
Area:	288 square miles
Population:	98,000
Capital:	Nuku'alofa
Languages:	Tongan, English
Currency:	Pa'anga (100 seniti)

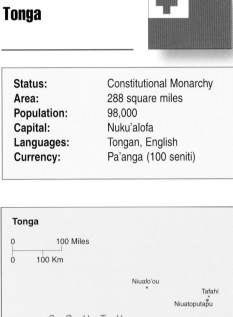

In 1773, when the explorer Captain James Cook visited Tonga, the islands' monarchy was already hundreds of years old. The king still has a great deal of power, although there are moves toward greater democracy. Britain governed the country as a protectorate from 1900 until 1970, when Tonga became an independent state and a member of the British Commonwealth.

Tonga's territory covers more than 170 islands that are clustered in three main groups—Ha'apai, Tongatapu, and Vava'u. Almost two-thirds of the people live on Tongatapu, the largest island, where the capital Nuku'alofa is located. People inhabit 36 of Tonga's islands. The rest are little more than coral reefs with a few coconut palms and grasses growing in the infertile sand. Volcanic soils on the larger islands support Tonga's agricultural economy. The government owns all the land, but all males of 16 or older are entitled to rent a plot, and three-quarters of all workers make their living in this way. The farmers grow breadfruit, yams, sweet potatoes, tapioca, and peanuts. Fishing provides the main protein in the diet. Bananas, copra, coconut oil, and vegetables are the principal exports. Meat, flour, fuel, and manufactured goods are the chief imports. New Zealand and Australia are Tonga's principal trading partners. Tonga's warm, sunny climate, beautiful coast, and stunning mountain scenery attract thousands of tourists every year.

Above: Fishing with a surrounding net in one of Tonga's shallow bays.

Left: An agile youngster climbing for coconuts in Western Samoa.

Cook Islands and Niue

Cook Islands

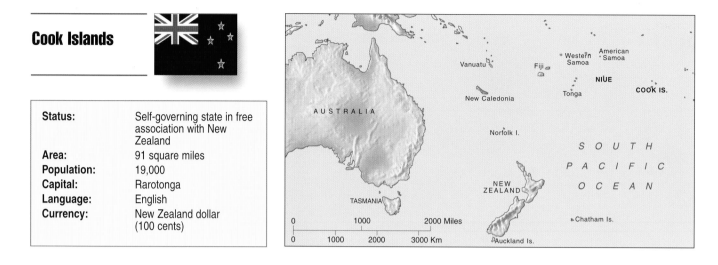

Status:	Self-governing state in free association with New Zealand
Area:	91 square miles
Population:	19,000
Capital:	Rarotonga
Language:	English
Currency:	New Zealand dollar (100 cents)

The 15 Cook Islands are spread across roughly 800,000 square miles of the southern Pacific Ocean and are grouped into two clusters—seven in the Northern Cook Islands and eight in the Southern Cook Islands. The northern islands are low coral atolls. Volcanic eruptions formed the much higher and more fertile southern group. The islands are named for Captain James Cook who, in 1773, was the first European to land on them. Britain passed administrative control of the islands to New Zealand in 1891, and the islands became self-governing in 1965. Under the free association arrangement, the Cook Islanders are New Zealand citizens, and New Zealand is responsible for the islands'

defense. Avarua, on Rarotonga Island, is the only large town and serves as the administrative and business center.

Most Cook Islanders live by farming. Bananas, coconuts (grown chiefly for copra production), pineapples, oranges, and limes are the principal export crops. Factory workers on Rarotonga process and can tropical fruits for export to New Zealand. Other islanders work in small factories producing clothing and crafts. Crews venture off the islands to fish commercially and catch shellfish closer to the coasts.

Below: Cook Islanders still use traditional outrigger canoes alongside modern sailing boats and motorboats.

Cook Islands

Penrhyn

Rakahanga

Manihiki

Pukapuka

Nassau

Suwarrow

S O U T H

P A C I F I C

O C E A N

Palmerston

Aitutaki

Manuae

Takutea   Mitiaro

Atiu   Mauke

Rarotonga

Mangaia

| 0 | 250 Miles |
| 0 | 400 Km |

Niue

Status:	Self-governing state in free association with New Zealand
Area:	100 square miles
Population:	2,300
Capital:	Alofi
Language:	English
Currency:	New Zealand dollar (100 cents)

Just 13 miles long and 11 miles wide, the coral island of Niue is a tiny speck in the southern Pacific Ocean between Tonga and the Southern Cook Islands. The people are Polynesian, and their language is closely related to that of Tonga. Although geographically part of the Cook Islands, Niue has been administered separately since 1904 and became independent, in free association with New Zealand, in 1974.

Niue's farmers grow vegetables, coconuts, bananas, passion fruit, and limes, and most of them also raise pigs and chickens. Copra and tropical fruits are the island's principal exports, along with the beautiful baskets and mats the islanders weave from the leaves of the pandanus pine. Fishing, as on most Pacific islands, provides the local people with an important part of their diet. A small, forested region in the middle of the island supplies timber to a sawmill, but the island has no other industry, and the economy depends heavily on financial assistance from New Zealand.

Left: Even in Paradise there's washing to be done.

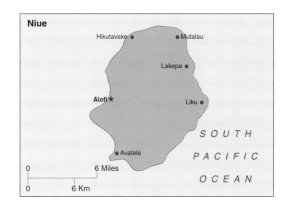

Niue

Hikutavake   Mutalau

Lakepa

Alofi ★   Liku

Avatele

S O U T H

P A C I F I C

O C E A N

| 0 | 6 Miles |
| 0 | 6 Km |

French Polynesia and Pitcairn Island

French Polynesia

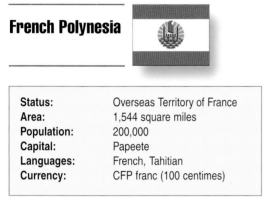

Status:	Overseas Territory of France
Area:	1,544 square miles
Population:	200,000
Capital:	Papeete
Languages:	French, Tahitian
Currency:	CFP franc (100 centimes)

French Polynesia comprises 130 islands scattered in five groups across a vast area of the South Pacific Ocean, halfway between Australia and South America. The five groups are the Society Islands, the Marquesas, the Tubuai (Austral) Islands, the Gambier Islands, and the Tuamotu Archipelago. Tahiti, in the Society Islands, is by far the largest of the islands. More than 60 percent of French Polynesia's people live on Tahiti—about 37,000 of them in Papeete, the largest town and the capital of the territory.

The islands of the Tuamotu Archipelago are low coral atolls rising only a few feet above sea level. Their thin, dry, sandy soils are difficult to cultivate, so farmers concentrate on growing coconuts, which are naturally adapted to those conditions. The phosphate mines on Makatea were exhausted in the late 1960s, but pearl diving and collecting mother-of-pearl shells remain important activities.

Volcanic eruptions on the floor of the Pacific Ocean created the other island groups. Rugged mountains fill their interiors, where the steep hills are covered in dense tropical rain forests. Deep river gorges separate the hills from one another. Fertile plains ring the coasts, and most of the islands are encircled by coral reefs enclosing shallow lagoons. Farmers grow sweet potatoes, breadfruit, and taro as their principal food crops. Chickens, pigs, and fish provide meat. Copra, coffee beans, vanilla, peppers, and sugarcane are the main cash crops grown for export, principally to France. The islands' beauty supports a thriving tourist industry that provides jobs in hotels, transport, sport fishing and other activities. Trade, tourism, and aid from the French government ensure a high standard of living.

Right: Polynesian men lift a feast of meat and vegetables from a roasting pit where it was cooked over hot embers, sealed in with palm leaves and earth.

French Polynesia

Makatea
Uturoa
Papeete
SOCIETY IS. Tahiti
MARQUISAS IS.
TUAMOTU ARCHIPELAGO
Mururua
Rikitea
GAMBIER IS.
TUBUAI IS.
Mataura
Rapa

SOUTH PACIFIC OCEAN

0   250   500 Miles
0   250   500 Km

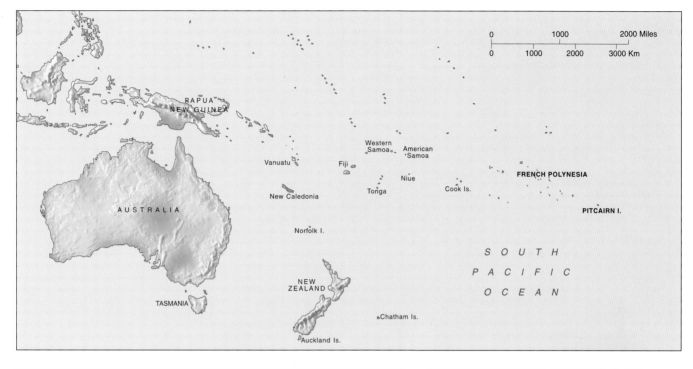

Pitcairn Islands

Sandy

Oeno

Henderson

S O U T H

P A C I F I C

O C E A N

Ducie

Adamstown
PITCAIRN

| 0 | | 50 | | 100 Miles |

| 0 | 50 | | 100 Km |

Left: The clear shallow waters of a reef-ringed lagoon lap silver sand shaded by coconut palms on Motu Is. in Polynesia.

Pitcairn Island

Status:	United Kingdom Dependency
Area:	212 square miles
Population:	70
Capital:	Adamstown
Language:	English
Currency:	New Zealand dollar (100 cents)

Pitcairn Island is mainly famous as the final destination of the mutineers from Captain Bligh's HMS *Bounty,* but it is also one of Britain's most remote dependent territories. This rocky island and its uninhabited neighbors—Henderson, Ducie, and Oeno Islands—lie in the southeastern Pacific, 5,000 miles east of Australia and just south of the Tropic of Capricorn.

The island rises steeply from the sea. The land's sheer cliffs lead to high inland areas, where the soil is fertile and the climate is mild and damp. The islanders, mostly descendants of the mutineers and the Polynesian wives they took with them, grow bananas, coconuts, taro, sweet potatoes, and pumpkins.

279

Antarctica

Antarctica

Status:	Protected International Territory
Area:	5.4 million square miles

Antarctica is a land of extremes. It is the highest, coldest, windiest place on earth. Although covered by water in the form of ice, Antarctica is a desert without a single tree in all its 5.4 million square miles. Seasonal birds such as penguins live on the continent when they breed and hatch their young.

The fifth-largest continent, Antarctica is almost one-and-a-half times the size of the United States but has no native people, no flag, no government, no farming, and no industry. Seven countries—Argentina, Australia, Chile, France, Great Britain, New Zealand, and Norway—have all claimed sectors of Antarctica. These claims fan out in pie-shaped slices from the South Pole to the coast and beyond. In 1961, all these countries set aside their territorial claims under the Antarctic Treaty, which preserves the continent for science alone and bans any form of military use, commercial exploitation, or environmental damage. Antarctica has no fixed population, but several thousand scientists and support personnel live there in the summer months. In winter, this number dwindles to less than a thousand, who carry out long-term research on climate studies.

Ice, averaging more than a mile thick, covers almost the entire continent. In a few places, the jagged tops of mountain ranges stick up through the ice, but most of Antarctica is a vast, smooth plateau of ice with an average elevation of 7,500 feet above sea level. The continent is lopsidedly centered on the South Pole and is divided into two contrasting parts—West Antarctica and East Antarctica—by the Transantarctic Mountains. This range stretches across the continent from the Weddell Sea to the Ross Sea.

Below: Summer on the Antarctic Peninsula, and the ice that covered the sea through the winter has broken up, littering the surface with wave-worn fragments. Only at this time of year can supply boats reach the scientific bases scattered around the edge of Antarctica.

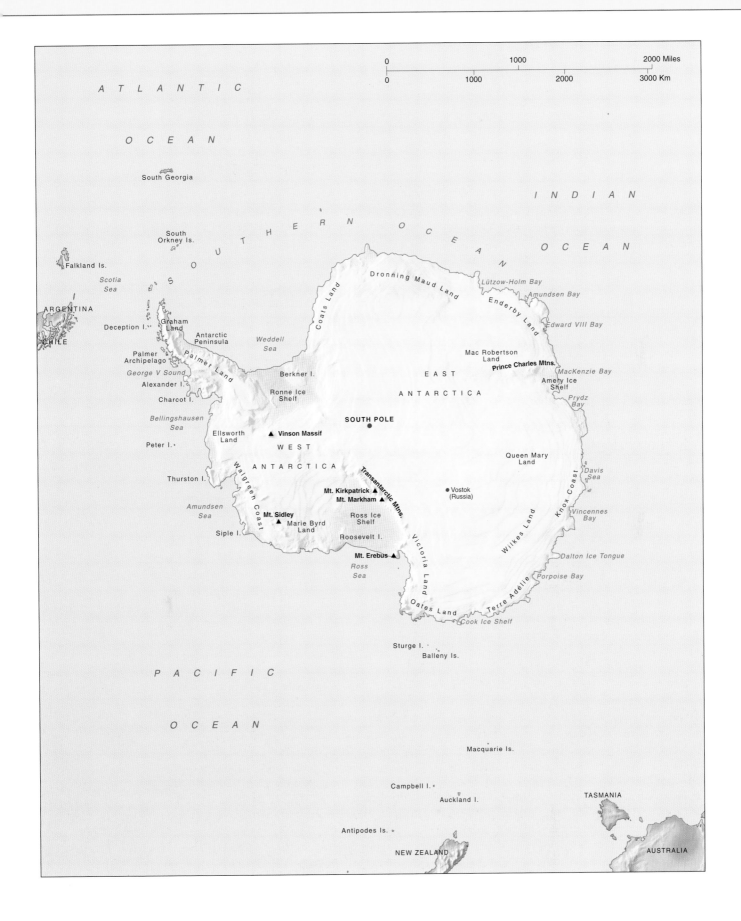

Antarctica

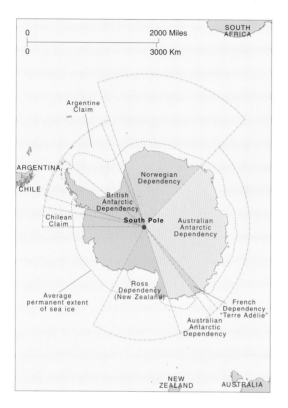

Above: After years of persecution which brought several species to the brink of extinction, many of Antarctica's whales are slowly recovering.

Left: Seven nations have set aside their territorial claims in Antarctica so that the continent can be used for peaceful scientific studies to benefit everyone.

Mountain ranges, basins, glaciers, and plateaus dominate West Antarctica. If the ice melted, this region would be a confusion of islands and seaways. West Antarctica reaches northward toward South America as a long, narrow S-shaped peninsula that is an extension of the Andes Mountains. Near the base of the peninsula, Vinson Massif, Antarctica's highest peak, rises to 16,860 feet. West Antarctica is much younger and more geologically active than East Antarctica is. Mount Erebus, Antarctica's most active volcano, occasionally spouts lava at the Ross Sea end of the Transantarctic range, and Deception Island near the tip of the peninsula erupted several times in the late 1960s.

East Antarctica is geologically much older. It is also much larger, covering almost three-fourths of the continent. A huge ice dome pushes up between the Transantarctic range and the mountains that rise along coastal sections of the Southern Ocean (sometimes also called the shores of the Indian and Atlantic Oceans). In the dome's center, the ice is more than 15,700 feet thick—deep enough to bury Chicago's Sears Tower ten times over. In places, the weight of the ice has pressed the underlying land surface far below sea level. This enormous mass of ice contains 70 percent of the earth's fresh water.

Temperatures at the South Pole average -56°F and often fall below -90°F in the winter months. In 1983 scientists at Russia's Vostok Station, which sits 11,220 feet above sea level, recorded the world's lowest-ever air temperature of -128.6°F. High winds frequently sweep across the plateau and down the mountain slopes and glaciers of the peninsula. Winds of 70 miles per hour can blow for days at a time, but the windiest place on earth is Commonwealth Bay on the Antarctic Peninsula, where meteorologists have recorded gales of 200 miles per hour. Surprisingly, little new snow falls on Antarctica. Yearly total precipitation is about six inches— half the average for the Sahara Desert. The blizzards that often reduce visibility to a few yards are full of granular snow and ice grains that have been picked up, blown around, and dumped again, over and over.

Ice hides most of Antarctica's coastline, so maps generally show the outer limit of the permanent ice, including the huge ice shelves that partly fill the Ross Sea and the Weddell Sea. These shelves are up to 2,000 feet thick where they join the coast and 600 feet thick at their outer edge.

In summer, huge slabs break off and drift out to sea as tabular icebergs. One of the largest in recent years measured more than 200 miles long

and 60 miles wide—an area almost as big as the states of Massachusetts and Connecticut combined. In winter, the surface of the sea freezes, and thick pack ice extends up to 900 miles from the coast. In summer the ice breaks up into ice floes and wave-worn lumps called brash. Only at this time of year can supply ships reach the scientific stations around Antarctica's coast. The stations that are far inland, like Vostok and the U.S. Amundsen-Scott base at the South Pole, are supplied by air.

Only two kinds of flowering plants and tiny lichens, algae, and mosses manage to survive in Antarctica's harsh climate. Around the coast, penguins, skuas, petrels, and other seabirds arrive to breed in summer, and seals haul themselves out onto ice floes and beaches to give birth to their pups. By contrast, the Southern Ocean teems with life. Plankton (tiny floating plants and animals) and their larger relatives, the shrimplike krill, feed fish and baleen whales. Fish and squid, in turn, provide food for seals and toothed whales.

Geologists have found copper, manganese, zinc, chromium, lead, and other minerals in Antarctica, as well as thick coal seams exposed in cliff faces in the Transantarctic Mountains. But any such mining is forbidden under the Antarctic Treaty. Oil and gas fields may lie beneath the continental shelves around Antarctica and its fringing islands, but these, too, are out of reach.

Antarctica's value to humans does not lie in a few hard-to-reach resources but in its value as a unique natural laboratory. Atmospheric scientists working in Antarctica first alerted the world to the hole in the ozone layer—the thin veil of ozone gas that protects the earth from damaging radiation from the sun. That discovery led to research into the cause of the problem—and to international agreements to phase out the industrial chemicals—called CFCs—that were found to be causing most of the damage. Glaciologists examine patterns of ice movement and the effects of global warming on the Antarctic ice sheets. Biologists study the sea and land life, including fish that have developed a natural antifreeze to prevent them from freezing in the icy sea. These and other studies continue to add to people's understanding of the natural environment.

Below: Adelie penguins dive into the water to hunt for fish.

The World relief

ARCTIC
OCEAN

Beaufort
Sea

Bering Strait

Gulf of
Alaska

NORTH

AMERICA

Rocky Mtns.

Gulf of
Mexico

PACIFIC

OCEAN

Greenland

Baffin
Bay

Hudson
Bay

Appalachian Mtns.

ATLANTIC

OCEAN

Caribbean
Sea

Atlas M

SOUTH
AMERICA

Andes

ARCTIC OCEAN

Barents Sea

Kara Sea

East Siberian
Sea

ASIA

Ural Mtns.

Sea of
Okhotsk

Bering
Sea

ROPE

Black
Sea

Aral
Sea

Caspian
Sea

terranean
Sea

Arabia

Iranian Plateau

Hindu Kush

Himalayas

East
China
Sea

PACIFIC

RICA

Arabian
Sea

Bay of
Bengal

South
China
Sea

OCEAN

INDIAN

OCEAN

Timor
Sea

OCEANIA

Australia

Great Dividing Range

Tasman
Sea

ANTARCTICA

The World political

ARCTIC OCEAN

GREENLAND

ICELAND

ALEUTIAN ISLANDS

CANADA

Newfoundland

IRELAND

UNITED
KIN

SPAI

PORTUGAL

MOROCCO

CANARY
ISLANDS

WESTERN
SAHARA

MAURITANIA

SENEGAL

GAMBIA
GUINEA-BISSAU
GUINEA

SIERRA LEONE

LIBERIA

IVORY
COAS

BU

HAWAIIAN ISLANDS

UNITED STATES OF AMERICA

BAHAMAS

MEXICO

CUBA
W E S T

JAMAICA HAITI

DOMINICAN
REPUBLIC

PUERTO RICO

I N D I E S

BELIZE
GUATEMALA HONDURAS
EL SALVADOR NICARAGUA

COSTA RICA

PANAMA

VENEZUELA

TRINIDAD &
TOBAGO

GUYANA

SURINAM

FRENCH GUIANA

COLOMBIA

ECUADOR

GALAPAGOS
ISLANDS

PACIFIC

FIJI

OCEAN

BRAZIL

PERU

BOLIVIA

PARAGUAY

CHILE

URUGUAY

ARGENTINA

FALKLAND/MALVINAS
ISLANDS

South Georgia

The Atlantic Ocean

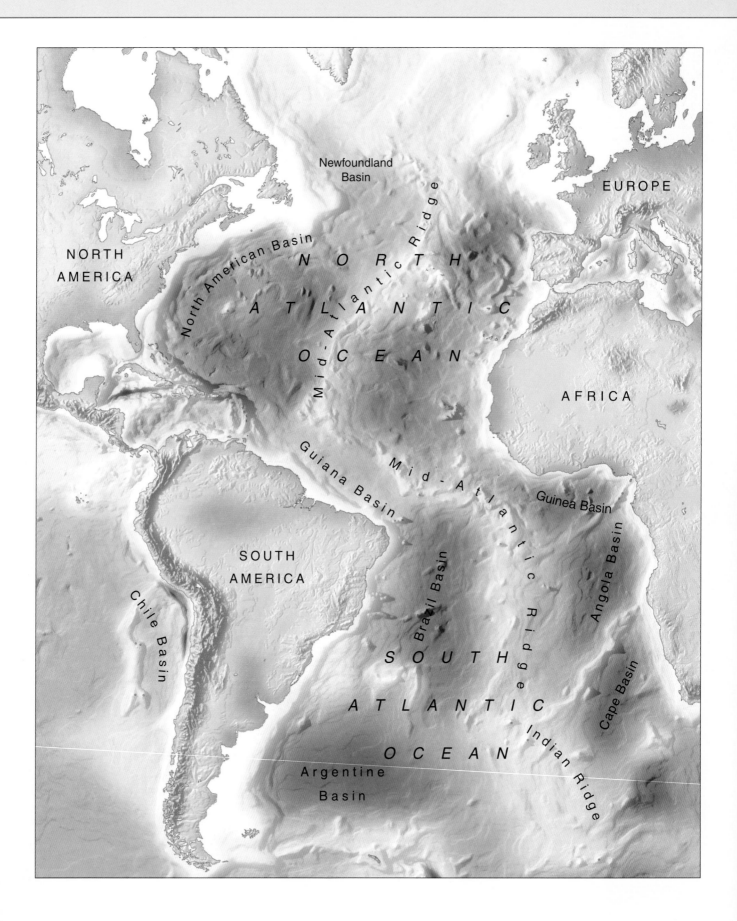

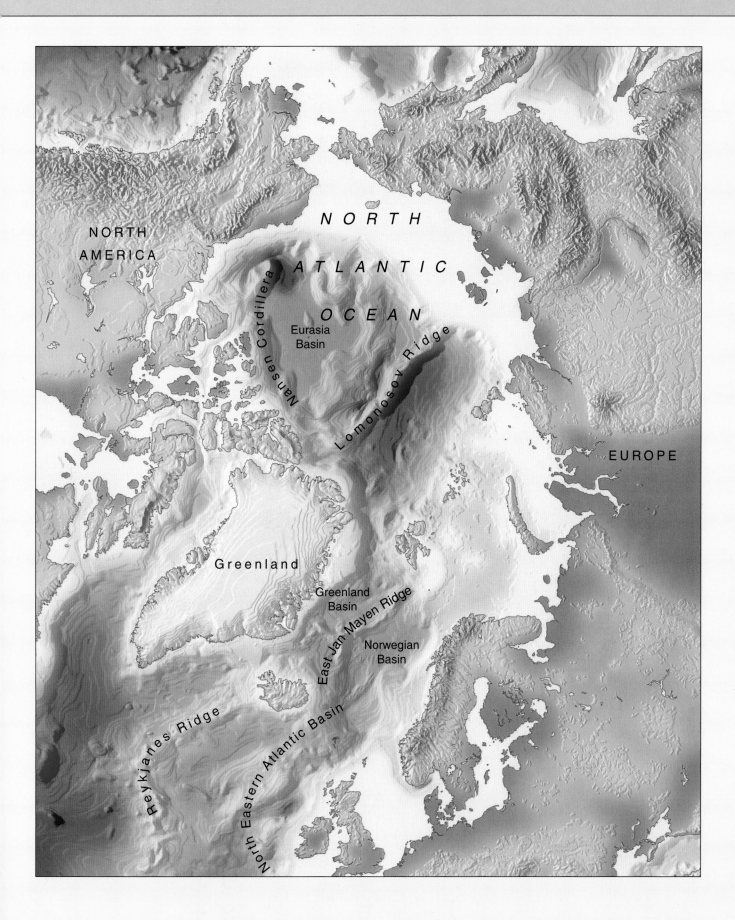

NORTH AMERICA

NORTH

ATLANTIC

OCEAN

Eurasia
Basin

Nansen Cordillera

Lomonosov Ridge

EUROPE

Greenland

Greenland
Basin

East Jan Mayen Ridge

Norwegian
Basin

Reykjanes Ridge

North Eastern Atlantic Basin

The Antarctic

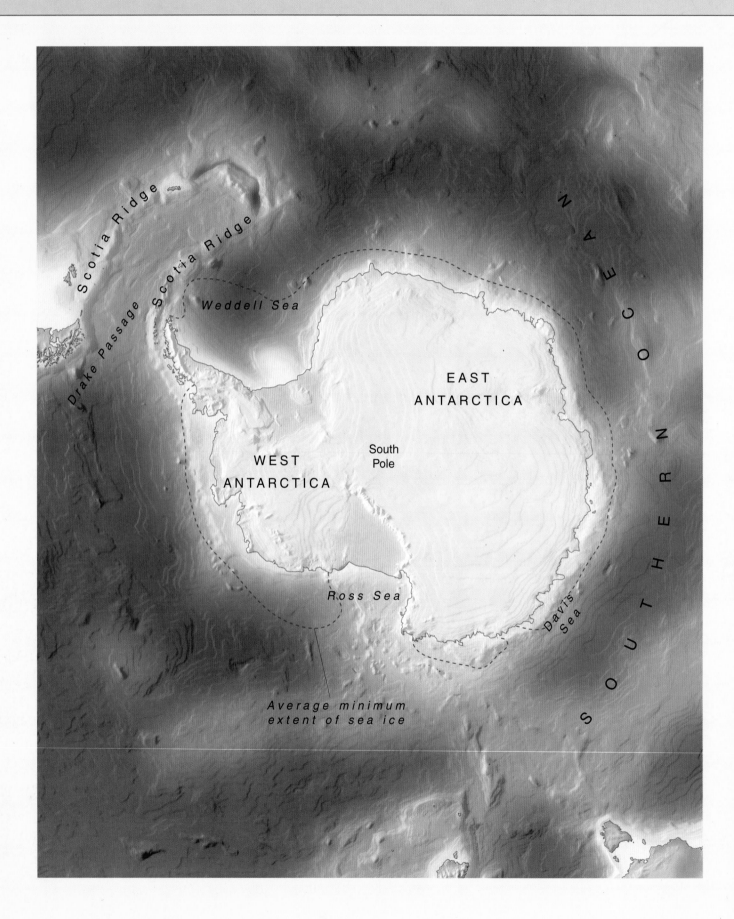

Scotia Ridge

Scotia Ridge

Drake Passage

Weddell Sea

OCEAN

EAST
ANTARCTICA

South
Pole

WEST
ANTARCTICA

Ross Sea

Davis Sea

SOUTHERN

Average minimum
extent of sea ice

The Pacific Ocean

ASIA

Bering Sea

NORTH AMERICA

Sea of Okhotsk

Aleutian Trench

Kurill Trench

Emperor Seamount Chain

Mendocino Seascarp

Sea of Japan

Mid-Pacific Mountains

Yellow Sea

Ryukyu Trench

Kyushu-Palau Ridge

South Honshu Ridge

Philippines Trench

PACIFIC

OCEAN

Pacific Rise

Kapingamarangi Rise

Arafura Sea

Coral Sea Basin

Lord Howe Rise

South Fiji Basin

Kermadec Trench

AUSTRALIA

Peru Basin

Pacific Ridge

South Australian Basin

Chatham Rise

South-West Pacific Basin

The Indian Ocean

The Gulf

Red Sea

Gulf of Aden

Ara
S

Ara
Ba

AFRICA

Carlburg Ri

Somali
Basin

Mascarene

Mascarene
Basin

Mascarene Ridge

Mozambique Channel

Madagascar

Natal
Basin

Madagascar
Basin

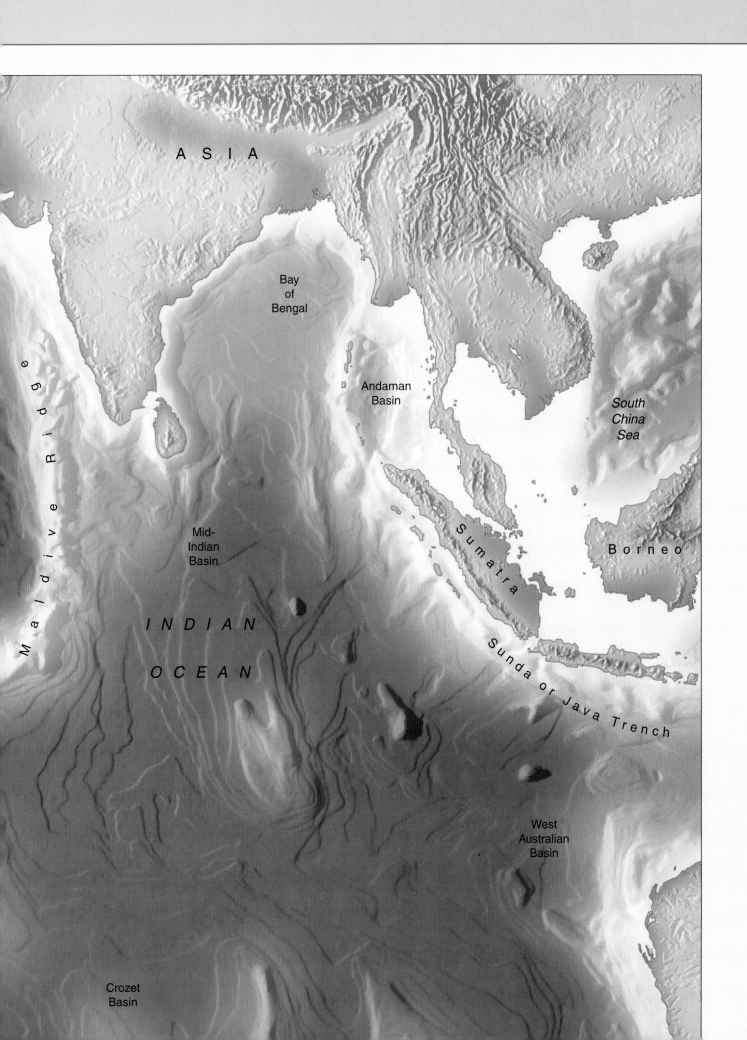

Glossary

abolitionist: a person who opposes slavery and works to end it

abyssal plain: a vast, fairly level, and very deep area of the ocean floor where no light penetrates

alluvial plain: a level tract of land bordering a river on which sediment has been deposited

animist: a person who believes that there is conscious life in nature and natural objects

apartheid: meaning "apartness" in Afrikaans, a policy of racial segregation in which a minority holds political power over a majority

Arabian Peninsula: a vast, mostly desert area of southwestern Asia whose political divisions are Bahrain, Kuwait, Oman, Qatar, Saudi Arabia, the United Arab Emirates, and Yemen

archipelago: a group of islands that stretches across a sea

ayatollah: a highly respected religious leader among Shiite Muslims

Bedouin: a member of the nomadic peoples who inhabit the desert areas of North Africa and the Middle East

British East India Company: a private organization that opened trade with India and eastern Asia in the 1600s and that received special trading rights from the British government

Buddhism: a religion of Asia founded by Buddha. It teaches that through living a good life a person's soul is freed from pain, sorrow, and desire.

cash crop: a crop that is produced mainly to make money and not feed one's family

caviar: an expensive food made from the salted eggs of certain large fish, such as sturgeon

colonial rule: a time of governance by an outside power that runs the territory as a colony

colony: a territory ruled by another country that is typically located far away

Communist: a person who supports Communism—an economic system in which the government owns all farmland and the means of producing goods in factories

coniferous: describing mainly evergreen trees that bear cones and have needle-shaped leaves

continental shelf: the seabed that borders the continents and that is covered by shallow water

coral island: a piece of land made up of coral, rocklike formations made of billions of coral polyp skeletons

coral reef: a ridge of rocklike formations made up of billions of coral polyp skeletons

deciduous: describing trees that lose their leaves at some season of the year

delta: a triangular piece of land at the mouth of a river

drumlin: a long, oval-shaped hill or ridge made of finely ground rocks

duties: taxes paid to a government on goods brought in from another country

emirate: a state under the rule of an emir, meaning "commander" or "chief" in Arabic
federation: a form of government in which states or groups unite under a central power. The states or groups surrender power to make some decisions but retain limited territorial control.

fjord: a long, narrow sea inlet bordered by steep cliffs

floodplain: a low, flat area next to a river or stream

fodder crops: coarse plants—such as cornstalks, hay, and straw—that are grown as food for cattle, horses, and other farm animals

fossil fuels: substances, such as coal and petroleum, that slowly developed from the remains of living things

fundamentalist: adhering to a strict and literal interpretation of a set of beliefs

geothermal energy: energy produced by the heat of the earth's interior

geothermal power: energy produced by the heat of the earth's interior

glacier: a large body of ice and snow that moves slowly over land

gum arabic: a substance obtained from acacia trees that can be made into inks, adhesives, or candies

hajj: the journey to the Saudi Arabian city of Mecca, defined as one of the five religious duties each Muslim must try to perform

heathland: an area of open land covered by heather, low shrubs, and other hardy vegetation

hemp: a tall plant having tough fibers that can be made into rope and heavy cloth
Hinduism: the main religion of India. It emphasizes performing one's duty, especially through the observance of certain rituals and social obligations.

hornbeam tree: a member of the birch family, having gray bark and hard white wood

Glossary

ice age: an ancient period when ice sheets covered large regions of the earth. The last ice age—the Pleistocene—ended about 10,000 years ago.

igneous rock: a type of rock from the earth's crust that has solidified from molten magma (hot, melted rock)

Imam: an Islamic leader who traces his descent from the prophet Muhammad. An Imam often holds civil as well as religious authority.

infant mortality: deaths occurring in the first year of life. The infant mortality rate is usually represented as the number of deaths per every 1,000 live births in a country, state, or region.

infrastructure: the basic system of public works (schools, hospitals, highways, docks, railways, etc.) that enable a country, state, or region to live and work

Islam: the religion of the world's Muslims. It emphasizes belief in Allah and in Muhammad as his prophet.

jute: a strong fiber that comes from plants that originated in eastern India. The fiber can be manufactured into twine and burlap sacking.

kapok: the silky fibers around the seeds of the tropical ceiba tree. The fibers are used to stuff mattresses, sleeping bags, and life preservers and as insulation.

karst: an limestone region with underground streams and caverns

League of Nations: an international organization formed after World War I (1914-1918) to maintain peace among the nations of the world

loess: a yellowish soil that is good for growing crops. The soil lies on the land and, during dry times, can be blown up into the air.

Massif Central: the plateau region of south central France that reaches to more than 6,000 feet above sea level

meseta: an extensive, heavily eroded plateau area of Spain's interior that covers about three-quarters of the country and that is crossed by several mountain ranges

mestizo: a person of Spanish and native Indian ancestry

Middle East: an unofficial term to describe the countries of southwestern Asia and northeastern Africa

monsoon: a rain-bearing wind that blows from the southwest in southern Asia during the months of April to October

moor: a wild stretch of usually elevated land that is covered with heather, coarse grass, and other hardy vegetation

muskeg: a bog in northern North America

nationality: a group of people who, because they share race, language, tradition, and origin, can be distinguished from other populations

oasis: a fertile area of a desert that is usually fed by an underground source of water. Oases can vary in size from a small patch surrounded by date palms to a large city that raises yearly crops.

pan: a naturally occurring low place that can fill with water during the rainy season

Papal States: lands, mostly in central Italy, that were once under the economic, military, and political rule of the Roman Catholic popes. In modern times, the pope only governs Vatican City.

plateau: a large, relatively flat area that stands above the surrounding land

polder: an area of land that has been reclaimed from the sea. The land is enclosed in a series of protective boundaries and is then drained by pumping the water into canals.

population density: the size of a population divided by land area, usually measured by the number of people who live in a square mile. The more people who live in the square mile, the denser the population is said to be.

prevailing wind: the dominant wind, indicated by direction, in a certain place

protectorate: a territory under the authority of another

Ramadan: the ninth month of the Islamic year, observed by fasting from dawn to sunset every day

republic: a government having a chief of state (usually a president) who is not a monarch. In a republic, supreme power belongs to a body of citizens who are entitled to vote and who elect representatives responsible to the citizens. These representatives govern according to law.

Sahel: an Arabic word meaning "coast" that refers to the belt of land bordering the southern edge of the Sahara Desert

savanna: a tropical grassland where rainfall varies from season to season
seiner: a fishing vessel that pulls a large net, call a seine, that encloses fish in a vertical trap

Semite: a member of any of the historic or modern peoples of southwestern Asia who speaks a Semitic language, such as Hebrew or Arabic

separatist: an advocate of independence or self-rule for one's group. Separatists want representatives of their own group to make the political decisions that affect the group and work to withdraw from any other political entity to which they are joined.

shea nut: the fatty fruit of a tropical African tree from which shea butter can be made

sisal: a strong, durable white fiber used in making rope or twine

slash-and-burn: a style of farming in which farmers clear, burn, and plow land before planting crops. The crops survive for only a few seasons, and the land is then abandoned.

smelting: the act of melting to get the pure metal of certain minerals or ores to separate away from the waste matter

steppe: a level, treeless plain

steppes: the level, generally treeless grasslands of Russia, eastern Europe, and central Asia

Strait of Hormuz: the strategically important transportation route that connects the Persian Gulf with the Gulf of Oman and the Indian Ocean. After having their holds filled with oil, tankers navigate the strait to bring the fuel to destinations throughout the world.

subcontinent: a large landmass that is a smaller but major division of a continent

subsistence agriculture: a farming plan in which a farmer produces only enough crops to feed the family, with little, if any, surplus for market

taiga: the belt of forested land lying to the south of the tundra. The trees in the taiga are mostly cone-bearing evergreens, such as spruces and firs.

teff: an African cereal grain that yields a white flour. Some teff is used to feed farm animals.

temperate: having a mild climate, with cool winters and warm summers

terrace: a flat platform of soil with sloping banks. A series of terraced fields, rising one above the other, can offer farmers more land for growing crops.

trade sanction: a restriction that prohibits or limits trade between countries

tributary: a river that joins a larger river

Tropic of Cancer: one of the two imaginary circles around the earth that parallel the equator. The other is the Tropic of Capricorn. The hot, humid area between the two circles is called the tropics.

tropical rain forest: a dense, green forest that receives large amounts of rain every year. These forests lie near the equator.

tropics: the hot, wet region that forms a wide belt around the earth's equator between the Tropic of Cancer and the Tropic of Capricorn

trusteeship: supervisory control by one or more countries over a non-self-governing territory

tsetse fly: an insect from tropical areas of Africa that can infect humans or animals with sleeping sickness

tundra: a region of treeless plains and permanently frozen soil around the Arctic Circle

tung tree: an Asian tree whose seeds yield a pale yellow oil used in making quick-drying varnishes and waterproofing agents

veld: the grasslands of southern Africa

wadi: a dry streambed or river channel that floods during heavy rainfalls

Woman leaning out of her highly decorated window, Thailand.

Index